HOKKAIDO

42°

HONSHU

40°

Niigata

Sendai

30°

SINGLE CROPPED RICE LAND

DOUBLE CROPPED RICE LAND : Rice - Rice,
Rice - Winter Wheat, or Rice - Winter Vegetables

DRYFIELD CROPS

HILLY LAND   Mostly Forest

TOKYO

Yokohama

EDO BAY

IZU ISLANDS

NUMBER OF PEOPLE
FOR EACH SQUARE MILE OF CROPLAND

JAPAN	
3400	

GREAT BRITAIN	
1620	

CHINA	
1400	

BRAZIL	
900	

INDIA	
570	

FRANCE	
530	

USSR	
290	

USA	
270	

36°

140°   142°   144°   146°   148°

The United States and Japan

THE AMERICAN FOREIGN POLICY LIBRARY

CRANE BRINTON, EDITOR

The United States and Britain
Revised edition. CRANE BRINTON

The United States and South America
The Northern Republics ARTHUR P. WHITAKER

The United States and China
Revised and enlarged. JOHN KING FAIRBANK

The United States and Scandinavia FRANKLIN D. SCOTT

The United States and Japan
Third edition. EDWIN O. REISCHAUER

The United States and France DONALD C. MCKAY

The United States and Turkey and Iran LEWIS V. THOMAS
and RICHARD N. FRYE

The United States and Mexico
Revised edition, enlarged. HOWARD F. CLINE

The United States and India and Pakistan
Revised and enlarged. W. NORMAN BROWN

The United States and Italy H. STUART HUGHES
Revised edition.

The United States and Argentina ARTHUR P. WHITAKER

The Balkans in Our Time ROBERT LEE WOLFF

The United States and the Southwest Pacific C. HARTLEY GRATTAN

The United States and Israel NADAV SAFRAN

The United States and North Africa
Morocco, Algeria, and Tunisia CHARLES F. GALLAGHER

The United States and the Arab World WILLIAM R. POLK

THE
UNITED STATES
AND
Japan

By

Edwin O. Reischauer

THIRD EDITION

HARVARD UNIVERSITY PRESS

Cambridge, Massachusetts

1965

LIBRARY OF CONGRESS CATALOG CARD NUMBER 64–8057

PRINTED IN THE UNITED STATES OF AMERICA

TO MY PARENTS

CONTENTS

PART V

The Postwar Japanese

MAPS

INTRODUCTION

TO THE THIRD EDITION

This volume centers upon the most crucial phase of Japanese-American relations, that is our occupation of Japan from 1945 to 1952. The story of the occupation is buttressed on the one side by a brief account of earlier Japanese-American relations and a detailed study of the nature of Japan and its society before we occupied it, and, on the other side, by an attempt to analyze the Japan that has emerged from the occupation experience and our relations with it. This book thus concerns three periods in time: prewar Japan, the occupation days, and what has happened since. It is therefore appropriate that, as it goes into its third edition, it is made up of chapters written at three different times: in 1949 for the original 1950 edition, in 1956 for the first revised edition, and now in 1964 for the third edition.

There are, of course, drawbacks to a book made up of materials written at different times. This is especially true when it concerns a country that has been changing as rapidly as Japan has since the Second World War. Points of view and basic assumptions, as well as objective facts, have changed amazingly between 1949, 1956, and 1964. But I feel that there are more advantages than disadvantages in keeping this book a mixture of materials written in different years. What is most important for an understanding of Japan and our relations with it is not the exact situation at any given moment but the direction in which Japan is moving. It would be virtually impossible writing today to recapture as fully and vividly the feel of the situation as it existed in 1949 or again in 1956. Thus the retention of the earlier materials gives a much greater sense of the rapid changes that have swept Japan than would a volume entirely rewritten from the vantage point of 1964. When the 1950 and 1957 editions appeared, they were criticized both in Japan and the United States for offering too optimistic a picture. But the reader will note that with each succeeding revision I have been forced to reduce the notes of pessimism and emphasize those of optimism.

Actually the time span between the various sections of this volume is greater than the three dates 1949, 1956, and 1964 suggest. The 1949 writing is primarily descriptive of prewar Japan, unmodified by postwar developments. Chapters 1 and 2, largely concerning prewar relations between the United States and Japan, would be little changed if I were to rewrite them today. Parts II and III (Chapters 4 through 9) are an attempt to describe the ways in which the prewar economy and the personality and experience of the people, as seen particularly in Japan of the 1930's, differed from our own.

The 1956 materials are largely an effort to describe the American Occupation of Japan and its immediate effects, as seen only four years after the end of the occupation when its aura still hung heavy over the land. These consist of Chapter 3 on "Japan and America: The Problem" and Part IV (Chapters 10 through 12) on "The Occupation."

Part V on "The Postwar Japanese" is the section that has been revised or newly written in 1964. The only other changes I have made at this time are corrections of fact on pages 239 and 252. It will be helpful to the reader if he keeps in mind the span of time treated in all the chapters as well as the specific years (1950, 1957, and 1964) in which individual chapters were first published in essentially their present form.

It would be quite fruitless for me to attempt to list all the persons to whom I am indebted for information and ideas which have found some place in this work. Many and perhaps most of them I am not aware of myself. Generalizations, for all their axiomatic inaccuracy, inevitably form the heart of any book attempting to cover a broad field in short compass. But generalizations usually cannot be documented by citing chapter and verse. Those in this book are the result of a long and slow process of accretion and synthesis. All I can do is to acknowledge my great indebtedness to my many teachers, colleagues, and also students in this country and abroad, and to all those who have helped amass the information on which this book has been based or who have struggled with the problem of interpreting these facts in terms of generalized concepts.

I also wish to express my specific gratitude to those who, by kindly reading and correcting the manuscript of the first edition, prevented the appearance of certain simple errors of fact and helped make the generalizations less inaccurate than they otherwise would have been. Among these kind friends and colleagues I owe a double debt of gratitude to Professor Serge Elisséeff and Sir George Sansom, who not only have taught me much that I know about Japan but also have been kind enough to correct my rephrasings of some of their own wisdom. Others who have given me many invaluable suggestions and corrections are Professor Edward A. Ackerman, Professor George H. Danton, Professor John K. Fairbank, Mrs. Richard N. Frye, Professor Eleanor M. Hadley, Professor James R. Hightower, Professor John Pelzel, Professor Richard N. McKinnon, and Professor Donald H. Shively. I also wish to express my sincere thanks to the editors of this series, the Honorable Sumner Welles and Professor Donald C. McKay, for their sympathetic aid and encouragement. Unfortunately neither is still with us to help in the editing of this present revision.

Edwin O. Reischauer

June 1964

EDITOR'S NOTE ON
THE THIRD EDITION

The books in the Harvard Foreign Policy Library, although they are by no means meant to be mere handbooks of current reference, lose much of their usefulness if they are not frequently revised and brought up to date. The wisdom of the original editors of the Library, Sumner Welles and Donald McKay, is especially clear in their choice of Dr. Reischauer to write on *The United States and Japan.* In spite of the many demands made on his time as American Ambassador to Japan, he has prepared this revision of his book entirely on his own initiative. The present editor, succeeding to the post after the untimely deaths of both the creators of the Library, would like to claim some of the credit for Dr. Reischauer's work, but cannot honestly do so. He is, however, extremely grateful for this most opportune and, as far as he himself is concerned, undeserved gift. Few books in the series are more important in their subject than this one, and none live up better than this to the high purposes of Welles and McKay in founding the Library.

Crane Brinton

Cambridge, Massachusetts
October 1964

INTRODUCTION

TO THE REVISED EDITION

(1957)

The admission of Japan to the United Nations in December last can be taken as marking the end of a cycle in that country's postwar history. When General MacArthur arrived on the Battleship *Missouri* eleven years before, Japan lay utterly defeated and impotent in the face of her conquerors. In the ensuing years she underwent a wide-reaching economic recovery, and, far more important, achieved a program of reform whose extent and breath-taking acceleration were perhaps without parallel in history. As a result of these developments, and even more, of her prewar experience, Japan has become the front runner of democracy in Asia, and American policy in that vast area hinges in very substantial measure on the success with which the Japanese maintain and extend free institutions in the coming years. At a time when the competition of the free and communist worlds is joined to win the allegiance of the teeming populations still uncommitted, the future of Japanese democracy poses a problem of capital significance for American policy. It is a tragic fact that, despite the central role which the United States has played in Japan's recovery and reform, the American people are still remote from that country in both interest and knowledge. It is precisely this situation which gives the present book its opportunity.

The decade of the forties proved one of fantastic and paradoxical vicissitudes for the Japanese. The sweeping initial successes of the war served only to arouse Japan's gigantic opponent from the isolationist lethargy of the thirties and so to prepare for the slow but ineluctable crushing of Japan's initially developed strength. And yet, from the grievous wounds of the war, this proud people has by its own effort, in the context of support and guidance from the occupying authority, risen to a position of new importance in Asia. Says Mr. Reischauer:

For Japan herself, the fifth decade of the twentieth century will probably prove to be the most momentous in all her long history. Never before in such a short space of years has so much that was old and accepted been burned out of Japanese society and so much that was new and unfamiliar been poured in. Each individual phase of the process represents a cataclysmic change in itself — the gutting of her cities by the blinding flash of atomic power and the less spectacular but equally destructive force of thousands of tiny fire bombs; the shearing off of a huge empire; the arrival on Japanese soil of a conquering army for the first time in recorded history; and the dynamic enforcement in rapid succession of a whole flood of reforms, remaking the government and economy and reshaping the whole social structure.

In this great effort the leadership lay in the hands of General MacArthur, on whose controversial figure the author has focused a laudable, and difficult, objectivity.

Few men who have found themselves in history's spotlight have better fitted the roles which destiny has given them than General MacArthur in his capacity as American proconsul in Japan and benevolent but absolute master of the fate of eighty million people. . . . While making him the personification of the power of the United States and regarding him as the sole source of all occupation policy, they also looked up to him as the prophet of the future Japan and their own national hero.

In his penetrating treatment of "Retribution and Reform," Mr. Reischauer has dealt, on one hand, with the negative aspect of this program: demilitarization — the destruction of the Japanese armed forces and immediate war potential and the shearing away of the varied elements in the far-flung empire. More important, he turns to the positive aspects — "the maintenance of a reasonable degree of economic well-being," first through massive American aid and later through the restoration of Japanese productive power; and finally, and of prime significance, to the process of democratization, resting on the new program of reform. These great changes have involved a new constitution drafted under the strong influence of the occupation authorities, introducing responsible government to Japan, and, by stripping the Emperor of his powers (which "he never really enjoyed anyway"), preparing the way for a complete recasting of his role in Japanese society.

In the field of social reform, Mr. Reischauer finds that, in an Asian setting at least, the impact of American ideals on Japan has been "more revolutionary" than that of Communist ideals on China. The dynamic character of these reforms he examines in changes running the whole social gamut: education, equality for women, greater independence for youth, curbing of the power of the great industrial combines, development of labor unions virtually from scratch, and a drastic land reform which "has met only with praise," despite the frustrating fact that it necessarily faces problems which are almost insoluble.

Mr. Reischauer points out that it is easier to catalogue the postwar reforms and to estimate their varying degree of individual effectiveness than it is to pass judgment on the overall success of occupation policy in turning the Japanese into a stable and peaceful democratic nation. Our problem has been to readjust the balance so that the peaceful and democratic forces already existing in interwar Japan could gradually win out over the militaristic and authoritarian forces, thus reversing the history of the thirties. The basic objectives of the occupation the author feels have been achieved, but the future of democracy in Japan depends on the temper and capacity of the Japanese themselves. Neither we nor any other nation, no matter how powerful or how well-intentioned, can do these things for Japan. On the other hand, we still have a large role to play, provided always we can summon the patience, tolerance, understanding, and capacity to make sacrifices in the present for real, but imperfectly revealed, objectives in the future.

Mr. Reischauer believes that the close coöperation of the two countries will probably continue "under existing conditions." But conditions can change; and we can affect conditions. We must be willing and able to guarantee Japanese security. Japan's economic collapse could be immediately disastrous. Japan's economy is dependent upon an America free from depression; and our tariff policies can have an important impact on her trade. We have a major voice in determining her crucial trade relations with China, and here clearly reason will be a better guide than emotion. We can in short contribute heavily to the strengthening of Japanese democracy, hence to her value as an ally, or we can choose deeply to damage her position — and our interests — through neglect or mismanagement. Mr. Reischauer concludes his work with these cogent words:

But one thing is certain. Japan's future depends far more on the United States than on any other foreign nation, and conversely America's future, at least during the next two or three decades, may depend more on Japan than on any other country in Asia.

Mr. Reischauer has of course treated not only the past decade of Japan's development, central as that is to our interest. He has been at great pains also to have us understand this development by giving us a picture in depth of Japan and the Japanese. He has described our relations with Japan over the century since Commodore Perry took the dramatic step of opening "the closed door of Japan a crack" — relations which have run the whole gamut from war to an almost frenetic Japanese enthusiasm for things American. He has analyzed the growth of Japan's population in massive increments during the past century until now the peasants are crowded on the land almost 1900 to the square mile, a pressure equaled in no other country in the world. He has followed for us the forced draft industrialization and the consequent shortages of raw materials, the whole providing the dynamic of Japanese imperialism in East Asia. And no part of this book appeals to the present writer as more perceptive than that which analyzes in detail the national character and the contrary pulls induced by westernization — toward greater individual freedom, on one hand, and toward "enforced totalitarian uniformity," on the other.

To the immensely difficult task involved in the writing of this book, Mr. Reischauer brings unusual equipment. He was born in Japan, is bilingual, possesses at once both that intimacy of knowledge and that large measure of detachment which this kind of experience can confer. He early elected a scholarly career and has been a life-long student of Japanese language, literature, history, and "culture" in the anthropological sense. In this last-named connection, he is one of those still rare scholars who has reached out boldly but discriminatingly to exploit the offerings of the neighboring social sciences in analyzing for us the meaning of key elements in Japanese culture as a whole.

The author has known not only Japan of the "old regime" (the decades prior to 1941) but has returned repeatedly to postwar Japan and has spent the academic year 1955–56 in reassessing that scene prior to the present revision of this work, first published in 1950. During the war Mr. Reischauer was Lieutenant Colonel in Army Intelligence, concerned with Japanese military intelligence. In 1945–46 he was a member of the State Department, working on Japanese and Korean policy and sitting as one of the Department's representatives on the State-War-Navy Coördinating Committee, the chief policy-making organ of the government at that time. He is presently Professor of Far Eastern Languages in Harvard University and Director of the Harvard-Yenching Institute, which has played a vital role in education in the Far East and which is currently bringing each year to Harvard for further special study a substantial group of younger professors of high promise from various ones of the free countries of Asia.

Mr. Reischauer's book was most warmly received in its initial edition. This current revision, written after the passage of some seven years, gives a whole new view of post-treaty Japan, with a correspondingly surer and more balanced estimate of what the defeat and occupation really meant. It will, we are sure, be no less appreciated.

Donald C. McKay

INTRODUCTION

TO THE FIRST EDITION

(1950)

By 1937 it must have been clear to any student of the Far Eastern scene that vast new forces—some of them still shadowy, but others already sharply defined—were rising rapidly in every part of Asia. It was equally apparent that the growing impotence of the great colonial powers of Western Europe was hastening the day when the end of the era of imperialism would be at hand.

Now Asia is engulfed in a tidal wave of political and social revolution.

Nationalism in its narrowest sense has become a driving factor throughout the Eastern world. It has, of course, for many years past been artfully stimulated by Soviet emissaries carefully trained for that purpose. There is much reason to believe that nationalism may yet prove to be a boomerang of fatal consequence to the Politburo's schemes for Moscow's domination of the Asiatic world. Yet no thinking American can fail to take stock of the situation which this nation will confront if the peoples of Asia choose the road that leads to Soviet dictatorship.

Our hopes that at the war's end a way could be found by which the forces of nationalist and of social revolution might be canalized into constructive channels as a consequence of cooperative measures undertaken under the aegis of the United Nations have for the most part vanished. Here and there, as in India and Indonesia, because of the individual genius of a few leaders, grounds for optimism as to the future are not lacking. Yet it would be idle to deny that during the past year the horizon has been steadily darkening in the Far East in so far as the prospects for the consecration of human liberties, for democratic self-government, and for economic reconstruction are concerned.

It would almost seem as if the Government of the United States had deliberately discarded every major advantage that this country possessed in determining a foreign policy that would make for a peaceful and a safe world.

I know of no more humiliating failure in the recent history of American diplomacy than the record of American policy in China during the past four years. It has been fatally vacillating. It has apparently been formulated in ignorance of Chinese history and of Chinese psychology. It has ignored the fact that in a world in which the Soviet Union is determined to play power politics the United States cannot successfully counter Soviet measures of aggressive expansion except by playing power politics herself. It is a policy that has left a prostrate Chinese people in the hands of an alien-inspired government bent, in so far as we can now see, upon making of the Chinese nation, rich in manpower, in raw materials, and in productive capacity, a subservient satellite of the Soviet Union.

Mr. Reischauer's volume, *The United States and Japan*, makes clearer than any other book that I have read that the United States still possesses through its special position in Japan a chance to atone for its mistakes of omission and of commission in the Far East and to repair to some extent the damage that has already been done to American security and to the safety of the democratic West.

While, as Mr. Reischauer properly emphasizes, the occupation of Japan is technically the common enterprise of those members of the United Nations that joined in bringing about her defeat, the occupation is primarily an American responsibility. Granted that there are justifiable grounds for criticism of certain aspects of the occupation, it nevertheless has to its credit a brilliant record of positive achievement. Soviet Communism has made but little headway among the Japanese people. Such Soviet policies as the refusal to return to Japan many hundreds of thousands of Japanese prisoners of war and their retention as slave labor have inevitably increased the realization of the Japanese people that the American occupation has been essentially humanitarian. They are traditionally suspicious of Russia's motives.

That Japan can later become a mighty bulwark against Moscow's domination of Asia can no longer be questioned. What Mr. Reischauer makes plain, however, is that the outcome will depend upon the awareness of the American people of the vital significance of the issues that are involved in this phase of their nation's foreign policy, and upon their realistic recognition of the major obstacles that they confront in making such a policy succeed.

Mr. Reischauer places a healthy emphasis on the many inherent good qualities of the Japanese people and of the progress that they had made in acquiring electoral and Parliamentary experience before the tragic days when they permitted their fanatics and their militarists to lead them into a disastrous war of aggression and to merit the hatred of their Asiatic neighbors and of the Western democracies. No one who lived in Japan, as I did, thirty-five years ago, before the Army had fastened its strangle hold upon the Japanese people, can fail to recognize the vitality of the forces of political liberalism that had sprung up among many sectors of Japanese society as an aftermath of the era of the Meiji reforms. During the past two decades those forces, it is true, have lost impetus. But they have not died. The question is whether the occupation and a sane and just peace treaty can restore that impetus and make those forces the new dominating factor in Japanese life.

At a moment when the military mentality in Washington seems to be so largely responsible for the determination of American foreign policy, it would be well for every American citizen to ponder this passage from Mr. Reischauer's book:

"We should not forget, however, that no matter how feasible it would be to make Japan our military ally, it probably could not be done without seriously endangering Japanese democracy. In view of Japan's strong militaristic tradition and the record of recent history in which the Japanese Army played the leading role in scuttling the young and still very imperfect democratic institutions of prewar Japan, it would be too much to hope that Japan could be both a military and an ideological ally. As the former she might render the United States valuable aid, if war were to come in the next few years, but she would unquestionably render a greater disservice by driving the rest of Asia away from us and presumably into the other camp. As an ideological ally, she could be of inestimable value in strengthening the cause of democracy throughout Asia. The choice to any but the narrowest of military minds should be an obvious one."

Nor should any of us fail fully to grasp the economic problems that the Japanese people must face in the years to come or the economic problems that we ourselves confront in carrying on our present occupation policy. Since 1945 the American taxpayers have been contributing half a billion dollars a year to keeping the Japanese people from starvation and making it possible for the wheels of Japan's industry to turn again. It is inconceivable that the American taxpayers are going to be willing indefinitely to continue such a drain upon their own resources even were the Japanese themselves willing to accept the indefinite continuation of conditions under which they are condemned to live upon a foreign dole. Yet Japan cannot grow enough food to feed her own people.

As Mr. Reischauer cogently states, "All Japan has to offer on the world market is her own energy—manpower and energy of coal and water. With these she can transform imported raw materials into goods for reëxport. The slim margin of profit from this reëxport trade must be sufficient to pay for all the imports Japan must have to support her own people. To do this Japan's export trade must be huge. But where is she to find her markets in a divided world and in a Far East disrupted by revolution and bitterly determined not to trade with her? Japan's situation is basically similar to England's, but infinitely worse."

Such staggering problems as these—the political conversion of the Japanese people into safe and coöperative members of international society and the economic reconstruction of Japan in order that the Japanese people may obtain a chance to prosper and to maintain higher living standards—are not going to be solved by sleight of hand. They can only be successfully surmounted through an American foreign policy backed by an enlightened American public opinion that keeps its sights set upon the ultimate objectives and which is prepared to devote the time and the material sacrifices that may be needed so that those objectives may ultimately be achieved.

Finally, there is one point that Mr. Reischauer brings out that seems to me to be of supreme importance, if American public opinion is to demand of its own Government that kind of policy in Japan that can promise to bring about the desired results.

Nothing could be more futile than for the American people to believe that the people of Japan can be re-created in their own image. Nothing seems to me more fantastic than for us to assume—and many are so assuming—that a new Japanese Constitution, drafted by American authority, will be retained by the Japanese people as their national charter once a peace treaty has been signed and Japan once more becomes an independent power.

If a true Japanese democracy is ever to come into being, it must be "made in Japan." American policy and the American occupation of Japan will only succeed in making the Japanese people an ideological ally of the West, and a bastion of individual freedom and self-government in the Far East, if they encourage and foster natural forces that derive their strength from the individual genius of the Japanese people themselves.

Sumner Welles

PART I   THE PROBLEM

1. Our Neighbor Japan

Japan and the United States face each other, but across the broadest ocean of them all. Once such a body of water was almost like the space between us and the moon. Man was a land animal, crawling slowly over the land surfaces of the world and not venturing far into the surrounding seas. Even a mere five hundred years ago, the civilized world was limited to the great Eurasiatic land mass and the contiguous portions of North Africa together with a few outlying islands. England and Japan, two island lands lying close to the western and eastern coasts of this land mass, represented the two extremities of the civilized world. Beyond them lay the vast and unknown oceans, the unquestioned ends of the world. The earth was indeed flat, and Europe and the Far East lay far removed from each other at the opposite ends of its flat surface.

In that day of slow and precarious travel, the peoples of the world had significant contacts only with close-by lands. The English might fight the French, but even Poland and Hungary were too far away to be of much concern to them, while India and China were little more than fairy-book lands. The Japanese might have dealings with Korea and China, but Java and India concerned them little, and they were blissfully ignorant of the very existence of Europe. Relations were largely between immediate neighbors and usually between peoples of the same cultural and historical background, who were bound together by far more that they shared in common than they were divided by elements that distinguished them.

But in the last five hundred years all this has changed. The oceans no longer are the great barriers they once were but have become instead the mortar holding the various pieces of the earth together in one economic whole. The world has undergone a cataclysmic shrinking, in the process of which the two ends of its once flat surface have curled up and come together. Man has circled the globe, first through extending long thin tentacles of exploration around its surface and then by slowly incorporating into the civilized world, through conquest and settlement, the lands which lay between the East and West on the far side of the earth. Europe, the Far West of the Old World, has straddled one ocean and then slowly spread across the land mass of the New World, until its cultural and racial offshoots have come to stand on the shores of the Pacific, facing the Far East across but a single body of water.

Even in this day of air travel and instantaneous communications, however, the Pacific remains a very broad expanse of water. Two weeks of plowing its long swells will prove this to the sea-voyager. A trip by air reduces the time but not the distance. With the magical aid of the international date line, it is now possible to stand on Japanese and American soil on the same calendar day, but not even the motionless speed of a plane suspended above the unchanging waters of the Pacific reduces the vastness of that ocean. Your sense of time, if not your sense of sight, tells you that you have flown the distance from New York to San Francisco and then repeated it again and again. A nonstop flight from Seattle to Tokyo would be as long as a flight from Florida to Patagonia or one from Maine to the Ural Mountains.

Navigable water, however, is in no sense a barrier such as mountains, desert, ice, or even masses of people. There is no intervening obstacle to communication between us and the Japanese. No other people come between us to divert our attention from each other. We are not like two city dwellers living almost cheek by jowl, as do the peoples of Europe, but

like two country dwellers living out of sight of each other
but still contiguously with no one else between them. We are
perhaps the world's most distant neighbors, but neighbors
nonetheless.

We have been slow and consciously reluctant to realize our
special relationship to Japan, but it has been forced upon us
by the irresistible sweep of history, culminating in war—the
most traditional of all relationships between neighboring peoples. Though our trade with Japan ranked first in our trade
with all Asia, though Japan was considered our only military
rival in Asia and perhaps the chief military menace to us in the
whole world, it took war and our subsequent occupation of
Japan to make us realize how closely involved we had become
in Japan and its problems. The Japanese, for their part, have
been more conscious of what America meant to them. For
many decades, the United States has been the country which
more than any other represented the Occidental world to them.
It had become the chief neighbor to the east, just as China had
always been the major neighbor to the west. And since the
war and its aftermath of American occupation, the United
States has appeared to many Japanese to be the only foreign
country of vital significance to them.

Man moving eastward and man moving westward have at
last met on the far side of the world in the vast expanse of
the Pacific and the lands that rim its shores. The recent war
in a sense represented the final shock of that meeting of forces.
In this naked confrontation of the peoples of the Far East and
the Far West, we find epitomized the difficulties and also the
challenge of the new world—the one world in which we all
now live. Man, who has never been able to solve the frictions
and conflicts between neighboring peoples of common racial
and cultural background, is now faced with the problem
of solving the still more basic conflicts between peoples of
widely divergent racial and cultural heritage.

In the meeting of Japan and the United States, the two
extremities of the world, the problems, the hazards, and, pos-

sibly, the benefits of this head-on convergence of races and cultures in a shrinking world stand out in a clearer, starker light than they do in other parts of the world, where the meeting has come about more slowly and has been between less spectacularly contrasting cultures. It is perhaps no mere coincidence that Japan, the easternmost country of the old civilized world, is now the most Westernized of Asiatic lands, or that America, the westerly extension of the westernmost part of the old civilized world, has taken the lead in bringing the Occident to Japan. America and Japan have for some time now been unconscious neighbors. The war and still more the occupation have brought home to us as well as to the Japanese the somewhat unhappy realization of what very close neighbors we really are.

2. Japan and America: The Record

1. EARLY RELATIONS WITH THE WEST

Japan's first direct contacts with the Western world came in the sixteenth century, a few years after Magellan had circumnavigated the globe, but centuries before the United States came into existence as a nation. In 1541 some Portuguese drifted ashore in Kyushu, the southernmost of the main islands of Japan, and two years later other Portuguese came, largely by accident, to Tanegashima, a small island lying off the southern tip of Kyushu. They were soon followed by other Portuguese and then by Spaniards, Dutchmen, and Englishmen, eager for trade with this newly discovered land. The merchant did not come alone. St. Francis Xavier, the great Jesuit missionary, arrived in Japan in 1549 and was soon followed by determined bands of other Jesuit and Franciscan missionaries from Portugal and Spain, as eager for spiritual conquests as the merchants were for economic gain.

The Japanese response to these unexpected new contacts was both immediate and enthusiastic. We do not know exactly what took place during the first Portuguese landings, but we can surmise the keen interest the Japanese showed in the firearms the Portuguese carried ashore with them at Tanegashima, for the name *Tanegashima-teppo*, "guns of Tanegashima," was for long the regular word for "gun" in Japan. A new religion was, of course, harder to assimilate than new weapons and technical skills, but here too the response was surprising. Conversions came slowly at first but soon in increasing numbers, until, by the end of the century, there may have been as many as 300,000 Catholics in Japan, a larger percentage of the population of that time than the Christians form in Japan today.

One cannot but wonder what might have happened if the Japanese had continued these fruitful contacts with the West uninterruptedly until today. Certainly the history of the Far East and perhaps of the whole world would have been far different. In the sixteenth century, Japan, like the other countries of the Far East, was only slightly behind Europe in matters of weapons, navigation, and scientific knowledge and perhaps ahead of Europe in many other respects. If Japan had continued for the next three centuries the rich Western contacts she had in the second half of the sixteenth century, she unquestionably would have caught up with Europe and remained abreast of the other countries of the world in every way. She would have gradually settled into her natural economic and political position in the world; she would have slowly absorbed what fitted her best from among the ideas of the early modern West and the concepts and techniques the West has produced since then. There would have been no sudden reëmergence from isolation in the nineteenth century, no forced marches to catch up with the rest of the world, which have so severely taxed the Japanese capacity for assimilation and adaptation; there would have been no mushroom growth of economic and military power, which has proved so upsetting to Japan and all her neighbors. In short, this book would have had a very different story to tell.

But this is, after all, idle speculation. Japan after less than a century of contact with the West put an end to these relations and withdrew into herself for over two centuries. By 1638 direct Japanese contacts with the West had been reduced to one closely supervised Dutch outpost, which was moved three years later to the tiny island of Deshima in the harbor of Nagasaki. For over two hundred years this small Dutch trading post and occasional licensed Chinese traders at Nagasaki were Japan's only links with the outside world.

One naturally asks why the Japanese imposed isolation on themselves and how they were able to maintain it so long in the face of the religious and commercial zeal of the Europeans. Isolation was possible first of all because Japan was an island country, well insulated by hundreds of miles of open sea from the rest of the world. Another factor was that in the early seventeenth century whatever superiority the Europeans may have had in the military arts was more than offset by the tremendous distance from Europe to Japan. Japanese mercenaries fought in the Portuguese and Spanish garrisons in the Far East. Japanese and Chinese pirates were able to drive the Dutch out of the island of Formosa in the seventeenth century. There was not yet the vast discrepancy in military power between Europe and Asia which was to remake the map of the Far East in the nineteenth century.

But still we have the question why the Japanese wished to retreat into an isolation which in the long run was to prove so disastrous for the nation. The answer comes from domestic Japanese history. The sixteenth century witnessed the slow and painful reunification of Japan after centuries of anarchic division of the land among a welter of petty feudal lords. Three strong men in succession brought increasing unity and order out of this confusion. The first two, while contributing greatly to Japan's political reunification, did not succeed in passing on their power to their heirs. The third, Tokugawa Ieyasu, who cemented his mastery over all Japan in a great battle in the year 1600, was keenly aware of his predecessors' failures. His guiding principle, and that of his heirs as well, was the retention of power within the family. Stability became the watchword. And to achieve stability, change or the threat of change had to be eliminated. This meant a freezing of society. It also meant destroying Christianity, which was felt to be an upsetting dogma in an Asiatic land.

The Japanese stamped out Christianity through bloody persecutions; the European missionaries were either driven out or executed. In the process most of the Western traders were expelled too, because of their association with the missionaries. The Japanese authorities even went so far as to prohibit the return of any of the thousands of Japanese then abroad, for fear that they might come back contaminated with Christianity, and they also banned the construction of large ocean-going vessels which might take Japanese abroad again. Foregoing the lucrative trade with the West and with the rest of the Far East as well was a high price to pay, but no price was considered too high for stability. That was what the Tokugawa wanted, even if it meant isolation, and that is what they got. The period from 1600 to 1868 is known as the Tokugawa Age, the period of the Tokugawa Shogun, and it was a period of unprecedented stability and peace in Japanese history.

2. THE REOPENING OF JAPAN

The West by the early nineteenth century was no longer the West that Japan had turned her back on two hundred years earlier. Western weapons, improving decade after decade, were now far superior to the antiquated firearms and swords and lances of Japan. Europe, just starting on her amazing industrial revolution, was forging an economic structure with which no Asiatic nation could compete. While Japan had been grimly preserving her political stability, the Europeans had been brawling their way to new power, until they had come to dominate virtually every corner of the globe. Now England, not Spain or Portugal, was in the forefront of European commercial and imperial expansion. English ships of a size and fire-power undreamed of two hundred years earlier and in numbers unknown in the seventeenth century were now plying Far Eastern waters. America, the western extension of Europe in the New World, was also represented in the Far East. Americans were joining in the pursuit of the fabled riches of the Canton trade and of the equally lucrative but less romantic whale.

Even before the reopening of Japan and before the spanning of our own continent by road and rail, the United States had begun to assume its position as Japan's Occidental neighbor. While British ships followed the traditional route between West and East around the Cape of Good Hope and the Malay Peninsula, New England clipper ships crossed the Pacific, passing close by the coasts of Japan on their way to Canton, and sturdy New Bedford whalers tossed in the cold waters off the northern shores of Japan. Americans were intrigued by the forbidding and forbidden coastal mountains of Japan. They in particular hoped for open ports in Japan in which to refit their ships and replenish their stores. Americans were shipwrecked on the rocky coasts of Japan in greater numbers than other Occidentals and were subjected to the harsh treatment of a backward feudal regime determined to keep a menacing outside world at arm's length. And with the coming of steam vessels, possible coaling stations in Japan immediately became a matter of particular interest to Americans.

Beginning in 1792, Russian, English, and American mariners frequented Japanese waters in increasing numbers, charting the coasts, attempting to open trade relations, returning Japanese castaways, or seeking shipwrecked countrymen. Between 1797 and 1809 American ships supplied the Dutch trading post at Deshima, which had been cut off from the homeland by the Napoleonic Wars. In 1837 missionaries and traders aboard the American vessel *Morrison* sought to establish amicable relations with the Japanese but instead drew the fire of coastal batteries in Edo Bay and at Nagasaki. An American naval officer, Commodore Biddle, paid another unsuccessful visit to Edo Bay in 1846, and Commodore Glynn of the American Navy visited Nagasaki three years later. Finally in 1851, the United States government decided on a full-scale effort to open the doors of Japan, and on July 8, 1853, Commodore Perry anchored his squadron at the mouth of Edo Bay. His "black ships" were unanswerable arguments, and on March 31, 1854, Perry signed with the Japanese the Treaty of Kanagawa, prying open the closed doors of Japan a crack.

Only two ports in addition to Nagasaki were opened for a limited amount of trade, but this was enough to pierce the armor of Japanese isolation. By 1858 the American Consul-General, Townsend Harris, arguing that America was a more friendly nation than the rapacious imperialists of Europe, was able to secure a full commercial treaty with Japan. Both treaties were soon followed by similar treaties between Japan and the principal European countries. The doors of Japan had been pushed wide open. America had assumed her role as Japan's Occidental neighbor and as the spearhead of Western penetration. We had established ourselves as the first and foremost Occidental friend of Japan. It is significant that the first mission which newly opened Japan sent abroad was not to her Asiatic neighbors or to the countries of Europe but to the United States to exchange treaty ratifications with us in Washington in 1860.

New wines cannot be poured into old bottles, and Western trade and diplomatic and military techniques were decidedly new wines for the old and decaying bottles of Tokugawa feudalism. Within a decade after the signing of the new trade treaties, the old order had crumbled. By 1868 a determined group of young revolutionaries—and revolutionaries they definitely were, so far as the old order was concerned—had seized the reins of government from the faltering grasp of the Tokugawa and had started to build a new and more highly centralized government in the name of the young Emperor, whose ancestors for some seven hundred years had lived in majestic but powerless dignity in their ancient capital at Kyoto. Calling the new era Meiji (1868–1912), or "Enlightened Rule," they launched Japan upon a rapid series of reforms, designed to regain in one mad dash the ground lost to the West over a period of two hundred-odd years.

The securing of military equality with the Occident was, of course, the clearest and most understandable objective of Japan's new leaders, because Japan's helplessness in the face of Western naval power had been made all too clear to them.

They were all obsessed with the fear that Japan, too, might go down the road toward colonialism already being followed by so many other Asiatic peoples. But they did not simply set their sights at military reform. With surprising perspicacity, they saw that military strength in turn depended upon industrial power, technical knowledge, and administrative efficiency and that it would not be enough merely to acquire the new Western weapons. Instead they embarked upon a broad and intensive program of economic, political, and even social reform, such as the world has rarely seen.

3. JAPANESE REFORM AND AMERICAN INFLUENCE

Fundamentally, reform meant learning as much as possible from the Occident and mastering the lesson as quickly as possible. It called for a supreme effort at self-education on a nation-wide scale, with every contact with the Western world exploited to the fullest. The United States, because of its preponderant role in the opening of Japan, took from the beginning a leading part in this Westernization of Japan. The Japanese, however, came to realize that conditions of life in the older and more tradition-bound countries of Europe approximated those of Japan more closely than did conditions in the still raw and half-settled lands of the New World. The United States in the nineteenth century, moreover, was still only a small and weak newcomer to the family of nations, lacking the prestige of the great and old powers of Europe. Quite naturally the Japanese increasingly went to England, Germany, and France for their models for military, economic, political, legal, and administrative reforms. But despite Japan's conscious effort to learn from Europe itself rather than from Europe's recent geographic extension westward, America was Japan's neighbor in a sense Europe could not be, and in the long run the Japanese probably borrowed more from the United States than from any one European nation.

Students flocked to the United States perhaps in greater numbers than to any other Occidental land. Many institutions, such as Japan's first banking system, were copied directly from America, and American business influence left an indelible mark on Japanese business practices. The colonization and development of the northern island of Hokkaido was carried out largely under the guidance of American experts, and the Sapporo Agricultural College in Hokkaido was founded at the suggestion and under the presidency of American nationals. So strong was the American influence in Hokkaido that even the agricultural landscape there today bears a startling resemblance to that of our own rural areas.

In the all-important field of education, American influence was particularly great. Fukuzawa Yukichi, the founder in 1858 of a school which was to grow into Keio University in Tokyo, accompanied the first Japanese diplomatic mission to the United States in 1860 and, after a trip to Europe two years later, again visited America in 1867. Joseph Niishima (Neesima), the founder in 1875 of Doshisha, one of Japan's earliest Christian educational institutions, and perhaps its most distinguished, secretly left Japan in 1864 to complete his studies in the United States. Dr. David Murray of Rutgers was brought to Japan in 1873 to serve as the educational advisor of the Minister of Education, and during his fruitful stay in Japan he profoundly influenced the whole Japanese educational philosophy and structure. Between 1880 and 1885 the Japanese even attempted to follow the American educational system before returning once more to European models which better fitted their needs. The Harvard zoologist, Edward Sylvester Morse, who arrived in Japan in 1877, was responsible for introducing the Japanese to the fields of zoology, anthropology, and archaeology; Ernest Fenollosa of Boston, arriving in Japan the next year, became an influential teacher of Occidental philosophy and inspired the Japanese to take renewed interest in their own art; and numerous other American scholars made similar though less striking contributions to Japanese scholarship.

It was probably through Christianity and the Christian missionaries that the United States exerted its chief influence on Japan. The Occidental business community, at least until the First World War, was dominated by the British, and only in the past three decades has it become primarily American. But from the start Americans led in the missionary movement in Japan. The Protestant missionaries in particular have always been for the most part Americans. The first missionaries to reenter Japan were Americans, and three American Protestant denominations, the Episcopalians, Presbyterians, and Dutch Reformed, started formal missionary work in Japan in 1859. Among the first American missionaries to come to Japan were such great figures as Dr. Guido Verbeck, who was an influential advisor to the Japanese government and played a large role in the development of the institution which was to grow into Tokyo University, and Dr. J. C. Hepburn, who has left his name on what is still the most widely used romanization system, that is, the method of transliterating Japanese into Latin letters.

By 1873 the Japanese government, reversing the strict ban on Christianity of more than two centuries' standing, decided on a policy of religious toleration, thus permitting Christians to propagate their faith freely in Japan. The missionaries from the start concentrated on education and in coöperation with native believers built up many of the pioneer schools both for boys and girls, founding no less than forty-three schools for girls in the first two decades of the Meiji period. For several decades American missionary schools, particularly at the secondary level, were in the forefront of the educational movement in Japan, and only in the twentieth century did they gradually drop behind in prestige and facilities to the government institutions, which had behind them the financial power and authority of the central government.

The Protestants, off to an early start in 1859, and the Catholics, building anew on the faint traces of the once prosperous Catholic church of Western Japan, have not had the same numerical success as their Jesuit and Franciscan predecessors of three centuries earlier. Protestants and Catholics together constitute today less than one half of 1 per cent of the population. But their influence is far greater than these statistics would indicate. Because of the consistent emphasis on education in the missionary movement, Japanese Christians are almost exclusively from the better educated classes. They constitute far more than one half of 1 per cent of Japanese leadership, and few among the educated classes of Japan have not felt the influence of Christianity in one form or another. The Christian churches of Japan are among the strongest and most self-reliant of the newer church bodies of Asia. It is no accident that there is a disproportionately high percentage of Christians in the present Japanese Diet or that one of Japan's postwar premiers was a Protestant Christian. Right up to the outbreak of the recent war, the strongest of all American influences in Japan was probably that exerted by our Christian missionaries there. It was a relationship of sincere friendship and good will, and this perhaps helps explain why the common Japanese people, even when they found themselves at war with us, continued to regard Americans with admiration and sometimes even with affection.

One other major influence exerted by America on Japan in recent years has been the unexpected influence of the Nisei, the Americans of Japanese origin. Nisei went to Japan in large numbers in the 1930's, seeking higher education or a livelihood, for the doors of opportunity in this country, never so wide open to them as to Americans of Occidental ancestry, seemed to be swinging shut, as the full effects of the depression were felt. Thoroughly American by birth and environment, the Nisei had a hard time in Japan. Handicapped in language and still more in social habits and outlook, he found it extremely difficult to make the adaptation to Japanese life which was demanded of him by his relatives and associates. Inevitably he remained to a certain extent a small island of Americanism, ultimately exerting a greater collective influence on the Japanese around him than they on him. Rejected by the country of his birth, he was nonetheless an ambassador of Americanism —an unheralded and unhonored ambassador, but still a very effective one.

There were several thousand Nisei in the cities of Japan during the decade preceding the war, and they contributed an even more specifically American flavor to the Westernization of Japan. Other factors helped. America was no longer a weak and insignificant country but a recognized giant among nations. More important, she had become not only Japan's chief Occidental neighbor but in many ways Japan's most important neighbor.

The predominantly American flavor in Japan's Westernization could be seen in many ways even before the war. If one traveled eastward from Europe through Asia, it would have been obvious during most of the trip that the dominant Occidental influences had been moving in the same direction from Europe eastward, but somewhere between South China and North China and between Indonesia and the Philippines one would have noticed that the prevailing currents had shifted and that the Occidental influences were coming from around the other side of the world. Korea and Japan, too, lay in the path of this prevailing westerly current from America.

One could see this in Japan in many fields. Baseball, or *besu-boru* as they pronounce it, has for decades been as much the national pastime of Japan as it is with us. Even in language, the American influence has been strong. The combined influence of Great Britain and the United States has made English the unchallenged second language of Japan. Far more Japanese make a sometimes desperate stab at speaking English than attempt to speak all the other foreign languages of the world together, including Chinese. The Japanese government has done its best to make it the King's English which is spoken in Japan, rather than American English, but the effort has met with complete failure. In pronunciation, the Oxford accent has been strongly pushed, but Japanese enunciation of English is usually so far from perfect that no one could tell whether the Japanese speaker were attempting to imitate an Oxford don or a Brooklyn Dodger. Most Japanese who claim a knowledge of English speak Japanese English pure and simple, and any resemblance to an Oxford accent or any of the American accents is likely to be accidental. If a Japanese has managed to progress beyond the usual Japanese mispronunciations, the chances are perhaps nine out of ten that he speaks American English rather than Oxford English.

As to vocabulary, thousands of English words have crept into Japanese, and all too frequently they reveal their obvious American origin. In a Japanese department store, or *depato* for short, or in an office building, which they abbreviate to *biru*, one rides up in an *erebeta*, not a "lift." One uses *gasorin* and not "petrol" in one's automobile. Passing a sandlot ball field, one will see the batter approach the plate after the traditional *uomingu-appu* period, while the crowd shouts for a *homu-ran*. Soon the crowd shifts to yelling *boru-pitcha* in an effort to rattle the pitcher by asserting that he throws only balls, but the umpire unmovedly announces his decisions: *boru, sutoraiki, auto,* and *sefu.* Yes, English in Japan, like most other borrowings from the West, is definitely Americanized, and the Nisei deserves no little share of the credit or blame for this.

In other ways, too, the Japanese-Americans have been an important factor in bringing the United States and Japan closer, though not always in an amicable fashion. China supplied the first cheap Oriental labor to our West Coast. Chinese were brought here in large numbers immediately after the gold rush had served to draw population to California and increase the demand for labor there, but within a few decades strong prejudices had grown up against them on the part of American workers in California, and in 1882 a federal law was passed excluding them. The Japanese then began to take their place to meet the continuing demand for cheap labor in California. By 1890 there were 2039 Japanese in the United States, and during the next two decades the number jumped first to 24,326 and then to 72,157. Meanwhile, many more had been brought under the American flag by the annexation of Hawaii in 1898. The population of Japanese origin in the continental United States before the war stood at approximately 127,000 and that of Hawaii at almost 158,000, which was more than 37 per cent of the total population of the islands.

The same prejudice which had resulted earlier in the exclusion of the Chinese immigrants began to operate against the Japanese as soon as they had become an important group on the West Coast, and discriminatory legislation began to pile up in the statute books. In 1906 a San Francisco municipal law forced Japanese children to attend special Oriental schools, and in 1913 California passed a law barring aliens from owning land. This hit the Japanese farmers very hard, for they, as Asiatics, were not eligible for naturalization. Meanwhile, in 1907 and 1908 a solution of the basic problem of Japanese immigration had been amicably arrived at in the "Gentlemen's Agreement," by which the Japanese government agreed not to issue passports to Japanese laborers seeking to come to the United States. During the next decade and a half, more Japanese men left the United States than entered it, though Japanese women married at long distance to eligible Japanese bachelors in the United States entered in considerable numbers as "picture brides." Anti-Japanese sentiment, however, continued to mount on the West Coast, and eventually in 1924 Congress passed a law excluding outright all Japanese on the basis of race, as the Chinese had been excluded forty-two years earlier. In practice this meant little actual change in the situation, but Japan, which by this time was recognized as one of the world powers, regarded it as a national insult.

Thus, the humble Japanese immigrants had unwittingly stirred up violent animosities against Japan among many

Americans, which in turn had led to a growing feeling of resentment against America in Japan. And the Japanese-Americans themselves had been left in the unhappy position of a people marooned between two cultures, removed in geography and, increasingly, in habits and thought from the race of their origin, but not accepted as equals by the country of their choice. Even their sons and daughters, born in this country, found themselves in an anomalous position. Japan embarrassingly claimed them as her own, which in language and psychology they were not; but we Americans were reluctant, on grounds of race, to accept them on terms of equality as fellow Americans, which they definitely were.

Fortunately, this situation seems to be passing. As we have seen, the Nisei, despite their unhappy lot in America, proved to be successful though unintentional American ambassadors whenever they went to Japan. They have done more than that. By building up a magnificent record of good will, loyalty, and bravery during the recent war, they apparently have won for themselves the position of equality in this country which was at first denied them, and at the same time they seem to have restored in American minds a basic respect for the Japanese and the realization that character means more than race. Their quiet and loyal acceptance of the grossly unjust treatment they received during the war is now a well-known story. There was hardly a word of complaint from them when they were moved from their homes to relocation centers, our own enlightened form of concentration camps. Even better known is the glorious story of the heroic all-Japanese 442nd Regimental Combat Team in Italy, which won wide acclaim as "the most decorated unit in the military history of the United States," and the equally heroic story of the Nisei combat interpreters with our forces in the Pacific. The Nisei paid a heavy price in blood and suffering, but there is reason to believe that their sacrifices have not been in vain. Now scattered more widely throughout the United States than they were before the war, they have found a new position of equality in our society.

More than that, they have turned a source of contention and bitterness between the United States and Japan into a bond of understanding and mutual respect. In a broader context, they have helped to bridge the wide racial and cultural gap between us and our neighbors in the Far East, between the two ends of the earth in this now unitary world.

The immigration problem was not the only complicating factor in the contacts between the United States and Japan. Economic relations between the two countries made steady and uniformly favorable progress, with America becoming the chief consumer of silk, which was Japan's prime export commodity, and Japan becoming the United States' best customer in all Asia. More and more American businessmen as well as teachers and missionaries settled in Japan, and the cultural and intellectual contacts across the Pacific became steadily closer. A warmer friendship, however, did not result from these increasing contacts as neighbors. Instead an attitude of suspicion and hostility began to characterize Japanese-American relations, as it has the relations of so many other neighbors of longer standing.

The first American reaction to Japan had been one of curiosity and then of enthusiasm. Japan, which, though our neighbor, was after all at the other end of the civilized world from America, was a fascinatingly topsy-turvy land to us, quaint and exotic beyond belief. It was a land of cherry-blossoms and charming ways—a picture postcard land of beauty and quaintness. The whole-hearted Japanese enthusiasm for learning from us was flattering. Our admiration was evoked by Japanese perseverance and success in rapidly building up a Westernized state on the fresh ruins of a feudal order, when the rest of Asia seemed to be fumbling ineptly with the problem of modernization. Little Japan's military victory in 1894 and 1895 over China, the monster sleeping dragon of Asia, was greeted with the plaudits of the entire Western world. During her uphill fight against Russia, the colossus of the north, Japan had no more sympathetic friend than President Theodore

Roosevelt, that lover of a good fight, and there was no small degree of friendship in his action in engineering a peace treaty in 1905 at Portsmouth, New Hampshire, before the shaky Japanese economy gave way and robbed Japan of the fruits of her military victories over the Russians in Manchuria.

4. DETERIORATING RELATIONS

But the Russo-Japanese War marked both the high-water mark of Japanese-American friendship and a sharp turning point in our relations. Many Japanese, in an excess of nationalistic fervor, felt that Japan had been deprived of the full fruits of victory at Portsmouth and blamed the United States for this supposed diplomatic defeat. More important, the Russo-Japanese War made Japan one of the two paramount powers of the Pacific area. The other, thanks to the Spanish-American War a few years earlier and the new American hold on Hawaii and the Philippines, was the United States. The great power vacuum of the far side of the world had been filled. For better or for worse, Japan and America now stood alone in the Pacific and face to face. Henceforth the United States Navy was the hypothetical enemy for all Japanese navy men, while Japan ranked first among hypothetical enemies in our navy circles. The friendly Occidental neighbor of Japan had suddenly become the potential adversary. The charmingly quaint and admirably quick Japanese had suddenly become for us the sinister Yellow Peril.

Soon, too, the United States and Japan found themselves clashing over conflicting interests on the Asiatic mainland. Japan, starting a little tardily in the game of empire-building, was determined to make up for lost time by an aggressive foreign policy, in much the same manner as Germany, another late comer to the game. Her early seizure of Formosa and the near-by Pescadores Islands from China in 1895 was accepted by the powers as being entirely in keeping with the spirit of the times. No one could quibble over her seizure from Russia

U. S. S. R.

U. S. S. R.

MANCHURIA
1931

SAKHALIN
1905

JEHOL
1933

KWANTUNG
1905

KOREA
1910

KURILE IS.

CHINA

THE
JAPANESE
EMPIRE

RYUKYU IS.

FORMOSA
1895

0   500
MILES

MARIANAS
1920   MARSHALL
CAROLINE

in 1905 of Southern Sakhalin and the Kwantung Leased Territory at the southern tip of Manchuria. There seemed to be a
certain grim justness in this, for Japan had won the Kwantung
Territory from China in 1895, only to be forced to disgorge
it a few months later by combined pressure from Germany,
France, and Russia, who cynically helped themselves to pieces
of China three years later, with Russia taking the disputed
Kwantung Territory for herself. Even Japan's establishment
of a protectorate over Korea in 1905 and the outright annexation of that land in 1910 evoked no protests from the rest of
the world.

The days of easy colonial expansion in Asia, however, were
fast drawing to a close. The tragedy for Japan is that, drunk
with her first spectacular successes and carried away by her
desire to rival the great colonial powers of Europe, she persisted in her attempts at empire-building despite the mounting
costs. A nascent nationalism in China and the other colonial
and semi-colonial lands of Asia was foretelling the end of
empire, and in the face of new problems the colonial powers
themselves were beginning to abandon the cruder colonial
concepts of the nineteenth century. Great Britain before long
had started her slow retreat from empire, which was so greatly
accelerated by the granting of independence to India a few
years ago. We Americans had briefly joined the scramble for
empire when we took the Philippines from Spain in 1898, but,
returning to our more traditional belief in the right of self-
determination, we soon became the open opponents of imperialism in Asia, championing instead the twin concepts of
the territorial integrity of China and the "open door" policy
there, meaning by that term equal economic opportunities for
all foreign business enterprises throughout China. While Japan
still flirted with the idea of "carving up the Chinese melon" or,
perhaps, even appropriating the whole of it for herself, we
sought to preserve an independent China which would be open
to American business enterprise.

The clash of American and Japanese interests in China became acute during the First World War. Japan, as a member of the Allied coalition, seized the German foothold and concessions in the Chinese coastal province of Shantung. She also took gigantic steps towards us across the Pacific by capturing the German-held Marianas, Caroline, and Marshall Archipelagoes, strung out for more than two thousand miles north of the equator. These islands Japan later received as a Mandate at Versailles. The war in Europe, by distracting the attention of the other great powers, also gave Japan the opportunity to exact from the Chinese in 1915 the greater part of a series of concessions, known collectively as the "Twenty-One Demands."

Naval and diplomatic rivalry between the United States and Japan was perhaps eased somewhat by the Washington Conference in the winter of 1921–22 and the accompanying Sino-Japanese agreement. The Japanese agreed to withdraw from Shantung, entered into multiparty understandings regarding China, in keeping with the American policy toward that country, and accepted an inferior naval ratio of 5–5–3 with the American and British navies. The effects of the Washington Conference, however, were short-lived. As has been previously indicated, our abrogation in 1924 of the "Gentlemen's Agreement" regarding Japanese immigration produced a deeply unfavorable reaction within Japan. Five years later the worldwide depression struck, putting national tempers on edge and straining international relations to the breaking point. In 1930 the Japanese entered into a second naval agreement at the London Naval Conference, but the reaction in Japan was intensely unfavorable, and within a year, on September 19, 1931, Japan struck in Manchuria, taking the first fatal step which led eventually to another world war and her own downfall.

The return of the Japanese at this time, after sixteen years of quiescence, to the now definitely outmoded concept of imperialistic conquest was in one sense the result of developments within the social and political fabric of Japan, which we shall consider later, but at the same time it was almost as much the product of external conditions over which the Japanese had little control. The impact of the West on Japan had brought industrialization, which in turn had resulted in a rapid growth of population and increasing dependence on the part of the Japanese people on trade with the outside world. The world-wide depression, which followed the collapse of the American stock market in 1929, seemed to threaten the very existence of Japan. As panic spread and nation after nation threw up higher tariff walls to protect those markets it itself controlled, the Japanese were faced with the specter of total exclusion from the markets of the world. Our own depression-born animosity for the mark "Made in Japan" and our fear of cheap Japanese goods flooding our stores was more than matched by Japanese fears that, denied the markets of the world, Japan would lack the exchange to purchase abroad the food and raw materials needed for the daily life of her people. It was argued with telling force in post-depression Japan that only the great empires of the world could survive a world-wide depression, great self-contained land empires like the United States and the Soviet Union or sea empires like Great Britain and France, but not small and isolated Japan.

Unfortunately for Japan, her Asiatic neighbors, and ourselves as well, her first reëntry into the game of empire-snatching was unexpectedly easy and successful. Manchuria, where she had long had dominant interests, fell into her lap like the proverbial ripe apple. China was still too feeble to retaliate with much more than an economic boycott and bitter hatred, although a protracted and entirely pointless battle was fought between Chinese nationalist forces and the Japanese in the environs of Shanghai. The European powers, through the League of Nations, futilely censured Japan, which, by ignoring the report of the Lytton Commission the League had set up and by brazenly withdrawing from the League, dealt it its first fatal blow as an effective organ of international order. The United States made clear her uncompromising disapproval of Japanese actions in China, but did nothing more. Thus, Japan's one powerful neighbor, immersed in her own compelling economic problems and dominated by a blind belief that she could isolate herself from the problems of the rest of the world, failed to act and by this failure permitted Japan and the world to rush onward toward the catastrophe which was soon to engulf us all.

Meanwhile, Japan had in February 1932 set up a puppet regime in Manchuria and at a minimal military cost had, for all practical purposes, absorbed into her empire China's most economically valuable provinces, with their overwhelmingly Chinese population of upwards of thirty millions. After the spectacular and easy gains of the so-called "Manchurian Incident," there was no stopping the advocates of imperialistic expansion in Japan—no stopping them until they had brought down the Far East in ruins upon the heads of the Japanese people.

It is disconcerting to note that deteriorating relations between the United States and Japan produced an increasingly ostrich-like attitude on the part of Americans. The more American and Japanese interests clashed and the more acute the disagreements between our two lands became, the more deeply and carefully we should have studied Japan and the Japanese, if not in an effort to understand them, at least in an effort to thwart them. Instead, we chose to ignore them, to attempt to make Japan insignificant by refusing to recognize its importance to us. Our reaction was basically emotional rather than rational. Instead of facing our problems realistically, we were almost like a primitive people attempting to vanquish their foes by sympathetic magic.

We grasped at straws of rumor to bolster our belief in the weakness of Japan. The result was a flood of entirely unfounded stories about Japanese ineptness and stupidity, passionately believed and gloatingly repeated by our self-appointed Far Eastern experts. The Japanese were so dishonest, it was said, that they had to have Chinese tellers in their banks. They had some mysterious visual failing which made them miserable fliers. They insisted on building top-heavy warships which constantly turned turtle. They had slavishly copied the accidental imperfections of an airplane model obtained from the British, with the result that none of the planes built on that model would fly. This last story was the best-loved tale of all, turning up in a hundred variations, all based on thin air.

On the other side, our compulsive desire to believe the worst about the Japanese pushed us towards believing only the best about the Chinese. Any Chinese success against the Japanese was magnified out of all proportion to reality. Chinese guerrilla resistance alone, we were told, would be enough to destroy the Japanese war machine. Driven by dislike of Japan as well as by a natural sympathy for a people fighting heroically to maintain their freedom, we gradually built up in our minds an idealized picture of China, which, when turned to disillusionment by later events, has done much to sour Sino-American relations.

Our Army, Navy, and Foreign Service did train a few men in the Japanese language, but the outbreak of war soon revealed how pathetically inadequate our efforts in this direction had been. More careful study of Japan probably would not have been enough to avoid the Pacific War, but it might have enabled us to delay it and thereby make its opening phases less costly to ourselves. We paid a heavy price for letting prejudice blind us to the necessity of studying our enemies as well as our friends.

After five years of consolidating her gains in Manchuria, Japan returned to the offensive in 1937. An exchange of shots between Japanese and Chinese troops at Marco Polo Bridge near Peking on the night of July 7 of that year signalized the renewal of Japanese efforts to slice off pieces of China. It was also the curtain raiser for the final climactic act. Japan was now attempting to seize parts of the heartland of Old China, and the Chinese were determined to resist to the bitter end. In a huge country like China, the bitter end can be a long way off. Chinese armies could not stop the better equipped and better trained Japanese military machine, but neither could Japanese bayonets kill the will to resist on the part of four hundred million Chinese. This time, there was no cheap and rapid success, as in Manchuria six years earlier. Instead, Japan found herself enmeshed in a long, costly, and inconclusive war.

Seizing the coastline and the major river and rail arteries of China was not hard for the Japanese, but making these conquests pay in the face of bitter guerrilla resistance and the sullen resentment of the Chinese masses was another matter. After four years of war, Japan in 1941 seemed further from victory than she had been at the outset. Worse than that, she was dependent on foreign sources for many of the sinews of war, and these foreign sources were gradually being closed to her. Oil in particular, oil to run her ships, planes, and tanks, was being denied her by the United States and the European. powers, newly awakened by the outbreak of war in Europe to the danger of allowing aggression to go unchecked. Time was running out for Japan.

At this point, a situation which had been a reality for many years finally became quite apparent to everyone. America and America alone could stop Japan, or, to put it another way, only America stood in Japan's path to empire. On the surface Japan was far less deeply embroiled with the United States than with a number of other countries. For four long years she had been engaged in the seemingly endless task of conquering China. Japanese troops glowered at Russian troops across the long frontier between Manchuria and Siberia, and twice the Russians and Japanese had tested each other out in full-scale border battles. But the Soviet Union had its own problems and was anxious to avoid any major involvement of its energies and military power in the Far East. In September 1940 Japan became the open ally of the Axis Powers, which were already engaged in a life and death struggle with England, France, and Holland. The British and French concessions in the cities of China were a thorn in the side of the conquering armies of Japan. After the fall of France, the Japanese bullied their way into French Indo-China. The Dutch and British colonial possessions farther south had the oil and other natural resources Japan so desperately needed to continue her war effort. In reality, however, America was more than ever Japan's one great neighbor and opponent. As long as the United States gave its moral support, the Chinese had hope and would fight on. As long as America stood firm, the other powers would stand with her, in the so-called ABCD coalition of America, Britain, China, and the Dutch, to frustrate the Japanese dream of hegemony over the Far East. The Japanese understood America's dominant role. When negotiations were undertaken in 1941 in a last-minute effort to avoid war, these negotiations were exclusively between the United States and Japan. When war came, the attack was directed primarily against our forces at Pearl Harbor and in the Philippines.

Historians will long discuss the might-have-beens of the recent war and the critical years that preceded it. Obviously we were psychologically ill prepared to achieve the most in our negotiations with the Japanese. At the least, we could have postponed the Japanese attack, by subterfuge if necessary, until we ourselves were better prepared for it. With a clearer understanding of the Japanese mentality and Japanese problems, we might even have been able to do more. Certainly our basic insistence that Japan first withdraw from her conquests in China before we would discuss her own legitimate or fancied grievances, though diplomatically correct, was hardly skillful diplomacy. Bargains are not arrived at by insisting that one party make major concessions before the other party has revealed its hand. Be that as it may, the Japanese-American negotiations of 1941 were the one fundamental effort to settle the Sino-Japanese conflict and avoid a general war in the Pacific. When they failed, a war involving the whole Far East and every corner of the Pacific became inevitable.

So set had we become in our psychology of avoidance with respect to the Japanese problem that it took the outbreak of war to awaken the American public from its indifference to Japan and to make us realize how important a neighbor she had become. The war in the Pacific, though involving a score or more of nations, was essentially a Japanese-American war. Some British, Canadian, and Dutch units were engulfed in its opening phases; Australian, Indian, and Chinese troops participated in the New Guinea and Burma campaigns; the Chinese continued, as best they could, their war of slow attrition throughout the length and breadth of occupied China; and the Russians came in during the last week of the war to smash the hollow shell of the once powerful Kwantung Army in Manchuria. Otherwise, it was almost exclusively an American war with Japan. American forces took the giant strides along the island steppingstones of the Pacific, until they reached the front door of Japan. American ships, submarines, and planes destroyed the Japanese Navy and the Japanese merchant marine. American B–29's burned out the heart of Japan. When the end finally came, it was but natural that an American general should receive Japan's surrender and that the United States should undertake the occupation of the defeated nation, creating, thus, a far closer and more vexatious bond than had ever existed before between our two nations.

3. Japan and America: The Problem

1. THE OBJECTIVES OF THE OCCUPATION

It is not true that wars never settle problems, but they often create greater problems than those they were fought to solve. The American forces moved into Japan with the light, springy step of self-confident men. When General MacArthur received the formal Japanese surrender on September 2, 1945, on board the battleship *Missouri* in Tokyo Bay, the modern name for Edo Bay, where Perry's "black ships" had forced the reopening of Japan less than a century earlier, we assumed that our troubles were over. The basic problem of the Far East seemed to have been solved by bullets and a rain of fire bombs. Japan, which had run wild through China for over a decade and had plunged half the world into war, had at last been brought to her knees. The bad boy of the Pacific had been tamed. The rest of the Far East could now return to normalcy, free from the fear of Japanese aggression. The future seemed rosy. And yet in a shorter space of time than it had taken to win the war, that rosy future darkened into a series of thunderheads more ominous than any we had ever seen before. Japan and the whole Far East appeared to be mired in a bottomless slough of new problems, more difficult than the old, and the United States was more deeply involved in the Far East and its problems than ever.

Fortunately, we started off in Japan at least in the right direction, even if we did not have an accurate idea of what the future held in store for us. There was no false start as in

Germany, the other major postwar "bad boy," where we briefly toyed with a plan to reduce Europe's leading industrial power to an agricultural and pastoral economy. Naturally we were forced to abandon this plan almost before we had started to put it into execution. During the war, the economic and cultural isolation of Japan and the consequent de-industrialization of her economy, too, had been a popular concept in America. Dressed up in the colorful but grim phrase, "Let Japan stew in her own juice," it had seemed a fitting and workable solution for the Japanese problem. Reduced to its simplest terms, "stewing in their own juice" would have meant the starvation of a few tens of millions of Japanese, specifically that portion of the population which was in excess of what an isolated and therefore largely agricultural economy could feed, clothe, and house. Luckily for us, for the Japanese, and for the whole Far East, we had already faced the problem of trying to reduce Germany to a sheep pasture before we ever put foot in Japan, and we knew better than to make the same blunder again. Our leaders had come to realize that this would be no solution of our Far Eastern problems but would leave a permanently sick Japan, which was economically a liability rather than an asset to the shaky Far Eastern community of nations, a source of infection for its neighbors, and a hopeless invalid who in desperation might welcome the brutal surgery of totalitarianism.

During the hectic summer of 1945, after Japanese surrender had become clearly imminent, our policy-makers, working through the State-War-Navy Coördinating Committee, drew up a basic guiding directive for our occupation of Japan, known as the *United States Initial Post-Surrender Policy for Japan*. This document, which was radioed to General MacArthur on August 29 of that year, proved itself to be a wise and practical statement of objectives. Broad in scope and flexible in detail, it provided us with an over-all program that proved to be sound in concept and on the whole feasible in execution. Despite rapid changes since the war throughout the Far East and in American understanding of what international realities actually were, this document remained an essentially valid guidepost for the occupation period, and it helped produce a Japan that, since the end of the occupation in 1951, seems to have been moving basically in the right direction. Certain aspects of this policy had to be modified and others abandoned, but by and large it stood the test of time very well, while most other American foreign policies required drastic revision not long after the close of the war.

The *United States Initial Post-Surrender Policy for Japan* outlined a three-point program. First came the demilitarization of Japan to prevent her from again disrupting the Far East by military aggression. Next was the more basic objective of creating "a peaceful and responsible government" in Japan, meaning, of course, a democratic government which, because of popular control, would be less likely than an authoritarian government to embark upon a warlike course. The final point was the realization that a peaceful and democratic Japan could exist only on the basis of a viable economy, that is an economy which would "permit the peacetime requirements of the population to be met." Changing circumstances both inside and outside of Japan produced changing interpretations of some of the specific details of this policy, but they did not alter its basic spirit or objectives.

2. JAPAN IN A DIVIDED WORLD

Where our policy-makers made a bad, but thoroughly understandable, miscalculation was not in the internal problem in Japan but in the general world situation and Japan's relationship to it. We were convinced that the only serious problem in the Far East was Japanese military aggression and that Japan's complete collapse had solved this problem. With Japan prostrate, the rest of the Far East could quickly find its way back to stability and prosperity, while we altruistically experimented with reforming the troublemaker. If we were successful, some day he would be allowed to return to the society of nations, a chastened and wiser citizen. If not, so much the worse for him. We were giving him a chance to reform, but the ultimate outcome was his concern, not ours. We were not vitally concerned, because Japan, once stripped of military might, could never again menace a united world.

The only thing wrong with this concept was that a united world failed to materialize, and the Far East outside of Japan, far from marching back toward stability and prosperity, broke out in a rash of civil wars and disturbances. Korea, restored in theory to independence after forty years of cruel Japanese oppression, was in reality divided between two mutually hostile occupying forces, which left behind them, when they eventually withdrew, two separate Korean governments. Then in June 1950 the Communist regime in North Korea invaded South Korea, which had been sponsored first by the United States and then by the United Nations itself. American and Chinese Communist forces were soon involved in the resulting struggle, and it grew into a major though basically inconclusive war that left behind it a still divided and now war-ravaged land.

China, escaping from the curse of foreign invasion, was soon plunged into an equally destructive civil conflict. Even after the expulsion from the mainland of the American-backed Nationalist regime by their Communist adversaries, this war went on smouldering, as Chiang Kai-shek's forces, with American naval protection, continued to defy the Communists from their island stronghold of Formosa and occasionally engaged them in minor clashes on the coastal islands of China.

French Indo-China was wracked by civil wars between the Communist-led Vietminh and the colonial authorities, and, when the French, finally bowing to the inevitable, withdrew, they left behind them in Indo-China a perilously weak Laos state, a scarcely more viable Cambodia, and a Vietnam precariously divided between the Vietminh Communists and a would-be democratic Vietnam, which rested heavily on American aid.

Somewhat the same picture repeated itself in Malaya, where year after year Communist guerrillas, drawn almost exclusively from the Chinese population in the peninsula, kept sizable British contingents continually on the go in a seemingly endless game of hide and seek in the jungles. With large parts of the land still guerrilla territory and with a population divided

between Malays, Chinese, and Indians, who have little solidarity with one another, Malaya faced a decidedly uncertain
future on the eve of its independence in 1957.

In the Philippines the situation for long was not any better
than in Malaya, but eventually the Communist Huks were
brought under control, and under the vigorous leadership of
President Magsaysay the newly independent land seemed at
last to be settling down to peace and stability. Indonesia too
was torn by war between the Dutch colonial administration
and the native nationalists, and even after the withdrawal of
the former the still very weak and inexperienced Indonesian
Republic was plagued by constant revolts in one or another
area of its far-flung domains. Siam since the war has had its
customary quota of *coups d'état*, while in Burma, despite the
ungrudging and gracious withdrawal of the British, there has
been frequent strife between the new government and various
intransigent political and tribal groupings.

And over the whole scene has lain the dark cloud of Communist and Western rivalry. The world outside the Far East,
far from being united, had drawn apart into two armed
camps. Once again there was talk of world war. Every political disturbance had its overtones of two-power rivalry, height-
ening the discords and injecting an ominous note into the
rumblings of social and political change in Asia.

Obviously no world order existed in which Japan might
some day take its place again. Certainly there is no community of nations in the Far East able to control even a drastically weakened Japan. Economically destitute and torn by
revolutions, the lands of the Far East are no more capable
of providing a firm international order than they were before the war. The original problem of Japanese military
aggression has not been solved for the future by the growing
solidarity of the rest of the world. The problem has in fact
taken on an entirely different aspect. Far from being worried
about possible Japanese aggression in the future, the great
powers have become more and more interested in Japan as a
political or, even possibly, a military ally. Instead of being
the bad boy who was to reform and penitently seek readmis-
sion into the one world club, Japan is now viewed as a poten-

tial candidate for one of the two mutually exclusive world clubs and is assiduously wooed by each.

We made another miscalculation in believing that the other lands of the Far East would quickly catch up in economic and military power to a bomb-gutted Japan, once the war was over. However destructive the war was to Japan, she has not lost her basic economic strength in terms of industrial assets and the technical abilities of her industrious people. Her neighbors, through war damage and civil disturbances, have lost proportionately as much as Japan. They have found difficulty in restoring even their feeble prewar economies and have been entirely unable to take advantage of Japan's defeat to achieve industrial equality with her.

Japan is still the paramount economic power of the Far East, economically as far ahead of her neighbors today as she was before the war. She is also the chief potential source of military power. China, through closer integration and nationalistic enthusiasm under her new Communist leadership, now produces much greater military power than ever before in modern times, but she still lacks the factory power and technical skills to produce herself the most important modern weapons of warfare. Only Japan in all of Asia has this capacity today, and, though she has very little military power in being, she nevertheless has the only significant potential for producing the means of military aggression. One might conclude that any unreformed Japanese militarist would have ample reason to gloat over the situation.

It is not surprising, therefore, that Japan's neighbors from Korea to Burma, which all have felt the heel of the Japanese conqueror, or even distant Australia, which was thoroughly terrified by the specter of Japanese conquest during the recent war, retain a very vivid fear of a revived Japanese militarism. For sixty years Japan fished with consummate skill in the troubled waters of the Far East to catch her erstwhile empire piece by piece, and no one can deny that once again the waters are mightily roiled up. Conceivably a skillful policy of playing Russia and America off against each other might prove very profitable to Japan, and she could in this way recreate her hegemony over the Far East.

Such fears on the part of the peoples of the Far East and Australia are thoroughly understandable, but when looked at judiciously and without emotion they prove to be anything but realistic. There is actually little if any danger that Japan will reëmerge as a major military power and reëstablish her political domination over her neighbors. In the case of Germany, the danger conceivably may still exist, but Japan, unlike Germany, is not the geographic center and natural economic heart of her part of the world. Neither is Japan at present — or potentially — so powerful a nation as Germany. Unlike Germany she does not heavily outweigh most of her closest neighbors in population but instead is numerically far inferior to two of them. Her ascendancy in the Far East has been to a large extent a historical accident rather than the inevitable result of geography. The Japanese, for a combination of reasons, got off to a head start over their Asiatic neighbors in acquiring new techniques from the West. Japan will eventually lose this temporal advantage, and China, far larger in size and richer in natural resources, will inevitably outstrip her some day.

More important is the fact that a shrinking world and the appearance of military powers of a new magnitude have transformed Japan from a giant among the military pygmies of Asia into a midget between the two great powers which flank her on either side. While Germany could conceivably rise again to rival the United States and Russia, it is out of the question that Japan could ever again threaten her neighbors, if either the United States or the Soviet Union disapproved. For fifty years a time advantage over her Asiatic neighbors and a spatial advantage over her more distant rivals gave Japan a dominant place in East Asia. The first factor, though passing, has not yet been eliminated, but the second has disappeared, and with it has gone the possibility of Japan's ever again becoming a truly first-rate power.

Of course, Japan theoretically could win back her old position of dominance if the major powers were to destroy each other or lead the world into international chaos, while Japan remained relatively intact, but in that case those of us who survived the holocaust would have other more pressing worries than Japanese aggression. Another theoretical possibility is that either the United States or the Soviet Union might permit and encourage a rearmed Japan to reconquer her former empire, but such a situation is actually quite inconceivable today.

This, however, does not mean that Japan is of no military importance in the modern world. Far from it. She may have no chance of becoming again an independent military power, even if the Japanese desired this, which they most certainly do not for the present. Ever since the end of the war there has been a strong revulsion against militarism in Japan, and even today the majority of the people seem strongly set against any great rearmament. On the other hand, Japan unquestionably is capable of being a weighty counter in the balance of power in a divided world. Obviously she is not of the magnitude of the three major centers of industrial and military power in the world — the United States, the Soviet Union, and Western Europe — but potentially she ranks close behind the fourth center, the British Isles, and far ahead of any others. For all our wishful thinking, it is the other lands of Asia that might conceivably be considered as still remaining outside the major stream of world rivalries, but certainly not Japan. These other Asian nations with their vast populations will inevitably come to count in the balance of power, if not within the next two decades, then perhaps in the next half century. But Japan counts right now. Like Western Europe, she is potentially part of the present balance of power — not just that of the year 2000.

Even an unarmed Japan has been of considerable direct military significance during this past decade. Under the occupation and since then by special treaty arrangement, Japan has served as our principal military base in the Far East. In fact, she has been the largest Western military outpost in all of Asia. Without it, we could scarcely have fought the Korean War at all and certainly not as effectively as we did. Japanese industrial facilities too gave direct support to our military effort in Korea that was indispensable.

For very obvious reasons we cannot assume, as we did at first, that Japan's ultimate fate is of no great concern to us or to the rest of the world. It is of vital importance to all of us, not because of the dangers of a Japanese return to military aggression but because of Japan's potentialities in a world that is divided by constant political strife and verges at times on open warfare. A Japan which actively supported the Communist program of world conquest might tip the scales disastrously against us first in Asia and then, through Asia, in the world as a whole. On the other hand, a Japan actively supporting the concept of a world order of international democracy could prove a valuable, possibly a decisive ally to the democratic side.

The problem is not purely a military one. More important is the economic capacity of Japan that lies behind her military potential. In the early postwar years it was hoped that the other nations of the Far East, with the aid of the transfer of machinery from Japan as reparations payments, would soon establish their independence of the factory power of Japan, which, when reformed, would have to find a new place for itself in a now more equalized Far Eastern economy. Reparation transfers of machinery from Japan to the countries she had devastated, however, were not carried out on any significant scale because of technical and political difficulties. The economy of the Far East remained flat on its back, and it has proved difficult to revive it to prewar levels, much less to raise it to levels that would maintain even minimum standards of health, education, and economic security.

Under such circumstances Japanese factory facilities and economic skills in general have taken on an unforeseen importance. Unquestionably the Communists eye them enviously. If they had the Japanese economic potential in their hands, there would be no doubt of the success of the great communist experiment in China, even though Japan might have to be bled white to provide China with the industrial blood it needs.

The Japanese economy soon came to appear equally important to us. Non-communist Asia was desperately in need of the goods, machines, and skills that the Japanese are capable of supplying. Many of these countries stood dangerously close to the edge of economic collapse, and in the background always lurked the shadow of communism. In such a situation we scarcely dared squander any of our economic assets, and certainly Japan was a major one. It seemed absurd to let Japanese industrial capacity lie idle at a time when the Far East was in such grave economic peril and Japan itself living miserably on an American dole. A more reasonable course was to encourage rather than prevent the industrial recovery of Japan, even if this entailed some curtailment of our reform program there. In this way Japan could be made self-supporting and would stop being the huge financial drag on us that it was during the early postwar years. More important, the Japanese industrial potential could be brought into play in building up the economic ramparts against communism throughout free Asia.

This change in American attitudes came about primarily in 1948 and 1949, but it proved a difficult task to get Japanese machines working for the economic recovery of the Far East. For one thing Japan herself recovered economically from the war far more slowly than any other major industrial power, in part for political reasons but more significantly because of the fundamental weakness of the Japanese economic base. It took three years for Japanese industrial production to be restored to half of what it had been about two decades earlier and a quarter of what it was in 1944. And it was a full decade before it recovered fully from the wounds of the war and living standards began to approximate and then inch above those of prewar years.

The attitudes of Japan's neighbors toward her have been an even more important reason why Japanese economic capacities have not as yet played a large role in postwar Asia. For the most part the other Asians are reluctant to have much to do with Japan, even if such a policy hurts themselves. They fear that an economically revived Japan might restore her wartime economic control over them. Like Japan eighty years earlier, they are anxious to build up their own factories so that they can compete with the economies of an industrialized Japan and the West. In addition, they hate Japan for past aggressions. They prefer to trade with any other country in the world rather than with her.

While the economic fears of Japan's neighbors are almost

as groundless as their parallel fears of Japanese military aggression, they are quite understandable and certainly very real. They will without doubt restrict Japan's economic role in the Far East for some years to come, but this role, nonetheless, is sure to become important in time and may even spell the difference between economic success and collapse in some of the countries of Asia. Japan, far from having been insulated economically from the rest of the world, remains the economic pivot of the Far East and a crucial economic factor in the global contest between communism and democracy.

In the political field our original attitude toward Japan was proved by postwar history to have been even more mistaken. We insisted on regarding Japan as an international pariah to be excluded from world society until reform had made her a fit associate for the other nations of the world. At first our occupation authorities rigorously isolated Japan from normal international contacts, while they pushed through reform after reform, designed to bring Japan up to a hypothetical world standard. But the unrealities behind these assumptions soon became apparent. There was no accepted world standard. The only policy all the victor nations shared with regard to Japan was the purely negative one of demilitarization. The United States was true to its ideals in attempting to shape a democratic Japan, with emphasis on the inalienable rights of the individual, a government responsible to the people, and as much free enterprise as could be reconstructed in the economic chaos of postwar Japan. But these were hardly Soviet standards. The Russians, with their rigid view of clear-cut spheres of influence, were outwardly willing to defer to the United States on most decisions affecting Japan, but, through the Communist movement within Japan, they steadily fought our basic policies there, with the hope of eventually subverting Japan to communism. Political reform in Japan, thus, was obviously part of the world-wide struggle, and as such it took on global significance.

The remarkable fact in all this is that the *United States Initial Post-Surrender Policy for Japan*, while drawn up on the assumption that Japan was to be reformed for membership in a unitary world order, still proved fundamentally sound even after we realized that the world was divided and saw clearly that our objective in Japan must be to enlist a reformed Japan on the side of democracy against communist aggression. Demilitarization was still necessary, because Japanese militarism, as it had existed, could never be a desirable or dependable ally of democracy; political reform and the creation of a stable and healthy democratic regime in Japan were even more essential in the new situation than before; so also was the economic recovery of Japan on which democracy depended. In fact, the only basic changes our policy planners might have made with the wisdom of foresight would have been to place slightly less emphasis on demilitarization and considerably more on economic recovery. In any case, the high degree of validity of this document under the vastly altered circumstances of the cold war show that it was not just a clever policy statement but a product of real statesmanship.

3. JAPAN AND THE FUTURE OF DEMOCRACY

As we have seen, however, there were some basic errors in American attitudes toward the future role of a defeated Japan. The original American attitudes, in fact, were not merely outmoded by the changing international situation; they were in many ways invalid from the outset. This was particularly true in the political field. Japan, far from being the one non-democratic nation in the Far East, was in fact the most promising prospect for democracy in all Asia.

Even before the war, Japan was the only significantly industrialized nation in Asia, the only one with a well-established system of universal education, and the Asian country with the greatest practical experience in democratic forms of government. Aided by the catharsis of military defeat and the tonic of American reform policies, she quickly began to show more promise of approximating Occidental standards of democracy within the foreseeable future than did any of her Asian neighbors. Instead of attempting to bring her up to a standard commonly accepted by the nations of the Far East, we were in reality attempting to push her even further ahead of them and closer to the standards of the Western democratic world. Japan, as the disturber of the peace of the Far East, was obviously in need of reform in a way the other countries of Asia were not, but her very ability to be the aggressor in Asia was the result of her greater advancement in Western techniques over her neighbors. She was still the pioneer in Asia, economically, educationally, and, if democracy has any future in Asia, then in the political field as well.

Viewed in this light, one can see the true significance of the American reform program under the occupation and of the whole history of Japan since the end of the war. Japan is a great ideological battleground, and the outcome of the battle there is of the greatest importance for us. We are anxious to prove that democracy is an article for export, that it can work and will work beyond the borders of the few really democratic states of today. We want to prove that the rest of the world does not have to turn to the seemingly simpler totalitarian panaceas of communism or fascism. We are anxious to have another people firmly on the side of democracy, one more nation to help keep the preponderant weight of the world behind the ideals of individual freedom and the acceptance of majority decisions in both domestic and international affairs.

This same ideological struggle repeats itself in various lands of Europe, but in Japan it has added significance. No one doubts that, if the Dutch and Finns can be thoroughly democratic, so also can the Germans and Poles. Their basic cultural backgrounds are sufficiently close. But Asia is a different matter. No non-Caucasian people has ever made democracy operate successfully over a long period of time. Throughout Asia democracy is given much lip service, and most of the newly independent countries of Asia are formally organized as democracies. Unquestionably many of Asia's leaders understand and thoroughly believe in democracy. But it is one thing to believe in democracy and to draft democratic constitutions and quite another to solve for long the manifold problems of a modern state through the agency of popular elections, particularly when faced with the ignorance, inexperience, pathetic poverty, and often the profound cultural and linguistic divisions of the peoples of most Asian states.

It is not surprising that democracy seems something of a chimera to many Asians, an admirable ideal, perhaps valid in the West, but at best of only limited applicability in countries where the masses are illiterate and primarily concerned with finding their next meal. Democracy to many in Asia, while a glamorous concept, seems to be a rather peculiar political product of one of the more peculiar corners of the world. Obviously the people of northwestern Europe, with their blue eyes and "red" hair, are different from men in general. Is it surprising that they and their cultural and racial extensions overseas should have a peculiar type of society which does not fit the more normal people of the world? Democracy at best seems a rather distant and uncertain goal, while benevolent despotism, always the Asian ideal and now provided with a startling array of powerful new techniques, stands ready at hand as an inviting and apparently easy short-cut. There is far more need for a demonstration that democracy works in Asia than there is in Europe, and this is what makes the whole experiment in Japan so important to us and to the world.

We Americans only slowly began to be aware of the significance of the task of reforming Japan we assumed so blithely in 1945. The recent history of Japan, as we shall see in a later chapter, indicates quite clearly that if Japan does not become democratic, then she is almost certain to turn to totalitarianism. But if the most advanced nation in Asia with the highest economic and educational standards and the longest and deepest experience in democracy were to turn away from it to totalitarianism, then there would be small hope for democracy anywhere in Asia. And if democracy cannot survive in Asia, then the people of the existing Western democracies will soon find themselves a hopelessly outnumbered minority, perhaps unable to maintain even their own democracy for long in an overwhelmingly totalitarian world. The democratic experiment in Japan is obviously not being conducted in a vacuum isolated from the rest of the world, as we at first believed, but is a crucial battle in the war between democracy and communism; it may actually prove to be the crucial battle as far as Asia is concerned.

Perhaps the best way to understand how deeply concerned

we are with the success of the democratic experiment in Japan is to consider briefly what are the alternatives to its success. The simplest and perhaps the most likely form of failure would be a situation in which democratic reforms, though partially successful, failed in the long run to maintain living standards at a tolerable level or failed to operate efficiently enough to win the mass of the people to a continued support of democratic institutions. Even though unrest did not develop to the point of revolution or result in drastic revision of the democratic political framework, still, if economic conditions were intolerable, if society were unstable and people restive, if the government were corrupt or merely ineffectual, democracy would be judged to have failed in Japan.

Such a state of semi-failure of our democratic reforms could very well develop into a situation even more disastrous to American foreign policy. A frustrated and disillusioned Japan could all too easily revert to the authoritarian and possibly militaristic concepts of the past and resume the pompous march down the glittering road toward totalitarianism. The details of a revived totalitarian system might differ from those of the prewar years; the symbols, the names, even the theories might be changed; but, as long as it meant rejection of the realities of democracy and a return to militarism and authoritarianism, it would be a catastropric defeat for American policy.

A third and, by all odds, the most likely way in which democracy might fail in Japan would be if she abandoned it for the more easily followed road to communism. This could come about as a result of direct Soviet pressure or, conceivably, invasion, though the latter seems only a remote possibility under present conditions. Communism is much more likely to come to Japan as a result of frustration and gradual disillusionment with democracy within Japan and the consequent espousal of the communist creed by the desperate masses as a more promising way to prosperity and happiness. In Japan, with its strong authoritarian traditions, this picture is not a difficult one to conjure up. In fact, any return to totalitarianism in postwar Japan seems unlikely except in the form of communism. At the same time, any prolonged economic depression or social unrest would probably not just stop there but would force the Japanese to turn to communism as a possible cure for their ills. In other words, it is hard to imagine democracy failing in postwar Japan without communism taking its place.

In any case, no matter how communism might come to Japan, the Japanese acceptance of it in place of democracy would be for the democratic world a defeat far greater than the one in China. It might very well spell the eventual end of all democratic hopes in Asia and certainly would place Japan at once in the opposite camp. The Japanese economic potential would be used for the benefit of communism, not the free world. So also would the entire Japanese military potential. While a democratic Japan may not be able to recreate its full military power for fear of the harm it might do democracy there, the Communists would be faced with no such problem. Militarism and communism go perfectly together. In more ways than one a communist Japan would greatly increase the menace to the security of our country and the whole democratic world.

4. JAPAN AS AN AMERICAN PROBLEM

The future of Japan is, of course, not a problem that concerns us Americans alone. It is of importance to all the peoples of the Western democracies and all the peoples of Asia as well. But in one way Japan has been and still is a peculiarly American problem. While all countries are involved in the outcome, it was the United States that had the chief responsibility for the reform of Japan during the occupation, and since the signing of the peace treaty the United States has continued to exercise far more influence on developments in Japan than any other foreign country — perhaps more influence than all the other countries of the world put together.

The occupation of Japan was in theory an allied occupation, and General MacArthur, as the Supreme Commander for the Allied Powers, or SCAP, was actually an international figure and not merely an American administrator. The supreme policy-making body for Japan was not the United States government, but the thirteen-power Far Eastern Commission in Washington, which included China, Great Britain, the Soviet Union, Australia, the Philippines, India, the Netherlands, France, Canada, New Zealand, Pakistan, and Burma. Ten of these states were members of the Far Eastern Commission since its inception early in 1946, and Pakistan and Burma joined the group on November 17, 1949. Great Britain, the Soviet Union, and China shared with us the veto power in this body, and the same three powers also sat with us in the Allied Council for Japan in Tokyo. Large contingents of Australian troops and some from New Zealand and India, acting in behalf of the whole British Commonwealth, also took part in the military occupation of Japan.

On the surface, thus, the occupation was quite international, but the simple truth is that behind this façade it was from start to finish an American show. General MacArthur, despite his glorified international title of Supreme Commander for the Allied Powers, was also the Commander-in-chief of all United States forces in the Far East and made no pretense of not being essentially an American proconsul in Japan. American troops had the primary responsibility for taking over and policing Japan. Chinese and Russian units were to have joined them in this task but never did, because of civil war in China and mutual distrust between the United States and the Soviet Union. The British Empire forces that did come to Japan undertook the military control of an important sector of western Japan, but they remained only a minority element among the tactical troops in Japan, without any direct involvement in the execution of the all-important reform program. MacArthur's huge staff of experts and advisers in Tokyo was always overwhelmingly American, and so also were the military government teams scattered throughout the nation. The few individual exceptions — a lone Australian Brigadier among the higher echelons in Tokyo, an occasional British oil expert, Italian scholar, or French secretary in the huge bureaucracy of the occupation — only served to highlight the obvious fact that the staff of the Supreme Commander for the Allied Powers was almost as exclusively American as the average federal agency in Washington.

More important than the personnel in Japan was the fact that all occupation policies were based on the *United States Initial Post-Surrender Policy for Japan*, which, while conforming to the simple terms of two international pronouncements — the Cairo Declaration of December 1, 1943, and the Potsdam Proclamation of July 26, 1945 — was essentially an American policy statement. The Far Eastern Commission came into being only as a result of the Moscow Agreement of December 27, 1945, four months after the United States had started to implement her own policies in Japan. Although the Far Eastern Commission was made in theory the supreme policy-making body, with the right to review all of General MacArthur's actions and directives as Supreme Commander for the Allied Powers, its hands were tied from the start. The United States' veto power in the Commission could effectively block any attempt to censure General MacArthur or make him reverse actions already taken. Similarly, no established United States policy for Japan, even if not yet implemented, could be changed without American consent. The United States could even continue to make new policy decisions unilaterally, because the Moscow Agreement stated that "the United States Government may issue interim directives to the Supreme Commander pending action by the Commission whenever urgent matters arise not covered by policies already formulated by the Commission."

Thus, in reality, the Far Eastern Commission could do little more than discuss and then approve, but not disapprove, previous American policy decisions. On June 19, 1947, it eventually adopted, with only minor changes, the *United States Initial Post-Surrender Policy for Japan* as its own basic policy. The Commission exercised a certain restraining influence on American policy-makers, but only infrequently did it have any positive influence on the formulation of major policies. Desiring to preserve the dignity of international organizations, if not their efficacy, the members of the Far Eastern Commission accepted its frustrating and impotent position with surprising good grace. The sessions of the Commission were unusually amicable for a postwar international body, and the veto was used only infrequently. The Far Eastern Commission gradually settled down to a genteel position of pompous futility. It had powers which made it difficult for the United States on its own initiative to modify fundamentally the nature of the occupation or to terminate it, but the Commission never had the capacity itself to control the occupation or formulate basic policies for it.

The case of the Allied Council for Japan was even sadder. Limited in its duties largely to consultation with and advice to the Supreme Commander, it degenerated almost at once into a debating society, in which the American and Russian members carried on an acrimonious argument in front of the embarrassed British and Chinese representatives. Then it lapsed into a moribund state. W. Macmahon Ball, for a year and a half the British member of the Council, has placed the blame for its failure primarily on us. He has accused General MacArthur's representative on the Council of having "treated it with frivolous derision" and General MacArthur himself of having "omitted to consult it on many major questions." Mr. Ball concluded that, "In these circumstances, it was inevitable that the Council should have been on balance a failure, and at times a fiasco." *

Despite the list of international controlling bodies and the theory of international participation, neither we nor our Allies on the Far Eastern Commission had any illusions about the essentially American nature of the occupation. Throughout the world it was frankly regarded as an American undertaking, the success or failure of which would be chalked up in large letters to the credit or debit side of American foreign policy. Particularly in Japan, where omnipresent realities outweighed the verbiage of international documents, the man in the street never thought of the occupation as being international. How could it be, when it was so manifestly and so completely American? For better or for worse, Japan was in our hands, perhaps as a sort of unregulated trusteeship on behalf of the Allied powers as a whole, but still in our hands and no one else's.

After the peace treaty ending the occupation was signed in

* W. Macmahon Ball, *Japan, Enemy or Ally?* (New York: The John Day Company, 1949), p. 33.

1951 and went into effect the next year, the situation on the surface, at least, was entirely changed, but in reality the United States has remained as deeply involved as ever in the islands and our influence almost as great as before. For one thing, a security pact was concluded between the United States and Japan at the time of the peace conference, permitting American armed forces to remain in Japan. This was necessary not only because Japanese bases were essential to the whole American military position in the Far East but still more because, without American protection, Japan would have been virtually defenseless before her hostile communist neighbors. The Japanese had readily given up their army, navy, and air force at our earlier insistence and were now reluctant to recreate them despite a greatly altered American attitude toward the problem of Japanese rearmament. Japanese public opinion as well as the national economy would permit only a very slow and feeble build-up of armed strength, and in the meantime strong American guarantees as well as sizable American forces were necessary to assure the safety of Japan from communist aggression or possibly a *coup d'état* at home.

The Japanese economy, too, remained heavily dependent on the United States. While the Korean War had greatly accelerated the pace of recovery, American defense spending in Japan and various other forms of economic aid were still essential to the economy. The influence of the American reform program and the multitudinous close contacts with Americans during the occupation period also continued to be heavily felt. And in the field of international politics, the now entirely independent Japanese government continued to cooperate with the United States almost as closely as before and looked to us for leadership. In a sense, we remained Japan's only real companion. She was viewed with intense hostility by the communist world and was blackballed from the United Nations year after year by the Russians, until she was finally admitted in 1956. She was hated by most of her neighbors and regarded with suspicion or at best unconcern by most other nations. Only the United States was unmistakably friendly and believed firmly in the postwar Japan she had helped fashion.

American influence and leadership, thus, while now dependent on persuasion and negotiation rather than dictation, has been almost as marked these past few years as during the declining days of the occupation. Americans, while now more circumspect, are as much in evidence in the cities of Japan as ever. The United States, while no longer the arbiter of Japan's fate, has become instead her sponsor in international society. In other words, the deep and exclusive relationship between Japan and the United States continues though in new forms. All democratic peoples should be deeply concerned in the fate of Japanese democracy because of what it may mean for democracy everywhere, but only we of all foreign peoples have had and continue to exert much direct influence on Japan's future. If democracy were to fail in Japan, it would be not only a major blow to the whole democratic cause but a direct and colossal policy defeat for the United States.

But how precarious, then, is the position of democracy in Japan? How likely is it to fail outright or, at least, fall short of full success? During the occupation our ears were filled with the alternate shouts of triumph of the optimists over the obvious success of democracy in Japan and the dismal moans of the pessimists over the complete failure of our reforms. What is one to believe? General MacArthur and his aides never lacked positiveness in their claims of success, and they unquestionably had a remarkable degree of success to point to. The occupation went more smoothly than anyone would have thought possible. The Japanese welcomed us with almost embarrassing friendliness and disquieting docility. Reform legislation was adopted swiftly, easily, and in monumental quantity. And since the end of the occupation, Japan has remained politically stable and has made remarkable economic gains. On the surface, certainly, things have gone very well. On the other hand, there are tremendous obstacles in the path of democracy in Japan, which, taken together, make an easy optimism seem puerile.

First of all, there is the problem of whether or not Japan, regardless of the political and economic system she eventually chooses, can maintain any satisfactory standard of living in the future. She cannot grow enough food to feed all her people. She cannot produce the greater part of the fibers from which she must spin clothes for her millions. She has very little oil or iron and is lacking in adequate quantities of most of the other minerals and raw materials needed to maintain a modern industrial economy. Nylon and other synthetic fibers have destroyed most of the demand for silk, the one major export item she produced entirely within her own boundaries. All she has to offer on the world market is her own energy — manpower and the energy of coal and water. With these she can transform imported raw materials into goods for reëxport. The slim margin of profit from this reëxport trade must be sufficient to pay for all the imports Japan must have to support her own people. To do this, Japan's export trade must be huge. But where is she to find her markets in a divided world and in a Far East disrupted by revolutions and bitterly determined not to trade with her? Japan's situation is basically similar to England's but infinitely worse. She is far less richly endowed with the vital resources of coal and iron than are the British Isles. She is less highly industrialized. She has no overseas empire to aid her but instead an international legacy of distrust and hate. And she has almost twice the population of Great Britain to support on her more meager resources. The economic situation in Japan may be fundamentally so unsound that no policies, no matter how wise, can save her from slow economic starvation and all the concomitant political and social ills that situation would produce.

There are other reasons for pessimism. History tells of no case in which an occupation of one country by another produced within a short span of years a sincere conversion to the beliefs of the conquerors on the part of the conquered. Many would say categorically that military occupation can never do this. Of course, history perhaps has no precedent for the curious relationship that existed between the United States and Japan. There have been many cases of conquest of closely related and associated people by each other; there have been colonial conquests by people of one culture with clearly superior military power over a people of another culture; civilized peoples have been overrun by barbarian hordes; but never has an Occidental land conquered and occupied an Oriental land of comparable military, economic, and intellectual advancement. There are no exact precedents, but the less specific parallels in history offer no cause for optimism.

Japan's particular cultural background, also, suggests that in the long run democracy may find it very barren soil. Once already within the past half century it has been tried and rejected there. The unparalleled docility of the Japanese masses and their willingness to follow any strong leadership, while giving us a false sense of rapid success in Japan, make a poor basis for democracy. Few people in modern times have reveled so openly in blatant militarism as the Japanese. Few, if any, have subscribed so wholeheartedly to the authoritarian ideal.

After our policy blunder in China, no one can look at the situation in Japan without some misgivings. Are we facing another and still more costly policy defeat? What are our prospects for success? We Americans have usually attempted to answer this last question primarily on the basis of our varied estimates of what we ourselves have done in Japan since the war. Because of ignorance about the Japanese and a natural egocentrism, we have often overlooked an even more vital factor — the Japanese themselves.

Are the obvious difference of the Japanese from us and the rest of the Western world so great and of such a nature as to make democracy unworkable in Japan? Will the Japanese be capable of maintaining for long the democratic society we helped them construct? Will they even want to have a democratic system? No one has a sure answer to these questions, but, in order to be able to make a reasonably intelligent guess, we should first look at the basic economic and social framework of Japanese life, at the physical realities of the livelihood of the Japanese and their psychology and habits of thought, and then consider the postwar record in Japan in the light of these fundamentals.

PART II

THE PHYSICAL SETTING

4. People and Land

1. INTENSIVE AGRICULTURE

Japan and the United States in many ways make a curious pair. The discrepancy in size alone between these trans-Pacific neighbors makes them seem not like just a Mutt and Jeff combination but more like two lands which are so different in size as to be different in species. Japan, with less than 150,000 square miles of land surface, could be fitted into the continental United States twenty times over. The state of California alone could accommodate the whole of Japan, though a fairer comparison might be to the combined areas of New York, New Jersey, Pennsylvania, and Ohio. But this is, of course, a crude two-dimensional comparison of a sort which would dwarf Great Britain beside the dead vastness of Greenland and equate France with Madagascar. National size is not simply length by breadth but has the added dimensions of natural resources, population, technical skills, and productive capacity. In fact, in measuring the strength of countries, population is certainly more significant than land surface, and productive capacity, which, in a sense, is the product of the multiplication of population times technical skills times natural resources, gives the clearest single figure for relative national size.

In thinking of countries, we tend to visualize maps, which by their very nature represent land surfaces rather than these

other dimensions. We should have more maps showing population, natural resources, and productive capacity. Perhaps
frankly distorted maps depicting each area in proportion to
its population or productive power would help to correct the
distorted picture in our minds of the relative size of the lands
of the world. Such maps would immediately show small Japan
to be one of the larger countries of the world, not so large,
of course, as the United States, but ranking not far behind her.
A considerably pruned postwar Japan still stands fifth or sixth
in population in the world, surpassed only by such colossi as
China, India, the Soviet Union, and the United States. Before
the war she did not rank much lower than this in the key
category of industrial production. Here she outstripped both
China and India, but yielded place to Germany, Great Britain,
and France, as well as to the United States and the Soviet
Union. But rank her fifth, sixth, or, because of her notable
weakness in natural resources, even as low as tenth; Japan
still is one of the great countries of the world, even though,
next to Great Britain, she is the smallest in land area of all the
great powers. The United States and Japan, though by no
means evenly matched, do not make the elephant and mouse
combination our maps would show.

Thus, Japan is, in a way, a giant among nations, but she
is an unhappily misshapen one in that her people far outbal-
ance her land and natural resources. Today over 80,000,000
people are crowded into her narrow islands, or rather, into
the narrow valleys of her narrow islands. Japan's precipitous
mountains make beautiful scenery but leave little space for her
farmers. In fact, even today only about 16 per cent of the land
is cultivated. No country, not even the teeming lands of India,
China, or Java, equals Japan's record of almost 1900 members
of the purely agricultural population to each square mile of
cultivated land. The average Japanese farmer has less than
one-fifth as much land to cultivate as the average farmer in
Belgium, the West's most densely populated country. Include
Japan's huge cities, and she has more than 3400 people per

square mile of cultivable land, putting her far above all competitors as the world's most crowded land. She has more than twelve times as many people to feed per square mile of farm land as the United States and approximately one-third more people to feed per acre than a thoroughly industrialized and urbanized land like Great Britain, which depends heavily on imports to meet her food needs.

Of course, even in agriculture, length and breadth are not the only dimensions. One must also take into consideration the fertility of the soil, the amount of rainfall or other water resources, the length and intensity of the growing season, and the efficiency of the agricultural methods employed. Japanese soils, on the whole, are not very fertile and would probably be left in part unworked, if they were found in countries more generously provided with agricultural terrain. The rainfall in Japan, however, is plentiful, the growing season is both long and intense, and the Japanese have applied to their agricultural problems unstinting labor and agricultural skills which, while seemingly backward when compared with the mechanized farming of our country, have succeeded in grubbing from the soil as close to its maximum possible yield as man has ever been capable of producing.

There is ample rainfall in most parts of Japan, but the industrious Japanese, not content with this alone, have utilized the heavy water run-off from their rugged mountains for irrigation wherever feasible. Rain-soaked fields, which could grow good crops of wheat or barley, can, through irrigation, grow even more solid fields of wet-field rice, the grain which gives the largest yield per acre. The investment in labor is great, but it is worth it to the Japanese, if a larger crop can be realized from Japan's minuscule fields. As a result, virtually all of the flat bottom lands of Japan are inundated by a network of small channels and dikes to form wide stretches of rice paddies, and smaller patches of flooded rice fields creep up most small valleys and ravines, and wherever water is available even climb the steep slopes of the hills in progressively narrower and higher terraces. Every scrap of land which can be made into a paddy field has been converted into a miniature swamp. The Japanese, by extending irrigation to its physical limits, have made the best use of their great asset of water and have thus added another dimension to their narrow fields.

With all this emphasis on paddy fields and rice, the Japanese inevitably are rice-eaters, as are most of the other peoples of southern and eastern Asia. Since prehistoric times rice has been an important crop in Japan, and today about half of the cultivated area is given over to rice for at least part of the year, and it constitutes well over half of the total value of farm produce. "Cooked rice" and "a meal" are actually the same word in Japanese. A Japanese feels that he must have rice three times a day and plenty of it. Lacking the variety and richness of the American diet, he depends on rice in quantities which would seem ludicrously excessive to most Americans to provide him with energy for his daily tasks.

Despite the extremely deep snows of northern Japan, most of the country is subtropical. Lying on the eastern fringe of the Eurasiatic land mass, it enjoys roughly similar climatic conditions to the comparable latitudes of our own East Coast, which has the same general relationship to the North American continent. The one major difference is that Japan, being an island country, has a somewhat more oceanic and less continental climate. Cold snaps tend to be less severe than on our East Coast and rainfall heavier. But, on the whole, the northern island of Hokkaido approximates New England in climate, northern Honshu our middle Atlantic States, and the bulk of Japan the South Atlantic States from North Carolina to Georgia. Saved from our devastating cold snaps, much of Japan thus enjoys a very long growing season, and double cropping is practiced extensively both in upland fields and in rice paddies wherever it is possible to drain them adequately in winter. While double cropping is impossible in the extreme north, in some sections of southern Japan virtually every field bears two crops a year. This, of course, means more back-

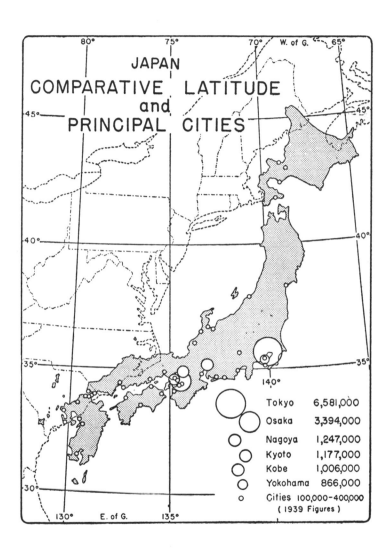

JAPAN
COMPARATIVE LATITUDE
and
PRINCIPAL CITIES

Tokyo	6,581,000
Osaka	3,394,000
Nagoya	1,247,000
Kyoto	1,177,000
Kobe	1,006,000
Yokohama	866,000
Cities 100,000-400,000	

(1939 Figures)

breaking labor, but it adds still another dimension to the meager land resources of Japan.

Japanese methods of agriculture, involving as they do an immense amount of arduous hand labor, seem primitive and inefficient to most Americans. With our simple faith in machinery, we often feel that mechanization of agriculture in Japan would not only save labor but would also increase production. Unfortunately, saving labor in a densely populated land like Japan means nothing unless the labor saved can be profitably employed in other tasks, and the concept that production can be increased by mechanizing farming is a complete fallacy as far as Japan is concerned. Tractors are used to a slight extent in the island of Hokkaido, but they are of little use in the narrow hillside terraces and tiny paddy fields that make up so much of Japan's farm land. And even on the broader stretches of flat fields, mechanization of the sort common in this country would on the whole decrease the yield rather than increase it. Machines have not been invented which till the soil as effectively as the great Japanese hoe with its two-foot blade. Nor have machines been invented which can equal the skill and loving care of the individual farm wife transplanting rice seedlings by hand. It would be as practical to mechanize the growing of flowers around an average suburban home in this country as to mechanize a Japanese farm. Japanese farming is really gardening, with the prolific farmer and his family lavishing as much work and care on each square yard of their land as an American family would on its prize flower bed. Farming by tractor could only make sense in Japan if two-thirds or more of her present farm population could be gainfully employed elsewhere and if great new sources of food were available to her.

Actually, Japanese farming stands at a high level of achievement, given the special relationship of man to land existing in Japan. The tools and techniques used, while recklessly extravagant of manpower, make the most of every cultivable scrap of land, which is as it must be wherever men are overabundant and land is scarce. Machines are used on a small scale for certain farm tasks but only where they do not reduce the yield. With government aid, better seeds have been developed and are utilized widely. Most important of all, fertilizer, which is essential to make Japan's infertile and overworked soil produce, is used lavishly and when available in close to maximum quantities, considering the cost of fertilizers, which has in recent years risen to about 20 per cent of the total cost of agricultural production in Japan. While chemical fertilizers and soybean cakes from Manchuria were commonly used before the war, the most universally available and therefore most widely used fertilizer in Japan, as in most of Asia, still is night soil. In the tight Japanese economy nothing can be wasted. As the cities grow, they require more food, but at least they produce in return more night soil with which to grow more crops and incidentally to impart that unfortunate olfactory atmosphere to Japan's farm lands which contrasts so sharply with their pleasant visual impression. All in all, Japanese farming techniques, though backbreaking and literally malodorous, produce virtually all that Japan's poor land could possibly grow under present conditions of scientific knowledge. Because of these intensive gardening methods, as well as Japan's plentiful rainfall and long and hot growing season, farmers throughout most of Japan produce two or three times as much per acre as most farmers in the drier, colder, and less labor-saturated lands of western Europe.

There is little hope that the yields from Japan's present farm lands could be greatly expanded in the near future or that food crops could be increased at the expense of less essential agricultural products. Already the grim struggle of man for food has forced the Japanese to a greater concentration on direct food crops than in almost any other land. An isolated Japan once produced her own cotton and hemp, but world trade now permits her to import most of her clothing fibers and devote the land once used for them to food. The only non-food crop of any importance in Japan is mulberry leaves, used to feed silk-worms, and these are grown largely on sandy upland soils, which, although capable of producing good sweet potato crops, could not grow much rice.

Japan does not even devote a large part of her area to the indirect and less efficient production of food through the growing of fodder for meat and dairy animals. That is a luxury she cannot afford. Instead, the Japanese eat fish, caught in the rich coastal and deep-sea fisheries around the islands, which, in a sense, extend their economic area by many thousands of square miles. What little land the Japanese have must be devoted to the production of the maximum number of calories, which means rice wherever possible and the other grains and vegetables where rice cannot be grown. It also means cultivating every plot of land, however small or barren, and coaxing from it the highest possible yield, no matter how prodigious the expenditure of labor required.

2. THE RATIO OF MEN TO LAND

Japan's food resources cannot be greatly increased by expanding her farm lands. Japan, in sharp contrast to the United States, has been a densely populated land for hundreds of years. In 1800, after almost two centuries of very slow population growth, she had close to 30,000,000 inhabitants, which was about three times as many as England and Wales at that time. The vast majority of these people were peasants, who even then occupied the arable land of Japan as fully as do their descendants today. The present agricultural population of Japan is considerably larger, but it has proportionately more to support it. There are the new fields of the frontier island of Hokkaido, which land-hungry Japanese peasants have gobbled up only in the past century. There are also larger yields per acre as a result of new manufactured and imported fertilizers, better seeds, more scientific knowledge, and better tools.

With the exception of Hokkaido, Japan's farm land has been

fully exploited for centuries. In fact, in their desperate effort to wring from the land the last bushel of rice or pound of sweet potatoes, the Japanese have long since passed the reasonable limit of profitable cultivation of the soil. No scrap of land is too small to be ignored. An abandoned roadway, the triangle formed by the convergence of two railroad tracks, the space between the foundation stones of a burned-out house—all are used to produce their quota of food. The indefatigable Japanese peasants have hacked their way up their boulder-strewn hills, leveling off with painstaking care pathetic yard-wide fields several hundred feet up the precipitous slopes. They have cut back the lower fringes of the hills to broaden the fields below. They have converted their tidal swamps into rice fields in a slow, bitter battle against nature. Ambitious drainage projects might add a few more square miles to Japan's farms, but no measures, however heroic, could possibly expand tillable acreage at the rate her population has been increasing. Japan was agriculturally an overpopulated land two or three centuries ago. The unbalance between man and land is even more drastic today.

During the two and a half centuries of rule by the Tokugawa Shogun, the population remained almost as stable as Japanese politics. An isolated Japan, dependent upon her own food resources, had hit the Malthusian limit. The poverty-stricken peasants were forced to practice a type of *ex post facto* birth control. This was called *mabiki*, an agricultural term meaning "thinning out," which referred to the tragic necessity of thinning out the children in a family through infanticide. Japan's reëntry into the world and her subsequent industrialization made it possible for her to concentrate her energies on her most productive specialties and to trade her manufactured goods for food from abroad. The Malthusian limit was raised, with the result that the population spurted from around 30,000,000 to about 90,000,000 in a mere century. But there could be no comparable increase in arable land or the over-all productivity of Japanese agriculture. Population growth has followed hard on the heels of the advancing Japanese economy and has far outstripped Japan's ability to feed her people from domestic sources. Japan today, with all the benefits of modern science and all the hard work of her industrious peasants, simply cannot produce enough food to feed 90,000,000 people, except at the barest starvation levels. She must feed approximately five people per acre of her infertile soil. For many decades now there has been a fairly steady deficiency of about 15 per cent in Japan's domestic food supplies, which has had to be met by imports. As Japan's population continues to grow, a more efficient and scientific agricultural system might conceivably prevent that percentage from increasing but it probably cannot diminish it. Japan, like England, faces a permanent food deficiency, and therefore, again like England, she is a country which depends directly and unequivocally on large-scale world trade to feed her people.

This heavy proportion of men to land over a long period of time has had profound social effects in Japan. For one thing, it has kept the farmers desperately poor. The rural population, which just before the war still formed virtually half of the total, is largely made up of a poverty-ridden peasantry, lagging decidedly behind the rest of the nation in its march toward modernization. Japan's new factories have not been able to draw to the cities more than the yearly increase in population. They could not drain the excess population from the farms. While Japan as a whole became a modernized and industrialized nation, her peasant masses were left behind, living not far above the miserable economic levels of feudal days. Moreover, by threatening to glut the labor market, they kept urban labor down to these same pitiful levels. The result has been something new and as yet unique in the world—an industrialized nation supported by the toil of people living not far above the subsistence level. We have yet to see how typical this picture may become of Asia as a whole and what the consequences will be for the rest of us if it does become the general pattern for the Asiatic half of the world.

An excess of men and a dearth of land have produced high rent rates in Japan. These have been accompanied by the inordinately high taxes on agricultural land through which the government was able during the past century to finance much of Japan's spectacular industrialization and the modernization of her war machine. High taxes tended to force peasants to mortgage part of their lands in bad years, and high rent rates often forced them then to sell the rest. The result has been an alarming growth of tenancy. High rents, however, have not been the result of any unusual depravity on the part of Japanese landlords but have been merely the normal outcome of Japan's particular economic conditions. Where labor is plentiful and land scarce, the agricultural worker has little bargaining power, and the landowner holds the cards. With rents averaging well over half of the annual crop, the rich grew richer and the poor poorer, until they hit the bedrock of the existence level. Japanese farms average only two and a half acres in size, even including the relatively large farms of the less productive north, but many peasants could not maintain their hold on even these miniature patrimonies. Before the war, almost half the arable land was tenant-operated and over a quarter of the peasants owned no land at all. At the other end of the scale, less than a tenth of the landowners held over half of the farm land. There was a dangerous dichotomy in rural society between a fairly small class of well-to-do landowners and the mass of the impoverished peasants. The minority controlled the majority not only economically but politically and spiritually as well. The bulk of the rural population simply continued the age-old pattern of following without question those who so clearly dominated their destinies.

The pattern and history of landownership in modern Japan, however, should not be compared, as it so often is, to that of the great feudal estates of eastern Europe before the war. With less than 1 per cent of Japan's landowners possessing as much as 125 acres of farm land, few if any of these agricultural holdings resembled in any way the Junker estates of Prussia

or the broad lands of the Polish and Hungarian nobility. Nor
were they often owned by nobles or descendants of the privileged classes of feudal times. The Japanese feudal lords of a
century ago depended largely and often almost exclusively
on the agricultural productivity of their domains. The privileged samurai class of hereditary warriors, who served as officers and retainers under these feudal lords, were usually paid
in turn in the rice produced from their lord's domains, but
they did not normally have any direct control over specific
tracts of land. Moreover, when the lords and samurai surrendered their feudal privileges in the early Meiji period, they
were paid off in government bonds and cash, thus losing for
the most part all direct contact with the land.

Even under the Tokugawa, the peasants' payments to their
lords amounted virtually to taxes, and they were effectively
used as such by the early Meiji government, after it had abolished the feudal framework. Capitalism was already so far
advanced in late feudal Japan that many peasants had lost full
title to their lands through mortgages to a rising landowner
class, consisting of richer peasants and petty industrial entrepreneurs of the rural areas. The outright ownership of these
lands by this new class was legally recognized by the Meiji
government, anxious to abolish all feudal claims on the land
and to create a uniform and simple system of landownership.
As early as 1873, about 31 per cent of the land was tenant-
operated, and the rate of tenancy grew steadily under the combined pressure of high taxes and high rents, until it reached 48
per cent in 1929. Since then its growth has been checked, and
in the 1930's tenancy even receded slightly to 47 per cent as a
result of national legislation by a government which had finally
become aroused to the plight of the peasants.

The grinding poverty of the lives of Japan's peasants, however, remains unchanged and, perhaps, unchangeable. Tenancy
itself may be diminished or even .abolished by law, but the
conditions which created it cannot be altered so easily. Some
of the symptoms may be eliminated, but the basic disease will

remain. A two-and-a-half-acre farm is too small to support a family at a reasonable level of well-being. And there are not even enough two-and-a-half-acre farms for all the farmers who need them in Japan or to produce the food to feed 90,000,000 people. Japan's land problem is insoluble in and of itself. Inevitably the Japanese have been forced to approach the problem from its reverse side as a population problem, because if the land and the food it produces are not elastic quantities, the solution to the problem must be sought by somehow reducing or at least limiting the number of people the land must support.

3. THE POPULATION PROBLEM

The population problem has long been a tragic one in Japan. Today, with Japan's economic and political place in the world greatly reduced, it is more terrifying in size and baffling in complexity than ever before. Various solutions have been proposed for Japan's population problem, some of them speciously by protagonists who utilized it as a justification for Japan's foreign aggressions. To them the simple fact that Japan had too many people was excuse enough for her to conquer her overpopulated neighbors and appropriate for her own people the positions of wealth and authority these countries could provide. But even at its height, the Japanese Empire offered only a partial and temporary cure for Japan's basic ill, while spreading a new and more virulent infection abroad. Japan's foreign conquests did absorb a significant number of men with technical education, who, if left jobless at home, might have been a source of social and political unrest within Japan. They drained off some of the more adventurous and less tractable citizens of the land who might have been troublemakers at home. But they did not reduce overpopulation in the Japanese islands. Even with strong government backing, few Japanese farmers wished to emigrate to Korea, Formosa, or Manchuria to compete with Korean and Chinese peasants accustomed to a still lower standard of living than the Japanese. Even at the height of the war, with about 6,000,000 soldiers and civilians abroad, the pressure on the overworked soil of Japan was not eased. And, in any case, how could Japanese overpopulation justify the exploitation of the people of other overpopulated lands for the benefit of the Japanese?

Japanese emigration without the aid of the flag has been no more successful than empire snatching as a solution for the population problem. It is inconceivable that Japanese immigration would be permitted anywhere in the world on a large enough scale to change the balance between men and land in Japan. The experience with Japanese immigration into the United States is perhaps typical. The entrance over a period of twenty-odd years of a few tens of thousands of Japanese, perhaps as many people altogether as are added to Japan's population every month or so, was enough to embitter Japanese-American relations for decades and bring war that much closer. Even the thinly populated lands of South America have been willing to take only very limited numbers of Japanese and a half-empty country like Australia almost none. Clearly the more established lands of the world will not absorb Japan's excess population.

The case of the underdeveloped and underpopulated colonial lands of the tropics is not so clear-cut. As seen from the Japanese point of view, there is no reason why the English-speaking peoples, who have actually multiplied during the last century and a half at a far more rapid rate than the Japanese, should have had the right to appropriate for themselves most of the lightly populated parts of the world which enjoyed a desirable climate, while the Japanese are excluded not only from these areas but also from the less desirable and still empty lands of the tropics, simply because they became candidates for emigration a century or two later than the English-speaking peoples. They naturally look toward the great unexploited islands south of them, such as New Guinea and Borneo, and dream of a New Japan which will redress the unhappy balance of the old. But, whatever may be the ultimate justice of the division of land and riches among the various peoples of the world, there is little possibility that Borneo or New Guinea will ever solve Japan's population problem. For one thing, there is the simple political reality that other peoples, including the present inhabitants, have prior claims to these areas. And, even assuming that they were thrown open to all peoples, immigration from other overpopulated Asiatic lands might leave little room for the Japanese. In any case, the difficulties and cost of successful emigration to the tropics would necessitate so slow a movement of people as to make possible only an insignificant reduction of the population pressures already built up within Japan's tight little islands.

In the long run, the only possible solution of the land-population problem in Japan is population control. If the land cannot be expanded, the population will simply have to be tailored to fit it. This can be done in four ways—by the age-old automatic controls of disease and famine, by conscious control through infanticide, as during the Tokugawa period, by the automatic reduction of births by changing social customs, such as the postponement of marriage, or by the reduction of births by artificial methods of birth control, against which the Japanese may have social prejudices but no religious scruples. One or more of these factors will inevitably become operative to keep the Japanese population within the inexorable bounds set by geography.

The one bright spot in the dismal population picture in Japan is offered by the graphs showing that the birth rate and, with it, the rate of population increase may be beginning to drop. Perhaps Japan too will follow the population curve already established by the more thoroughly industrialized lands of the West, like England. England's rate of population-increase during her period of rapidly expanding industrialization and urbanization equaled any records Japan has been able to produce more recently but then gradually leveled off. Social changes incidental to urbanization and industrialization are usually given the credit for this process. If these same forces operate in Japan and if she follows this same course, some day her population may automatically stabilize itself. If not, there can be nothing but disaster ahead for the Japanese people.

But even if a balance between births and deaths is finally achieved, this will not come about until well after the 100,-000,000 mark has been reached—until the unbalance between land and people is just that much worse than it is today. There already is a big overhang of population beyond the agricultural foundations of the land, which can be only supported by foreign trade, That overhang will inevitably grow far greater before it reaches stabilization. Already Japan's national structure rests heavily on industry as well as on agriculture. In the future, industry must bear an even greater share of the load, because agriculture can carry no more. With a fixed agricultural base and a growing population, the vital question for Japan is the future of her industry and foreign trade.

5. Men and Machines

1. NATURAL RESOURCES

The miracle of modern Japan has been her rapid and dramatic industrialization during the past century. Her fate during the next several decades depends on the ability of her industries to continue to bear the increasing load of population, which agriculture cannot carry. An industrially growing Japan might be able to maintain reasonable standards of living for an expanding Japanese population—a foundation of well-being without which no democratic structure could long stand. An industrially stagnant Japan could only mean starvation and unrest. The agricultural potential in Japan is an all too rigidly fixed quantity. Population growth is an alarming but predictable hazard. The future of Japanese industry is the unknown factor which spells the difference between a healthy nation and chaos.

Modern industry depends on three essential elements—men to operate machines, power to run them, and materials to be worked on by them. Japan is adequately supplied with only the first two. She lacks the materials to feed her machines, and in this lack lies the great question mark regarding the future of Japanese industry and of Japan herself. Japan's whole imperialistic course over the past several decades and the recent war itself can be interpreted as an effort by the Japanese to snatch from others the materials she herself lacked. Defeat and the altered balance of power in the world have put a permanent end to this attempt by the Japanese to build a solid basis for Japanese industry at the expense of other peoples. We have yet to see if any other solution of the problem is possible and if Japan, with only men and power at her disposal, can compete industrially with countries which have men, power, and materials.

Japan is lavishly supplied with men, but her sources of power, though sufficient to have enabled her to become a first-class industrial nation, are far from abundant. As in every other important manufacturing area of the world, coal has been the major source of power in modern Japan, accounting for over nine-tenths of Japan's power fifty years ago and perhaps two-thirds of it before the war. Without relatively large quantities of easily accessible coal, primarily in northern Kyushu, Hokkaido, and along the coast of Honshu north of Tokyo, Japan could never have started on her amazing climb to industrialization. But her coal resources fall far below those of her major industrial competitors. Although she is at present the greatest coal-producing country of East Asia, her per capita reserves are only about one-fortieth those of Germany or Great Britain and an infinitesimal fraction of those of the United States. Even at her present rate of consumption, they will last only a century or two. If in the future her industries require much more coal than in the past, or if the Japanese were to abandon their Spartan custom of living in virtually unheated houses all winter and were to start to use coal for domestic heating purposes, the reserves would vanish far more quickly. Moreover, much of Japan's coal is of poor quality and occurs in very narrow and broken seams, which are both difficult and costly to work. She is deficient in anthracite and was forced in the past to import coking coal for her steel industry. Thus, Japan, though possessing fairly large reserves of coal, had to look before the war to Korea, Manchuria, China, and French Indo-China for roughly 10 per cent of the coal she consumed.

The situation with regard to petroleum, another major power source, is much worse. With only small fields along the northwestern coast of Honshu and in Hokkaido, Japan could not supply even one-tenth of her prewar needs. Although much of this prewar demand was for her army and navy, even a completely demilitarized Japan would require heavy imports of oil. The Japanese do not have tractors but wield the less costly hoe. They do not have the luxury of private automobiles for commuting and pleasure-riding but rely on trains, streetcars, busses, and the ubiquitous bicycle. They have very few good roads for transporting interurban freight but utilize instead cheap coastal and inter-island water transportation and their efficient rail system. But they still cannot get away from the internal combustion engine. Municipal and rural bus lines and a great deal of short-distance trucking are unavoidable in any modern nation. Wartime conversion of taxis, busses, and trucks to cumbersome charcoal-burning devices offered no permanent escape from the need for gasoline. And in other fields the demand for oil is even more pressing. Industrial lubricants are still required, and Japan's huge fishing fleet, which has made the high seas a passable substitute for the prairies and steppes of broader lands, runs for the most part on imported petroleum. Oil is a vital deficiency in the Japanese economy, and it must be supplied from abroad.

The third source of power in Japan affords a more optimistic picture. This is water power, which, while quantitatively limited, fortunately is inexhaustible over the years. Japan's rivers, which are all short, shallow, and subject to extreme seasonal variation of flow, are for the most part worthless as communication channels, but, in their precipitous descent from the mountainous core of Japan, they provide a cheap source of power which the country desperately needs. The heavy rainfall on Japan's mountains, thus, can first be utilized for hydroelectric power before it fills the irrigation ditches of the lower valleys and narrow coastal plains. The Japanese were quick to exploit this power source and have harnessed a high percentage of their streams over a large part of their exploitable descent.

Japanese hydroelectric dams and power stations are quite different from those of the United States. There are no Boulder Dams or even any long and massive barriers like those on the Tennessee. There are few large reservoirs. Instead, their dams are usually unimpressively small but efficiently placed barriers to trap the waters of a mountain stream, which are then piped along the side of the steeply descending valley until the pipes suddenly drop down to a small hydroelectric station near the stream-bed below. Almost at once another dam snatches the water out of its normal channel, and the process is repeated. Japan's longest river, the Shinanogawa, has ninety such plants along its 229-mile course. Japan, thus, has hundreds of hydroelectric power plants, which, though usually tiny in scale, in the aggregate make Japan probably the world's fourth largest producer of hydroelectric power, surpassed only by the United States, Canada, and perhaps the Soviet Union, which are all lands of far grander scale and incomparably greater rivers.

Over four-fifths of Japanese electricity is generated by water power, while coal-burning thermoelectric plants are utilized to a large extent as auxiliary stations, primarily to offset the deficiencies of hydroelectric power during the drier months. Japan's balance between hydroelectric and thermoelectric power, thus, reverses that of the other major industrial nations, easing in this way the strain on her indifferent coal supplies. Cheap hydroelectric power, over half of which is applied directly to industrial purposes, has come to provide about one-quarter of her total power supplies. Next to Japan's abundant population, it is perhaps Japan's single greatest industrial asset, without which her industrial future would indeed be black.

If coal is the major source of power for industry, iron is its most essential material. Mankind entered the iron age more than two thousand years ago, and we still today live in a civilization held together by steel girders. All of the great industrialized areas of the world, almost by definition, have great supplies of iron ore—that is, all except Japan. Her known resources of iron ore are so small that they would not last the United States three months, and most of them are found in deposits so insignificant and so scattered throughout her rugged terrain as to be scarcely worth mining. In recent years more than six-sevenths of her iron ore has come from abroad, largely from Korea, China, the Philippines, and Malaya. This means very long haulage, but, since much of Japan's coal is found virtually at tidewater, the over-all transportation costs are probably no greater than the combined water and rail hauls to bring iron ore and coal together in the United States or the shorter rail hauls in parts of industrial Europe. There remains, however, Japan's need to purchase large quantities of iron ore abroad if she does not wish to make even more costly outlays for pig iron or steel.

Japan's shortage of iron ore is not offset by rich supplies of any other industrial minerals. Her hydroelectric capacity makes her a natural producer of aluminum, but she is dependent upon foreign sources for the necessary bauxite. For many centuries, including even her period of almost complete isolation from the rest of the world, she was an exporter of copper, but in recent years domestic demand has caught up to the output of her low-grade mines. She has some gold and silver and an exportable surplus of sulphur, but is markedly deficient in virtually all of the other minerals, importing about two-thirds of her zinc, three-quarters of her tin, and nine-tenths of her lead. A demilitarized Japan may have less demand for iron ore and some of the other metals, but she will clearly remain a heavy importer of ores and minerals.

Japan's supply of materials for light industry is only slightly better than in the case of the heavy industries. Until recently, spinning and weaving were the backbone of her machine production, employing about half of her factory workers three decades ago and accounting at that time for almost two-thirds of her exports. Japan, however, does not produce a large part of the fibers she uses. Once she grew her own cotton, but the opening of Japanese markets after 1858 to cotton grown in countries far better suited to its cultivation rapidly drove out the domestic product, and the land once used for cotton has long since been shifted to food crops. Cotton spinning and weaving, Japan's two largest industries a decade or so ago, depended entirely on imported raw materials. The smaller woolen weaving industry also had to be fed from abroad, for Japan never has produced wool. Only in silk did she produce her own fibers. Her hardworking peasants, living off the stony uplands of the central mountain massif of Honshu, proved to be the most efficient producers of silk in the world, and Japan soon captured a major share of the world trade in silk. Unfortunately for her, however, silk makes a relatively costly fabric, and the demand for it has always been limited and in recent years has almost vanished as the result of the development of rayon, nylon, and other artificial fibers. With silk no longer a major article of foreign trade, Japan faces the prospect of becoming even more dependent than formerly on foreign sources of raw material for whatever she can salvage of her textile industry.

Of course, Japan can manufacture at least some of the artificial fibers which are threatening her silk market. Before the war she was for a short period the world's largest producer of rayon. Rayon and staple fiber goods, however, are made from wood pulp, and Japan, even before losing the southern half of the island of Sakhalin to the Soviet Union as a result of the war, was dependent on the United States, Canada, and the Scandinavian countries for some of the pulp she consumed. The problem of wood pulp brings us to the larger and more vital problem of Japan's over-all wood resources.

Next to men and the power resources of coal and water, wood is probably Japan's greatest natural resource. With over half the land devoted to forest, Japan is among the more heavily forested of the civilized countries of the world and unquestionably the most heavily forested of the populous lands. Her poverty in agricultural land has meant a larger proportion of terrain preserved from the farmer's hoe. The country is rugged, but little of it is too high for forest growth, and relatively warm temperatures throughout most of the forest lands plus ample rainfall everywhere mean excellent growing conditions.

But the ratio of men to forest land in narrow Japan, while not so disastrous as the ratio of men to agricultural land, is precarious. The per capita acreage of forest land is only about one-fifth that of the United States. With timber lands so limited and with so little else to treasure, the Japanese have been forced to tend their forests with a care undreamed of in a land like ours, which has been more bountifully provided by nature. Up until the outbreak of war with China, attempts were made to cut no more than the annual growth, and reforestation over the years had gradually expanded the forest area. In the three southern islands, artificially planted forests account for about one-fifth of the total, making curious patterns of symmetrical rows of conifers, like some great corn field, in the mountain fastnesses of Japan. Careful cutting and planting practices have spread over the hills a patchwork pattern of different types and sizes of timber, resembling the patchwork patterns of agricultural land. The ratio of men to land in Japan has left man's imprint even on her wild mountains and rugged hills.

Japan is almost as dependent on a maximum yield from her forest lands as from her farms. While far richer in wood than are many of the lands of Asia and Europe, she depends upon her wood supply for greater and more vital services than does any other nation. The chief of these is for building material. Ninety million Japanese live in houses built primarily of wood. Despite tile, thatch, or tin roofs, mat floors, paper and glass sliding partitions, and walls made in part of mud plastered on bamboo lattice, wood forms the framework and bulk of the building materials in every house. The frequency of serious earthquakes throughout the land makes the utilization of stone or brick for houses somewhat hazardous. Lightly built wooden houses will sway safely with the motion of the tremor, where more rigid walls of stone or brick crack and fall. Only steel-framed office buildings and reinforced concrete offer a better answer to the earthquake menace than wood. With inexhaustible supplies of cement and sand available, the Japanese can build permanent concrete structures which will gradually replace many of their wooden buildings, thus relieving their forests of the necessity of providing materials for the periodic reconstruction of their flimsy wooden houses, which are destroyed in huge numbers by disastrous urban fires and more slowly but also more inevitably every few decades by the elements. In time, then, this major drain on Japan's wood resources can perhaps be diminished, but other demands will remain and even grow.

As an industrialized nation, Japan needs huge quantities of wood for railroad ties, telegraph poles, and mine timbers. The petty handicraft uses of wood and bamboo, which must be classed with it as a forest product, are numberless. Short of other materials, the Japanese use wood and bamboo for a thousand things for which we can afford to employ more costly materials. Japanese buckets may not be oaken but they are still made of wood. Simple wooden chopsticks take the place of our more complicated cutlery. Bamboo, an unbelievably versatile material, turns up in hundreds of surprising and ingenious uses. Japan also depends on wood, normally converted into charcoal, for what little heating her houses have and for cooking fuel wherever city gas supplies, made from coal, are not available. The Japanese, by holding their hands and wrists over charcoal braziers or by placing their feet in or close to specially designed heating devices, derive a considerable amount of warmth and cheer from a tiny spot of heat in an otherwise frigid house. But even this niggardly use of charcoal, when 90,000,000 people are involved, means a great demand for wood. This in turn necessitates scrub growths suitable for making charcoal on many mountain lands which might otherwise grow real timber.

And over and above these direct uses of forest products is

the growing demand for wood pulp. The Japanese have had a famous paper industry for about a thousand years and have developed some ingenious uses for paper. Pasted on sliding partitions and screens, it is an important architectural material. Long ago the Japanese, who suffer a great deal from winter colds, developed the sanitary use of fine paper tissues in place of the handkerchief. As a nation of voracious readers today, they absorb huge quantities of paper for books, magazines, and newspapers and would use far more if they could get it. As a great producer of paper as well as rayon, Japan's capacity for pulp consumption is almost unlimited.

With such demands for both wood and pulp, Japan inevitably needs more than she can produce. As already noted, she has had to purchase some of her pulp abroad, and she has been importing roughly one-quarter of her lumber. Wood is a major Japanese resource, but, as in the case of her domestic supplies of food, there may be a permanent shortage. In time, further reforestation and more scientific forestry can increase the yield considerably, but, even with a reduction of wood consumption in domestic architecture, the over-all demands for wood and pulp may remain in excess of production.

2. INDUSTRIALIZATION

Such a listing of Japan's industrial assets inevitably emphasizes her deficiencies instead. The wonder is that the Japanese were able to industrialize at all in the face of these lacks. Her tremendous manpower resources in no way distinguished her from the other major lands of Asia, and, in any case, excess population has often operated rather as a hindrance than as an aid to industrialization. Her power resources were meager by the standards of the other industrialized nations and her material resources wholly inadequate by any standards. And, despite these drawbacks, Japanese industry has been forced to provide, in the face of determined competition abroad, sufficient salable exports to pay not only for her deficiencies in food, cotton,

wood, rubber, iron, and various other vital materials to be consumed at home but also for the vast bulk of the materials out
of which her exports were fashioned. How under these circumstances was Japan able to outstrip all the other Asiatic
lands in the rapidity and thoroughness of her industrialization
and make herself a rival of the major manufacturing nations of
the West?

This question is by no means easy to answer. The more
difficult the problem of industrialization becomes for Japan's
Asian neighbors, the more miraculous her success appears.
Perhaps part of the answer lies in the rather nebulous field of
national characteristics. As we shall see, the Japanese have
done much to make their dogged belief in the superiority of
will power over matter seem plausible. Another part of the
answer may lie in the realm of basic historical factors. The
Japanese already in the middle of the nineteenth century were
a closely knit, nationally conscious people, and their economy,
while partially feudal, bore more resemblance to that of the
West than did the economies of the other Asian nations. Perhaps for these reasons, the Japanese were better able than the
other Asian peoples to make a smooth transition from relative
isolation to membership in a world society dominated by the
economic and political patterns of the West. They were able
to devote all their efforts to reconstructing Japan, while their
Asian neighbors were dissipating their energies in perhaps
unavoidable but certainly profitless friction. The result was a
temporal advantage for Japan over the other Asiatic lands
which Japan was quick to exploit.

Two seemingly minor factors contributed greatly to Japan's
vital head start. One was that Japan's coal resources, though
not particularly rich, were close to the sea and therefore could
be transported cheaply. If an extensive rail system had been
necessary before this essential power source could be exploited,
Japan's industrialization might have been considerably delayed.
The other factor was silk. A contagious silkworm disease had
blighted the silk industry of Europe shortly before the opening

of Japan, and thus there was an immediate demand for Japanese silk and silkworms when Japan was first opened. Silk reeling also happens to be an industry which can be mechanized quickly and cheaply. Hundreds of small filatures soon sprang up throughout central Japan, producing a uniform product which was definitely superior to the hand-reeled silk of the other Asiatic countries. A great cash export was thus provided Japan just when she needed it most to pay for the early stages of industrialization. If the European silk blight had not come just when it did, if silk reeling were not an easily mechanized industry, or if present silk substitutes had existed eighty years ago, the Japanese attempt to industrialize might have encountered insuperable financial obstacles.

With the quick start provided her by coal and silk, Japan went on determinedly and rapidly to expand her industrial base. She built up a communications network which far excelled that of any other Asiatic land. She concentrated heavily on cotton spinning and weaving, which are relatively easy industries to establish. Building up these and the other light industries at a fantastic rate after 1880, she soon found herself far ahead of her neighbors in industrial skills, experience, and equipment, at a time when they were taking only their first hesitant steps towards industrialization. She also lengthened her industrial lead by utilizing the military power it gave her to seize near-by territories, which she exploited in such a way as to derive from them maximum support for her own economy.

But the industrial advantages of a quick start could not be maintained indefinitely. Japan enjoyed no permanent economic advantages which could prevent her neighbors from eventually establishing their own light industries which would inevitably cut deeply into Japan's essential export trade. To keep her advantage, she was forced to forge ahead into new and more complicated industrial fields, which her less experienced neighbors could not develop as rapidly as they could the light industries. For this fundamental reason and also because of a more immediate desire to build up her war machine in preparation for further conquests, Japan, during the 1930's, swung rapidly from light industry as her primary manufacturing base to heavy industry, the chemical industries, and the manufacturing of fine machinery. In this way she developed a new type of export market which might not be lost so quickly as her textile markets.

Japan's industrial progress, thus, has been no steady, inevitable growth, based solidly on obvious economic advantages, as in the case of America's rise to industrial leadership. It has been more like the erratic progress of a broken-field runner, fighting his way against great odds by a quick getaway, brilliant improvisations, and daring reversals of the field. Utilizing to the fullest her one advantage over the West of cheap manpower and her one advantage over Asia of greater industrial skills, she has threaded her precarious way toward industrialization between the far greater industrial potential of the West and the still cheaper labor of the rest of Asia. With her industry-swollen population, there can be no turning back. She cannot even stand still, for her less industrialized neighbors are always threatening to catch up with her and wipe out the technical advantages on which her people now live. The Japanese are engaged in a desperate "Alice in Wonderland" race with time, and there is no end in sight. To stay where they are, to live at all, they must keep forging ahead industrially to ever greater productive levels and higher technical skills.

Japanese industry, which has only men and power to support it, will inevitably be forced more and more into the fields in which materials count least and labor and skills count most. Japan must go increasingly into the fields in which her cheaper labor costs give her an advantage over the West while the greater skills of her workers give her the edge over the rest of Asia. This means less emphasis on textiles and a growing emphasis on industrial art products, precision instruments, fine machinery, shipbuilding and ship repairing, and the like, which require a high ratio of skilled labor to materials. But even with the most careful rationalization of her industrial potential, the future of Japanese industry is certainly precarious. Even with determined efforts to maintain technical leadership over the rest of Asia on one side, balanced on the other by a willingness to accept a far lower standard of living than the industrialized peoples of the West, the Japanese have ahead of them, at best, a very uncertain future.

But, whatever may be the ultimate fate of Japanese industry, it has already laid a heavy imprint on Japan and the Japanese. It has made Japan into a land of huge cities and sprawling factories, of whirring machines and crowded commuters' trains. Today Japan boasts two of the eight or nine largest cities of the world and four more which have around a million residents.

Urbanization, however, is not a strictly new phenomenon in Japan. It has merely been greatly accelerated by the industrialization of the past century. Even under the outwardly feudal regime of the Tokugawa, Japan had her great and small cities. Edo, the modern Tokyo, had a population of about one million at the beginning of the nineteenth century, making it then, as now, one of the three or four largest cities of the world. Such a huge city in a supposedly feudal land can be explained only by the high degree of political centralization which underlay the feudal façade. Each feudal lord was forced to maintain at least one mansion in Edo, where he spent about half of his time and his family remained permanently, while the Shogun, in addition to maintaining his tremendous castle, the central core of which at present forms the spacious Imperial Palace grounds in Tokyo, supported a vast and complicated governmental structure to administer his own broad lands and supervise the other feudal domains, which collectively ruled over almost 30,000,000 people.

Another great city, Osaka, showed the extent to which domestic commerce and handicraft industries had grown beyond the bounds of a feudal economy. Although a purely commercial city, Osaka before the opening of Japan had a population approaching a million. Then, there was Kyoto, the ancient capital of the emperors, dating back to the end of the eighth century, which survived as a city of fine handicrafts after its decline as a political center. And all the many castle headquarters of the feudal lords were surrounded by thriving administrative and commercial towns, which have grown into the medium-sized cities of today. Japan in 1800, though an outwardly feudal land, was almost as urbanized as were the leading industrial countries of the West at that time. It is not surprising that, with the advent of machines, Japanese cities have kept pace with the cities of the Western world in size.

The cities of Japan tend to be more geographically concentrated than those of most other lands. All her great cities and the vast bulk of her industries lie in a narrow coastal strip on the southern shores of Honshu from Tokyo to the tip of the island and then continuing along the north coast of Kyushu. If you draw a straight line from Tokyo 540 miles down the Inland Sea to the northwestern tip of Kyushu, you will find that within forty miles of this line and either on the sea or close to it are located thirty-three of Japan's forty-seven largest cities and more than half of her cities of medium size. One reason for this unusual concentration of cities and industries is that along this same strip were located the chief centers of population before modern times, and, with men her chief industrial asset, industries naturally grew up where labor was the most plentiful. Moreover, this narrow belt has the advantages of cheap maritime transportation and closeness to the major sources of power. North Kyushu has the richest coal supplies of Japan, and the whole Inland Sea area up to the great complex of cities at its head can easily draw on these supplies. Farther east, the industrial centers along this line lie close to the rich hydroelectric resources of the central massif of Honshu.

Even within this long coastal strip there are several nodes of still more highly concentrated population and industry.

The northeastern corner of Kyushu, with its coal fields and blast furnaces, is one. Another is the great industrial city of Nagoya in central Honshu. But the two largest remain the old population centers of Tokyo and Osaka. Tokyo had passed the 8,000,000 mark by 1956, and its port of Yokohama has for long been close to 1,000,000. There are also a great number of small cities and large towns clustered around Tokyo and Yokohama, making this one of the greatest concentrations of population in the world. Another similar concentration is found at the head of the Inland Sea. It consists of Osaka with well over 3,000,000 population, Kyoto and the port of Kobe, each with around 1,000,000, and four other nearby cities, each with more than 100,000. But even where these large urban nodes occur, the strip of heavy population and roaring factories remains narrow. A few miles from any of these cities one will find sparsely inhabited mountains and tiny farms which look little different from those of feudal times.

3. THE INDUSTRIAL WORKER

Men with machines in their hands produce far more than hoe-wielding peasants, and productive power means more wealth. Industrialization in Japan, however, has not brought significantly higher wages to the Japanese worker or put more food upon his table. Pitifully low wage scales apply not only to the industrial laborers themselves but also to all wage and salary earners in Japan. White-collar workers and technicians receive proportionately no more than manual laborers. All down the line workers receive only a small fraction of what their services would be worth in the United States.

One explanation of this situation is that the high profits taken by selfish industrialists have robbed the workers of their rightful share. Instead of building up a healthy local market for their produce and permitting an equitable division of wealth to ensure adequate purchasing power at home, Japan's industrialists are said to have concentrated on the more lucrative production of export goods to be sold in markets where purchasing power already existed. Whatever may be the validity of this concept—and we have no clear evidence that profits in Japan were in excess of those in comparable fields with comparable risks elsewhere at the time—it is at best only a small part of the truth. A more important factor, as we have seen, was Japan's inescapable need for large-scale exports to pay for large-scale imports. We need no hypothesis of unnatural cupidity on the part of Japan's businessmen to explain her large export trade. Then, there was the need for Japanese industry to make lower labor costs compensate for her lack of materials. Another factor was the reinvestment of an unusually large percentage of the profits of industry to expand the industrial plant. Japan's rapid industrialization during the past seventy years has depended primarily on the reinvestment of profits instead of their consumption either by capitalists or by their employees. Still another factor was the diversion through taxation of as much of the national income as possible to a long-range and eventually disastrous investment in military power. And behind all these factors stood the inescapable economic laws of supply and demand, which apply as well to labor as to goods.

The excess farm population has been and still is the chief reason why the wages of Japan's industrial workers have been kept down to the barest minimum. With the burgeoning rural population always ready to provide more workers than industry could absorb, Japan's urban laborers have had little more bargaining power than their country cousins. In so far as skilled labor was involved, bargaining was sometimes possible, but only for brief periods and at very low levels. By and large, the industrial proletariat has been so closely tied to the economic levels of the peasantry as to constitute a sort of urban peasantry itself, basically no better off than the tenant farmers of rural areas.

The close interrelationship between peasants and workers

in Japan is seen in many ways. Although the city dwellers of Tokugawa times account for a certain proportion of the present urban population, most city folk are in origin country people or the sons or grandsons of country people who have been forced from the farms by the excess of births over deaths and drawn to the cities by an expanding labor market in industry. Typically only the eldest son of a family remains on the farm; his younger brothers must go to the city to seek their fortune. These urbanized peasants maintain close contacts with their relatives in the countryside and tend to return to the farms to live at a subsistence level whenever they lose their means of livelihood in the cities. In fact, Japan, despite its great urbanization, has so far been spared the cost of social security programs by this more primitive system of letting the jobless be cast back upon their rural relatives for support.

In some cases, there is no real line between peasants and industrial workers, for a large number of the latter are at the same time peasants. Silk filatures, located as they are in the countryside close to the supply of cocoons, have naturally operated on the excess labor supply of these rural areas, while hundreds of simple industrial processes, either complete in themselves or else parts of some more complicated process, are farmed out to rural families to be performed on a piecework basis. Moreover, many peasants commute by train to city factories. Thousands of peasant girls in their late teens also go to the cities to work for a few years in light industries, either to help salvage family finances or else to build up a dowry for marriage. Living in compounds under strict supervision, these girls often are little better than indentured laborers, providing Japan with an extraordinarily cheap supply of workers but helping to keep urban wage scales tied to the miserable living standard of her farmers.

Low wages, factory girls living in company dormitories, and sweatshop practices have earned for Japanese industry the epithet of "feudal." The word "feudal," in its modern journalistic use as a broadside term of condemnation, certainly does apply, but not as any exact comparison with the economic, social, and political patterns of feudal Europe or feudal Japan. There is no historical connection between modern Japanese factory practices and Japan's feudal past. In fact, the rise of industry in Japan under the Tokugawa had as disastrous an influence on Japanese feudalism as it did on the feudalism of Europe. Certainly none of the major evils of the Japanese industrial system is based upon feudal concepts or feudal patterns of life. They are thoroughly modern phenomena. Perhaps they are the inevitable outcome of the meeting of machines and masses of people living at the subsistence level. If the pattern of labor exploitation set by Japan were merely a Japanese phenomenon, growing out of Japanese feudalism, it would still be distressing, but it would not be alarming for the world at large. Unfortunately, the other Asiatic lands with no feudal past are beginning to show many of these same characteristics, as they start to industrialize. One comes to the gloomy conclusion that, wherever the basic factors of overpopulation and grinding poverty exist, the results of industrialization may not be very different from what they were in Japan.

The one element in Japan's modern industrial practices which might be traceable to feudalism is by no means its worst feature. This is the strong emphasis on personal relationships between employer and employee in Japan. All the way down the line management expects more personal loyalty from employees than in the United States and in return takes a more paternalistic attitude toward its workers than is common in this country. The size of a worker's family is considered an important factor in determining his wage, and once employed the worker is felt to have a lifetime right to his job. Often the mere lack of work to be done is not considered adequate reason for dismissing a man from a no longer existent job. This emphasis on personal relationships, as a holdover from Japan's close feudal past with its dominant emphasis on personal obligations, has all the unpleasant connotations of a master and servant relationship, but at the same time it injects a certain note of humanity into an otherwise ruthless exploitation of labor and keeps alive the personal factor, which we are attempting to recapture in American industry today.

The low scale of pay in Japanese factories does not mean that industrialization has not benefited the people of Japan at all. Although most of the direct profits which industry has brought to Japan have been turned to the creation of more industry and a profitless war machine, nevertheless industrialization and the modernization of government based on it have enriched the Japanese people in many ways which do not appear in wage tabulations, and it is these benefits which have put the Japanese standard of living markedly above that of the other Asiatic lands. Extensive hydroelectric power has meant cheap electricity, with the result that in Japan perhaps a higher percentage of the homes have electric lights than in any other of the major countries of the world. Before the war Japan had excellent and cheap train service as well as equally good postal and telegraph service and the other basic services of a modern country. The government afforded extensive police protection and more medical and sanitary services than are enjoyed by any other Asiatic people. There is also a widespread and highly specialized school system, with free education at the elementary level, which actually accommodates a higher percentage of the children of elementary school age than we have as yet been able to put in school in the United States. And factories mean cheap industrial goods to take the place of the more costly products of hand industries and foreign imports. The rubber boots and bicycle of the modern Japanese peasant or laborer are clear indications of a higher standard of living than his father enjoyed, even though the money in his purse and the rice in his bowl may be no more plentiful.

4. THE "ZAIBATSU" SYSTEM

The statement that a high percentage of the profits from Japanese industry was not consumed by either the capitalists or by their workers but was reinvested in capital expansion perhaps needs some explanation. Limitation of consumption is possible in countries like the Soviet Union, in which the government controls all industry and therefore can determine what percentage of the profits will be diverted to reinvestment, but how could Japan, just emerging from feudalism and innocent of both socialist theory and practice, accomplish this feat? Part of the answer lies in the government's zealous efforts to build up industry, but another factor was the heavy concentration of Japanese industry in the hands of a very few individuals, which resulted in the accumulation of wealth in such great quantities that the owners were unable to consume it all and almost automatically plowed a large part of the profits back into industry.

The early Meiji government pioneered in virtually all of the major industrial fields in Japan. This was not because of any predilection for government-owned industries, though government ownership of some of the means of production has always been common in the Far East, but rather because the need was urgent and private capital too weak and also too timid to meet the demand. Japan herself lay defenseless before the warships of the West, and her handicraft industries were equally defenseless before the machine products of the Occident. With the example of European colonialism throughout Asia before them, the Japanese were not eager to call in foreign capital, even if European bankers had felt that Japanese industry was a good risk. At the beginning of the Meiji period, the only possible course for the Japanese, if they were to build up industry in order to save their economy from foreign goods and their independence from foreign guns, was to pay for new industries out of taxes and government credit, which meant tax receipts in advance.

Placing the tax burden squarely on agriculture, the government started building Japan's rail network and factories in various industrial fields. Some of these were munitions plants, which were an end in themselves, but others were model plants,

designed to demonstrate the feasibility of new industrial processes and smooth the way for private capitalists with more
limited financial resources than the government. Only in silk
reeling, where mechanization was cheap and easy, was such
direct governmental encouragement largely unnecessary. But
all this was at a time when most Japanese factories were not
yet bringing in a profit. It was only later, certainly well after
1880, that industry really began to pay, and by that time the
government was out of most of the industrial fields, maintaining its leadership for the most part only in the field of railroads,
still largely a government monopoly, some of the armament
industries connected directly with military strength, and monopolies for revenue purposes, such as tobacco.

The chief credit for the process of capital reinvestment,
which so markedly accelerated the speed of industrialization
in Japan, goes to the peculiar concentration of Japanese industry and commerce in the hands of a few great families—in
other words the *zaibatsu* system, which has been in many ways
the curse of modern Japan but at the same time a factor which
greatly increased the speed of her industrialization. Nowhere
in the world, before the appearance of the totalitarian governments, has such a large percentage of national industrial power
been controlled by so few people, and possibly nowhere else
has industrialization been achieved so rapidly.

It has been a world-wide phenomenon during the past century that the number of independent industrial enterprises has
been decreasing, while a few giants have come to control the
production of an entire industry among themselves. The steel
industry in this country, the oil industry, and the manufacturing of automobiles clearly illustrate this tendency. The
individual Japanese companies, with the exception of the almost
monopolistic Oji paper interests, rarely controlled greater per-
centages of the particular industry in which they were engaged
than did comparable companies in the United States. What
made big business in Japan different from big business in
America was the association of huge companies, operating in

many different fields, in a single giant combine, to a large extent owned and definitely controlled by one family and its immediate and loyal henchmen. It was as if United States Steel, General Motors, General Electric, Standard Oil, the Du Pont interests, several of our major banks, a few of the major shipping and export firms, and a host of less well-known but equally important companies in less prominent fields were all owned and controlled by a single American family. In Japan the component companies were not as large as the American industrial giants listed above, but they were proportionately as important to the Japanese economy as United States Steel or General Motors are to the American economy. At least two of these fantastic combines numbered their employees in the millions.

Obviously the profits of such combines were far greater than their owners could reasonably spend, particularly in Japan where the people tend to be frugal. Where ten thousand or even a thousand owning families might well have spent most of the profits for moderately luxurious living, one family obviously could not, and so a large surplus could be turned back into new capital investment. Moreover, the collective financial strength of such great combines meant adequate resources for pioneering in new industries. A series of well-established and profitable ventures could be used to support within the framework of the combine the great financial risks entailed by each new industrial undertaking.

The *zaibatsu* system has played such a significant role in Japanese industrialization and has been so dominant a factor in the shaping of modern Japan that many people have assumed that it was deliberately created during the second half of the nineteenth century by a group of Japanese government planners, anxious to establish a centralized big business system to parallel the centralized political system they were building. But, of course, such theories presuppose an understanding of economics and a capacity for long-range planning on the part of the statesmen of the Meiji period such as no statesmen elsewhere had ever exhibited before. These men were confronted with immediate financial and industrial problems of the greatest difficulty. Their chief concern in the economic field was to build up industry as fast as possible without reducing Japan's finances to chaos. They were willing to try anything that promised to achieve this result, and they frequently changed their course. It seems much more reasonable to suppose that, in their concern with immediate problems, they had little realization of what the long-range effects of their acts would be and that, in this sense, the development of the *zaibatsu* system was to a large extent accidental and not a premeditated plot on the part of the Meiji statesmen.

The chief factor which lay behind the development of the *zaibatsu* system was the paucity of private capital in Japan at the beginning of the modern period. During the Tokugawa era, a rich merchant class had grown up and had come to dominate the culture as well as the finances of this politically feudal land, but the accumulations of capital were relatively small and largely in the hands of men more accustomed to trade and moneylending than to industrial production. At the beginning of the Meiji period, the merchant class was understandably reluctant to leave its accustomed field and risk its modest capital in pioneer work in hitherto unheard-of industrial enterprises. Most of what little private capital there was for industrial ventures came from the former feudal classes, the old feudal lords and the higher ranking samurai, who in the 1870's were paid off in cash and government bonds in return for the relinquishment of their old feudal privileges. Some of these men founded modern banking enterprises with these new assets or moved cautiously into the industrial field. But even this new private capital based on government credit was not great. Thus, the total amount of private capital was limited, and the few merchants or samurai who had a little capital and daring were in a position to gain rich profits from successful industrial and commercial ventures. Where labor is plentiful and capital scarce, profits inevitably are high, and those who got a head start under such circumstances were in a position to accumulate wealth rapidly. Moreover, the government, anxious to see industry advance, gave them direct and indirect assistance of a sort which would now be branded as patently scandalous.

An important step in the creation of the *zaibatsu* system was the government's sale during the 1880's of many of the industrial plants it had built. Japan at the time was facing a financial crisis, and most of these factories were still a drain on the government's budget. It was felt, therefore, that the government would have to unload most of these significant but costly ventures for whatever prices could be obtained and concentrate on the more specifically military industries, leaving the bulk of the other industries to private capital to develop as best it could. In the course of the 1880's, plant after plant was sold, often at ridiculously low prices. In some cases these prices were the result of collusion between government officials and businessmen, but usually the low prices simply meant that no one had been willing to pay the higher prices first demanded. Naturally the buyers of these plants were the very few men who had some money. Shortly after this transfer of government factories at extremely low prices, Japanese industry for the first time really began to pay. The few owners of modern industrial and commercial enterprises in Japan had started on their rapid growth to become some of the greatest financial and industrial magnates in the world.

Once well established there was no stopping the *zaibatsu*. They entered one new field after another, until the roster of the interests of the bigger *zaibatsu* combines was virtually a catalogue of the full extent of the Japanese economy. With their immense and varied resources they could engage in price slashing which would have been suicidal for smaller competitors. They grew by gobbling up their smaller business rivals, until the Japanese economy came to be divided for the most part between the *zaibatsu* combines themselves, with only the crumbs of less profitable and small-scale industries left to the independent businessman. The *zaibatsu* all along had profited immensely from government patronage, and they always did their best to stay close to the political powers for protection and for further favors. By providing bureaucrats with lucrative positions and politicians with campaign funds, they maintained their close relations with the government long after they had outgrown all need for direct government assistance. In fact, they increasingly became the patrons and the politicians their grateful beneficiaries. With the passing of time and the growth of Japanese industry and trade, the *zaibatsu* system became ever more entrenched.

An obvious question is how the *zaibatsu* combines were able to hold together over the years despite their unreasonable size and extraordinarily diverse interests. Several factors account for this. Originally, each had been owned and controlled by a single family, with its own strict laws carefully formulated to assure the continuance of family solidarity and family control of the sprawling industrial and commercial empire it had created. But, in time, the growing complexity of economic problems and the inevitable ups and downs of business talent within a single family put the immediate control of most *zaibatsu* enterprises into the hands of a managerial class of business executives with no blood ties to the family.

This process was well advanced by the 1930's, but the *zaibatsu* combines showed no signs of falling apart. For one thing, there were great advantages in the association of many powerful business enterprises together for the sake of protecting themselves and exerting influence on the government. There was also the centralized selling technique of the *zaibatsu* combines, which kept the member companies dependent for the sale of their products on the combine's trading organs. Another factor was the careful hierarchical arrangement of the component companies. At the top was a holding company, normally owned by the family itself, which more or less controlled through the stocks it held certain major affiliates, which in turn controlled lesser affiliates, and so on down the line. But this control was not merely a matter of majority ownership of stocks, for frequently this was not the case. More important than the formal structure was the strength of personal bonds within the organization. Here, perhaps, was another holdover from the feudal emphasis on personal obligations. Young men, upon graduation from university, would enter the service of a *zaibatsu* company, and, though they might be shifted from company to company as they advanced, they expected to remain with that particular combine for life. Only by giving it their full loyalty could they expect to get ahead, and, by the time they had reached the top as high executives, they were almost as much a part of the combine as the *zaibatsu* family itself. These men could be trusted to hold the combine together, even if the family no longer had the executive talent to do so. The top executives, through a complicated system of interlocking directorates and an invisible bond of personal loyalty and club feeling, were the real links which held the combines together even more than the stocks owned by the *zaibatsu* family.

It has never been established just which combines were large enough to be called *zaibatsu* and which were not. The Japanese often refer to the old and the new *zaibatsu*, meaning by the latter the combines which came to prominence after the Manchurian venture of 1931. These, on the whole, tended to be less widely spread in different industrial and trading fields than were the older combines. The big four among the *zaibatsu* have always been Mitsui, Mitsubishi, Sumitomo, and Yasuda, and among these the first two are the greatest of all and really form a class by themselves.

Mitsui grew out of a Tokugawa merchant firm, which had its humble beginnings in the early seventeenth century as a *saké* brewery. In time, it grew into a prosperous dry goods and money-lending enterprise, which made loans to the Shogun and to the Imperial court. During the Meiji Restoration, the Mitsui family gave strong financial support to the new regime, and presently, in keeping with the spirit of modernization of the times, they changed their old money-lending firm into

Japan's first modern banking corporation. They also rapidly modernized their commercial interests into great trading companies and entered the mining field and various industries. By 1933 they had established some degree of control over no less than 130 different companies. Before the war the chief Mitsui affiliates were in trading and commerce, mining, banking, shipping, steel, machinery, textiles, food products, chemicals, aircraft, light metals, lumber, and building and warehousing.

Mitsubishi had a very different origin from Mitsui. It was founded shortly after the Restoration by a samurai called Iwasaki, who had been the financial administrator of the Lord of Tosa, an important fief on the island of Shikoku. Iwasaki started in the shipping business and provided transportation facilities for the expedition sent by the government in 1874 against the aborigines of Formosa, ostensibly to punish them for having killed some mariners from the Ryukyu Islands but really to test out the European game of empire-building. As a reward for this service, he received from the government the extraordinary gift of thirteen steamships, originally purchased by the government for $1,568,000. He also derived huge profits from the transportation of government troops during the Satsuma Rebellion of 1877, and eventually his shipping interests grew into the great merchant fleet of the Nippon Yusen Kaisha. The rest of the story is much like that of the Mitsui. The Mitsubishi interests were extended to other fields—notably heavy industries, mining, commerce, banking, chemicals, and electric goods—and in time the Iwasaki came to control almost as many different companies as the Mitsui.

The *zaibatsu* system may have had a vital role in building up Japanese industry, but it has also left a legacy of major political and social ills. If the uneven division of ownership of Japan's agricultural land is cause for concern, the vastly more lopsided division of economic strength in industry and commerce can hardly be condoned. Obviously, the concentration of so much economic power in the hands of so very few people could have nothing but a deleterious influence on attempts to build up democracy in Japan. The enormous differences in wealth produced by such a system were also not a healthy social phenomenon and engendered bitter resentment against the *zaibatsu* on the part of large groups in Japan, particularly intellectuals, low-paid government workers, and army and navy officers. The term *zaibatsu* itself is proof of this attitude, for it is a pejorative, meaning "financial clique" and carrying with it all the venom with which many Americans use the term "Wall Street."

Even before the war there existed growing resentment in Japan against the *zaibatsu*, and we Americans singled out the whole combine system as one of our major targets for postwar reform, but still the *zaibatsu* should not be denied their historical due. They did have a mighty part in the industrialization of Japan; because of the very size of their enterprises, they were able to inject some diversity of point of view into the monolithic totalitarian system Japan's bureaucrats and militarists were attempting to create before and during the war; and they gave an over-all integration to Japanese industry and commerce which the Japanese will find hard to replace today. Many economists feel that the combines were not really economically efficient organizations but were overly diffuse in their ramified interests. That may well be correct, but the combines, at the same time, afforded an integration in Japanese industry which may not be replaceable except by a system involving a high degree of governmental control.

However unfortunate a social and political influence the *zaibatsu* have been, the industry they built remains as the main support of the Japanese economy today. Japan must continue to be a highly industrialized land, and, if she is to attain even moderately adequate living standards, her factories must be constantly expanded and the skills of her workers continuously improved. Japanese industry faces a most uncertain future, but it is Japan's only hope. The Japanese people, who have almost trebled in number because of the greater economic opportunities industrialization has given them, now are entirely dependent on industry to live, and industry in turn depends on foreign markets. The history of modern Japan is the story of expanding industry, permitting an expanding population, which in turn has resulted in an increasing dependence on foreign trade. The inexorable laws of economic necessity have forced the Japanese to choose one of two diametrically opposed courses to secure the trade they must have. Either they must fight for empire, or else they must be champions of peace, world order, and more international trade. The unalterable factors of geography and economics have given them these two alternatives, but other considerations besides geography and economics have determined their varying choices in the past and will do so again in the future.

6. The Japanese and the Outside World

1. GEOGRAPHIC ISOLATION

The economic realities of modern Japan stand out in an all too stark and ugly light, but a nation is not merely a huge economic unit. It is made up of millions of individuals with well-established patterns of conduct and habits of thought. The outer limits of their activities may be defined by unchangeable geographic factors, but within these broad bounds there is room for a thousand significant variations, primarily determined by other more subtle but equally important influences. Even when given similar geographic environments and comparable economic opportunities, the various peoples of the world have met their problems in a bewildering variety of ways. A hundred minor variations have produced in permutation a myriad differing patterns of society, sometimes contrasting sharply with one another despite their similar physical backgrounds. The steppe lands of the western part of our own country support an entirely different civilization from that found in the steppe lands of Central Asia or North Africa. The Canadians and the Russians are two very different peoples; Brazil and India have little more than geographic and climatic resemblances in common; and the Japanese have fashioned a very different society with very different potentialities from the societies built up by other peoples in somewhat similar areas—say the Italians or the English, the inhabitants of our own East Coast, or even Japan's closer neighbors in Korea and China.

Culture, civilization, national character, whatever you wish to call it, is not subject to the same clear measurements that can be applied to geography and economics. You can say that one people has twice the per capita coal resources of another, but it does not mean anything to say that one people has one-half the per capita bravery or loyalty or honesty of another people. You can only make vague generalizations which not only are statistically unverifiable but are even based on undefined and perhaps undefinable standards. The very concepts of honesty, bravery, and loyalty and the types of situations in which they are considered applicable may differ so radically between cultures as to offer little basis for comparison. And within any large national grouping the individual variations with regard to such qualities are so great as to make any concept of per capita averages meaningless. All one can do is to say that, in terms of the accepted standards of one people, these qualities appear on the whole to be deficient or in excess, to a greater or lesser degree, in another people. For example, we can note those qualities of the Japanese which seem to be sufficiently exaggerated or minimized in many, if not most, Japanese as to strike an American as being departures from his own norms. This, of course, involves no value judgments, for the process in reverse would reveal many American characteristics unduly stressed or minimized when measured against Japanese norms. It also does not imply any invariable uniformity with regard to these characteristics on the part of any individual Japanese. Such comparisons merely provide an arbitrary means of expressing broad cultural differences which might make the Japanese react differently from Americans to any given situation and which, therefore, must be kept in mind by Americans whenever they attempt to evaluate what has happened or is happening in Japan and still more when they attempt to predict future developments there.

It is never safe to state unequivocally that certain geographic influences have produced certain specific cultural characteristics. One can so easily find other places in the world where similar geographic conditions had no such result. And, in any case, a culture is not a series of unrelated phenomena but is always a complicated pattern, in which a large number of different factors so act upon one another as to achieve a total balance. One geographic factor, however, stands out as a dominant one in Japan's cultural heritage and an element which distinguished Japan from all the other older civilized lands of the world. This factor is isolation. In pre-modern times, no other important group of people consciously participating in the rich culture of the Eurasiatic land mass lived so far removed from all the other civilized peoples. The straits between Japan and Korea are five times as wide as the Straits of Dover, which have had a significant influence in shaping England's history and the character of her people. The distance between Japan and China, the homeland of her civilization, is even greater. Only in recent centuries have peoples of the civilized world come to live at greater distances from the Eurasiatic land mass, and by that time vastly improved techniques of navigation and, now, instantaneous communications have wiped out the factor of isolation.

One obvious influence of isolation on Japan has been the creation of a highly homogeneous race of people there and, what is more important, a very homogeneous culture. The Japanese as a race are primarily a Mongoloid people, as are all the major groups of that part of the world. They differ no more from Koreans and Chinese than Englishmen differ from Frenchmen or Germans. Statistically certain physical variations appear between the Japanese, Koreans, and Chinese. The Japanese show more signs of negritic and proto-Caucasoid admixtures than do their continental neighbors. It is impossible, however, to be certain on purely physical grounds that any given individual is a Japanese rather than a Chinese or Korean. Clothing, even of Western style, and, still more, haircuts and mannerisms often differentiate them clearly, but not any invariable physical characteristics.

The problem of the origin of the Japanese has fascinated a great many scholars and casual students of Japan and has led to many pseudo-scientific attempts to explain the Japanese in terms of racial origins. Some have been intrigued by the continued existence in Hokkaido of small settlements of Ainu, a people who obviously were once more widespread in the islands and probably account for the proto-Caucasoid strain in Japanese blood, which evinces itself in the ability of many Japanese to grow more luxuriant mustaches and beards than their continental neighbors. Other scholars hold strongly to the view that the Japanese are most closely akin to the peoples of Malaysia and the islands of the Pacific. There certainly are strong cultural similarities between Japan and the islands to the south in their seafaring habits, their lightly constructed houses, their mythology, and many other things, but no crude theory of the movement of peoples from the south into Japan stands up under the test of archaeology. Possibly a diffusion of peoples, perhaps from South China into the islands to the south and to Japan by way of Korea, accounts for some of these resemblances. Other scholars emphasize the well-authenticated movement of peoples from Northeast Asia down through the Korean Peninsula into Japan. The archaeological evidence for this is clear. At least one important element in the Japanese race and the group which slowly built up the Japanese state of early historical times came to Japan from Korea and had close cultural resemblances to the peoples of Northeast Asia.

The Japanese, thus, like all other peoples, are a blend of many diverse elements, but their exact racial composition is, in fact, little known and makes less difference. What is important is that there have been no significant additions of blood to the Japanese race for well over a thousand years. They have had plenty of time to become thoroughly mixed together to form as unified a people as exist anywhere in the world.

Their culture, though repeatedly enriched by foreign borrowings, has also had time to become extremely homogeneous, particularly during the two centuries of Tokugawa isolation. The Japanese culture of the mid-nineteenth century was perhaps more uniform than the culture of any European country of comparable size. Some observers feel that the Japanese have achieved greater cultural uniformity throughout the length and breadth of the land and throughout the vertical stratifications of their society than has ever been achieved in a country of Japan's size, and they compare Japanese cultural homogeneity to that of a primitive tribe.

But it is doubtful that this, if true formerly, still holds today. The rapid influx of Western ideas and techniques during the past century has injected a time differential into contemporary Japanese culture. Certain classes and certain areas have been affected more rapidly and more thoroughly by these new influences than others, the intellectuals notably more than laborers, for instance, and the city people more than the peasants. Although the Japanese do not have the great geographic differences of a broad country like ours or the differences we inherit from immigrant forefathers of differing races, cultures, and religions, there are tremendous contrasts in conduct and in thought as well as in external ways of life between a university professor in Tokyo and a peasant in southern Kyushu. These differences, though far less obvious, are not much less profound than the differences between a New York broker of Yankee stock and a Negro sharecropper in Mississippi.

Some observers, struck by the startling mixture of East and West in the daily life of the urban Japanese, have gone to the other extreme and attributed to the Japanese a sort of cultural schizophrenia. They feel it incongruous to find cultural elements with which they themselves are familiar mixed in with what is to them strange and bizarre. They feel that a Japanese who dresses in a business suit on weekdays and a kimono over the weekend or eats his luncheon with knife and fork at an Occidental type of restaurant and his breakfast and supper with chopsticks while kneeling on the floor at home must feel as self-conscious over these contrasts as they would themselves if they were suddenly forced to adopt Japanese ways for part of each day. But actually the diverse origin of these various elements in their culture disturbs the Japanese no more than the mixed use of Latin letters and Arabic numerals disturbs the average European. It seems no stranger to a Japanese to alternate between a business suit and kimono, depending on the occasion, than it does to an American woman to don a kimono at night after having worn slacks all day. The Japanese have had railroads, telegraphs, electric lights, and printing presses about as long as any of us and feel just as much at home with them as we do. It is no more incongruous or upsetting to them to wear a ski hat or eat a dish of ice cream than it is for an Englishman to drink a cup of tea.

Another clear influence of geographic isolation on Japan has been the infrequency of close contacts with foreign lands throughout Japanese history and, conversely, the heavy waves of influence from abroad whenever close contacts did exist. Most other parts of the civilized world have been subject throughout history to a continuous stream of foreign influences, so steady and uniform as to have gone virtually unnoticed most of the time. In Japan, however, the very paucity of such influences at most times meant that, whenever close contacts were feasible, there was likely to be heavy, almost frantic borrowing from abroad. The first such period was from the beginning of the seventh century through the first half of the ninth, when the still very backward and primitive Japanese state, in an amazing display of energy and ambition, attempted to model itself after the T'ang dynasty of China, which at that time was unquestionably the richest, strongest, and, in many ways, the most advanced state in the world. Then came several centuries of only desultory contacts between Japan and the outside world, followed in the thirteenth to sixteenth centuries by a period of increasingly close relations with China and Korea, culminating in a few decades of contacts with the Western world in the second half of the six-teenth century. This time there was no conscious effort to remodel Japan on the pattern of either China or Europe, but foreign influences, nevertheless, were strong. The swing of the pendulum then brought two centuries of almost complete isolation during the Tokugawa period, followed in turn by the frantic period of Westernization during the past hundred years. For a second time in her history, Japan was consciously attempting to follow a foreign model.

Even within this last period there have been ups and downs in the rate of borrowing. It started with the mad rush Japan made during the Meiji period to catch up with the West. This gradually slowed down, until by the 1930's the Japanese were self-consciously rejecting everything Western which was not already well entrenched in Japan. Their defeat has made them eager once more to learn from the West, meaning specifically the United States this time, and at least for the moment there is again an unquestioning acceptance of anything from abroad.

It is doubtful whether Japan's jerky start-and-stop method of learning from the outside world has resulted in any greater sum total of foreign influences than are to be found in any other land of comparable size. In fact, a good case could be made for the opposite thesis. It can be argued that, in almost every phase, Japanese culture differs more from other cultures than, say, the cultures of Germany, Persia, or Siam from those of their respective neighbors. Japan's graphic arts, her industrial arts, writing systems, poetry, prose styles, drama, culinary arts, domestic architecture, clothing, political and social institutions, and even her religions and philosophy show, for better or for worse, a distinctiveness that few if any other lands can boast.

But the alternation of periods of rapid borrowing and comparative isolation has resulted in a clear awareness on the part of the Japanese of the whole process of borrowing. They have been so acutely conscious of this wholesale learning from abroad during certain periods in the past and have so emphasized this aspect of their history that they have helped create the myth that they are nothing but a race of copiers, a monkey-like people lacking any originality or creative powers themselves. Their careful labeling of this element in their culture as having come from Korea in the sixteenth century and that from China in the eighth has left little but the most primitive elements to be cherished as "native," thus strengthening the impression gained by foreigners during the past century of heavy borrowing from the West that nothing Japanese is really "Japanese" at all and that they, unlike other peoples, can only copy but not create.

While forced by geographic isolation to develop alone more of their own civilization than have most other peoples, they have been overwhelmed with the concept of borrowing from abroad and have, in compensation, emphasized supposed "native" elements more than other nations have. A clear-cut contrast between Western influences and the native culture before the impact of the West exists throughout Asia, and the nativistic reactions in Japan to this contrast have not differed from those of other Asiatic lands and, for that matter, have been only greater in degree but not different in type from the nativistic reactions of America at various times in its history. The Japanese, however, are unique in having kept alive a distinction between what is considered to have been natively Japanese before the seventh century and what resulted from the contacts with China from that time on. It is as if the French were obsessed with the idea that only that part of their culture which was derived from pre-Roman Gaul was native and labeled all else as foreign borrowings. Such an attempt would send the British back to the druids for their native culture. Naturally, in Japan, it has resulted in a ridiculous emphasis on the primitive and an impossible search in the only hazily known early years of Japanese history for some mysterious source for Japan's later greatness. It has also been the background for a great deal of mystical nonsense about Japan and the Japanese, which has been used to justify a host of absurd political and social doctrines and a particular virulent brand of nationalistic dogma.

There has been, however, one very good result of Japan's consciousness of foreign borrowing. The Japanese take the process of acculturation for granted and are not afraid or ashamed, when circumstances dictate, to borrow whatever they need from abroad. Without the historical example of Japan's heavy borrowing from China a thousand years earlier, it might have been more difficult than it was for the Meiji leaders to conceive the idea of repatterning Japan on Western models and to justify this course of action both to themselves and to their people. Certainly that concept came much more slowly and far more painfully to most of the other peoples of Asia. The Chinese, with their age-old belief that China was the unique civilized land of the world, surrounded by bar-barians of varying degrees of inferiority and loyalty to China, found it particularly difficult to accept the idea that anything important could be learned from the West, much less that the Chinese economic and political structure would have to be remade on Western lines. But in Japan it seemed evident that, if the land had been converted into a miniature China in the seventh and eighth centuries, it could be made into an Asiatic England or Germany in the nineteenth. Even today, the con-cept of another great transformation, dictated this time from abroad, seems less strange and less repugnant to the Japanese than it would to most peoples.

By and large, isolation may have had the curious effect of making the Japanese more ready to accept new things from abroad than were most other peoples—and they certainly have always demonstrated a great enthusiasm for the new—but at the same time isolation has also permitted them to cling more persistently than other nations to the old. The result is Japan's particular form of conservatism, which is the cherishing of the old and outmoded while enthusiastically embracing the new. Perhaps because international friction was less intense in this isolated corner of the globe and the struggle for cultural survival, therefore, less acute, many of the outmoded aspects of Japanese civilization could continue to exist side by side with the new. The Imperial institution itself is a case in point. The Emperors of Japan by the twelfth century had become incongruous survivals of an earlier age. Almost anywhere else in the world, the struggle for national survival would have forced the abandonment of such outgrown forms, but Japanese isolation permitted the coexistence of the old political institutions in theory and the new feudal institutions in practice. Another example in the cultural field is the survival until today of virtually every aspect of religion that has ever existed in Japan. Where other lands have seen new religions or new religious movements sweep the whole land bare of many earlier religious forms, in Japan each new religious movement has simply taken its place beside the old. Drama is an even more surprising case in point. The Japanese still enjoy the *No* theater, which they perfected in the fifteenth century, along with the puppet theater of the seventeenth, the *Kabuki* theater of the eighteenth, and their still feeble attempts at Western dramatic forms and their vastly popular adaptations of Hollywood techniques. The Japanese are like us in that they are always ready and even eager to adopt the new, but at the same time they are very unlike us in their strong tendency to preserve the old and outmoded.

2. NATIONAL SELF-CONSCIOUSNESS

The Japanese concern with what is "native" and what is borrowed in their culture shows a heavy self-consciousness which may also be associated with isolation. They are figuratively, as well as literally, an insular people, like the English, but in a very different way. The British are conscious of themselves with a certain air of self-satisfaction, which is by no means wholly unjustified. Japanese self-consciousness contains a large degree of embarrassment and the fear of inferiority. Perhaps the difference is that between a people isolated enough to feel slightly set apart and a people so isolated throughout their history as to have feared that they did not belong at all.

The Japanese attitude has certainly been strengthened by the painfully obvious contrast throughout most of their history between small, backward, remote, and young Japan as opposed to China, the admitted home of civilization, which was far larger, far older, and far grander than Japan could ever hope to be. It was as if the British had always been set off against a unified continent held together by a continuing Roman Empire. Perhaps the contrast with China in size, age, and prestige was enough to give the Japanese collectively a certain sense of inferiority with respect to the outside world, though, as we shall see, the existence of this same pattern on an individual scale within Japan suggests the possibility of an entirely different origin for it. Conceivably, their shortness of stature as compared with the European peoples or even the Koreans and northern Chinese has also contributed to their feeling of inferiority. In any case, the Japanese show a national self-consciousness and a sense of inferiority which, while not altogether unknown in a self-assertive America just emerging from a position of cultural inferiority to Europe, is far more ingrained and compulsive with the Japanese than with us. Where we are inordinately interested but also amused by the unending flow of half-truths about ourselves from visiting English pundits, the Japanese evince an unquenchable and decidedly morbid interest in every expression of opinion on Japan by any foreigner, no matter how poorly informed or unqualified he may be to render judgment.

The Japanese have reflected these characteristics in the alternating periods in their history between abject humility toward outside civilizations and arrogant cultural independence and self-assertiveness. The hero of one period is the broad-minded leader who openly condemns Japanese failings and extols the virtues of foreign cultures. Sooner or later he is replaced by a very different type of hero who points out the corrupting influences of inferior foreign civilizations and calls for a return to native Japanese virtues. But, whichever type dominates a period, both are equally conscious of the contrast between Japan and the outside world. The hundred miles of open sea between Japan and Korea, still more the five hundred miles of water which lie between western Kyushu and China, seem to cut the Japanese off from the rest of the human race. The classification "Japanese" seems almost a more significant classification than "human being." The native-born Japanese abroad rarely loses himself in another civilization. He remains always a self-conscious representative of Japanese culture, never quite able to forget his national identity. Even the Japanese at home, with no foreign contacts to stimulate his national consciousness, maintains an unusual awareness of a surrounding alien world. The fellow villagers of an Olympic swimming champion are not just proud of the hometown boy who made good. They are proud of him as a Japanese who has demonstrated Japan's superiority to the outside world. The gulf which the Japanese feel between themselves and their fellow men is almost as real as the water barrier that isolates their land.

This national self-consciousness has strongly influenced Japanese reactions at home as well as abroad. However pugnaciously self-assertive the Japanese may be or however insistent upon the unique virtues of Japanese culture, there is never any self-complacency about them. They are usually either engaged in an attempt to catch up with some other country or else are vigorously trying to demonstrate their superiority to an unconvinced world. They feel the eyes of the world are always upon them, not only when they venture abroad but also in their life at home. To the average Japanese, the actual indifference of the rest of the world to Japan would seem incredible. He assumes that the whole world is aware of and marvels at Japan's high rate of school attendance or whatever else he takes pride in and that all foreigners are equally conscious and scornful of Japan's various shortcomings. Exposed, as the Japanese assume themselves to be, to the merciless light of world-wide publicity, they can never relax but must always play to the grandstands. If an unsympathetic audience fails to applaud them for their obvious virtues, at least they will force the audience to gasp at their derring-do.

All this stands in sharp contrast to the Chinese, who, except for a small group of strongly Westernized apologists, have until recently tended to remain blandly secure in their knowledge of China's long superiority over all her neighbors and content to let the outside barbarians discover China's virtues for themselves. Conquering hordes have come to China many times in the past but have always been absorbed eventually by the superior Chinese culture—always except for the Mongols who were driven out again after a mere century of rule. The inconsequential military superiority of the crass Europeans or the even more despicable Japanese was, therefore, nothing to become hysterical about. China, the "central land," would always remain the center of civilization. Thus, the Chinese, with their easy-going assumption of superiority, have appeared to the rest of the world relaxed and genial, whereas the Japanese, fearful of the scorn of the outside world and eager for its plaudits, have made others vaguely ill at ease by their self-consciousness and definitely annoyed by their insistent demand for appreciation.

National self-consciousness has probably also contributed to the Japanese inability to see a problem from another people's point of view. Of course, it is futile to make comparisons between the relative inabilities of various peoples to put themselves in some other people's shoes or sandals. Man, individually and collectively, demonstrates a determined adherence to his own particular point of view. But the Japanese do seem at times a little less able than some to recognize the possibility that other people can have honest differences of opinion from themselves. Any point of view but the Japanese is likely to bring from them the boringly repetitious charge of "insincerity." The absurd doctrine of the white man's burden was maintained in the West only so long as the colored peoples of the world remained stunned into silence. The Japanese managed to retain faith in the justness and practicability of Japanese hegemony over Asia in the face of the uproarious opposition of all the peoples who were supposedly being benefited by the Pax Japonica. They repeatedly guessed wrong about the reactions of the Chinese people. In fact, the whole eight-year war with China and most of its major campaigns were fought with the mistaken expectation of an imminent collapse of Chinese opposition as a result of continued Japanese successes.

Similarly, the Japanese decision to fight the United States was based on a colossal misjudgment of the American people. The Japanese government knew perfectly well that we had the material resources to crush them, but they seem to have assumed that we did not have the will power to deny ourselves new automobiles and all the gadgets we love so dearly in order to devote our industrial energies to a distant war. Japanese will power, they felt, would thus triumph over American material superiority, and on the basis of this reasoning they launched a brilliantly successful attack which instantaneously created among all Americans a determination so strong that it was more than enough to see us through to the complete destruction of Japan. Misjudgments of this sort lie at the heart of most international strife, but the Japanese in recent years have made more than their share of such disastrous blunders.

3. NATIONALISM

A national sense of inferiority might also be associated with the early appearance of nationalism in Japan. Nationalism, as opposed to a primary loyalty to religious groupings, as in India, or a cultural grouping like that of traditional China, has become a significant force in the greater part of Asia only in the last few decades, but it was a dominant influence in Japan in the middle of the nineteenth century and was an important factor in Japanese history at least as far back as the thirteenth century. This early rise of nationalism was partly the result of the clear-cut geographic and linguistic delimitations of Japan, which have set it apart as a separate country ever since early days, but another factor seems to have been the sense of inferiority. A study of nationalism which included the early experience of Japan might reveal that a sense of inferiority— the contrast of the lesser unit with the obviously greater unit —has had a larger share in the shaping of this tremendous modern force than has often been recognized. Certainly in Europe, nationalism grew fastest in the peripheral areas of the classic world and perhaps had its most spectacular growth in small and isolated England. In the United States, periods of galling inferiority to Great Britain or Europe in general gave rise to some of the most blatant expressions of American nationalism. And in Japan, ever since the thirteenth century, nationalism has been expressed primarily in terms of mystical national traits of superiority—the divine origin of the Japanese people or the divinity of the land itself—which were conjured up in an effort to compensate for China's indisputable superiority in size, power, age, and prestige.

Whatever isolation may have had to do with the early rise of Japanese nationalism, there can be no doubt that nationalism deserves a large share of the credit for Japan's recent Cinderella success story. An essential ingredient of the modern nation-state naturally is nationalism itself, and it is no mere accident that the one Asiatic land with a strong national consciousness in the early nineteenth century far outstripped all the others in the speed of its modernization along Western lines. A ready-made nationalism provided the nucleus around which the Japanese could concentrate their energies in their drive toward modernization. In the other Asiatic lands, basic Westernization was virtually impossible until this binding force had been slowly and painfully developed. If any one factor is to be singled out to explain the difference between Japan's rapid modernization and the slowness of the process in the rest of

Asia, this factor is nationalism. Similarly, one of the chief distinctions between Japan today and the rest of Asia is the greater maturity of her nationalism. In most of Asia, nationalism is a dynamic new force with creative and destructive potentialities which are as yet incalculable. In Japan, as in America and Europe, it is a tremendous force but nothing new. It has long since demonstrated its terrible power. It is a known quantity and not a new and unpredictable force upsetting the previous balance of society.

All in all, isolation has probably contributed as greatly to the formation of Japanese culture as any single identifiable external factor, and it certainly has done much to determine the relations of the Japanese to other people. It has permitted them to live apart from the rest of the world more than any other major people. It has also meant relatively less experience in relations of either an amicable or warlike nature with other people. Little accustomed to foreign contacts, the Japanese, recently thrown into the international maelstrom of the modern world, have shown very little finesse in their dealings with other nations. They have been like the one child in a group which is not accustomed to playing with other children—uninhibitedly selfish, uncertain of what is expected of him or what effect his acts will have on others, and always painfully self-conscious. Like all self-conscious people, the Japanese have an unhappy suspicion that they are always putting their worst foot forward, and, in their case, this suspicion is not altogether unjustified.

Perhaps these are all only minor surface characteristics which should not have much influence on the Japanese at home, but the Japanese cannot withdraw again into their isolation of former days. The modern world does not permit that luxury to any nation, and the Japanese, above all other peoples, are unable to cut themselves off again from the rest of the world but must buy and sell abroad to live. Gross ineptness in their dealings with foreign peoples, culminating in a disastrous war against all their neighbors near and far and a goodly number of nations at the other end of the world, has contributed heavily to the sad plight in which the Japanese find themselves today. No people in the world, with the possible exception of the Germans, have earned so much ill will from their fellow men. Somehow the Japanese must overcome this disadvantage and the poor start it has given them. They must learn how to earn the good will of other peoples, so that they can again trade without discrimination abroad, for, if they do not do this, they will certainly starve at home.

7. Emotion and Conformity

1. EMOTIONAL EXPRESSION

As Ruth Benedict has pointed out in *The Chrysanthemum and the Sword*, there seem to be a number of absurd contradictions in Japanese character—that is, absurd contradictions when one presupposes American norms.* They are contradictions to us only because we do not understand the substratum of forces within Japanese culture which has produced the particular surface patterns which we see in Japanese behavior. There are contradictory forces in all societies which tend to hold one another in a dynamic balance. Those in Japanese society may not be, on the whole, any more contradictory than those in other civilizations, but, in so far as they differ from the underlying forces in our society, their tensions and points of balance will be different, resulting in what may seem to us contradictions and irreconcilable traits within the Japanese character.

Among such underlying forces, two which tend to balance each other, but with a markedly different degree of tension and point of equilibrium in different lands, are, on the one hand, the basic emotional drive toward self-expression and the counterbalancing social force of conformity. The dynamic balance between these two forces is as fundamental to our civilization as to that of Japan, but the degree of tension created between these two forces seems in some respects to be greater in Japan and their point of balance there seems to us decidedly

* Houghton Mifflin Company (Boston, 1946), pp. 1–2.

off-center. The emotional drive toward self-expression appears to be, if anything, greater among the Japanese than with us, but at the same time the Japanese have developed a counter-force of social conformity which is far stronger than anything with which we are familiar. They have seen fit to bridle their free emotional expression as severely as any major people in the world, thus establishing a tension between these two forces and a point of balance between them which are sufficiently strange to us to create in our eyes many apparent inconsistencies in their conduct.

The Japanese so successfully submerge their spontaneous emotional expressions or so warp them to fit their rigid rules of conduct that they have won for themselves the reputation of being a race of "deadpan" robots, and many casual observers consider them as deficient in feeling as any people could be. The man whose only reaction to a suicidal order is a flat, stereotyped statement of acceptance, who submits to an unjustified berating without changing expression, or who giggles nervously when telling of his wife's death that morning seems to have no emotions at all. We are likely to be so misled by the concealing mask of conformity which the average Japanese wears that we cannot see beneath its unchanging lines the heavy play of emotion in his heart. Of course, relative degrees of emotional drives are not easily measured, particularly between national groups each of which shows tremendous variation within itself. Some people who express their emotions readily may have fewer strong emotional drives than others who so conceal them as to seem virtually emotionless. This is as true of peoples as of individuals. But any close study of the Japanese will reveal that the Japanese are an emotional people or at least a people whose emotions are so pent up by other forces as to have more explosive powers than we would consider normal.

All the peoples of the Far East, when studied closely, seem by our standards to be highly emotional and, as we would say, frequently irrational. Northrop's characterization of Eastern civilization as primarily aesthetic in contrast to the theoretic bias of Western civilization has much to recommend it, at least in so far as it applies to the Far East.* The peoples of East Asia have consistently given a greater place in their higher culture to direct emotive response to outside stimuli and have shown far less interest than we in systems of logic. A graphic example carries far more weight with them than the neatest syllogism. Emotional expression in art or poetry is more their forte than a reasoned analysis. Throughout their history, they have placed a greater emphasis on graphic arts and poetry than have we in the West. Of course, we, too, have our art and literature, which may or may not be greater than theirs, but increasingly we have left it to poets and artists, masters and specialists, to produce our art and poetry for us. In the Far East, these are not the prerogatives of the specially talented but are the common coin of all cultivated men.

No matter how "deadpan" a Japanese crowd may be, no matter how monotonously they stick to their formalistic routines, their whole history betrays their basic emotionalism. Our earliest clear picture of the Japanese, in the seventh and eighth centuries, shows them responding with startling enthusiasm to the more advanced civilization of China and particularly to Buddhism, the popular Chinese religion of the day. The Japanese drank eagerly and deeply at the springs of Buddhism, which offered not only far more satisfactory spiritual concepts than any they had previously known but provided them with an emotionally satisfying pageantry and new fields and new techniques of artistic expression, which appealed to the Japanese more directly and more strongly than the philosophy which lay behind them. They embraced first the new religion and then the whole Chinese culture in which it was embedded with the enthusiasm of faddists, which they have ever since shown themselves to be. There has never been anything lethargic about their responses. In the nineteenth century, as

* F. S. C. Northrop, *The Meeting of East and West* (New York: The Macmillan Company, 1946).

in the seventh, they showed a wild enthusiasm for the whole-sale adoption of a foreign civilization. Crazes have repeatedly swept the land, whether they were new sleeve lengths for kimonos, new twists to poetry, or the recent world-wide crazes of skiing, amateur photography, or even existentialism. The Japanese are not the phlegmatic conservatives they appear to be but a people given to fads and enthusiasms.

It was only centuries after the introduction of Buddhism that the Japanese began to make notable philosophic contri-butions to the new religion, but they mastered almost at once the Buddhist arts of architecture, sculpture, and painting. Some of the buildings of the Horyuji, a monastery erected in the seventh century near the old capital of Nara, still stand as the oldest wooden structures in the world and the best surviving examples of Far Eastern architecture of the T'ang period; and the "Golden Hall" of the monastery is crowded with superb pieces of religious sculpture in bronze and wood, dat-ing from the same time. It also has some of the world's finest religious murals, which survived the ravages of time, only to be badly disfigured in 1949 by a fire, resulting, ironically enough, from modern electric equipment. Near by, in the old capital of Nara itself, stand many other beautiful Buddhist monasteries with more paintings and magnificent Buddhist statues, providing even more lavish proof of the extent of Japanese artistic production in the eighth century and the consummate mastery the Japanese exhibited even at that early date in adopting the sophisticated artistic language of China and adapting it to their own use.

From then on, each new age, each century, produced a wealth of great new artistic works. In some periods, the Japa-nese showed their creative genius by developing brilliant new aspects of art. In other periods, they drew new inspiration from the ample artistic springs of China. Every major aspect of Chinese art has its parallels and interesting variations in Japan, and there are in addition the largely native developments, such as the highly original domestic architecture evolved in early medieval times and the picture scrolls of the same period which portray, in a distinctly native style called *Yamato-e*, continuous scenes of breath-taking motion, illustrating the episodic development of a battle, the history of a monastery, or the life of a saint. There were also the late medieval arts, such as landscape gardening and flower arrangement, which, though originally of Chinese inspiration, were completely reshaped and brought to greater perfection in Japan, whence they have recently spread to the Western world. There was also the realistic genre painting of Tokugawa times and the woodblock prints which developed from it and which were greatly admired in the West in the late nineteenth century. The Tokugawa wood-block prints of beautiful landscapes and famous actors represent one of mankind's earliest and most successful attempts at producing fine artistic works at cheap prices for the general public. One might conclude from this that there was, perhaps, a larger and more discriminating popular demand for pictorial art in Japan at this time than in any other country in the world.

It is dangerous to say that one people has more artistic genius or a greater aesthetic bent than another, but certainly the speed and skill with which the Japanese adopted the highly developed art of China contrasts sharply with the slowness and clumsiness of the north European attempt to master the arts of the classic world. And throughout their history the Japanese have shown an enthusiasm for beauty in all its forms which is almost unique. An inordinate passion for the beauties of nature has filled their literature since earliest times and is an important part of Japanese character today. They flock to their "famous" beauty spots the way we throng to football games, and no part of the world is more amply provided by nature with scenic beauty. The Japanese are keenly aware of the play of the seasons on nature around them. Cherry blossom viewing is a national pastime, and the chrysanthemums and maples receive their due in the fall.

The Japanese show a flare for designs and color combinations in clothing which excite the admiration even of those who inherit a very different artistic tradition. They exhibit an amazing refinement of taste in their interior decorating. The wicker basket which a humble craftsman makes or the cheapest pottery bowl shaped and painted by the simplest artisan is often a veritable work of art. The Japanese in their adaptations from the West often show a distressing misunderstanding of our artistic canons, but, from the top to the bottom of their society, they exhibit a high artistic appreciation for what is in their own tradition and uniformly good taste in a myriad of intimate details of their daily life. There is relatively little of the dichotomy we find in our own culture between the self-conscious good taste of the self-appointed artistic minority and the bad taste and artistic vulgarity which they so deplore in others.

Naturally, artistic creativeness and good taste are not merely unrestricted expressions of the emotions. The Japanese, too, have their strict artistic canons, but the fact that Japanese art has never been reduced simply to sterile imitativeness indicates the depths of the emotional springs which feed it. The Japanese passion for natural beauty, their repeated triumphs since ancient times in the field of art, and the high level of artistic taste exhibited throughout the nation give strong evidence of their basic emotionalism, however devoid of feeling they may seem to be superficially.

2. LITERATURE

Most foreign observers of Japan would perhaps agree that her graphic arts are the finest aesthetic expression of her culture, but the Japanese themselves might point to poetry instead. Throughout the Far East, poetry has always been considered the greatest of the literary forms, and it is certainly the earliest true literary expression we find in Japan. During the seventh to ninth centuries, the Japanese seemed willing to substitute almost anything Chinese for their older heritage and were particularly enamored of the Chinese written tradition, so much so, in fact, that for several centuries thereafter educated Japanese felt it beneath their dignity to write in their native tongue, but their love for their own poetry remained unchanged, and the Sinophile Japanese courtiers of the day still fell back on pure Japanese poetry for the most sincere expressions of their emotions. The *Manyoshu*, a collection of about 4500 contemporary or earlier poems, was compiled shortly after the year 759, attesting to the popularity of Japanese poetry at the very height of the period of borrowing from China. The *Kokinshu*, another great anthology of about 1100 poems, was compiled in 905 by Imperial command, and twenty similar Imperial anthologies were compiled during the next five centuries, representing one of the few significant activities the Imperial court continued after it had been replaced politically by the feudal structure of medieval times.

Japanese poetry is always emotive, rather than didactic, impressionistic, rather than expository. It thus shows the primary concern of the Japanese for aesthetic rather than rational expression. Its very form, as well as long established tradition, has helped to preserve its impressionistic, emotive bent. Ever since the time of the *Manyoshu*, the standard poetic form has been the *tanka*, or "short poem," consisting of thirty-one syllables, arranged in five verses of 5–7–5–7–7 syllables respectively. Since Japanese is a polysyllabic language of very simple phonetic structure, this allows only a very few words per poem, far fewer than we can cram into a thirty-four-syllable limerick. If much is to be expressed, it must be through suggestion—the creation in the mind's eye of a vivid scene by a brief mention of its key detail and the stimulation of an emotional response by a mere symbol or the juxtaposition of two contrasting images. The typical Japanese poem tersely conjures up a picture, usually a beautiful scene from nature, and then by a deft turn transforms the visual impression into a surge of emotion.

Since all the syllables in ancient Japanese were open syllables ending in one of the five Japanese vowels, *a, e, i, o,* or *u,* rhyme was too boringly inevitable to have any significance, and, since there is no stress accent like ours in the language, meter, as we know it, was impossible. Instead, the Japanese rely for interest in their poetry on skillful plays on words and deftness in the sleight of hand which transforms a few over-worked verbal symbols into living scenes and poignant emotions. All this, together with the tremendous linguistic, as well as psychological, differences between Japanese and English, makes it almost impossible to translate a Japanese poem literally without making gibberish or pedantry out of it, but the following simple and, to us, particularly understandable example, taken from the *Kokinshu* and presented in transliteration and parallel translation, may give some idea of what the *tanka* is like:

Haru tateba	When spring comes
kiyuru kōri no	the melting ice
nokori naku	leaves no trace;
Kimi ga kokoro mo	Would that your heart too
Ware ni tokenan	melted thus toward me.

In ancient times, the Japanese sometimes composed longer poems than the *tanka,* and they were always thoroughly familiar with the more elaborate poetry of China, but they remained true to their own short poetic form. The only significant development in later times was its further abbreviation to seventeen syllables by the omission of the last two verses. This form, known variously as *haiku, haikai,* and *hokku,* reached full maturity in the seventeenth century and became the favorite poetic form of the Tokugawa period, but in the last several decades the *tanka* has returned to its traditional place of preference. The *haiku,* while retaining the basic approach of the *tanka,* required even greater density: a scene tersely suggested by two or three words, with the emotional impact, which in the *haiku* frequently was humor, carried by an equally terse juxtaposition of unexpected concepts or merely by an overtone. Some idea of the genre may be gained from the following simple examples, which illustrate a few of the aspects of the *haiku*—wit, mood, and the sudden spark of insight:

Tsuki ni e o	To the moon, a handle
sashitaraba yoki	add—a good
uchiwa kana	fan indeed.
Kare eda ni	On a withered branch
karasu no tomarikeri	a crow rested
aki no kure	—the autumn dusk.
Asagao ni	In a morning-glory
kyō wa miyuran	today I seem to see it
waga yo kana	—my life!

Japanese poetry may strike us as a highly restricted medium, but it has never lacked popularity among the Japanese, who have found in its channeled emotionalism a needed medium for self-expression. In ancient times, poetic ability was perhaps more highly prized by the upper classes than any other skill. Love-making without the composing of poems at each meeting and parting was unthinkable. Poetry was as indispensable for all other types of social contact and was an important tool in government itself. In time, other forms of literature became popular—by the late tenth century the sentimental diary and romantic novel, by the thirteenth century the romanticized accounts of the exploits of warriors, by the fifteenth century the deeply Buddhistic *No* plays, and in the seventeenth century the more dramatic and realistic but equally emotional puppet and *Kabuki* plays and a new type of romantic novel—but, throughout, poetry remained the most highly regarded literary expression of each age. In time, more and more people adopted the aristocratic affectation of composing poetry on all memorable occasions. Today, the Japanese find nothing unusual in the holding of an annual national poetry contest, sponsored and participated in by the Emperor himself. Every educated man is expected to be able to compose an appropriate poem on demand. A gathering of old friends may end with the inscribing of poems in a special book the host keeps for such occasions. The successful politician returning home is likely to be asked by the local paper to write a poem for it to publish. Poetry is an important emotional outlet for the Japanese, and they continue to show for it an enthusiasm that the richer and more varied poetries of other lands have rarely evoked.

Anyone reared in our own rich musical tradition will naturally wonder about the position of music in Japanese culture. It has had much the same place with them as with us, appearing in all the roles which we have given it—folk music and the more elaborate music of the court and the cultivated classes, the music of religion, and the music of the stage, both instrumental and vocal. In Japan, however, and for that matter in the whole Far East, there has not been the same rapid development of music which the West has seen in the last few centuries. Like the Chinese, the Japanese failed to explore the possibilities of harmony and polyphony. Their graphic arts in some respects have been far ahead of ours both technically and in aesthetic development, but their music has technically lagged behind ours in modern times. As a result, although their tradition of painting still stands, for the most part, little affected by Occidental artistic traditions, Japanese music is on the verge of rout before our music. Put a pencil in the hands of an educated Japanese, and what he draws will probably be unmistakably Oriental. Ask him to sing a tune, and he is as likely as not to essay "Home Sweet Home."

3. RELIGION

Religion has been a major emotional release for people everywhere, and the Japanese are no exception. In fact, they have shown a consistently greater interest in religion than their Far Eastern neighbors, on the one hand, and, on the other, have stressed the purely emotional aspects of religion more than we have. Their religions have usually been so thoroughly emotive that it is often hard to see in their culture where aesthetics leaves off and religion begins.

Shinto, the religion of the primitive Japanese and the backbone of Japanese religion today, is in essence a nature cult. Its typical cult deities are natural phenomena which by their superb beauty or their mysterious power create a sense of awe in the breast of the onlooker. The term for deity in Japan (there is no word for "god" as we understand it) is *kami*, which means simply "superior." Peerless Fuji or any other lofty peak is perforce a deity. So is any waterfall or any stately tree. One of the commonest sights in the Japanese countryside is a miniature shrine before some towering cryptomeria or perhaps just a sacred straw rope around a gnarled oak. Every Shinto shrine stands in a place of beauty—if nothing else, at least an ancient grove of trees. The thunder and the storm are, of course, deities, as are also the vital forces of fertility, sometimes symbolized by that sly and mysterious creature of the fields, the fox. What could be more natural than that the sun itself is the supreme deity, personified as Amaterasu-omikami, the "Sun Goddess" and progenitress of the Imperial family? There is no line separating man from nature. Awesome and superior men, too, are *kami*—the storied ancestors of old, the heroes who have died in battle, or the mysteriously remote Emperor.

Primitive Shinto went little beyond the simple appreciation of nature and a sense of awe before its more fearsome manifestations. It brought together the local community through common membership in the village shrine group and joint participation in the local festivals. There was attached to it also a primitive mythology, which was preserved in writing in all its naive crudity by the courtiers of the early eighth century, who, even in that age of immoderate admiration for all things Chinese, sought to fashion out of Japan's mythology a history which could rival China's glorious past and, in doing so, unfortunately created a series of national myths which have cast a shadow over rational thought in Japan ever since. Primitive Shinto's closest approach to ethical concepts was the stress it placed on ritual purity, which entailed a great deal of bathing and bodily cleanliness along with avoidance of the ritually impure. It was almost more an aesthetic concept than an ethical one. To the love of beauty, thus, the Japanese added the love of cleanliness, which in Japan never needed to be justified by hygiene or bracketed for emphasis with godliness. The Japanese have always loved bathing, making a virtual cult out of their nightly scalding baths. As a result, they have probably been throughout history one of the most washed and cleanest people in the world, and only recently has the bathtub and shower mania of us Americans, coupled with the wartime lack of fuel and soap in Japan, pushed them into second place.

During the ages, Shinto witnessed many new developments —the influence of Buddhist philosophy and ecclesiastic organization and repercussions from various other forces in the culture—but the main stream has remained little changed. That is why almost every Japanese is to some degree a Shintoist, close to nature and awed by its majesty. But above this simple foundation has been reared in recent time a superstructure of very different aspect. During the nineteenth century, individual religious leaders, some of them women, founded a series of so-called Shinto sects, which were really eclectic religious movements, called Shinto largely because of the Shinto origin of their principal deities. Many of them are openly nationalistic, and several stress faith healing. The adherents of some of these so-called Shinto sects number in the millions, but, despite their popularity, they have had very little influence on the simple main theme of Shinto itself.

An even more spectacular outgrowth of Shinto has been the utilization of its shrines and symbols for blatant nationalistic propaganda. There is nothing inherently nationalistic about primitive Shinto, but, in so far as it is identified with the oldest native tradition of Japan and with the land itself, it has naturally been used by the self-conscious Japanese throughout their history as something native to which to point with pride in the face of the overwhelming superiority of the outside world. Time after time, zealots have turned to Shinto for evidence to support their nationalistic prejudices. The work of such propagandists in the eighteenth and early nineteenth centuries helped create interest in Amaterasu-omikami and still more in the long-ignored line of Emperors descended from her, who in ancient times had walked out of the haze of mythology onto the stage of history. The Imperial line provided a rallying point for all the dissatisfied elements in Tokugawa Japan—rival feudal clansmen, reformers, or reactionaries. When Commodore Perry and Townsend Harris pushed open the doors of Japan and thereby unwittingly undermined Tokugawa feudalism, these men quickly raised the cry of an "Imperial Restoration" and soon brought down the feudal edifice in ruins. Jealously guarding the Emperor as their symbol of unity, they marched on Edo, renamed it Tokyo, the "Eastern Capital," and started the amazing series of reforms which was to transform Japan during the Meiji period.

The Japanese were already a more nationalistic people than any other in Asia, but that was not enough. A far greater nationalistic drive and a fanatical willingness for self-sacrifice were necessary if a suspicious and reluctant people were to be driven through the startling and upsetting reforms needed to change a feudal country into a modern nation-state. The emotional force of Shinto lay ready at hand for the new leaders to exploit. They carefully reshaped the major Shinto cults, turning them slowly into instruments of nationalism. With unlimited resources for pageantry and propaganda at the government's disposal, it was possible to develop a new cult, Emperor worship, and make it the greatest cult of the land. School children were indoctrinated through compulsory visits to the leading shrines, which were now regarded as holy places of nationalism. Small shrines, containing pictures of the Emperor and Empress, were erected in every school, and the children were taught to bow whenever they passed them.

Where the Nazis made a ridiculous attempt to revive the long dead cults of the Teutonic gods, the Japanese found comparable cults still vigorously alive and merely needed to warp them to fit their own nationalistic ends. Thus, so-called State Shinto was created during the last few decades and, to meet the objections of Buddhists and Christians, was defined as being non-religious. Cults of hypernationalism are not unknown even in the democratic lands of the West, but State Shinto was unique in that it tapped the chief religious current of the land. It was a typically modern perversion of the religious instinct, diverting it away from its original bed and into nationalistic channels. State Shinto has been an essential part of the hypernationalism of modern Japan, but, if once this unnatural link is broken, Shinto itself should return to its normal course of appreciation and wonder before the beauty and mystery of nature.

Though Shinto has remained the backbone of Japanese religion, Buddhism has formed most of its flesh and blood for over a thousand years. Buddhism, as it was developed in India almost two and a half millenniums ago, was a religion based on a number of premises which the Japanese and the other Far Easterners have never fully accepted. The Indians believed in an endless cycle of lives and the transmigration of the ego from one life to the next through an endless chain of *karma* causality. They also took it for granted that life was indisputably painful. The Buddha sought to break the chain of causality by cutting the individual's attachment to life and thus allowing him to escape from the never-ending cycle of existence to *nirvana*, which literally meant "extinction" and was compared to the going out of a candle but was, somehow, something more than mere nothingness. To achieve the necessary state of enlightenment, the Indian Buddhist practiced austerities and held, if possible, to a monastic life of celibacy.

Nothing that man could conceive is more remote and incomprehensible to the Far Easterner, with his love of life and sense of family continuity, than these Indian ideas. Buddhism could never have spread to China or Japan or survived in the latter country as its greatest religion if it had not been profoundly modified. The Japanese of the seventh century were attracted by the magnificent ritual of Buddhism, its glorious art, the worldly wisdom of its continental missionaries and of the Japanese monks who had studied abroad, and the power of the many deities it had acquired on its long journey to Japan. Unknown though these gods were to early Buddhism, they had taken on far greater powers by the seventh century than were ever attributed by the Japanese to their own simple deities. So powerful were they, in fact, that they began at once to swallow the whole Shinto pantheon. The old, familiar deities of Japan, it was explained, were merely the local manifestations of the universal Buddhist deities. The two were not at all incompatible but existed simply on two different levels —the local and familiar, the universal and supreme—and, ever since, most Japanese have considered themselves to be both Shintoist and Buddhist without any sense of incongruity or conflict.

Buddhism spread only slowly from the Sinophile court circles down to the people at large, but by the eleventh century it had so worked itself into the whole culture as to have produced a religious excitement among the people, which grew with a rising crescendo until it exploded in a great outburst of religious fervor, reflected in the creation in the late twelfth and thirteenth centuries of a number of new, popular Buddhist sects. But in this great Buddhist awakening of medieval Japan, everything that was stressed was diametrically opposed to the teachings of early Indian Buddhism. *Nirvana* had become a beautiful paradise, a glorious afterlife, which compensated for the pain of the life on earth. And the way to paradise was no lonely road of self-denial and mortification of the flesh. *Bodhisattvas*, enlightened creatures who, though infinitely wise, had themselves postponed entrance into *nirvana* in order to help their weaker fellow creatures, stood ready to save anyone who but called on them. The ideal of *jiriki*, salvation through one's "own strength," had been replaced by the easier doctrine of *tariki*, salvation through "the strength of another." Amida, the Buddha of the "Western Paradise," had vowed to save all sentient beings. It was enough merely to chant *Namu Amida Butsu*, "Hail to the Buddha Amida." The layman could hope for salvation as well as the cleric. There was no need to turn away from this life. The priests of most sects were allowed to marry and raise families, as nature had ordained. Buddhism had become a happy, positive religion, which, while destroying none of the older Japanese religious beliefs, had added a great new dimension to religious experience in Japan.

The *Bodhisattva* concept of service to others created a great ethical ideal of social service, but there was no idea of mortal sin—in fact no clear doctrine of sin at all. Buddhism encouraged good works but did not insist on any restricting ethical code. A single expression of belief was enough to win salvation from the compassionate gods. There was no rigid dogma. All things were encompassed within Buddhism—the hairsplitting metaphysics of the Indians or the simple faith and hope of the medieval Japanese. The Shinto love of nature could also be added. Everything fitted into the tolerant comprehensiveness of Buddhism. The Zen sect, drawing heavily on the naturalistic Taoist philosophers of China, as well as on the Japanese love of nature, became the most important Buddhist movement of late medieval times. Emphasizing meditation and the sudden flash of intuitive knowledge which transcends all rational perception, the Zen practitioners sought to achieve a oneness with nature, an understanding of the basic principle of the universe, through intuitive understanding of one of its humble natural manifestations. Zen, which is undefiledly aesthetic in its approach and belligerently opposed to all that smacks of the theoretic, was the final distillation of the alien Buddhist doctrines over the fires of Chinese Taoism and Japanese nature worship.

Thus, religion in Japan, whether Shinto or Buddhist in form, is largely aesthetic in expression. A code of ethics and a system of philosophy are secondary, or perhaps entirely irrelevant. What is important is the sense of awe and wonder, the act of worship, the comforting sense of belief. Religion means the gay shrine festivals, where *saké* flows freely to help break down the emotional inhibitions of the celebrants. Religion means a feeling of awe before the plunging waterfall and the half-instinctive bowing of one's head and clapping of one's hands before something superior, with little thought of direct benefit or any clear rationale for one's act. Religion means praying before a mysterious image of the Buddha, while the priests chant the liturgy and the beauty of serenity enters one's heart to match the beauty of the world outside.

Art, poetry, and religion are some of the more important outlets the Japanese use for the expression of the emotionalism they so carefully hide in most of their daily life, but there are also other permitted channels of emotional expression in Japanese society. They lavish a love on little children which contrasts sharply with the formality they show in most relations between adults. They drink without reserve but rather with a carefree desire to get as much emotional release as possible out of a very small quantity of *saké*. As a result, there tends to be a great deal of boisterous conviviality in Japan with only an inconsequential amount of alcoholism. They are far freer about sexual matters than are we in the West, where sex and sin are so closely linked. Japanese men feel little but economic restraints against extramarital relations, and throughout Japanese history homosexuality and masturbation have been accepted with no sense of shock. They also allow themselves a great deal more sentimentality than we do, crying on occasions when we would suppress tears, and assuming a degree of sentimental attachment to home, friends, school, and all other old associations which we would stoutly deny if we felt. Their language has a much used set of words expressing nostalgic longing, which find no parallel in common English speech. They are as inveterate lovers of sensationalism as are the readers of an American tabloid. They show the same wild enthusiasm for the subject of suicide that we devote to crime, although the suicide rate of Japan, like the crime rate of America, is no higher than that of several other lands less engrossed by these subjects.

In their literature, in particular, the Japanese show their love of the sentimental. It has permeated their literature ever since the great *Tale of Genji*, written shortly after the year 1000, and is often found to a degree we would consider cloying. Modern writers frequently indulge in morbid introspection, which the reading public laps up. The Japanese, though probably no better able than the average American to understand the great Russian writers, devour their descriptions of the emotional conflicts and outbursts of their characters with an enthusiasm known here only to a small coterie of devotees. And the whole Japanese theater drips with emotion. The Japanese do not want happy endings. They go to the theater to weep over frustrated lovers who finally die in a love suicide. They go to see actors struggle visibly under their emotions, faces taut and voices cracking, in a way the members of the audience never permit themselves to act, regardless of the emotional strain.

4. SOCIAL CONFORMITY

Thus, in a great variety of ways, the Japanese show themselves to be a strongly emotional people, but what strikes the foreign observer first is not at all their emotionalism but rather the heavy cloak of conformity which so covers the surface of Japanese society as to all but conceal the lines of emotion below. How is it that such emotional people have been able to so control their emotions as to transform themselves into an ant-like society of willing coöperators? Why are the Japanese not like the Koreans, whom they resembled so closely in the early days of their history and who still stand closer to the Japanese, culturally as well as racially, than any other people? Anyone will admit that the Koreans are emotional. They are erratic individualists—self-assertive sometimes to the point of anarchy. No one has accused them of conformity or of blind obedience.

The contrast between the Japanese and Koreans in this respect may actually be of fairly recent origin. The Japanese, too, seem to have been an openly emotional and unrepressed people during much of their history, perhaps until as late as the sixteenth or seventeenth century. The unending quest for love and beauty on the part of the hero of the *Tale of Genji* typified the courtier of ancient times. Murder and treachery, uprisings and feuding, passionate outbursts and equally passionate devotion characterized the feudal age. The Confucian insistence on decorum and the "doctrine of the mean," though perhaps the keystone of the Chinese system which they sought to borrow, made relatively little impression on the ancient Japanese. There was nothing moderate about them. The Portuguese and Spaniards in the sixteenth century did not find them unduly repressed emotionally or more prone to conformity than the Europeans themselves.

The two centuries of stability and peace of the Tokugawa period, however, seem to have brought a great change in Japanese society. The land was filled up by then. There were great cities, densely packed with humanity. For a long period people lived in close proximity to one another under the stern and watchful eye of an oppressive regime. Perhaps in a heavily crowded land such as Japan has been since the seventeenth century, established patterns of conduct must be more rigidly observed than in lands where people live with more room about them and a wilderness to conquer. The contrast between us Americans and our more law-abiding and class-conscious cousins in Europe may be a case in point. The lack of privacy within the Japanese house may also have contributed to the growth of social conformity in Japan. With sliding partitions of flimsy paper taking the place of solid walls, the niceties of genteel living within the family depend upon careful observance of mutually understood rules of conduct. Japanese observers of the West have been amazed by the locks on the doors inside our homes and have correlated locked doors with individualism. Flimsy paper partitions should, perhaps, be correlated with conformity. But, whatever the cause, the modern Japanese, unlike their more remote ancestors, are a nation of conformists, of followers of the rule books, and the book of rules in Japan is amazingly detailed and explicit.

It is significant that, with the advent of Tokugawa stability, the Japanese suddenly took a much greater interest in Confucianism than ever before. The Tokugawa period is the golden age of Confucianism in Japan. A stable, peaceful Japan needed a detailed book of rules, the way a war-torn land did not. Confucianism, heavy with the wisdom and prestige of China, fitted the need admirably, providing a perhaps overly emotional people with the external controls they required to form a well-regulated, peaceful society.

Confucianism, the way of life taught by the Chinese sage and his disciples more than two millenniums ago, emphasized etiquette and ceremony. It exploited the sound psychological principle that one learns proper attitudes by starting out with proper conduct. There were Confucian virtues, but the heart of Confucianism, as it had evolved through the ages, was the strict outer form, the almost ritualistic embodiment of the virtues in specific patterns of conduct. These were a great boon to the emotional Japanese. It is easier to conform to an outer pattern than to a general precept. Strict rules allowed no chance for doubt, whereas vague virtues alone would have left room for the emotions to slip back in and determine the course of action. The use of ritualistic etiquette as a curb for the emotions was by no means new in Japan, but this aspect of her culture was greatly strengthened in the Tokugawa period through a conscious reëmphasizing of Confucian rules of conduct, backed up by a ruthlessly severe and ever watchful government.

Confucianism stressed human relationships and the creation of a more perfect society on earth through the proper regulation of these relationships. The combination of inner uprightness with external etiquette, they taught, would produce the supreme virtue, *jen*. *Jen* is a homophone for the Chinese word for "man" and is written in Chinese with the character 仁, which is made up of the two parallel lines of the symbol for "two" and the character for "man" or "human being" on the left. Thus it clearly means "humaneness" in the sense of the proper conduct between two men—the way human beings should treat each other. But this does not mean simply benevolence or love, as it might according to our Christian ideas. Confucianism emphasized the "five relationships," which were those between ruler and ruled, husband and wife, father and son, elder brother and younger brother, and friend and friend. Significantly, all but the last of these relationships is between a superior and an inferior, and they all are particular relationships, not general ones. Here is the fundamental ethical difference between the Far East and Europe. In the West we have tended to build up a universalistic ethic which equates all individuals in their relationship to God or to society. In the Far East, all relationships tend to be specific. Proper ethical conduct cannot be generalized but depends upon the particular relationship between the two individuals involved. Is the other man your ruler, your father, an uncle, an older cousin, a younger brother, a neighbor, an acquaintance, or a stranger? The way you treat him should differ accordingly. Treating a stranger as a cousin would be doing an injustice to your cousins. Treating an acquaintance as your father would be insulting to your parents.

The particularistic bent of Confucian ethics merely strengthened the natural tendencies within the feudal society of Japan. Any feudal society is, by definition, a society of many very specific personal relationships—a great pyramid of individual rights and obligations. The loyalty due a feudal lord is different from that due a friend. The rights of a peasant are not the same as those of a knight or samurai. There is no universal ethic. Proper conduct depends upon the specific status of the one man and his particular relationship to the other. With such a feudal background, it was natural that Tokugawa ethics became phrased largely in terms of specific obligations—obligations to feudal lord, to parents, to family, and, perhaps most important of all, to oneself, in the sense that one must properly play the role assigned to one by fate in a society of hereditary status. Life entailed a complicated mass of obligations on every side—to those above, to those below, and also to one's own position.

There could be no general guideposts equally valid for all men. Such vague virtues as faith, hope, and charity all had their place in Buddhism—and the Tokugawa, for security purposes, forced all persons to be registered as parishioners of some Buddhist temple—but these Buddhist virtues had no more to do with the normal obligations of society than did the Shinto love of natural beauty. If each man were to perform his specific obligations properly, he must have detailed and explicit instructions, not just general guiding virtues. Each situation must have its specific rule for each category of person. Generalized rules applicable to all would lead only to confusion and conflict in a society in which status, and therefore obligations, differed so radically from individual to individual.

The result of all this has been a far more rigid adherence to a detailed set of social rules than we know in the West. This is what makes the Japanese seem to be the politest people on earth, though they may be essentially no more courteous than we, but simply more punctilious. The Japanese are sticklers for etiquette. Each situation calls for an exactly correct act or a precisely prescribed phrase. Following the rule book exactly should see anyone through any situation, however complicated or unpleasant. To us, with our more individualistic concepts and the high premium we place on originality, such an inflexible adherence to rule appears slightly ludicrous. The endless stereotyped phrases of polite conversation, the machine-like alternation of bows between two friends in a solemn greeting on the street, the painfully exact exchange of presents, and a thousand other rigid formalities of Japanese daily life seem to us excessive and even absurd. Though not different in spirit from our own daily stereotypes, they occupy a much greater share of normal social life than they do with us. This is, of course, stultifying to what we would consider normal friendly relations, smothering them under a heavy blanket of time-consuming and sometimes expensive formalities. But, at the same time, it provides the sensitive, emotional Japanese with a protective armor of acceptable responses for all occasions. There need be no embarrassing situations, no painful quandaries.

This, of course, does not mean that there are no conflicts within Japanese society. There are occasional clashes even between obligations, as in the famous story of the "Forty-Seven *Ronin*." In this historical incident, which occurred in the years 1701 to 1703 and became at once a favorite theme of Japanese literature, a group of samurai broke their obligation to the Tokugawa regime to keep the peace in order to fulfill their obligation of vengeance to their dead lord. Their lord had been insulted by another lord and had drawn his sword in anger within the castle grounds of Edo. As punishment he was forced to commit suicide. The forty-seven samurai, made *ronin*, or unemployed samurai, by their lord's demise, paid their obligation to him by taking his enemy's head, and then made amends to the regime by committing suicide themselves.

An even more common conflict in Japanese society is the clash between obligation and "human feeling," as they call their emotions. This conflict between *giri* and *ninjo*, to use their terms, is typified by the love suicide or by the samurai who sacrifices his dear ones to fulfill some higher obligation. The Japanese are aware of this conflict and dote on it in their novels and plays. They also realize that *ninjo* should temper *giri* and that *giri* should modify *ninjo*. At the same time they try to minimize the conflict between *ninjo* and *giri* in actual life by attempting to keep them in separate compartments. The emotions are directed into accepted channels where they will not wash against the social structure. A man may visit courtesans and prostitutes all he wishes and make whatever romantic attachments he can financially afford, but, when it comes to marriage, the family will choose a proper mate for him. He has religion, poetry, and art in which to express his emotions, but the serious business of life is no place for him to exhibit temperament. He may weep over the beauty of the moon and pour out his soul in verse, but he should never betray upsetting anger or excitement before his family or friends.

The system works well enough. The Japanese manage to live their formalistic lives with perhaps no greater emotional tensions than we in the West who have left room in our cultures for a far less fettered play of the emotions. There is, however, one great weakness in the system. The Japanese who ventures out beyond the boundaries of his rule book is more completely lost than those of us who live by more generalized precepts and fewer exact rules. When he enters another culture, he is baffled by the vagueness of its rules of conduct. If he sticks to his own precise rules, he appears ridiculous. If he seeks to follow the other man's rules as strictly as he follows his own, he is little better off.

Still worse is the unexpected situation not accounted for in his formal training. The unaccustomed human relationships created by war mean a clearer break with all past experience for the modern Japanese soldier than for our G.I.'s. Our peacetime virtues may seem to lose some of their validity in battle, but his more meticulous code of conduct becomes clearly inapplicable in many of the situations he meets and he consequently may disregard it completely. Whereas at home he is far less given to physical violence than are we in the United States, on the battlefield brutality comes as less of a shock to him than to us. Torture in war and meticulous politeness in peace seem less of a contradiction to him than organized mass murder and simple friendliness under our more universalistic ethic. The loyal Japanese soldier, who was never prepared for the possibility of capture, had nothing to guide him, if, by any chance, he did fall into our hands. The prisoner who had participated willingly in the suicide charge of the night before saw nothing inconsistent in volunteering his services to aid the Americans the next day. The unforeseen had happened, and obviously none of the old rules were any longer applicable.

On the other hand, this same situational ethic also permits more rapid adjustments to new situations and a sensible flexibility of conduct which we sometimes lack. Perhaps this tendency has been strengthened by a basic fatalism conditioned by the uncontrollable ferocity of nature, which periodically ravages the Japanese islands. Few parts of the world are more subject to devastating earthquakes or are more frequently visited by destructive hurricanes—the dread typhoons of the Far East. Probably more than 100,000 persons were killed in the great Tokyo earthquake and fire of September 1, 1923, the greatest natural cataclysm that mankind has ever suffered. Repeatedly the Japanese have had to pick themselves out of the wreckage of their cities or farms and patiently start over again.

But whether or not natural disasters have forced the Japanese to show greater flexibility in their conduct, there can be no doubt that their situational ethics has often permitted them to reverse their attitudes suddenly when convinced that the situation required a new approach. The bitterly anti-foreign sentiment of the late Tokugawa period was transformed almost overnight into a wild enthusiasm for learning from the West, once the Japanese became convinced that the outside world could no longer be kept at arm's length. As invasion and ultimate defeat in the recent war began to stare the Japanese in the face, almost to a man they remained calmly determined to go down fighting—to resist to the end, even if it meant opposing our heavy armor with nothing more than sharpened bamboo sticks. That was their duty to Emperor and country, and there could be no doubt about it. And then came the surrender, correctly arranged by their leaders according to the rules. The situation had changed. There was no longer any virtue in suicidal resistance. Now it was their duty to show friendliness toward the Americans and wholehearted coöperation. It was not a matter of emotion but of two different sets of duties to meet two different situations. The change was incomprehensible to us who were fighting, not out of duty so much as because we were "fighting mad" with righteous indignation.

But, as we have seen, the Japanese, if they ever lose their ethical bearings, are perhaps more helplessly at sea than we would be. They are accustomed to a narrow prescribed course. We have more often ventured out upon uncharted waters. Deprived of their familiar situational guideposts, they seem to fall into panic somewhat more easily than we. How else can one explain the slaughter of Koreans by the usually polite and law-abiding citizens of Tokyo after the great earthquake of 1923? Although not different in spirit from the race riots and lynchings of our own country, the massacre of Koreans in Tokyo was on a far larger scale. Thrown off balance by the horror and devastation of the earthquake, the ordinarily mild and good-natured city crowds were transformed by entirely groundless and absurd rumors into blood-crazy packs of predatory animals, butchering defenseless Koreans on sight. The specific situational code of the Japanese works well enough on ordinary occasions, perhaps with less friction and strain than our own more individualistic code of conduct, but it seems to break down more completely than our more generalized ethics when confronted with the unexpected, throwing the Japanese back on their unguided instincts.

8. Shame, Obedience, and Will Power

1. SHAME AND SELF-RESPECT

The Japanese, as we have seen, are an emotional people, but their drives for self-expression are not bridled by any clear concept of sin or any categorical religious sanctions. How, then, can one explain the power of social conformity in Japan and the rigid adherence to specific rules of conduct? What is the power which enforces these rules and prevents willful and socially disruptive self-expression, if religion offers no firm precepts and conscience does not curb the passions with a sense of guilt? In the West, an emotional people with no sense of sin and no religious sanctions might be undisciplined and anarchistic libertines, but this description hardly fits the Japanese. They obviously have a substitute for our Western religious sanctions and our sense of guilt as means of preventing individual infractions of ethical codes. This substitute is a sense of shame before society. In their culture shame enforces the ethical system and inhibits individual deviations from acceptable conduct. Guilt and shame, of course, are not mutually exclusive. Both are known in Japan as well as in the West, but, where the sense of guilt carries the major load in our own sin-conscious society, shame is the primary force in the honor-conscious society of Japan.

"Good child" and "bad child" are important conditioning phrases for Japanese children, just as "good girl" and "bad boy" are for our own, but "good" and "bad" in the West soon become linked with a series of abstract but absolute virtues and sins, while in Japan the criterion always remains primarily the approval or disapproval of society in general. Worse than the phrase "bad child" is the more explicit statement, "People will laugh at you." The child is taught not to eschew sin but to avoid *faux pas*, embarrassing or costly errors which would cause others to laugh at him or his family to be ashamed. Although he is taught to acquire certain general virtues, the emphasis is on winning specific approval and praise. His family's devoted admiration serves as a substitute for the approval of society only in his early years. By the time the child starts to go to school, family approbation and disapproval merely mirror the judgment of society. The family instead of offering the child protection from the scorn of society, blames the child for having brought shame on the family. There is no crying and running to mama. The family uses the harsh judgments of society to teach the child conformity and obedience.

This emphasis on the judgment of society makes the individual Japanese a very self-conscious person. "What will they think of me?" is always his first thought, not "What do I think of them?" Even the most humble Japanese feels himself to be on a stage before his fellow countrymen and the whole world. More than that, he has a keen awareness of playing a role on the stage of history. As true Far Easterners, the Japanese have a much stronger sense of history than we do in the West. The individual soldier who stubbornly sought death alone in the jungle was steeled to his act by the feeling that, even if no compatriot were there to report his deed, it was illuminated by the footlights of history. The Japanese are taught to feel shame before society and to fear it. The result is a self-consciousness which borders on an inferiority complex. This could be part of the origin of the national sense of inferiority the Japanese sometimes exhibit toward the outside world. But it does not seem to have produced among individuals in Japan much overt aggressiveness, largely because individual aggressiveness is strongly condemned by society.

With the approval or disapproval of society the ultimate

criterion by which he judges himself, the Japanese, however, is inevitably a highly competitive individual. Life for him is one great competition—competition to win more approval than the next man. Competition so pervades life that the Japanese tend to avoid any dramatization of it. They love our Western competitive sports but decry their effect. They make entrance into all schools beyond the elementary level a brutally competitive matter and then minimize further competition between students once they have been admitted. They are far more rank-conscious than we in America, but are afraid of promotions by merit, preferring to stick wherever possible to the less competitive system of promotion by age. They encourage individuals to measure up to fixed standards or to improve their own records as a stimulus to work, leaving competition with others the ultimate but unmentioned measure of success. Thus, they try to avoid overt competition, but they cannot eliminate their strong competitive spirit or the bitterness of failure, which they perhaps feel as keenly as any other people on earth. Every Japanese has his stories of officials who took their own lives when they failed to perform acceptably their appointed tasks and of students who committed suicide when they failed in their entrance examinations.

To avoid shame and win approval the Japanese must preserve "face" and self-respect. He must avoid errors; he must fulfill all his obligations however onerous; and, above all, he must live up to his own concept of his position and duties. Anything else would be to lose "face" and self-respect, if not openly before others, at least inwardly to himself. A sense of shame and the need for self-respect provide the Japanese with much the same individual driving force that we derive from conscience and a sense of guilt. Self-respect can be as hard a taskmaster for them as conscience was for the Puritans. To persons raised in our guilt-conscious society, they appear to be in some respects undisciplined and licentious and in other respects rigid adherents to pointlessly strict rules of conduct. To them, reared as they are in a society which stresses shame, we appear at times amazingly prudish and at other times strangely lacking in discipline and self-respect.

We Americans are thoroughly familiar with the concept of saving "face," even though we have borrowed an Oriental term to express it, but we profess to consider the desire to save "face" more of an amusing weakness than a virtue. To the Japanese, it is a basic aspect of their ethics. Without it, the whole ethical structure would collapse. The individual must have a strong fear of aberrations from accepted standards which others will laugh at or condemn. He must also have a compelling desire to win praise by excelling in approved patterns of conduct. Sensitivity to the judgments of society is the chief ethical sanction in Japan.

With "face" such an important matter, one should no more deny another "face" than willingly sacrifice it oneself. No one should be made to appear ludicrous, whatever happens. No one should be shown to be in error, because to look silly or to be wrong is too damaging to the personality in a society which stresses the avoidance of error or ridicule as we stress the avoidance of sin. The Japanese language not only is lacking in blasphemy but does not even have many terms of abuse or revilement. Omission of the proper honorific expressions is usually as close as the Japanese permits himself to come to open insult, not because he feels anger less keenly but because ridicule and abuse are far more serious offenses in Japan than in the West. To laugh at another man or to expose his errors is to show no knowledge of human nature and deserves the devastating condemnation of "insincerity." A man who allows himself to do such things is patently not living up to the rules of the game. He is not just impolite. He is striking at the roots of the other man's character.

If laughing at a man is such a terrible thing, Japan is obviously no place for practical jokes or hearty laughs at another's expense. The Japanese do not laugh easily with strangers or even acquaintances and as a result have won for themselves the reputation of being humorless. Their punctilious observance of etiquette and their sometimes curious adaptations of borrowings from the West strike us as being amusing, and we do not see why they do not join in the joke. But the Japanese, although they do not always laugh at the things we find funny, have their own well-developed sense of humor. Their literature since ancient times has had a broad stream of humor in it, which has shown no sign of shrinking. Even their art has its humorous aspects. Japan eight centuries ago had her Walt Disney, who painted delightfully satirical animal scrolls, depicting fat, solemn frogs as pompous monks and religious dignitaries. The Japanese dote on puns and plays on words of every kind. They can be hilariously funny among their friends, but except when with the most intimate of comrades they do not laugh at others or participate in the good-natured but insulting banter and chaff we enjoy.

The Japanese have developed many stratagems whereby the normal business of life can be accomplished without causing anyone to lose "face." The whole formalism of their social and official relationships is part of this system. If strict routines of conduct are always followed, no one can be embarrassed by unexpected developments. The insistence in Japanese domestic propaganda during the war that every development was what had been expected is an indication of how deeply they fear the unforeseen. A business call in Japan will normally start and close with polite conversation which serves as a sugar coating for the unpleasant necessity of making a request and possibly being refused. And one never makes a simple refusal in Japan. There must always be an excuse, however transparent, to make it appear to be not unwillingness to comply but rather a reluctant bowing to fate. But the best loved stratagem is the go-between—that is the use of a third party or, often enough, two third parties to bargain and make arrangements in behalf of the principals, so that the latter will not be forced to lose "face" or be impolite to each other. This is how marriages are arranged, how most embarrassing or important requests are made, and how many business deals are transacted. It is a cumbersome system, but it is highly effective in minimizing the unpleasant personal contacts which occur in all societies but are particularly distasteful to the Japanese.

In Japan, which was an essentially feudal land until less than a century ago, "face" and self-respect have created a concept of "honor" not unlike that of feudal Europe and a corresponding need for revenge, not so much to wipe out insult as to wipe out shame. The man who proves you wrong may not have insulted you by our standards, but he has caused you shame according to theirs, and revenge may be called for. But anger or chagrin alone are not enough reason for revenge. To be bested by someone who is admittedly superior to you is no cause for shame. The Japanese were maddened before the war by our refusal to take them very seriously, because our obliviousness to the Japanese threat implied a certain degree of contempt. But our victory over them produced a very different reaction. We had proved ourselves to be unquestionably superior. Losing to us was no cause for shame. The Japanese need for self-respect, instead, induced them to magnify our virtues and picture us as a race of supermen, and many an American in Japan, overwhelmed by the power and prestige of his position in an occupied country, accepted the new role without a blush.

Despite the glorification of the revenge motive in Japan, particularly in such well-loved feudal tales as that of the "Forty-Seven *Ronin*," revenge plays only a very minor part in daily life. Today the Japanese are much more likely to turn resentment inward against themselves. Perhaps something of this is to be seen in their masochistic self-mortification since the war and the insistent admissions of guilt so many Japanese now indulge in. The result of such inverted resentment is often morbidity or even suicide. In fact, in modern Japan suicide is glorified far more than revenge. It is not a sin to them but something almost romantic. It is the one sure way to wipe out shame, to find escape from any situation. Suicide, however, is not entirely an inversion of resentment. It also has a positive function, as when a Japanese man committed suicide in front of our embassy in Tokyo in protest against the Exclusion Act of 1924. To commit suicide on your enemy's doorstep is to put the finger of shame on him for having driven another to such a desperate act, and he, of course, loses "face."

But "face" is not merely keeping up appearances and avoiding embarrassment. As we use the word in English, it is exclusively a matter of outward appearances. But in Japan it also means self-respect. Maintaining "face" to oneself is far more important than maintaining "face" before others. One must fulfill one's obligations, even if they are unknown to the world and one's sacrifices unappreciated by others. One must live up to one's position, regardless of how unpleasant or even embarrassing the immediate consequences may be. "Face" is something you win or lose yourself rather than an attribute others can bestow or steal. The Japanese, unlike the Chinese, do not put great emphasis on the concept of "giving 'face.'" It is better to accept insults than to lose self-respect by showing anger. The man who undergoes indignities with composure gains "face." The man who loses his temper also loses "face," no matter how justified his anger or effective his tongue or fists.

There are a myriad obligations which must be meticulously fulfilled, if self-respect is to be maintained. Among the most burdensome is the obligation to one's family. The child inevitably becomes heavily indebted to his parents and his family in general, and a life of selfless service to family interests is not too much repayment. In feudal times there was also the primary obligation to one's lord, which necessitated unwavering and unquestioning loyalty at all times. This obligation has been transformed in modern times into unlimited loyalty to the Emperor, serving as the personification of the state. The individual, as the recipient of the heritage of a long civilization, is unendingly indebted to society, usually thought of as the state and symbolized by the Emperor. No sacrifice, however great, can be more than partial payment of this debt. Absolute and fanatical devotion to the service of the state is thus built into the foundations of Japan's ethical code.

Such obligations to family and state are unlimited, and the individual Japanese is willing to bear a very heavy burden in their name, but in addition there are many other specific obligations which differ from individual to individual. Any benefit received from another carries with it obligations which should, if possible, be repaid. One's teachers deserve unending loyalty. Once a disciple always a disciple, and the disciple never doubts or corrects his master. One's employer or supervisor is due his share of loyal service, if he in turn has lived up to his obligations. The bond between master and servant is likely to develop into a lifelong exchange of patronage for loyalty. In fact this is the pattern for all relationships between superiors and inferiors. Between equals a careful balance of favors must be maintained. Gifts are not to be received with casual thanks. They must be paid in kind if one is to maintain self-respect. A present for a present is the inflexible rule in Japan. The language itself reflects their heavy consciousness of indebtedness. Where we easily wipe out a minor favor or kindness with a casual "Thank you," the Japanese emphasize their indebtedness by using phrases which literally mean, "It is hard to have," "This calls for awe," "I am indebted to you," or "I have caused you trouble." It may not be more blessed to give than to receive in Japan, but it certainly is much more pleasant. Nowhere in the world are people more determined to repay casual favors as well as real indebtednesses, and nowhere else are they more capable of devoted loyalty to those who have aided or befriended them.

Self-respect in Japan calls for "sincerity." But "sincerity" is by no means to be associated with frankness, as it is in the United States. Frankness to the Japanese often appears to be nothing more than rudeness. "Sincerity" to them means knowing what is expected of one, or rather what one should expect of oneself to maintain self-respect, and then having the strength of will to do it. It means being too "big" to act improperly, no matter what the other man does. To be sincere one must know the rules—that is, one must recognize the authority of the rules and be obedient to them—and one must also have the will power to live up to the rules in the face of any difficulty.

The whole Japanese ethic is based on the individual's unquestioning acceptance of society's judgment of him and his assumption of fixed obligations within society. An outside authority is taken for granted. There is no concept of a social contract; no premium placed on individual freedom; no emphasis on personal initiative. Instead, each member of society is expected to accept without question already established rules and obligations. The individual has no responsibility *for* these rules and obligations, but he is completely responsible *to* them.

One can even say that in Japan the individual is less the unit of society than in the West. In theory the individual does not even exist as an individual but only as a member of certain larger groupings—family, school, community, or nation. There are no individuals but only sons and fathers, students and teachers, citizens and officials, subjects and rulers. The interests of society are not just the collective interests of its individual members. Nor is the judgment of society merely a tabulation of individual preferences. The Japanese whenever possible avoids individual decisions and individual responsibility. Group decisions and group responsibility seem to him the way to achieve group interests.

2. THE ACCEPTANCE OF AUTHORITY

Every society depends to some degree on the willingness of the individual to subordinate his interests to those of the group and his acceptance of the authority of society, but, on the whole, the Far Easterners perhaps show a greater readiness to submerge themselves in society and to accept its authority than we in the West, at least in modern times. The authority of tradition, for instance, weighs far more heavily with them than with us. Their whole emphasis on history and its value as a guidebook for human conduct is evidence of this. Where our thinkers boast of their creative concepts, even when they are merely revamping old ideas, the philosophers of China consider themselves to be antiquarian scholars who have rediscovered the true ideas of the ancients, even when they are blazing new intellectual trails.

Some would trace the more ready acceptance of authority in the Far East to the so-called "Asiatic" type of society which was characteristic of the ancient centers of civilization in Asia as well as in Egypt. According to this theory, for example, a fundamental, shaping influence on Chinese society is to be found in the necessity since ancient times of maintaining large-scale public projects on the plains of North China, the homeland of the culture, in order to prevent the Yellow River from flooding and to control irrigation. These large-scale enterprises, it is assumed, made it necessary for the few to organize and direct the labor of the many, producing in turn a clear division since ancient times between a small ruling class and the masses and leading by the end of the third century B.C. to the creation of a unified empire under an all-powerful Emperor, a form of monolithic, authoritarian state which has remained until recent decades the Chinese political ideal and the political reality during most of the intervening centuries.

This theory may have some validity for China, but it has little direct applicability to Japan. No large-scale water-control projects were needed there, and only rarely before modern times did the Japanese succeed in achieving a truly unitary state like the Chinese empire. The Buddhist church was able to maintain much greater independence and authority in Japan than in China; the Emperors, who were always considered to be the ultimate source of all temporal authority, exercised none during most of Japanese history; and even the military rulers of Japan were divided into warring factions as often as they were united under a single authority. Authority throughout Japanese history has been no more unified than in a typical European land. The emphasis on obedience to authority, however, may well have been brought to Japan from China as part of the Chinese culture which Japan borrowed, and in this sense Japan may have become a stepchild of the "Asiatic" type of society.

Another basic reason for the greater readiness on the part of the Far Easterners to accept authority is found by some in the Chinese writing system. If, as most scholars believe, the Sanskrit alphabet, like those of Greece and Rome, derives from the ancient Phoenician alphabet, which in turn was derived ultimately from Egyptian hieroglyphics, then all the living systems of writing in the world, except for the Chinese and its derivatives, stem from a single source. Only in the Far East has a pre-alphabetic system of writing survived in competition with the more efficient phonetic notations invented in the ancient Near East. Chinese characters are the greatest unifying bond in Far Eastern civilization and at the same time the greatest element of cultural distinction between the Far East and the rest of the world.

The Chinese writing system, like that of ancient Egypt, is pictographic in origin, but our earliest remaining examples of it, dating from more than three millenniums ago, show that it had already by that time developed into a highly complex and sophisticated system. Over two thousand years ago the Chinese characters had become established in essentially their present form, with few if any suggesting to the uninitiated any pictographic element at all. Ever since earliest times, however, the basic principle of the Chinese writing system has been that each word, or, in cases of polysyllabic words, each syllable of a word, should be represented by a separate character. Naturally there have been irregularities in the system. Semantic developments and graphic substitutions have resulted in some characters having two or more independent meanings and sometimes more than one pronunciation, but, by and large, the Chinese have kept to the principle of a different character for each lexical element. This means that several thousand symbols are required to write Chinese, as opposed to our twenty-six letters, and because of their very number many of these symbols must be extremely complex. Whereas none of our letters requires more than four strokes, as the Chinese would count them, hundreds of Chinese characters are written with more than twenty strokes.

Such a complicated writing system has inevitably had a profound influence on Chinese culture. It has been a serious limiting factor, making the recording and transmission of knowledge and ideas harder than in India or the West. It has also made the learning process essentially one of rote memory work. There has been less room in Chinese education for reasoning or the exercise of judgment. Instead, education has been primarily the painful and literally endless task of accumulating characters—of adding piece by piece to the store of factual knowledge about characters and their uses, which only a teacher can impart and which the student must accept without question. Knowledge and wisdom have become essentially the accumulation of facts from books and teachers, not a dual process of study and thought.

The very difficulty of writing has given great prestige and authority to that which is written and also to the few who are literate. All cultures have tended to attribute special merits to the surviving literature of antiquity, but nowhere in the world is this truer than in China, where the so-called Classics have enjoyed the prestige and authority most other people reserve for their most honored religious books. Even today the average Chinese regards the written word with an awe which we, conditioned by the gibberish of printed advertisements, find ludicrous. And with education limited to the privileged few who have the time and opportunity to learn the difficult writing system, those who can control the magic of the characters tend to have greater power and prestige than we in the West have ever been willing to give to the educated. The scribe or even the scholar has been a relatively humble member of our civilization, but in China the social and political ideal for more than two thousand years has been rule by the best educated. Empires, there too, were won by the sword, but the only justification for rule has been moral superiority, always closely associated in the Chinese mind with education. Thus, the prestige of writing and education in China has produced a more willing acceptance of tradition and a higher degree of obedience to the authority of the learned than we know in the West.

The use of Chinese characters has produced much the same result in Japan and many additional problems as well. Perhaps the greatest single misfortune in the history of Japan was that, because of her geographic position, Chinese characters and not one of the Western alphabets became the basis of her writing system. The Near Eastern alphabets spread north of China through Central Asia as far as Manchuria. The Indian alphabet spread south of China to Siam and Malaysia. The ancient Japanese, however, although aware of alphabetic systems of writing, derived so much of their higher culture and its vocabulary directly from China that they inevitably came to adopt the Chinese writing system along with the rest. But Japanese, which structurally bears a close resemblance to the Altaic languages of north Asia, such as Korean, Mongolian, and Turkish, is a polysyllabic language characterized by the addition of one inflection after another at the end of words through a process of agglutination. Not only did the Chinese characters, each representing a Chinese word, fit the Japanese vocabulary only very imperfectly, but the Chinese writing system offered no way of recording the Japanese inflected endings.

It was probably more difficult for the ancient Japanese to write their language in Chinese characters than it would be for us to write English that way today. The Latin alphabet could have been adapted almost overnight to the needs of Japanese, but it took centuries of painful effort before the Japanese evolved from Chinese a workable though highly inefficient method of writing their language. For long the Japanese evaded the problem by writing only in the Chinese language and not attempting to write Japanese. Then they developed from the Chinese characters two different and at first chaotic phonetic systems, known as *kana*, in which highly abbreviated characters represented individual syllables of the Japanese phonetic system. But their cultural heritage was expressed so largely through Chinese characters that it was hard for them to write on any technical or scholarly subject without the use of characters. Eventually they combined these two radically different systems of writing, using characters for most uninflected words and for the roots of the inflected words and reserving the *kana* to write inflected endings and all words for which reasonable character substitutes did not exist.

This mixed writing system, which is still used today, has the advantage over the Chinese system of having the supplementary phonetic scripts. These have made possible the gradual elimination of the less commonly used characters, until the number used in most standard printing projects had been reduced before the war to less than two thousand. There is, however, the tremendous disadvantage in this system of multiple readings for most characters. A Chinese word, represented by a single character, sometimes corresponds to several different words in Japanese, resulting in several different readings for the character. Conversely, a single Japanese word sometimes spreads in meaning over several Chinese words, with the result that it can be written with as many different characters. Moreover, during the past fourteen hundred years the Japanese have borrowed a huge number of words from Chinese, just as we have from Latin, Greek, and French. These are written in Chinese characters and are pronounced according to the traditional Japanese rendering of the original Chinese word. Thus each Chinese character will have a Japanese pronunciation derived from Chinese—and usually there are two or more readings of this type representing geographic and historical variations in Chinese pronunciation—and at the same time most of the characters will correspond to one or more and sometimes as many as six or seven different native words. With only context determining the proper reading of each character, the deciphering of even the simplest Japanese sentence takes on some of the aspects of solving a puzzle. The net result is probably the most difficult writing system which is still in use anywhere in the world.

The important point in all this is that education in Japan, as in China, requires a tremendous amount of memory work, which seems to have had the same result in Japan of strengthening the authority of tradition and the emphasis on obedience. In any case, there can be no doubt that in modern Japan there has been unconscious emphasis on indoctrination in education and a conscious effort to utilize the educational system as a tool for inculcating obedience. Even in the early years of the Meiji period the government used the schools to teach new and as yet generally unpopular ideas—Western concepts of hygiene, new economic ideas, compulsory military service, and absolute devotion and obedience to the state. The cult of Emperor worship was spread primarily through the school system, and in recent decades school children have drunk in a virulent brand of jingoistic hyper-nationalism with every character they mastered. The propagandistic use of an educational system has become a thoroughly familiar totalitarian device, and Japan is certainly not unique in this respect. The Japanese, however, have been not just copying the West in this but have been, if anything, pioneers in this unsavory field. It may well be that the nature of the reading and writing problem in Japan, tied as it is to the slow process of learning Chinese characters by rote memory, makes education there more susceptible than in the West to use for purposes of propaganda.

3. HEREDITARY AUTHORITY

The emphasis on obedience to authority is very similar in China and Japan, but the nature of authority in the two lands is not. Over two thousand years ago China began to progress from the concept of strictly hereditary authority to that of authority because of individual merit. True, the supreme position of Emperor has always been primarily hereditary in China, but ever since a man of humble origin established the great Han dynasty in 202 B.C., few dynasties have attempted to prove their right to rule because of descent from former rulers. Chinese Emperors theoretically ruled because they had *t'ien-ming*, "the mandate of Heaven," demonstrated by their moral superiority and the willingness of the people to obey them. Below the Emperors, no offices or posts were in theory hereditary. The Chinese ideal has been that superior persons, regardless of origin, would distinguish themselves and rise to the top. For over a thousand years this theory has been institutionalized in an elaborate system of government-administered examinations for the selection of superior men. Naturally, practice and theory always diverged to some extent, but the Chinese remained true to the concept that authority was not inherited but was won by demonstrated superiority.

The Japanese have been much more like the post-Classic Europeans in their attitude toward authority. They have a strong aristocratic tradition and have always looked upon heredity as the basic source for authority. Most of the peoples who, during the past few thousand years, have radiated out from the central steppe lands of the Eurasiatic land mass have shown a tendency toward a tribal, aristocratic society. This was true of our own Indo-European ancestors, whose hereditary tribal chieftains developed into hereditary kings. Only in recent centuries has the divine right of kings given way in Europe to other more modern ideas. The Altaic peoples of the steppe lands, such as the Mongols, have always had an aristocratic form of society and have emphasized hereditary rule, and it seems probable that the continental invaders of ancient Japan who eventually set up the historical Japanese state brought with them from Korea not only the long straight North Asiatic sword and the equestrian habits of northern Asia but also this same concept of hereditary rule. But hereditary authority is also characteristic of Polynesian society, which, as we have seen, may be related in some way to primitive Japanese society. In any case, all our evidence indicates that Japanese society from earliest times showed a strong emphasis on hereditary authority and class distinctions. Chinese records tell us that in the third century of the Christian era Japan was divided among a number of small tribes, each controlled by a hereditary high-priest or in many cases a high-priestess, for matriarchy was probably once the rule among the Japanese. Rulers were buried in huge tumuli, some of which are the largest man-made tombs in the world, and servants and followers were once buried alive with their masters. Workers were organized into hereditary groups, and the primitive Japanese state was simply a hierarchic association of such hereditary functional units.

The borrowing of the Chinese system in the seventh and eighth centuries made the priest-chief into a full-fledged temporal ruler. Ever since, the Japanese Emperor has been in theory both a Japanese high-priest and a Chinese type of temporal potentate, but the concept of hereditary authority—the unbroken line from ages eternal—remained unaltered. Even when the Emperors lost all their powers, no one dared usurp their throne. Or perhaps it was not a matter of daring. Usurpation in Japan was simply unthinkable. The Chinese system of selecting men of talent by examination for government posts, though outwardly copied in Japan, had little actual influence. Almost all appointments continued to be determined by hereditary prestige and not by merit. Many posts were frankly hereditary. Prime Ministers had to be descendants of the ancient clan of the Fujiwara. Almost all of the later feudal lords speciously claimed descent from the Fujiwara or more often from the Minamoto or Taira, two offshots of the Imperial clan. In fact, it became a tradition that only descendants of the Minamoto could become Shogun, even though this was clearly a post won by the sword.

This emphasis on hereditary right in political matters is perfectly understandable to Westerners with their own aristocratic traditions, but the Japanese went even beyond the Europeans of pre-modern days. They have kept their genealogies far more carefully, with the result that many aristocratic families can trace their lineage with complete reliability back to the sixth century. They also have insisted on the hereditary principle in various fields in which we consider heredity could scarcely play any great role. Schools of poetry, acting, painting, and all the lesser arts and skills have usually been organized along family lines, even though the transmission from father to adopted son or disciple is more common than that from father to natural son. Even Buddhist sects and schools of philosophy have their "family" genealogies of successive generations of masters and disciples. The Japanese have been able to place so much emphasis on hereditary rights in part because they pay little attention to actual blood descent. A family line, like an artistic school, can be maintained as satisfactorily by adoption as by the birth of a legitimate heir. The important thing is the transmission of hereditary rights, not the continuance of a blood line.

Strong hereditary rights inevitably have meant rigid hereditary class distinctions in Japan. It has never been easy in China for members of the lower classes to rise to the top, but the theory for long has been that the peasant with sufficient ability could become Prime Minister. In feudal Japan, the peasant could no more become an aristocrat than he could in medieval Europe. One's status in society tended to be fixed by birth, not by ability or even by wealth.

The highest social class has always consisted of the Imperial family and the old aristocratic families around it, who emerged into the light of history in the sixth century as the rulers of Japan and maintained this position for the next five or six centuries. During the past thousand years the old court nobility has had virtually no political power and has for the most part lived in relative poverty, but even today no one questions its social supremacy. Next came the warrior class, or perhaps one should say the "new" warrior class, for the old court aristocracy had in its heyday been the military power of the land. The "new" warrior class came to prominence from the eleventh century on, winning its supremacy through its monopoly of the martial arts. Men of early feudal Japan, like those of Europe, fought in armor on horseback. The cost of a soldier's equipment made it an aristocratic profession and set up a clear functional distinction between the military ruling class and the peasantry. From the former came the Shogunal lines, all of the later feudal lords, and the samurai who were their administrators and soldiers.

The appearance of the foot soldier as the backbone of Japanese armies some time before the sixteenth century actually wiped out the fundamental basis for this class distinction, and the fifteenth and sixteenth centuries as a result witnessed a period of unprecedented social mobility, with men of low birth, such as Hideyoshi in the late sixteenth century, fighting their way to the top of the political heap, though scarcely to the top of the social pyramid. The Tokugawa, however, with their primary emphasis on stability, reimposed stricter class distinctions in the seventeenth century. They borrowed the ancient Confucian concept of four classes, which placed the merchants at the bottom, the artisans next, the peasants third, and the scholar-administrator class, which in Japan was of course the warrior-scholar-administrator class, at the top. But this theory hardly squared with the facts. The city merchants were obviously superior to the artisans they employed and also to the impoverished peasants, and, in any case, there were no strict class lines between merchants, artisans, and peasants. The theory, however, did help to maintain a strong barrier between the samurai and the mass of the people, despite the poverty of many samurai and their growing indebtedness to the city merchants.

The adoption of the Western pattern during the Meiji period meant for the most part the abandonment of hereditary authority and the lowering of class barriers. This was accomplished with amazing ease, in part because both hereditary authority and class distinctions had in reality been undermined during the Tokugawa period (1600–1867). The Tokugawa administration was in the hands of feudal lords and samurai, but these men had been selected from among their social equals because of ability, not because of heredity. Similarly, most of the feudal domains were administered, not by the lords or their hereditary high officials, but by lesser samurai of outstanding ability, and these were the men who came to the fore in the Meiji Restoration. More important, the two-class society was already breaking down. Despite rigid laws, rich merchants were marrying their daughters into samurai families, and poor samurai were dropping to the status of commoners. When the Meiji reformers swept away the old restrictions, Japanese society rapidly readjusted itself to new levels, not unlike those of a modern European country.

A new nobility was created, consisting of the old court nobles, the former feudal lords, the ambitious samurai who had carried through the Meiji reforms, and an occasional merchant leader, like Mitsui, but except for the last two groups of newly risen men, the nobility enjoyed far more prestige than power. Some of the samurai and city merchants and a few men of still humbler origin pushed their way up to positions of leadership in government, business, and the intellectual life of the land. Although most of the samurai, who had constituted something over 5 per cent of the population, sank back into the lower classes, a far larger percentage of the samurai than of the other classes achieved positions of leadership, because they had behind them prestige, influential connections, more education, and the tradition of leadership. With each generation greater social mobility was achieved, with some institutions, such as the army and navy, serving as particularly effective mediums for bringing talent from the lower classes to positions of high authority. Social mobility in modern Japan has never equaled that of the United States but has perhaps been more like the social mobility of England or Germany during the same period.

The Japanese feeling for class distinctions and for hereditary authority, however, remains strong. The Japanese has a much clearer sense of belonging to a class than does the American. The *eta*, or so-called "outcasts," have enjoyed full legal equality with other Japanese for many decades, but social discrimination against them still remains severe. Constituting perhaps 2 per cent of the population, the *eta* appear to be Japanese who during earlier centuries came to be despised by their countrymen on account of their trades, which, because they involved butchering or the working of animal products such as leather, fell under the Buddhist prejudice against the taking of animal life. The Japanese also maintain a strong awareness of the family standing and occupation of all their fellow citizens. If a son can follow his father as the principal of a school, everyone is delighted. They show a deference to the wellborn, regardless of their actual position in society, which is rare in this country. Conversely, the wellborn and those who would appear to be wellborn attempt to live up to a high standard of *noblesse oblige*, showing remarkable graciousness and tolerance toward their servants and subordinates. In Japan, as in the comparably aristocratic society of England, there is relatively little of the ostentatious display of wealth and authority which has been a by-product of social egalitarianism in China·and also in the United States.

Thus, the Japanese, while moving away from a society of hereditary status, retain many of the attitudes of such a society. Although the achievement of a position of leadership in Japan today depends, as with us and the Chinese, primarily on the ability of the individual to prove superiority, authority in Japan continues to retain much of the absolutism which it naturally had when heredity was the only criterion. Throughout Japanese society, authority is accepted with the unquestioning obedience one would expect only if the right to authority were unqualified and not merely a matter of comparative superiority. If a man reaches a position of authority by demonstrating better qualifications for that position, then theoretically he should retain it only so long as he continues to demonstrate this superiority, but in Japan, once the authority is achieved in free competition, it tends to become more absolute than in our society.

4. HIERARCHY

With obedience to authority so stressed throughout Japanese society, a primary problem is that of hierarchy among the different types of authority. No major people in the world places greater emphasis on hierarchy than do the Japanese. *Nippon-ichi*, "the first in Japan," is a ubiquitous phrase applied to anything or anyone from the nation's leading poet down to the biggest eater of raw fish. Proficiency in *judo* wrestling or the minor arts is graded and regulated like our Masonic orders. Almost anyone can tell you the order of prestige of the Japanese universities. Each person, each thing, fits into an accepted order of prestige and power. Position on this scale must be clear so that one can distinguish the superior from the inferior and know where authority lies. A committee without its chairman, a delegation without its chief makes the Japanese uneasy and unhappy. They, like the Germans, love titles and use them wherever possible, not only on the calling cards they exchange on every conceivable occasion but also in direct address, for titles take the place of pronouns in polite conversation. Their whole language, with its precise gradations of politeness, implies a hierarchical society, even though most humble forms today merely denote "I," "me," and "mine," and polite forms "you" and "yours." Some students of Japan even feel that the Japanese emphasis on strict hierarchic order influenced them to attempt to fight their way up in a hypothetical international hierarchy. In any case, they are certainly highly conscious of the relative prestige of the countries of the world and are as insistent for the moment on calling Japan a third-rate or even sixth-rate nation as they once were on proclaiming her a first-rate power.

There are many different types of hierarchy in Japan, but perhaps the most fundamental are those of age and sex. Age is, of course, a source of authority in all cultures, particularly in family relations, but in Japan the authority of parents tends to continue throughout life, and age carries with it much greater prestige and power than with us. Youth, far from being a time of self-assurance and exuberance, as it is in the United States, means to the Japanese strict obedience and un-limited deference to the authority of parents, teachers, the boss, and the forces of authority in general.

As we have seen, Japan, with a Sun-Goddess as her supreme native deity, probably once was a matriarchy, and until the middle of the eighth century many women occupied the throne in their own rights. Even as late as early feudal times, women could inherit property and feudal privileges, but in the course of the last several hundred years, probably under the influence of Chinese concepts, women have been pushed down to a position of legal and social inferiority to men. Tradi-tionally a Japanese housewife walks a few feet behind her lord and master, carrying the baby or the bundles, while he strides unburdened ahead of her. It often takes a discerning eye to distinguish the mistress of the household from a servant by the treatment accorded them. And what few social contacts upper-class men and women have in Japan are usually charac-terized by male domination of the conversation and appreci-ative tittering on the part of the women. The modern Japanese have followed the Chinese dictum, perhaps more literally than the Chinese themselves, that a woman obeys her father in her childhood, her husband in middle life, and her son in old age.

Such relations of clear superiority and inferiority between the sexes and different age groups have produced in Japan a strictly authoritarian type of family, such as is to be found in China today and was by no means unknown in the United States a few decades ago. Primogeniture has been the rule since medieval times, and each member of the Japanese family has a clearly defined position in a hierarchical order. So clear are the status implications of family relationships that hierarchical relationships throughout Japanese society are often expressed in these terms.

The Japanese family, however, does not have the complicated relationships of authority between different generations and distant branches which one finds in the extended family system of China. When great family power was involved, as in the leading families of feudal days or even among the *zaibatsu* in more recent times, highly complicated and far extended family relationships were maintained, and both feudal and *zaibatsu* families had their own domestic laws which determined family relationships and individual conduct. For the vast majority of modern Japanese, however, active family relationships are no more complicated than those of the American family of a few decades ago. The group living together tend to be husband, wife, and children, with perhaps a grandparent or two and possibly a nephew living with them while he goes to school. The Japanese expect somewhat more economic coöperation between close relatives than we do today, and they hold family councils far more frequently, but rarely does such close coöperation involve persons more distantly related than first cousins, and the decisions of such family councils have little more authority than they would in the United States. The typical modern Japanese family unit, while not so small or so loosely bound together as the contemporary American family, is closer to it than to the sprawling extended family unit of the Chinese upper classes.

There are many other types of hierarchy in Japan, which affect different individuals—business, religious, social, intellectual, and artistic hierarchies—but the one which takes precedence over all others is the political hierarchy. In late feudal times the supreme loyalty, the supreme obligation, was due one's feudal lord and through him the Shogun. The family as a unit was definitely inferior to the feudal realm. The real moral of the story of the "Forty-Seven *Ronin*," when viewed in the context of the Far Eastern milieu, is that these forty-seven men ruthlessly sacrificed their families, in some cases sending wives and daughters into prostitution, in order to fulfill their obligations to their lord. The clash between family and national interests is not unknown in China, but few Chinese before contemporary times would have accepted such complete submergence of family interests to those of the ruler. But centuries ago the superiority of the political unit over the family had been clearly established in Japanese ethics. The chief battle of the modern nation-state had already been won. The Meiji reformers did not face the major obstacle to Westernization which the family-centered ethics of China has proved to be on the continent. Expanding the basic political unit from the feudal realm to the nation during the past century in Japan has proved to be a far easier task than establishing the superiority of national interests over those of the family in China.

No difference between China and Japan is more fundamental or has had more profound influences on the history of these two lands in modern times. Japan has emphasized family relations far more than the modern West and has held to a more particularistic, situational type of ethics. But the Japanese family was smaller than the Chinese family and weaker in relation to the government, and Japanese concepts of ethics, at least in so far as family-state relations were concerned, were more universalistic and like those of the West. One reason for this may possibly have been the greater influence of Buddhism in Japan than in China, for Buddhism, like Christianity, emphasizes the individual and his personal relationship to the problem of salvation. Japanese religious leaders have often stressed the Occidental-sounding concept of the equality of all men in the "Law," as they often call Buddhism.

Another reason for this basic difference between China and Japan may be Japanese feudalism itself, for it inevitably placed strong emphasis on legal rights and obligations. With his feudal rights, a man inherited his feudal obligations, which normally made his relationship to his lord far more important than his relations with his brothers and relatives. Since

ancient times in China, laws have been considered simply the
regulations a ruler made to enforce obedience from his subjects. They had no higher validity and were, therefore, subject to sudden revision at any time and were always subordinate to the personal opinions of the judge or administrator.
Feudal Japan developed a far stricter concept of law, because
society and government depended entirely on the maintenance
of feudal rights and obligations. With their Chinese cultural
background, the Japanese never went on to formulate the clear
legal concepts of the West and always permitted broader dis-
cretionary powers on the part of the judge. High motives often
were allowed to redeem specific infractions—as could be seen
as late as the 1930's, when ultra-nationalistic political assassins
were given ridiculously light sentences because they had been
motivated by the "praiseworthy" desire to rid the Emperor
of "bad" advisors. The Japanese, however, entered the past
century of rapid Westernization with a concept of law far
more like that of Europe than was Chinese legal theory and
a belief in the supremacy of the political unit which resembled that of the modern West and contrasted sharply with the
family-centered social and political concepts of China. These
factors are obviously part of the explanation of the great difference between the Japanese and Chinese reactions to the
problem of Westernization.

With the government the supreme authority in Japanese
society, there has been a tendency to tie in all the lesser
hierarchies under the political. Government recognition, in
fact, established many of them. Since ancient times the placing of members of the Imperial family as abbots in certain
monasteries helped bring the religious hierarchy into line,
and in modern as well as ancient Japan a complicated system
of court ranks was used to place those of prestige in all fields
in proper sequence within a single hierarchic system controlled by the government. The bureaucrat, the diplomat, the
army officer, the leading doctor, the university professor, all
fitted into the same scale and were neatly tabbed so that every-

one might know the authority and prestige each rightly had. As in China, connection with the government, either through direct service or through official recognition of this sort, carries with it particular prestige. There is a strong cleavage between those who belong in this way to the government and the mere common people. Even the poor policeman, post office employee, or stationmaster on the government railways derives considerable prestige and authority from his uniform and connections with the government. The Japanese show a respect—one might almost say reverence—for the government and its officials, both high and low, which, though known in many parts of Europe, is entirely foreign to the United States. The prestige and power of the official and the meek subservience of the common citizen make a psychological soil in the Far East which is not congenial to the growth of democracy.

The government functionary who has enjoyed the greatest prestige in modern Japan has been the soldier. We in the West have seen enough of this in our own cultures not to be surprised, especially in view of Japan's recent feudal past, when the whole ruling class as well as all government officials were first of all military men. With close to a thousand years of warrior leadership behind them, it is small wonder that the Japanese have continued to give a special measure of respect to their military men or that the Japanese army felt that it was not just an arm of the government but was itself directly responsible for the physical and moral well-being of the nation. Even the kings of contemporary Europe masquerade in military uniform. Naturally the Japanese Emperor, too, wore a uniform and reviewed his troops astride his white steed. Since primitive times in Japan, the sword has been one of the so-called Three Imperial Regalia, the three sacred objects which were the symbols of Imperial authority; feudal Japan gloried in the sword—and incidentally produced some of the finest blades the world has ever seen—and in recent years the sword has been revived again as Japan's primary symbol. The cumbersome long samurai swords which the Japanese officers lugged into battle in the recent war were as much their standards as the sun flag itself.

The military hierarchy has been perhaps the single most important hierarchy in modern Japan. In feudal days it was reserved for a limited hereditary group, and the common citizen could only hope to rise in some other hierarchy—perhaps that of business. But in the more mobile society of modern Japan, the reverse has become the situation. Entrance into the civil bureaucracy and the intellectual and professional fields depends on advanced education, limited largely to those who can afford to pay for it. Business depends somewhat on hereditary wealth and associations. But the army represented a hierarchic ladder reaching down to the peasant masses of Japan. The bulk of the officers were drawn from the lower middle classes of the countryside, the sons of small landowners or well-to-do peasants, who commonly started their official military schooling at the end of the sixth grade, after passing stiff competitive examinations, on the basis of which sometimes as few as one in sixty of the overly abundant applicants were accepted.

The conscripts too came overwhelmingly from rural Japan. Man power was always in excess of demand for the standing army in Japan, and as a result the more rugged and tractable peasant boys could, for the most part, displace the less hardened and more sophisticated city boys in the ranks. The army was the peasant boy's best road to escape from the humdrum poverty of farm life. For two years he became part of a uniformed hierarchy reaching up to the uniformed Emperor himself. He was a part of the government—a hero to his family and friends. For the remainder of his life, as a reservist and a member of the Ex-Service Men's Association, he had special status in his community. With far more Japanese actively participating in this particular hierarchy and with most Japanese predisposed by tradition to accept the military man as a selfless servant of the Emperor and state, in contrast to the greedy businessman and self-interested politician, the army had pres-

tige and power unequaled by any other group in modern
Japan.

Since Japan is an island country, like England her pride and
strength in recent decades has been her navy, but strangely the
navy has not played a role comparable to that of the army in
modern Japanese politics and society. For one thing it lacked
the mass base of the army, being inevitably a smaller and more
select organization. The army, on the other hand, was in close
touch with a far larger segment of the population than was
the navy and, in keeping with the national emphasis on indoctrination and propaganda in education, concentrated on the
indoctrination of its recruits and of Japanese students in general. It went into the business of propaganda heavily and,
perhaps more than any other group in Japan, became the victim of its own propaganda. Developing a more virulent brand
of jingoism year by year, it succeeded brilliantly in convincing the peasants of Japan, whose ancestors for centuries had
been denied the right to own or use swords, that they were a
warrior race, but in the process the officers of the Japanese
army drew the blinders of propaganda before their own eyes
until they themselves could see only the single path which
eventually led them to destruction.

Japanese navy officers, far less involved in nation-wide propaganda, remained a more technically efficient group, retaining
a commendable breadth of vision and sense of reality. While
army extremists continuously pushed for war, navy spokes-
men tended to be understandably reluctant and pessimistic.
In contrast to the rantings of a Tojo, navy leaders usually
spoke in the more restrained vein of Admiral Yamamoto. The
ill-fated Admiral, whose plane was intercepted and shot down
by American fliers in the Solomons, was vilified in America
during the early years of the war for having boasted that he
would dictate peace terms in the White House. The real pur-
port of his famous statement, which is far more in keeping
with his own personality and the attitude of the Japanese navy,
was that Japan should not start a war with the United States

unless she were prepared to see it through to a dictated peace at the White House—in other words, Japan could not count on an easy, localized victory in the Pacific but would have to perform the virtually impossible feat of conquering the United States in order to win. Japanese army leaders, however, ignored his daring warning, and Yamamoto lost his life in what he had predicted would be a hopeless cause.

Hierarchy must have a beginning and an end. Some supreme figure, some starting point, is as essential to a hierarchy as the number one is to a numerical system. The political hierarchy and all other hierarchies below it in Japan find their ultimate apex in the Emperor. That is why even today most Japanese literally cannot conceive of a political and social system in Japan without an Emperor to give it its basic orientation. To them, Japan without an Emperor would not be Japan. Thus, millions of Japanese have been willing to accept any changes we wished to make in Japan so long as we did not do away with the Imperial system. They have been indifferent to constitutional changes which deprived the Emperor of all power but have insisted that at least a purely figurehead Emperor remain as the theoretical apex of Japan's hierarchic system.

The Emperor has, perhaps, been a particularly necessary element in the Japanese system during the past century, simply because rapid changes have seriously upset the old order and produced conflicts in authority which were hard to solve. Of course, a major reason why the Meiji statesmen and their successors did all in their power to build up Imperial prestige was that the old loyalties to feudal lords could be more easily transferred to the person of the Emperor than to the abstract concept of the state, and the blind devotion of the people to their Emperor gave the men who controlled him unprecedented power. At the same time, however, the Japanese people themselves contributed to the building up of the modern Emperor myth because of their desire to find some fixed and unchanging source of authority in an unstable time. As Japan modernized herself, the interests and attitudes of military officers, civil officials, politicians, industrialists, and intellectuals diverged more and more, and it became increasingly difficult to maintain a single standard of authority. Who was right when there were differences of opinion—the army, the civil government, the business interests, scholars and literary men, or even the representatives of the people in the Diet?

Japan's unilinear system of hierarchy was breaking down. It was necessary that all the divergent groups be held together by the supreme authority of the Emperor. It made no difference that in reality this authority was merely a fiction—that the Emperor in practice expressed no opinions but acted only at the instigation of his advisors. In fact it was better to have his supposed supreme authority preserved in the noncontroversial atmosphere of theory. The more divergent the sources of authority became in Japan, the more the Japanese felt the need for a single and unquestioned symbol of authority. The Japanese ethical system demanded uniform obedience and conversely unitary authority. Even more than the underlying pragmatism of modern Occidental thought, the rapid political, economic, and social changes which Westernization brought Japan have shaken the foundations of united authority there. This ethical earthquake has made the essentially obedient Japanese cling all the more blindly to the supreme, mystical authority of the Emperor.

5. SELF-DISCIPLINE

As we have seen, Japan's shame ethic depends on the one hand on a strong sense of obedience to authority, but at the same time the maintenance of self-respect also calls for the exercise of will power. More important than external conformity to avoid ridicule and shame is the inner force of will power to bolster self-respect. Self-discipline parallels obedience as a fundamental force shaping Japanese character. The self-respecting Japanese can find no more satisfaction in hidden shame than the God-fearing Westerner in concealed sin. The "sincere," self-respecting man must have will power, and to achieve will power he must employ self-discipline.

The aesthetic Japanese glories in the Spartan virtues. Poet, artist, nature lover though he be, at the same time he believes in subjecting himself to an ascetic regime in the name of self-discipline. Cold baths in winter, strict dietary limitations, and other such dismal austerities are the stuff of which will power is made. Army recruits are hardened by being denied sleep for several days. Where we Americans follow medical regimes to strengthen our bodies, the Japanese perform physically damaging austerities to strengthen their will power. Much of the theory and even the details of such ascetic practices stem from Indian mysticism, but the motivation is essentially different. Where the Indian mortifies his body in order to overcome the desires of life and escape beyond the suffering of this world, the Japanese performs his austerities in an effort to perfect his personality and thus to get the most out of life. All special skills, the Japanese believe, start with self-discipline. Expertness in calligraphy or fencing, painting or *judo*, depends on the ability to place an iron control over the emotions. The emphasis in archery is more on the self-composure of the archer than on his ability to hit the target. Complete self-discipline will raise the individual above the troubling doubts of shame or the fear of failure. Miracles can be accomplished by the man who knows self-discipline and has true will power.

The Japanese have an idealistic belief in the power of will over matter, which reminds one of the German idealists and stands in sharp contrast to the pragmatism of the Chinese. They can on occasion come down to earth with cold realism, as after their recent defeat. But the whole history of modern Japan is the story of a people who, with little more than sheer energy and determination to support them, came close to carving out what might have been the greatest empire the world had ever seen. Their expectations of victory over us were based on their belief that their will power would triumph over our greater material resources. Accustomed to a grim and sometimes brutal cultivation of self-discipline in order to develop will power, they could not believe that Americans, with their dislike of unnecessary self-denial, could have any will power at all. Believing that they could not lose because they refused to lose, they calamitously misjudged their own and their adversary's strength. Repeatedly the Japanese will to win resulted in battle reports which so consistently substituted determination for results that higher echelons often had a drastically erroneous picture of the progress of battle.

And yet, although this belief in will power has been in certain situations a Japanese weakness, it is at the same time their greatest strength. It has carried them to amazing accomplishments in the past and keeps them buoyed up now in what would otherwise be a sea of despair. The British in a far less unfavorable situation display one of their finest qualities in their dogged determination to "muddle through" somehow. The Japanese, faced with economic and political problems of unparalleled grimness, remain supremely confident that they will be able to fight their way upstream. They feel certain that they can solve any problem, so long as they can maintain their self-discipline and rally their will power.

This concept of will power has contributed to the Japanese emphasis on personal responsibility. This emphasis is perhaps to be traced to the old Chinese practice of holding individuals personally responsible for whatever occurred under their jurisdiction, whether or not they would be held legally or even morally responsible according to Occidental ideas. The Chinese believed that the mistakes of subordinates or even unseasonable acts of nature were a reflection of character defects in the ruler. The Japanese belief in will power complemented these ideas —although the Japanese have carefully placed the Emperor above the realm of personal responsibility. For all other men, failure of any sort is obviously a sign of a character defect—a lack of will power. An inadvertent slip, an error by a subordinate, even a natural catastrophe can be blamed on the individual who did not have enough strength of will to prepare for every eventuality.

The Japanese emphasis on self-discipline, combined with the essential poverty of the land and the narrow margin of life, has resulted in a veritable cult of neatness and a love of the small and the simple. The physical devastation and moral corrosion of the war years have left behind today a far from tidy Japan, but under more normal circumstances the average Japanese shows a passion for meticulous order which contrasts sharply with Chinese obliviousness to neatness and American love of large-scale grandeur at the expense of detail.

The very nature of life in Japan helps to enforce neatness. The peasant learns it from his farm, where he must devote painstaking care to each square foot of soil. The amount of uncultivated land around an American farmhouse is often as large as an entire Japanese farm. Where fields are measured by the square yard and not by the acre, the farmer learns to leave no weedy margins to his paths and no rounded corners in his fields. The Japanese city home and garden offer the same general picture of necessary neatness. Most houses are small, crowded, and flimsy, and their occupants must observe habits of extraordinary neatness unless they wish to live in squalor. With gardens sometimes as small as three or four square yards —and the nature-loving Japanese always prefer even such miniature gardens to nothing—each twig or blade of grass is treated with individual care and each fallen leaf is scrupulously removed.

This love of neatness, thus, grows from the environment, but the Japanese have made it part of their philosophy. Like all neat people they feel the satisfaction of perfection, even though it be only in one small part of their lives, but, more than that, they consider the discipline of neatness, of maintaining perfect order in some restricted area, a way of developing will power. Neatness is not just a commendable habit but is an indispensable part of character-building.

The Japanese have developed the love of neatness into a cult of the small and simple. They have done wonders with dwarfed trees, some of which are many centuries old, and they have developed the amazing minor arts of tray landscapes, made either with sand or colored clays. Their love of disciplined simplicity is perhaps best shown in their concept of flower arrangement, which in recent years has become a world-wide craze. Where we in the West usually gather the floral beauties of the fields and stuff them by the armful into vases, the Japanese create works of art with a mere handful of blossoms or sprays. Instead of relying simply on the prodigal floral wealth their islands provide, they create beauty by a sparing use of flowers and a lavish use of disciplined skill.

The Japanese concept of interior decorating is the opposite of either the Victorian or baroque ideals. They use plain unpainted woods in their houses, relying on natural textures and the rustic charm of nature's masterful symmetries and infinite variations. They derive beauty from the natural grains or twisted shapes of trees, where Europeans have sought to improve on nature with the knife, chisel, and paint brush. Artistic adornments, instead of choking every corner and dripping from all the walls, are limited to a few carefully selected items, placed in a special alcove where they can really be seen and their beauty enjoyed.

The Japanese, who have produced rich, varied porcelains of dazzling beauty, themselves look upon *temmoku*, a rough, dark brown, and often slightly misshapen ware produced in South China some five or six centuries ago, as the finest product of the potter's art. The slow rhythmic ritual of the tea ceremony, with its disciplined movements and concentration on a few simple objects of beauty, represents this artistic theme of simplicity translated into action. Japanese kimonos show an astounding combination of daring and good taste, both in color and in design, but there is no harsher word of criticism in the Japanese artistic lexicon than "showy" and no higher praise than *jimi*, which might be translated "restrained," "sober," or merely "plain."

This cult of the simple, as the meeting point of aesthetic and ethical concepts in Japan, has deeply influenced basic attitudes as well as art and literature. The Japanese have a fundamental suspicion and dislike of ostentatiousness and even of wealth. The contempt of the impoverished samurai for the wealthy merchant of feudal times has been continued as a general hostility toward the rich and a disdain for the profit motive. There can be no greater contrast anywhere than that between the Chinese passion for gambling and the Japanese scorn for even more legitimate means of amassing money. Wealth itself is not necessarily bad, but yielding to the morally enervating enjoyment of wealth is. Frugal living, if not poverty itself, builds strong character.

The Japanese ideal is that of loyal, disinterested service, based on Spartan self-discipline. In feudal times this was represented by the fearless, self-sacrificing samurai, who bolstered up his will power with the strict mental and physical discipline of Zen. In modern times, it has been represented best by the military hero or by the poor but respected civil servant or scholar, but not by the rich and powerful men of business who created the industrialized Japan of today. The typical hero is a General Nogi, who, although made a viscount after his fabled exploits in the Russo-Japanese War, continued to live a simple life of devotion to the Meiji Emperor and with his wife followed the Emperor in death by committing suicide. The shame-conscious Japanese may place a heavy emphasis on "face" and on success, but their highest respect goes not to the man who displays wealth and authority or even the man who has been successful in amassing riches and power, but to the man who has rendered great services to the state and taken little in return for himself, thereby demonstrating his superior self-discipline and will power.

9. Change and Conflict

1. WESTERNIZATION

Any account of the Japanese which gives the impression that theirs is an unchangeable or even unchanging society would be extremely misleading. All the major cultures of the world, at least in modern times, have been characterized by a rapid and, it would seem, accelerating rate of change. This is understandable to anyone in the United States, where change, particularly in the form of "progress," is a familiar and cherished concept. But the Japanese have unquestionably changed more rapidly during the past hundred years than we have ourselves. The Japanese of today are in no sense the Japanese of earlier times. In some respects they resemble the contemporary Europeans more than their own ancestors of the Tokugawa era. Naturally certain Japanese traits have persisted, at least in modified form, giving to their culture the continuity and distinctiveness which have made it characteristically Japanese from primitive times until today. Despite the growing uniformity of our modern world cultures, the Japanese as a people are not likely to become indistinguishable from the Chinese, Italians, or Americans. Japanese society, however, is a society in rapid motion. No aspect of it is immutable.

Change has brought with it extreme diversity and also startling contradictions. Not all Japanese have changed in the same way or at the same speed, nor have all aspects of the culture adjusted in perfect timing with one another. Japan today is a land of vivid contrasts and fundamental conflicts.

Obviously she will continue to change and change rapidly, until a far more stable balance has been struck than exists today. No one can be certain of what further changes will take place, but the direction of the motion is as important an indication of what Japan will be in the future as are historical characteristics, however basic, and present realities, however pervasive.

Japan in the past hundred years has witnessed not just superficial modifications but a fundamental social as well as economic and political transformation. Many students of the Far East have held that Japan has borrowed only the outer forms of Western civilization but has failed to understand or appreciate the inner content of our culture, and they even contrast the superficiality of Japanese Westernization with the more basic influences the Occident is said to have had on other Asiatic countries.

Behind this theory is the contrast between the Japanese intellectuals of today and many of the intellectuals of China and India, for instance. The Japanese, though thoroughly familiar with the history, philosophy, and literature of the West, has received his education in the Japanese language in Japanese schools and universities, whereas his Chinese or Indian counterpart, in so far as he is well versed in Occidental lore, probably has received a good part of his education in the English language and some of it in the Occident. The linguistic barrier, if nothing else, makes the Japanese intellectual seem less Westernized than the Indian or Chinese. But this is no measure of the degree of Westernization in these lands. The Japanese receives his training about the West as part of a normal Japanese education. The Indian or Chinese must go outside of his native culture to learn much about the West. While tens of thousands of Chinese students and even some Indians have gone to Japan during the past fifty years to learn the science of the West, no Japanese have gone to China or India for that purpose. And below the intellectual classes, the Japanese office worker or shopkeeper, laborer or peasant, not only knows vastly more about Western culture than his counterpart in China or India but is far more deeply affected by Western influences in his daily life and even in his thought.

The very idea that there is a distinction between the outer forms and the inner content of a civilization is a curious misconception. The Meiji leaders may have had this misconception too; they probably never dreamed how profoundly their reforms would remake the Japanese people. Of course, Japan remains in many ways essentially Japanese, and yet industrialization, universal education, and all the other external innovations from the West could not leave the Japanese basically unchanged. The Oxford-trained Indian and the Chinese with a Columbia Ph.D. may be more obviously Westernized than the graduate in English literature from Tokyo University, who, though well read in Shakespeare and Milton, has never been abroad or even had many opportunities to speak English, but the Japanese people from Cabinet Minister down to the humblest peasant have been influenced by the West in a way that is entirely unknown among the masses of India or China.

A great deal is heard today of the titanic social revolution which is beginning to sweep Asia, but it should be remembered that the initial convulsions of this continent-shaking revolution swept through the Japanese islands decades ago. The nationalistic awakening, industrialization, the spread of education, the revolutionary concept that the common man should participate in and perhaps even control government, all hit Japan long before the rest of Asia, but, perhaps because of some basic difference in the underlying geologic formations of society, the upheaval was less destructive in the islands than on the continent and passed almost unnoticed by the rest of the world. Japan for long has been a thoroughly nationalistic country; she has already made her adjustment to the machine age; her society has been transformed by universal education; and the Japanese have had a longer history of encouraging successes and disheartening failures in the field of representative government than any other people in Asia. While most of the rest of Asia is being shaken to the core by these same forces and the ultimate outcome is far from clear, Japanese society has adjusted quickly and easily, yielding to the force of the upheaval the way the light, frame buildings of Japan move with the motion of an earthquake, instead of standing rigid until cracked and thrown to the ground like the brick walls of China.

But these were only the initial shocks of the temblor. Japan weathered them gallantly, only to be faced with the new and even more complex problems of an industrialized and modernized state, such as face the countries of Europe. The clashes of contemporary Japan, while carrying Asiatic overtones, are basically not unlike the discords of modern Europe. Her problems find a closer parallel in England or Italy and still more perhaps in Germany than in neighboring China or Korea.

It seems safe to assume that the other lands of Asia, too, will find their present travail simply a prelude to new and equally difficult problems. The Japanese experience should make it clear that industrialization and universal education, however necessary or desirable they may be, offer no panacea for Asia. But the Japanese experience can certainly not be taken as any exact forecast of future developments in the rest of Asia. The very speed of the early stages of the revolution in Japan shows that there are fundamental differences between her and her Asiatic neighbors—differences which may affect their respective courses in the future as much as they have during the past hundred years.

Many have explained the greater speed of the Japanese reaction to the Western impact as a result of Japan's smallness and insular position, which made her more susceptible to rapid physical penetration by Western influences than were the vast stretches of China's landlocked interior provinces. This geographic factor, however, was probably not the major one. More important were Japan's ready acceptance of the concept of borrowing from abroad, her long established nationalism, her experience during feudal times with legal concepts somewhat similar to those of the West, and other basic points of resemblance to Europe. Japan in the early nineteenth century, far from having achieved the monolithic ideal of China, actually came closer to approximating the early modern states of Europe in her multiple authorities and her social as well as political diversity. She had also laid a firmer foundation than China for the development of a capitalistic economy, which, together with nationalism, serves as a cornerstone of modern Western civilization.

Japanese feudalism, in theory, had no more room for capitalism than had the feudalism of Europe, and yet Japanese feudal lords and retainers were heavily in debt to capitalistic moneylenders, and the feudal realms financed themselves by selling their surplus rice in a national market and by collaborating with businessmen in setting up trade or production monopolies. Many feudal realms maintained financial agents at Osaka to sell their rice and arrange for necessary purchases. The great rice markets at Osaka and Edo, with their dealings in futures and their delicately synchronized fluctuations in prices, closely resembled the major wheat markets of postfeudal Western Europe. The influence of the Chinese attitude of contempt for trade and the trader had strengthened Japanese feudal prejudices, resulting in the preposterous theory that the merchant class was the lowest social grouping, but in reality the city merchants dominated not only the economy but also the literature and art of the late Tokugawa period. Culturally a bourgeois revolution had already taken place in Japan, and the economy, despite the feudal façade, was in many ways an early capitalistic economy, not unlike that of Western Europe in early modern times.

Small wonder then that the Japanese rapidly adopted and exploited the capitalistic practices of the West. Small rural entrepreneurs quickly saw the advantages of capital investments to mechanize silk reeling and thus created Japan's first truly successful export industry; merchants cautiously converted their enterprises into modern banking or merchandising firms; and former feudal lords and samurai used their government bonds to become modern industrialists and bankers. While the capital of China for the most part remained tied by tradition and governmental caprice to the land or to short-term investments, Japanese capitalists were building up some of the greatest economic empires the world has ever seen.

Why the Japanese alone among the peoples of the eastern periphery of the Old World had these basic resemblances to the peoples of the western periphery is not a question which can be easily answered, nor has anyone seriously sought to answer it. Certain possible explanations, however, suggest themselves as worthy of further study. For one thing, Japan resembles Western Europe geographically and climatically more than do the other countries of Asia, with the single exception of her close neighbor, Korea. Even more significant is the complex of fundamental traits which followed one another in somewhat the same order in both Japan and Europe. Appearing independently of each other at the two opposite ends of the Old World, these parallel groupings and sequences of cultural characteristics suggest interesting causal relationships. Behind nationalism and an at least incipient capitalism in both areas lay a feudal experience, which in fundamental characteristics was amazingly similar in Japan and Europe; and behind feudalism lay the meeting in each case of an aristocratic, tribal society with a universal religion of salvation and a classic civilization which stressed a unified, authoritarian state. In most of Western Europe the tribesmen absorbed some of the classic civilization in the process of conquering and destroying it. In Japan they imbibed deeper draughts of the classic civilization by the more unusual procedure of consciously importing it to their own land. The process was different, but the basic ingredients were by no means wholly dissimilar.

Thus, behind Japan's spectacular Westernization in recent years lay earlier resemblances to the West. Perhaps Japan is not merely the most Westernized land of Asia but is more significantly the most "Western" land of Asia. It is fundamentally and unmistakably a cultural daughter of China—an integral part of the civilization of the Far East—but at the same time it has been the country which has diverged the most consistently and markedly from Far Eastern norms, and these points of difference have been, by and large, points of basic resemblance to the West.

2. TOTALITARIANISM

If this is true, then it is not surprising that Japan, in contrast to the rest of Asia, survived the initial shock of the Western impact with relative ease, only to run headlong into the problems which grip the West today. These are not only the economic problems of the industrialized and specialized economies of the West—serious enough though they be, particularly in countries like Japan and England, which are entirely dependent for life on the maintenance of a huge import and export trade. As we have seen, the rise in productive power resulting from specialization and industrialization permitted a spectacular growth in Japan's population, which in turn made Japan pitifully dependent on foreign trade. The economic problems which industrialization has brought Japan are far more complex and baffling than any a pre-industrialized Japan ever faced. A vastly more difficult problem which Westernization has brought Japan, however, has been the clash, or perhaps more properly the conflicting pull, of the two great forces produced by the modern techniques of machine production and universal education—the pull toward greater individual freedom, toward intellectual independence and democratic political rights, and the often conflicting pull toward a stricter integration of society, toward governmental controls over economy, and enforced totalitarian uniformity.

We lack terms both comprehensive and precise enough to describe this sharply drawn and pervasive struggle within modern civilization. Perhaps "democracy" and "totalitarianism" come closest to being the terms we need, but both convey too little in exact scope and at the same time too much in emotional overtones. But the clash exists and nowhere more clearly than in Japan. It is surprising how quickly and strongly these two forces manifested themselves in Japan after the introduction of Western ideas and techniques and how completely they dominate the history of modern Japan. In fact, modern Japanese history can be interpreted without great distortion primarily in terms of a curiously ambivalent and fitful progress in these two different directions and growing swings of the pendulum between these two roads of simultaneous advance as they increasingly diverged from each other.

The authoritarian background of Chinese political theory and Tokugawa practices gave from the start a totalitarian flavor to the new Japanese government. The newly centralized political structure was in the hands of a small group of men dedicated to the task of remaking Japan in the image of a militarily powerful Western state. The vision was different, but the process was not unlike the Russian Revolution of exactly a half-century later. The enlightened few were determined to reform the unregenerate many, who were usually apathetic and often openly hostile. Every possible pressure, from wholesale propaganda to naked force, was brought into play. Heads did not roll in the street, but social classes were liquidated nonetheless. The feudal lords quietly passed off the stage of history grasping their fat bundles of government bonds, but the samurai, who received only trifling monetary compensation for their loss of feudal income and privilege, often tried to fight it out with the new regime. A series of unsuccessful samurai revolts finally culminated in the great Satsuma Rebellion of 1877, in which it was proved, once and for all, that there was no road back to feudalism. Hereditary privilege and feudal diversity were rapidly leveled by the steam-roller tactics of the new regime, and the whole people were pressed into the same molds of compulsory education and military service. Japan began to approach closer to the Chinese ideal of a unitary society and a fully centralized government than she ever had when consciously following the Chinese model.

The early years of reform were the most dangerous. Each

successful reform gave the government greater security—a new weapon with which to enforce its will. The modernization of the organs of government gave it new efficiency and strength. A modern postal system, telegraphs, and railways drew the whole nation close to the watchful eye of the central government. The centralized French prefectural system of local government permitted a uniform and detailed control over all parts of the nation which contrasted sharply with the indirect control of most of the land in Tokugawa times. The Tokugawa system of secret police was broadened into a modern police organization, which spread its tentacles into every city alleyway and remote mountain valley. Closely associated with the police was the new army, which in its early days was designed more for the maintenance of peace at home than for the conquests abroad that later became its major task. Industrialization gave a sounder economic basis for the new government, strengthening it militarily as well as financially. And universal education, presaged in the Educational Code of 1872, provided the central government with a means of shaping its subjects' minds, which in the long run was a vastly more effective force than external supervision and control by army, police, and an all-pervasive civil bureaucracy.

Thus, the long road toward centralization which Europe has traveled during the past few centuries was covered in as many decades by the Japanese. For the first time modern Western techniques of organization and control had been superimposed on the age-old authoritarian traditions of Asia, and the mixture inevitably had a strong totalitarian tinge. Theories of governmental omnipotence—of abject obedience on the part of the common man and of unlimited sacrifice by the people for the sake of the state—came naturally in an Asiatic setting, even in Japan, where centralized authority has often been relatively weak. And now for the first time the new Western techniques made it possible for the government to approach omnipotence in fact as well as in theory. The Occident provided the rulers of Japan with better tools than they had ever known before to enforce abject obedience and, more important, to inculcate blind loyalty. The Meiji reformers rapidly coalesced into a band of oligarchs who enjoyed far greater actual power than any Japanese ever had before them.

Perhaps modern Japan does not offer an accurate picture of what Westernization will mean in the rest of Asia, but in this one respect there can be little doubt that the Japanese pattern is part of a broader Asiatic pattern. Oriental authoritarianism plus the Western techniques of mass education and propaganda, centralization, and police supervision add up to something very close to the modern Occidental phenomenon of totalitarianism. Throughout most of Asia the drift in that direction has been an inescapable corollary of Westernization.

3. DEMOCRACY

But the new Western techniques led in another direction also—toward social freedom, economic independence, and even toward democratic liberties and privileges. The Meiji reforms made it possible for men of ability to rise from the lower classes more easily than ever before. Men of humble birth became leading politicians and honored generals. Merchants and samurai, protected by the new laws, built up business empires which in wealth and economic power rivaled the feudal realms and principalities of earlier ages. And there even rose a swelling cry for the right to participate in government.

At first this cry was merely the demand of ambitious samurai who had been excluded from the Meiji oligarchy for some share in the power and prestige of government. Associated as this movement was in its early years with samurai unrest and reaction and producing as an offshoot in later years the chauvinistic patriotic societies, such as the Black Dragon Society, the samurai demand for a place in government obviously was no purely democratic movement. But in only a few years, under the inspiring leadership of men like the Tosa samurai, Itagaki, it began to transform itself into a democratic ground swell, such as had rocked the ships of state in Europe some-what earlier. Businessmen and landowners of the countryside took up the cry for a part in government and started to flock into organizations which were really incipient political parties. A popular demand for democratic forms of government was fast taking shape.

The democratic movement, however, was still very weak and might have been eliminated completely if it had not been for one accidental factor, which incidentally distinguishes the Japanese case history from that of the other lands of Asia today. Unlike the Chinese Communists of our time, the Meiji leaders assumed that parliamentarianism was an integral and indispensable part of the Western system. The fact that the strongest and most advanced of the countries of the West had parliaments was proof enough for them that a parliament helped make a country strong. In the spring of 1868, before the new government had consolidated its power, the group around the throne had the young Emperor issue a "Charter Oath," in which he promised that an "assembly" would be established and all measures would be "decided by public discussion." Even a decade and more later, when the oligarchy was well entrenched and the police, army, and other organs of government made it invincible, some of the oligarchs believed in the value of a parliament and others felt it to be at least a necessary nuisance, which would serve to divert popular discontent into harmless channels. In 1881 the government promised to establish a national assembly by 1890, and in 1889 the Meiji Constitution was promulgated, creating a bicameral and largely elective Diet to participate in affairs of state. Ito, the primary framer of the Constitution and an open opponent of parliamentary rule, saw to it that the document did more to enhance Imperial prestige and, through the Emperor, the power of the oligarchy, than to grant rights and powers to the people. The Emperor was expressly described as being "sacred and inviolable" and "invested with sovereign power," and he retained sufficient specific powers to give the oligarchy which controlled him complete dominance over the representatives of the people. But the idea of popular participation in government had been accepted and had been given expression in modern Japan's most sacred document.

The first Diet, which was elected in 1890, was a small and frail opening wedge, but it was enough. The concept of popular government, aided by the stimulus of universal education, produced a steadily growing demand for more democratic rights. Within a few years it had become a runaway force which would have appalled the cautious Meiji statesmen had they still been alive. Japan crowded into the four decades between the promulgation of the Meiji Constitution and the 1920's much of the same history of parliamentary growth which European nations had experienced over the centuries. A stiff tax qualification limited the first electorate for the Lower House to a mere 450,000 out of a total population of 42,000,000. But as education spread, there was constant pressure for lowering the tax qualifications and increasing the number of voters. By 1919 the electorate had increased from 450,000 to 3,000,000 and in 1925, after a long and bitter fight, universal manhood suffrage was adopted.

More significant, the powers of the Diet expanded year by year. From the start it refused to be the simple safety valve for public discontent which the oligarchs had planned. It made a major nuisance of itself, until Ito himself decided it would be easier to work with the Diet rather than against it and in 1900 founded the Seiyukai, which for the next four decades was to be Japan's leading political party. The next year he decided to retire from the troublesome forefront of political life, and thenceforth he let his political protégé, the court noble Saionji, take his place as premier and head of the Seiyukai party. By 1918 Saionji had passed on the premiership to Hara, who was in no sense an aristocrat or oligarch but a simple commoner and Seiyukai politician. Hara, a product of the ballot box and parliamentary give and take, formed the first strictly party cabinet. The Diet in gaining control over the cabinet had won a slow but nonetheless spectacular victory over the oligarchy.

By the 1920's the new forces unleashed by the Meiji reforms —one might better say the Meiji Revolution—were finally felt in their full power, and at the same time the growing divergence of the two paths down which they were leading Japan became apparent. Until the First World War the ultimate leadership had been in the hands of the old oligarchs, themselves products of the feudal age, who had started the revolution and had not been created by it. But with their disappearance from the stage, the Japanese Revolution came to full fruition, as leadership passed into the hands of men who were products of the revolution. The link with the past suddenly melted away. Japan was clearly out of sight of the stability of feudal times, and there was no way back. More important, the unity which the common samurai background of the Meiji leaders had given Japan suddenly vanished. The second generation of leaders had no such bond of common experience. They were the products of different backgrounds—of party politics, of *zaibatsu* business enterprises, of the rigid civil bureaucracy, or the regimented ranks of the military.

In this sense, the disappearance of the Meiji oligarchy marked a crucial turning point in the Japanese Revolution—a turning point which its more recent Russian counterpart has not yet fully reached. The Meiji oligarchs—one might even call them the "old revolutionaries"—dominated the scene for five decades, first as titular heads of the government and then in the less precise but more highly venerated role of *genro* or "elder statesmen." The *genro* system was typically Japanese—a product of the Japanese respect for age and dislike of the ostentatious display of power or of positions involving individual responsibility. Time after time in Japanese history, the real leaders have been a group of men behind the figurehead ruler or possibly behind a whole series of figureheads. It was altogether in keeping with the Japanese tradition for Ito and his colleagues to withdraw behind the scenes as "elder statesmen" in order to avoid the petty annoyances and dangers of public life while still retaining ultimate control over the premiers and cabinets which held the limelight. But the oligarchs could not live forever. Ito himself was assassinated by a Korean in 1909. General Yamagata, the chief builder of the modern Japanese army, died in 1922 and Matsukata, the last of the original oligarchs, two years later, leaving only Saionji, Ito's younger protégé, as the last remaining *genro* until his death in 1940. As long as he lived, Saionji, like the Emperor, remained a unifying force in Japanese politics, helping to gloss over the fundamental fissure in Japanese society, but all attempts to create a new body of "elder statesmen" to continue this function met with failure. The products of the new age, politician and admiral alike, were themselves part of the dichotomy of forces which was rending Japan.

The First World War, coinciding as it did with the disappearance of the older leadership, gave tremendous impetus to the drive toward democracy and greater individual freedom. The victory of the three great democracies of the West—Great Britain, France, and the United States—and the collapse of the three more authoritarian states—the German, Austro-Hungarian, and Russian Empires—seemed positive proof that democracy was the vital force behind the amazing strength of the West. A wave of enthusiasm for democracy and internationalism swept Japan, bringing with it not only Hara's rise to the Premiership and the adoption of universal manhood suffrage but also Japanese withdrawal from Shantung and the Maritime Province of Siberia and the reduction in 1925 of the standing army by four divisions.

Perhaps more important than the First World War was the full-fledged development by this time of a significant new class which had been created by fifty years of Westernization. This was the urban white-collar class, or, as the Japanese more accurately call it, the *sarari-man* ("salary man") class, produced by the need for technically competent and educated men in business, government, and the professions. Ranging from the university professor, doctor, and lawyer down to the shop clerk and office worker, this new urban class has dominated the culture of modern Japan even more completely than its cultural predecessor, the merchant class, dominated the arts and letters of Tokugawa times. Under its patronage the great city dailies, centered in Tokyo and Osaka, developed into powerful organs with circulations in the millions. Magazines of every degree of sophistication or vulgarity and every shade of opinion made their appearance together with a vast flood of books, as Japan became a nation of avid readers. Every artistic or philosophic current in the Western world produced its own little eddy in Japan. The urban intellectuals and white-collar workers found that education had opened for them the doors to the outside world, and they happily rushed out to bask in the light of a common world culture.

This was not merely a spiritual awakening. Growing intellectual independence inevitably produced in turn social individualism. Family authority began to disintegrate, as young people questioned the right of the family to choose their mates for them, thereby creating one of the most difficult of Japan's contemporary social problems. The younger generation joined in a world-wide social revolt, and Japanese flappers and their male companions, known respectively as *moga* and *mobo*, standing for the English words "modern girl" and "modern boy," delighted in shocking their elders. Some intellectuals began to question all authority, and a series of small radical movements sprang into existence. The spirit seeped down to members of the urban proletariat, another new class created by the Meiji reforms, and for a few years after the war Japanese industry was racked by strikes and labor disputes. Communism made its appearance among small groups of intellectuals, city workers, and even in some peasant communities. And in each successive election after the adoption of universal manhood suffrage, the white-collar residents of the cities showed their growing independence and disdain for established authority by voting in constantly growing numbers for socialist candidates.

4. THE CLASH OF FORCES

A casual visitor to Japan in the 1920's might have concluded that the drift away from authoritarian traditions and toward political democracy and beyond that toward socialism would go on unchecked, as Japan followed the road blazed by the British in recent decades, but appearances were deceptive. Social individualism and political independence were largely confined to the cities, and democracy was infinitely feebler than in England. The Diet had won intermittent control over the cabinet, but its powers were still strictly limited. Even during the 1920's some cabinets were frankly nonparty governments, and, despite the limitation of naval expansion at the Washington Conference and the reduction of the standing army in 1925, there was doubt as to how fully the Diet and party cabinets could control the army, navy, or even parts of the civil bureaucracy. Still worse, the party system rested on a relatively narrow base and was sufficiently inefficient and corrupt to estrange the sympathies of many public-spirited Japanese. Electoral dishonesty was rampant, and Diet members were often venal servants of *zaibatsu* interests. And, in any case, the Diet for the most part represented only one narrow segment of the population, the small landowners and businessmen of the countryside, rather than the people as a whole. The backward peasantry and the equally impoverished city proletariat were unable to take full advantage of the vote, even when finally given it, and the city white-collar classes, while politically vocal, were inexperienced latecomers to the game of politics.

Thus, despite the obvious strength of the pull toward individual liberties and democratic rights, the conflicting pull toward closer integration and greater authoritarian control of society proved the stronger of the two forces which emerged from Westernization. However emancipated, intellectually and socially, the better educated residents of the cities might be, the mass of Japanese tenant farmers and day laborers unconsciously continued in the old paths of quiet obedience and deference to authority, and the vast weight of tradition still stood firmly in the way of democratic growth. Perhaps even more important was the mounting strength of the new forces of authority and conformity which Westernization itself had fostered—the highly centralized economic empires of the *zaibatsu*, the huge and omnipresent civil bureaucracy, the all-seeing, all-knowing police, and, worst of all, the closely knit and fanatical corps of army officers.

All of these enjoyed more or less independence of the forces of democracy as manifested in the Diet. The *zaibatsu* scarcely feared it, for they bought and sold Diet members themselves. And the fiction that the Emperor actually ruled and that the civil bureaucracy, army, and navy were his direct representatives gave the latter not only theoretical but often actual freedom from Diet control. The remaining *genro*, the Privy Council, and the whole high bureaucracy, which had succeeded the Meiji oligarchs as the men around the throne, stood both in theory and in practice above the elected representatives of the people. Through their figurehead, the Emperor, they had the power to choose premiers and to issue Imperial Ordinances. The Diet did not even have complete control over the purse strings, for the budget of the previous year continued in effect if the Diet refused to grant the government its new budget. Yamagata, the army builder and determined opponent of parliamentary government, had seen to it that the army and navy retained their independence. As early as 1895 a ruling was established that only active generals or lieutenant generals could serve as army ministers and similarly only active admirals or vice-admirals as navy ministers. This ruling, confirmed on two later occasions, gave the army and navy each a veto over any cabinet. By refusing to let one of their officers join it or remain in it, they could destroy any cabinet, whatever its backing in the Diet or bureaucracy.

The army perhaps best represented the totalitarian tendencies within the new Japan. Inheriting the warrior traditions of the samurai and all the prestige that a thousand years of feudal rule had given the soldier, it was a major link with Japan's authoritarian past, but more significantly it was an entirely modern product of Westernization and a chief shaper of modern Japanese totalitarianism. The new army of peasant recruits crushed the samurai revolts; it, more than any other major institution, broke down the old social classes and created a hierarchy of merit in which the sons of peasants could rise to the top; and finally it espoused many of the theories of socialism, championing the cause of the impoverished peasant against the wealthy urban industrialist. In short, the Japanese army, as seen against the background of Japanese feudalism, was almost as revolutionary an institution as the Diet itself.

Thus, the army that Yamagata and the other samurai generals of the Meiji period created was thoroughly modern. It had no place for class distinctions or hereditary power. It depended for solidarity on no vague forces such as common social background but created its own solidarity by indoctrination. Officer candidates were selected young and subjected to long and intensive indoctrination. Indoctrination of the conscripts was considered as important as military training and was carried on intensively in the barracks and before that in the school rooms. Building on the strong foundations of the habitual obedience of the feudal Japanese and utilizing the propaganda techniques of the modern West, the Japanese army built itself up into as solid a pyramid of hierarchic authority as the world has ever seen. While this organization was in the hands of the samurai generals of Meiji times, it could be made a harmonious part of the total power structure of the state. But when its own propaganda-fed products began to reach the top, cooperation between the army and the Diet or even between the army and civil bureaucracy became difficult. The army officer simply lived in a different world from that of the party politician or civil servant.

Perhaps the most important area in which the two conflicting forces of democracy and totalitarianism met in Japan was in the field of education. Education was in a sense the key to Westernization itself. Universal primary education, advanced technical training, and all the associated means of spreading information through the printed word, moving pictures, and the radio, which collectively make up modern education, are what produced the technical skills on which industrialization, modernized forms of government, and the new army and navy depended. Unfettered education not only taught men new skills but opened their eyes and made them think. It inevitably produced a growing demand for democracy in Japan, as it already had in the West. It was the factor which made modern democracy so different from all earlier forms of democracy, in which some privileged group, but not the people as a whole, used electoral processes in government.

But education at the same time was perhaps the greatest of all the modern forces producing uniformity and regimentation in Japan. Controlled education, through the schools and the various modern media of information, could standardize thought and regulate society. In the hands of unscrupulous leaders it was a far more powerful weapon for enforcing obedience than guns or prisons. Education in its broad modern sense is perhaps the chief factor which makes totalitarianism something more than the many types of authoritarianism which the world has known in the past. As the Japanese army discovered all too soon, indoctrination through modern educational facilities was an invaluable weapon for gaining power.

While education, thus, had helped produce the pull toward democracy in Japan, it was at the same time the strongest weapon in the arsenal of Japanese totalitarianism and the factor which above all others made any return to the feudal patterns of earlier times out of the question. Through the Ministry of Education the central government directly controlled the curriculums and teaching materials in every private as well as public school throughout the country. The key struggle between democracy and totalitarianism in modern Japan was the slow, hidden fight in the schools and newspaper offices. As education was gradually forced into the strait jacket of indoctrination, the triumph of totalitarianism became certain.

During the 1930's, the fight between the forces of democracy and totalitarianism came into the open in Japan, but only after the issue had already been settled. Despite the liberal, international flavor of city life during the 1920's, there had appeared unchallenged new dogmas of nationalism and new concepts of mystical authority, which were all the more powerful because of their vagueness. "Japanese spirit," "national polity" (*kokutai*), and other empty terms had been built up into solid realities in the public mind, and the violation of their undefined principles had been accepted as a heinous crime. Accusation of such a violation was enough to discredit the accused, for neither guilt nor innocence of such mystical crimes was susceptible of proof. People also had come to believe that there was such a thing as the "Imperial will," even though the Emperor carefully followed the dictates of his supposed advisors. A political fanatic or assassin could claim that he was following the "Imperial will" in opposing or even murdering the Emperor's ministers, and the public would condone his act.

Still worse, the inexperienced supporters of parliamentary rule in Japan saw no reason to defend the rights of minority groups. They saw no danger in the utilization of the powerful Home Ministry and the efficient, centralized police force it controlled to stifle freedom of speech, when beliefs they themselves did not share were involved. They even permitted the bureaucrats and police to establish the principle that it was a crime to think "dangerous thoughts." The so-called "Peace Preservation Laws," which were the government's chief means of suppressing all supposedly dangerous movements, were greatly strengthened in 1928, accelerating the persecution of labor organizations and leftist political sympathizers, which had been mounting ever since the wave of strikes at the end of the First World War. The incipient labor movement had already been crushed, and now all "labor" and "peasant" parties were banned. The weight of police control fell especially heavily on Japanese students, who because of their schooling tended to be more independent in their thinking than their less educated compatriots. Since Japanese police methods included torture and indefinite detention merely on the grounds of suspicion, the weight of police control could indeed be heavy, and thousands of Japanese university students were imprisoned and tortured until they recanted the "dangerous thoughts" they were accused of harboring.

With the battle of intellectual freedom already lost, there was little hope that the forces of democracy would win, but even then the fight was long and confused. Other factors tended to overlie it and conceal the more essential struggle beneath. There was, for example, the dispute over foreign policy, which was in a sense merely one manifestation of the clash between these two forces. As we have seen, the world depression made the problem of Japanese foreign trade and empire more pressing, but the groups which favored foreign conquest were essentially the elements favoring totalitarianism within Japan, and the opposition was primarily the social groupings which stood behind democracy. The clash was precipitated by the dispute over the best methods of maintaining Japan's foreign trade, but behind it lay the more fundamental dispute over the basic organization of Japanese government and society.

The army's independence of the civil government permitted it to embark upon the seizure of Manchuria in 1931 and the conquest of all China in 1937, without the prior approval of government authorities or the people. The jingoistic fervor these wars of foreign aggression engendered then permitted the army and the other forces of totalitarianism to sweep aside all democratic opposition and transform the Diet into a meaningless rubber stamp—another of Japan's many anachronistic survivals from earlier days. The army stubbornly clung to its costly and inconclusive Chinese venture because it was aware that not just a foreign policy but a whole system of rule was at stake. It realized that, if Japan could disentangle herself from China once war had broken out in Europe, she would be in a favorable position to make solid economic and political gains, such as she had achieved under similar circumstances during the First World War. But retreat from China was impossible, because it would have been an admission of failure on the part of the army and might have permitted a resurgence of the democratic forces at home.

Another overtone of the great struggle was the nativistic reaction at this time against internationalism and Westernization. The Japanese were experiencing a perhaps unavoidable reaction to many decades of rapid borrowing from the West. But one should not conclude that this meant any return to the feudal past. That was definitely and irretrievably dead, and no revival of primitive symbols of nationalism or Confucian and feudal virtues could give it life. Instead, the reaction attached itself to the army and the totalitarian ideal it was fostering as the more acceptable of the two products of Westernization. The result was a strange mixture of mystical Shinto doctrines, feudal mouthings, socialistic dogma, and army discipline, unified only negatively by the common antipathy for democracy and Western liberalism in general.

The economic overtones of the struggle were perhaps as confusing to the American observer as any aspect of the clash. We tend to visualize modern political and economic theory in a single dimension from right to left, not utilizing even the two dimensions of the paper on which we usually record our thoughts. The result is an obvious confusion between political and economic "rightism" and "leftism." The extreme left and right take on a curious identity in communism, and the gulf between a leftist England and a leftist Russia is vastly though inexplicably greater than the distance between a socialist England and a capitalistic United States. The use of two dimensions instead of one, though resulting still in an absurd oversimplification, permits a somewhat clearer picture both for Japan and the West. With the vertical axis running from democracy down to dictatorship and the horizontal from socialism to capitalism, we find Communists, Nazis, and wartime Japanese regimes all near the bottom of the graph, while Great Britain, the United States, and the other democracies, though some distance apart on the left to right scale, remain near the top of the graph. Over the decades both the democracies and the totalitarian regimes appear to be moving from right to left, that is away from pure capitalism and closer to pure socialism, but while the one group appears to be slowly rising in the graph toward complete democracy, the other appears to be sinking closer and closer to absolute dictatorship. The fundamental dichotomy of modern society immediately shows itself to be on the vertical scale rather than the horizontal, and the socialist leanings of the authoritarian Japanese army are seen to be a thoroughly typical modern phenomenon.

The Japanese army, drawing its strength from the less privileged rural classes, understandably became the champion of the peasants and the poorer classes in general. The army ideal was the traditional Japanese ideal of service rather than profit. Rich industrialists seemed to be wicked men to the Spartan army officers and their peasant recruits. The corruption of the Diet made possible an easy identification of avaricious capitalists with degenerate politicians, to the detriment of both. While the urban white-collar worker himself was drifting toward socialistic ideals, the rural radical distrusted the "city-slicker" socialist and tended to throw in his lot with the army. At the same time, capitalistic *zaibatsu* interests, while distrustful of army fanaticism and apprehensive about the military's program of foreign conquests, were more interested in suppressing popular radicalism and the labor movement than in forestalling the army's rise to power. Thus, the socialist-capitalist cleavage, though an important one in modern Japan, was not the principal rift in Japanese society. In the great struggle of the 1930's, socialists and capitalists stood firmly on both sides of the fence or attempted hopefully to straddle it. The real struggle was between democratic and authoritarian forms of government, as the bewildered and disorganized politicians of the older, conservative parties together with urban socialists bowed before anti-capitalistic army officers, supported grudgingly by pro-capitalistic bureaucrats and the great *zaibatsu* interests themselves.

It is disheartening to note how small a shift in the balance of forces within modern Japan produced the tremendous swing from the democratic tendencies of the early 1920's to the totalitarianism of the so-called Showa Restoration in the 1930's. The army, without changing its basic views but merely by increasing its intransigence, started the whole kaleidoscópic regrouping of forces to form an entirely new pattern. Secure in its virtual independence of the civil government and emboldened by the growing economic crisis in the world and the success of totalitarian ideas in Europe, the army began to knock the props from under democratic government by "direct action." "Direct action" abroad meant undeclared wars, which stirred up chauvinistic support for the army within Japan. "Direct action" at home meant political assassinations conveniently committed by a lunatic fringe of officers and civilians but benefiting the whole army's cause by intimidating the potential opposition, party leaders, high bureaucrats, and *zaibatsu* executives alike. The army had the tacit support of the public, excited by the wars and as much blinded as enlightened by the half-propagandistic education it had received, and public opinion was hard to resist in Japan, where right and wrong were admittedly determined by the judgment of society.

The other power groups in modern Japanese society either adjusted to the army's strengthened stand or meekly gave way before it. The high civil bureaucrats, the chief spiritual inheritors of the Meiji oligarchy, had for decades been con-

cerned primarily with the problem of curbing the democratic
upsurge by riding with the tide and controlling it. Now the
bureaucrats sought to retain their supremacy in the face of the
new menace by employing the same subtle, conciliatory tactics on the army, but each successive government saw the
bureaucrats a little weaker and the army men a little stronger,
until finally in the autumn of 1941 General Tojo became premier, and the army's totalitarian program at home and aggressive plans abroad became accepted national policy. *Zaibatsu*
suspicion of military extremism gradually thawed before the
expanding economic opportunities which the army's Manchurian conquests gave them, while the army swallowed its dislike of the *zaibatsu* once it discovered that its own economic
inexperience made *zaibatsu* aid imperative for the exploitation
of Manchuria and the development of heavy industry in Japan.
The conservative democratic parties and their rural middle-
class backing, which had the most to lose from the collapse
of representative government, were swept by the chauvinistic
tide of war into weak acquiescence in their own destruction.
Only the urban, white-collar classes remained for the most part
firm though timidly silent advocates of democracy, voting
heavily for the few liberal candidates who were still allowed
to run in the now meaningless elections, but even in this group
there were serious defections, as many intellectuals climbed
aboard the army's militaristic band wagon and the urban socialist parties took on a strongly totalitarian hue. And the
masses of the people—the peasants and city workers—simply
stood apathetically by, ready to follow whatever leaders should
emerge.

The strange multi-cornered struggle in prewar Japan between army officers, civil bureaucrats, *zaibatsu* executives,
party politicians, terroristic demagogues, and liberal intellectuals offers a uniquely Japanese picture, but, after all the curious Oriental detail, such as Shinto mumbo-jumbo, "Imperial
will," and samurai prestige, have been removed, the stark outlines of the picture bear an all too clear resemblance to the

major outlines of Western history in recent decades. In fact, the Japanese picture perhaps helps to sharpen our own myopic vision and enable us to see behind the bewildering surface patterns of intense nationalistic rivalries the outlines of the titanic struggle between the forces of democracy and totalitarianism in our own half of the world—and for that matter wherever the complexities of machine production have resulted in high standards of popular education and the close integration of society on a national scale. The conflict is not always so clear-cut or so evenly balanced as it was in prewar Japan, but it exists in some form or another throughout the whole political spectrum of the modern world. The extreme integration of society in the modern totalitarian state depends on education, and education inevitably tends to breed the desire for individual freedom. On the other hand, education and the economic basis for individual freedom as we know it today depend on the extreme integration of an industrialized society, and integration in turn tends to produce limitations on individual freedom. The strongly democratic lands of the West all show a rapid and apparently irresistible drift toward greater governmental controls over individual freedom of action, while each totalitarian regime ostentatiously maintains a show of democratic electoral procedures and is vociferous about its democratic aims. The point of conflict is different, but the nature of the conflict is basically the same. The two forces of democracy and totalitarianism are inevitable concomitants of machine production and universal education, and their harmonious reconciliation is no easy matter.

The struggle between democracy and totalitarianism was not merely a passing phase of prewar Japanese history. The fires of war and the surgery of defeat have brought physical and spiritual changes within the body politic of Japan, but this fundamental struggle goes on. The American occupation itself, with its educational programs and external controls, inevitably pulled in both directions. And when the occupation ended, the struggle went on, and it will unquestionably continue to go on for some years to come, determining in large measure the future of Japan and the role she will play in the world. In turning our attention to the postwar period, we must bear in mind not only the physical framework within which Japanese society lives and the spiritual heritage which is its life blood but also the power of these two related but antagonistic forces within modern Japanese society.

PART IV   THE OCCUPATION

10. The Victors and the Vanquished

1. THE WOUNDS OF WAR

The history of the American occupation of Japan will some day form one of the most fascinating and important chapters in the history of the world in modern times, telling a story which is both dramatically unique and universally significant. Whether judged a success or failure, the occupation will stand as one of the most crucial phases of the clash between the forces of totalitarianism and democracy in modern society and at the same time one of the most important as well as spectacular episodes in the epochal meeting of East and West, which may become increasingly the dominant theme in the history of mankind in our age, recasting or even overshadowing the present ideological cleavage which rends the world.

For Japan herself, the fifth decade of the twentieth century will probably prove to be the most momentous in all her long history. Never before in such a short space of years has so much that was old and accepted been burned out of Japanese society and so much that was new and unfamiliar been poured in. Each individual phase of the process represents a cataclysmic change in itself—the gutting of her cities by the blinding flash of atomic power and the less spectacular but equally destructive force of thousands of tiny fire bombs; the shearing off of a huge empire; the arrival on Japanese soil of a conquering army for the first time in recorded history; and the dynamic enforcement in rapid succession of a whole flood of reforms, remaking the government and economy and re-shaping the whole social structure.

The story of each one of these destructive or constructive modifications of Japanese society can be related in full, but not the history of the decade as a whole. It is evident that old forces have been destroyed and new ones created, but no one can say what the eventual balance of forces will be. Some of the details of the picture may be clear enough, but we still cannot be sure of the composition as a whole. Some small innovation, almost unnoticed now because of the momentous events which overshadow it, may serve as the catalyst for a great social transformation, while many of our most vaunted reforms may prove to be no more than sand castles, which will be washed away by the high tides of nationalistic reaction or the storms of war. A century of rapid movement within Japanese society has culminated in a decade of still more frenzied change. No final description of the course covered is possible so long as the forward motion remains so precipitous and unpredictable. The best that one can hope for now and for some years to come is a progress report on Japan's tortured convolutions and her apparent direction of forward motion—an attempt to determine on the basis of her known past which are the main underlying currents today and which are just the eddies and surface countercurrents.

While the major ingredients which make up postwar Japan are essentially the same as those which formed the Japan of earlier years, one should not underestimate the fundamental changes that Japan has undergone during the past two decades. The soldiers who embarked for China in the summer of 1937 or set sail for the conquest of the Philippines and Singapore in the declining months of 1941 returned after the war to a Japan changed physically and spiritually almost beyond recognition. Even for those who stayed at home there is a strong before-and-after feeling — a clear break in their lives which came when the physical world they had known disappeared in fire and when the spiritual world they had inhabited vanished as suddenly in the stunning blow of defeat. The physical and moral destruction of the recent war and the bewilderment of surrender and occupation by an enemy power are as much facts which shape the Japan of today as are the older samurai heritage or the timeless poverty of the peasants. Defeat struck the average Japanese with the speed of lightning, but its effects have lingered on, burning themselves deeply into the Japanese soul. It was a traumatic experience, and its effects remained long after the numbness of the shock began to wear off — the burned-out cities, the daily scramble for a few sweet potatoes to eat, the American flag floating proudly in the breeze, while for three and a half years no one was allowed to display the Japanese flag, the railway car reserved for Allied personnel, looking clean and empty beside the other dirty and overcrowded cars in the train, with their broken windows boarded up and people hanging from the doors. Japan is not and cannot be the same country it was before the war. Defeat and the occupation which followed have altered it permanently. They too are now part of the ineradicable heritage of Japan.

Physical destruction alone was enough to change Japan permanently. It is estimated that 1,850,000 Japanese lost their lives during the war, 668,000 of them in Japan proper as a result of air raids. During the first few years after the war, over 6,000,000 soldiers and civilians who had been abroad, many of them for decades, were dumped back in Japan, providing just that many more mouths for the overtaxed land to feed. Forty per cent of Japan's aggregate urban area was destroyed or damaged, and some 2,252,000 buildings were totally destroyed. Hiroshima was wiped out by a single atomic bomb with the loss of perhaps as many as 100,000 lives; but Hiroshima was a small city, and its destruction came after most Japanese had been numbed by repeated disasters. More of them remember with far greater po·gnancy the two great fire-bomb raids on Tokyo in the spring of 1945. As each B–29 unloaded its bombs, a wide swath of houses burst into flames. The panic-stricken citizens of Tokyo, fleeing from one fiery outburst, would suddenly find a new wall of fire blocking their path. A hundred thousand civilians may have been burned to death in a single night; in all the various raids it suffered, Tokyo lost a total of some 695,000 buildings. The population shrank from about 6,700,000 to around 2,800,000, as destitute bomb victims and their terrified neighbors fled to the country. The same tragic drama was repeated on a smaller scale in every other major city in Japan, with the single exception of Kyoto, the ancient capital, which fortunately was as insignificant strategically as it was important culturally. Osaka, Japan's second largest city, shrank from a population of over 3,000,000 to approximately one-third that size, while two other great cities, Nagoya and Kobe, lost more than half of their population, and scores of smaller cities suffered proportionately greater destruction.

The Japanese houses, unlike the stone structures of Europe, burned to the ground, leaving no traces except for foundation stones, an occasional safe, and brick chimneys and mud-walled storage houses where the rich had once lived. Built of wood and closely packed together, thousands of Japanese homes burned as the result of a single bomb load. The terrible possibilities of total war, only partially realized in Europe, were demonstrated far more vividly in Japan, where a mere handful of airmen were able to destroy whole cities, thus undermining the human base on which industrial production and military power rested. But the Japanese, with their passion for neatness, soon started the sad work of cleaning up the wreckage; showing the same courage and resignation they have always evinced before the destructive powers of nature, they bravely and almost cheerfully set about the herculean task of reconstructing their ravaged cities. A scum of temporary shacks soon spread over the bomb-made deserts which marked the central portions of virtually all the cities of Japan. The better residential sections could not be rebuilt so quickly, because the universal lack of money and materials prevented the reconstruction of the more substantial homes of prewar days, but in these areas the land-hungry Japanese soon planted vegetable gardens, which softened the jagged lines of broken walls and fire-chipped foundations. War damage was far less in evidence in Japan than in many parts of Europe, but only because it was more complete. For miles on end in the larger cities of Japan everything was so thoroughly destroyed that there were no ruins to see — only the endless rows of new shanties, which make a superficially pleasanter but essentially more sobering sight than the partially destroyed and partially rebuilt cities of Europe.

But the destruction of Japan's cities, while bitter enough for the millions who lost relatives and all their worldly possessions to the flames, was not as serious for the nation as the collapse of the economy at the end of the war. The same tragic story is found in virtually every graph showing industrial production of any sort. Industrial production as a whole had more than doubled between 1930 and 1941, but in 1946 it sank to less than a third of the 1930 total and a mere seventh of the 1941 figure. In terms of monthly production, the picture was even worse. The production of coal, Japan's largest source of power, had fallen by November 1945 to one-eighth of the monthly average of 1940. Pig-iron production that same month was only about one-twentieth of what it had been in January of that year and a seventieth of the monthly average in 1942. Textile production at the beginning of 1946 was scarcely more than a twentieth of what it had been in 1937. Less than a tenth as many electric motors and truck chassis were being made at the beginning of 1946 as in 1939 and 1941 respectively. Machine production, which is so indispensable to the livelihood of the modern Japanese, had come virtually to a halt, and the nation had been thrown back on agriculture as its sole support.

The collapse of Japanese industry is not to be blamed primarily on war destruction. Even in the more seriously damaged industries, such as machine tools and rolling stock, direct and indirect war damage together accounted for the destruction of only a quarter of the productive facilities. The lack of adequate maintenance during the war seriously impaired the efficiency of the industrial plant, and wartime bombing hindered essential communications and often scattered the working force. Far more serious, however, were the starvation of Japanese industry toward the end of the war because of the lack of materials and its complete disruption following the surrender. In some cases production was forcibly stopped by the occupation authorities on account of the military nature of the product, and in the coal industry production fell drastically because the surrender brought release and eventual repatriation to thousands of Korean laborers who had been forced into the mines, where they had constituted 32 per cent of the working force. In most industries, however, production had started to drop sharply even before the surrender, not so much because of bombing raids as because materials were lacking. After the surrender the decline became even worse because the materials still were lacking and Japanese industrial leaders were too confused and too apprehensive in the face of threatened reparations and the American reform program to attempt to rehabilitate their enterprises.

The disappearance of the Japanese merchant marine, largely in the year 1944, was in reality the death warrant for Japanese industry. Month by month during that fateful year the toll of Japanese ships mounted, as American submarines roamed the waters of the Pacific in increasing numbers and American planes began to scour the seas and mine the harbors of the Far East. By January 1945 virtually the whole of the once great Japanese merchant fleet had sunk beneath the waves. Oil, rubber, ores, coal, and cotton ceased to flow into Japan, and stockpiles began to shrink rapidly. Japanese industry was living on borrowed time, and by the summer of 1945 that time was running out. Years before, the wartime conversion of industry to military production had put an end to Japan's normal export trade. Now her imports too had stopped, and the tremendous foreign trade on which modern Japan had been living was at an end. Still worse, war and revolution abroad combined to destroy Japan's former markets in the Far East, and war-born animosities and new patterns of trade threatened to prevent the revival of her trade elsewhere as well. Japan's foreign trade had not just been temporarily suspended; it was for all practical purposes dead. And with its death, the heart of the Japanese economy almost stopped beating, and Japan sank into an economic coma, from which only a strong revived flow of life-giving foreign trade could raise her.

With industrial production almost at a standstill and the cities of Japan in large part destroyed, the wealth of the nation was reduced for the most part to the agricultural land and its products. The Japanese peasant, while producing no more food, suddenly found himself in possession of a far greater proportion of the national wealth than ever before. His house stood intact, and his bombed-out city relatives were clamoring for admittance to it. During the first few years after the surrender he was actually producing less than before the war, because there were no longer any imported fertilizers, and the production of chemical fertilizers in Japan had fallen as low as all other industrial production. But the city dwellers were producing almost nothing, and, with foreign trade at an end, they depended all the more desperately on the food the Japanese farmer grew. The government program for the collection of foodstuffs from farmers and their rationed distribution to consumers was already beginning to falter as Japan staggered toward defeat, and after the surrender had undermined government authority it broke down still more. Food rations decreased dangerously, while the price of food in the black market began to soar. The peasant found that he could reap greater profits than ever before in his life merely by selling a part of his produce through illicit channels. Money was fast losing its value, and so he often accumulated fancy kimonos and family heirlooms from the desperate city folk in payment for his food. And he ate comparatively well—perhaps better than ever before—while his urban compatriots sank to near starvation levels.

The relative prosperity of the peasants was merely a sign of the disastrous collapse of living standards in the city. Fire had destroyed almost half of the property the city dwellers had owned, and long months of refugeeing in the country had eaten into their savings. Slowly they drifted back to their old homes to live in shacks a mere fraction of the size of their former houses, small though those had usually been. They found little fuel for cooking and virtually none for heating or bathing purposes. Even electric lighting often failed them. Commuting in the few dilapidated and perilously overcrowded trains, streetcars, and busses which remained at the end of the war had become a prolonged nightmare each morning and evening.

But worst of all was the desperate search for food. The government ration at reasonable prices often amounted to less than a thousand calories a day and was never enough to sustain life adequately. Virtually all city people were forced to resort to the black market for some of the food they needed, but few could afford to purchase enough from this source because of the prohibitive prices demanded. The desperateness of the situation is revealed by the cold statistics, which show that while more than 60 per cent of the income of the urban family went for food during the first few years after the surrender, only rarely did consumption rise as high as 2000 calories per capita and at times it sank below 1500. Those who could find a scrap of land to cultivate attempted to grow some of their own food, planting rows of vegetables between the foundations of their former homes or hacking out fields on the precipitous slopes of near-by hills. School teachers spent much of their energy cultivating patches of sweet potatoes. Office workers appropriated the margins of the roads in front of their homes to raise a few vegetables. Thousands of others took exhausting weekly trips by train to remote rural areas to trade clothes and household furnishings for a rucksack full of sweet potatoes. They wryly called it a "bamboo-shoot existence" or else "onion existence," comparing the piecemeal trading of their remaining possessions for food to the process of peeling off the successive layers of a bamboo-shoot or onion until little or nothing was left.

The drastic fall in production inevitably resulted in a runaway inflation. It had started during the war but accelerated rapidly with the collapse of industry and the loss of public confidence in the government after the surrender. In the weeks between the surrender and the formal occupation of Japan, the authorities gave added impetus to the financial rout. Money in circulation rose rapidly as the government paid off war workers with handsome bonuses. The army, in anticipation of the blow it knew would fall and anxious to placate the disgruntled public, hastily liquidated its holdings, permitting the vast stores of goods it owned to pass into private hands and thence to the black market. As money rapidly depreciated in value, the postal savings and bank deposits which millions of frugal Japanese had laboriously amassed became virtually worthless paper. Inflation also meant a precipitous drop in the real value of all salaries and wages, despite repeated spectacular raises which always turned out to be too little and too late. The man who had lived comfortably before the war on a salary of a hundred yen a month came in time to receive ten thousand or even twenty thousand yen but still could not support his family on it. The city man was sinking helplessly in the financial mire of postwar Japan, and only increased industrial production could give him again the firm footing he so badly needed.

Only the black market flourished, as it always does when production is low and a country disorganized. Shady operators and minor racketeers prospered as inflation profiteers and soon came to be the only group in the nation with ready money. Themselves unfit to lead the economic regeneration of Japan, they drained the energies of the nation like some cancerous growth, sapping the economy of its remaining vitality.

The United States and Japan

A complicating factor was the presence in Japan of hundreds of thousands of Chinese and Koreans who at first after the surrender refused to recognize the authority of the Japanese government and thus helped to nullify attempts to stifle the black market and regulate trade. Although repatriation of all such foreigners in Japan was offered by the occupation authorities and well over a million persons, mostly impressed Korean laborers, returned to their homelands, large numbers of Chinese and Koreans elected to stay in Japan, and many Koreans, discouraged by the conditions they discovered at home, later attempted to return illegally to Japan. The Chinese, who were largely merchants of long residence in Japan, showed their customary business acumen by taking advantage of their position as victors to ignore government restrictions on native traders, with the result that they quickly won ownership of a significant proportion of the retail trade in the cities. The remaining Koreans, who numbered some 600,000, were for the most part day laborers, but, claiming the status of quasi-victors, many of them flouted Japanese law and brazenly entered the black market. Thus, both groups constituted a serious problem in postwar Japan, aggravating the menace of the black market and winning the animosity of the Japanese public.

Laborious reconstruction and slow economic recovery gradually hid the physical destruction and economic wounds of the war and early postwar years, but other injuries which Japanese society suffered cannot be repaired so quickly. These are the grave injuries to morale and the moral fiber, which, though largely invisible, have perhaps been more harmful to Japan than any of the external damage.

It started with the black market, which made its appearance during the war and erupted into feverish activity after the surrender. The meticulously law-abiding Japanese found it increasingly necessary to patronize illegal dealers in order to live. The occasional incorruptible soul who tried to obey the law died of malnutrition. As conditions deteriorated, numerous other petty infractions of the law became necessary. Common sense justified all these minor departures from strictly legal behavior, but to the Japanese, with his emphasis on detail rather than on general ethical precepts, any conscious violation of the rules cut at the foundation of his character. He took the only possible course, but the damage to morale and self-respect was serious.

The impossibility of maintaining cleanliness and neatness during the war and postwar years was almost as injurious to morale, for the Japanese value perfection in physical detail as much as in ethical codes. Soap all but disappeared; bathhouses were closed for lack of fuel; and the Japanese went dirty for the first time in history. Japanese crowds on trains and busses began to smell. With all national energies and resources being devoted to the war effort, everything deteriorated from industrial plants and railways to parks and private homes. Clothing disappeared from the stores, and the individual Japanese became shabbier year by year and his suit more threadbare and soiled. As the cities burned, the women's beautiful kimonos burned with them. During the war many women changed from kimonos to the ugly *mompei* trousers which peasant women wear in the fields, and after the surrender they shifted to ill-fitting Western dresses or to sweaters and slacks, which did not enhance the beauty of their short and often stubby figures. Even in the countryside old army uniforms in part replaced the traditional peasant attire, and throughout Japan the kimono, like the peasant garbs of Europe some decades earlier, began to disappear, as the more utilitarian costume of the West displaced what was one of the most beautiful but least practical garments man ever devised for himself.

Courtesy fell victim to the war as much in Japan as in the other participant nations, but in Japan, where etiquette is such a major part of morality, the results were more serious. People fighting over a toehold on a streetcar or scrambling for food for their families become oblivious to the niceties of life, and in Japan this meant becoming callous to one of the fundamentals of ethics. The more informal and casual manners of the American occupation forces also created a new standard for personal relations, which, while attractive to many younger Japanese, undermined long-accepted precepts of conduct. In Japan the flippant bellhop and the boy and girl nuzzling each other in the public park are not just showing the callowness and bad taste of youth. They are challenging the authority of age and family and threatening the whole social order.

The black market not only sapped the moral stamina of its patrons but it also bred open lawlessness on the part of those who prospered from it. Gangsterism grew at an alarming rate after the surrender, as powerful black marketeers defied the police and terrorized honest tradesmen. New recruits were brought into the underworld, as inflation and industrial collapse robbed thousands of any possibility of making an honest living. Petty crimes and juvenile delinquency increased rapidly. Close police surveillance, strict parental authority, and popular respect for law had made Japan as free of petty crime and juvenile delinquency before the war as any major country in the world. Unguarded baggage was reasonably safe in a city railway station, and a package forgotten on a streetcar was likely to turn up in the lost and found department. But nothing movable was safe in postwar Japan. Professional criminals broke into locked houses, and bands of hoodlums smashed the windows of parked cars belonging to occupation officials and rifled them.

One of the most terrifying phenomena of postwar Japan was the rapid spread of gangs made up of the *oyabun*, or "big shot," and his *kobun*, or "little shots." Originally a widespread type of organization, particularly among artisans and day laborers, resembling the organizations of the Italian padrones, the *oyabun-kobun* groups became identified with gangsterism in postwar Japan. Protection rackets became common, and many such gangs terrorized whole neighborhoods and could only be brought to heel by direct intervention on the part of the occupation authorities.

Behind the rise of gangsterism was the collapse of police power and prestige in postwar Japan. The once all-powerful and arrogant police found that the surrender of the government they represented had pulled their pedestal from under their feet. They also were singled out by the occupation for drastic reform, many of their number being purged and their national organization being atomized to the municipal level. Suffering from the same economic ills as other salaried Japanese, many policemen fell to taking bribes, and all, demoralized to the core, presented a sorry spectacle of pusillanimity and ineffectualness.

Perhaps even more serious than rampant lawlessness was the public collapse of morale. The inconceivable defeat of Japan and the exposure of their most cherished beliefs as the figments of deceitful propaganda shook the confidence of most Japanese in all authority, even though the acceptance of authority was a kingpin in their whole ethical system. They showed their disillusionment in their contempt for the once feared police, their ridicule of the returning soldiers who had left home as heroes, their scorn for Tojo and his bungling attempt at suicide, and their abundant abuse of Japanese political leaders both past and present. But nothing took the place of the lost authority, except the new alien authority and the still somewhat vague ideal of democracy. Democracy was on everyone's lips, but the word had little specific meaning to many Japanese, and to others the liberties of the new age meant only license.

The normally disciplined and determined Japanese seemed confused and even dazed. Forgetting their belief in the strength of will power over matter, many of them became apathetic and dispirited. Lotteries of every sort flourished, although few of the frugal and sober Japanese had ever shown much interest in such speculative sports before. Graft and corruption, which had always existed in government circles, multiplied dangerously. Worst of all, the resourceful and hard-working Japanese even lost their self-confidence. Before the war many Japanese had been perhaps a little too self-assured and certainly too self-important, but now they became pathetically willing to believe the worst about themselves and to assume that others were always right. They often carried this attitude to ludicrous extremes, accepting the word of ill-informed Americans as if spoken by an oracle and even assuming that they themselves had failed to understand correctly when an American's statements became too obviously inaccurate or absurd. Of course, thousands of tough-minded military officers, bureaucrats, politicians, and business leaders maintained their self-confidence and clung to their old ideas, responding to the new situation by subsiding into watchful silence, waiting for the day of resurgence, or else fighting guilefully to protect their individual interests by affable deference to the wishes of the occupation authorities and carefully concealed sabotage of their efforts, but to the vast majority of Japanese surrender brought with it a disastrous collapse of morale and a dangerous loss of bearings.

2. SAVING VIRTUES

At the same time, many of the best qualities of the Japanese also came to the fore and helped them to survive these years of shame and anguish with surprising dignity and even self-respect. They stoically accepted the catastrophes that had overtaken them, and displayed an amazing capacity for cold realism. Wasting little time or emotional energy on mourning what might have been, they quietly accepted the finality of defeat and resigned themselves to occupation as the expected and unavoidable result of surrender. History had dealt them a new and very different hand, and they concentrated their attention entirely upon it and its possibilities, without a glance back at the far more promising hand they had just lost.

The Japanese showed this laudable realism individually as well as collectively. They spent no time on useless and corroding self-pity. They did not even permit themselves the luxury of blaming their woes on scapegoats. They had lost respect for Tojo and the government, for the police and the army, but they did not make them shoulder the whole blame. Most Japanese were ready to admit that they personally had believed all the jingoistic twaddle of prewar years and had enthusiastically supported the war. They were willing to accept their share of the blame for the disastrous war Japan had forced on the world. When, finally, almost three and a half years after the surrender, Tojo and his major colleagues received their sentences from the international tribunal judging them, the reaction of the Japanese man in the street was overwhelmingly one of pity, for had not they all shared the same delusions? Why should these few old men alone forfeit their lives or be imprisoned, while their younger compatriots went free?

This Japanese attitude contrasts significantly with the eagerness of most Germans after their defeat to place the blame on someone else, arguing that they personally were never in sympathy with Nazi ideas. Where the average German seems to have retained throughout Hitler's regime an uneasy feeling that Nazi doctrines might not be right and therefore apparently emerged from the war with a guilt complex which has made him both resentful and somewhat intractable, the ordinary Japanese believed naively and wholeheartedly in the propaganda he was fed but avoided any guilt complex after the war by frankly admitting his former folly. All that he had been taught in school, all that he had read in the newspapers, made it seem that Japan was right and the rest of the world unfair and deceitful. Under the circumstances, who could have believed otherwise? But now the situation had changed, and he had discovered how mistaken he had been before. Naturally he must change his attitude and admit his former errors, but there was no reason for shame or resentment. Instead he should do his best to profit from the new situation to discover all his past errors and correct them.

This attitude on the part of the Japanese is one of the reasons for the unexpected coöperativeness they showed the American occupation authorities — a coöperativeness so amazing, in fact, that many Americans interpreted it as the result of a vast, diabolical scheme to trick us into complacency and then to outwit us when we were off guard. Naturally there were thousands of Japanese who thought in these terms, and they were probably found in the greatest numbers among the old ruling groups, who had the most to lose from the changes surrender brought Japan. Our occupation authorities from the start had to be on guard against concealed opposition and subtle sabotage from these men. Others readily accepted our leadership with the cynical realization that the more coöperative they were the sooner the occupation would end. But it is absurd to think that the coöperative attitude of the vast masses of Japanese under the occupation was the result of a carefully laid plot. Such a theory is a reversion to wartime concepts of the Japanese as supermen, for it would take supermen indeed to carry out such a complicated scheme, particularly in the face of the disruption of government and the collapse of morale which accompanied the surrender.

The sincerity of the attitude of most Japanese since the end of the war is clearly proved by the very differences in their points of view. While the ideas of most Japanese changed markedly after the war, the various types of Japanese reacted in ways which were entirely consistent with their own particular backgrounds, the professional and white-collar classes differently from businessmen, students differently from bureaucrats, and urban laborers differently from peasants. Most groups were coöperative and basically friendly toward us, not mechanically in accordance with some formal plan, but spontaneously and genuinely.

As we have seen, there are many factors which may explain the coöperativeness of the Japanese since the surrender: their situational ethics, which permitted a sharp about-face; their respect for power and authority of any sort; the fact that they were fighting the war primarily out of a sense of duty and

not because of personal hatred or fear; the underlying friendship and admiration in Japan for the United States, despite
the prewar years of mounting friction; the realism of the
Japanese, which made them recognize that coöperation was
the only practical course; and their admirable willingness to
accept new knowledge and admit past errors. But, whatever
the causes for this coöperativeness, there can be no denying
that it was the single most important factor in the history of
the occupation, accounting in large part for the degree of
success we had in Japan and helping to explain why this was
the first military occupation in history which met with the
expressed approval and appreciation of the vanquished.

Another Japanese virtue which has been much in evidence
since the surrender and has strengthened their coöperative attitude has been their appreciation of favors, even when they
came from former enemies, and their desire to repay these
favors or at least to show themselves worthy of them. To most
people the presence of hated enemy soldiers on their native
soil would overshadow every other consideration, but the Japanese from the start showed no more personal animosity toward
our G.I.'s than they would have shown toward a storm cloud.
Instead they emphasized the good our soldiers did and even
the evil that they avoided. Convinced that the victorious
American troops would give themselves over to pillage and
rape in the traditional manner of conquering armies, the Japanese were visibly relieved and openly appreciative of the
discipline and good will our soldiers demonstrated, while the
latter, half expecting at first to feel knives in their backs, were
puzzled and then charmed by the essentially well-mannered
and law-abiding Japanese. The result was a strange fraterniza-
tion between American battle veterans, who often had a bitter
hatred of the Japanese they had just been fighting, and Japanese civilians who had lost loved ones and all their possessions
in American air raids.

As the fundamentally just and humanitarian objectives of the
occupation became known, the Japanese man in the street be-

came increasingly grateful to his conqueror. He had steeled himself to accept cruelty and injustice. But the Americans were obviously trying to be fair and to work for what they considered the betterment of Japan. As the sorry story of the conduct of the Japanese soldiers at Nanking and Bataan and a hundred other places came to light, Japanese gratitude was strengthened by the humiliating contrast between the conduct of American and Japanese soldiers in victory. What is more, the Americans brought food and gave it to the Japanese, thousands of tons of American wheat, which for long years spelled the difference between short rations and outright starvation in all the cities of Japan. Overlooking the many irritations and indignities which were inevitable in any occupation, the Japanese attitude toward their conquerors became primarily one of gratefulness and admiration. A relatively small investment in effort and goods — small as compared to what we poured into the far less populous countries of Western Europe since the war — paid off in Japan in a spectacular amount of good will.

Naturally some of this good will was worn thin by the disappointments and frustrations of long years of foreign occupation and economic chaos. Many Japanese came to resent the assignment year after year of between a quarter and a fifth of their national budget to defray the costs of the occupation; they became increasingly disillusioned with many of our policies and restive under American controls; they resented the luxurious homes we commandeered from them for our occupation officials or the snug new bungalows we built at Japanese expense, while most Japanese continued to live in pitifully inadequate quarters; they resented the more than ample heating of occupation homes and offices, while they all lived and worked without heat; they resented the comparative luxury of the Allied trains and a hundred other special privileges which the victors naturally arrogated to themselves. But, despite all these irritations — irritations of a sort which have always bred bitter hatred for the conqueror in other defeated lands — the Japanese remained essentially well disposed toward us and determined to coöperate as best they could and to repay us in some measure for the fundamental fairness and generosity of our conduct as conquerors.

The Japanese, despite their many adversities, in time began to recover their basic sense of optimism. Encouraged by the helping hand the occupation proved to be, they remained essentially cheerful and slowly regained some of their confidence in themselves. From the start they displayed amazing energy in tackling the discouraging tasks of reconstruction. And in time they came again to believe that determination and will power would see them through. Even now, they cannot hide from themselves the gloominess of Japan's future prospects — her basically unsound economic foundations and her political isolation in a still hostile world — but their determination injects the chief ray of hope into the picture. If the Japanese do manage to solve their many economic problems and make their country a stable and respected member of the family of nations, it will be primarily because there is something to their belief that will power is stronger than matter.

3. MAC ARTHUR AND HIS STAFF

The Japanese people may have largely determined the atmosphere of the occupation, but it was the American authorities who guided the course of early postwar Japan. Although they numbered only a few thousand individuals, backed at first by a sizable army of occupation troops but later by no more than a token force of 100,000 men or less, they dominated the scene, making themselves an indelible part of Japanese history in one of its most crucial phases. A mere handful of men, they vigorously and confidently undertook the task of remaking a nation of eighty million people. The nineteen million Japanese school children and students alone roughly equaled the total population of the United States zone of Germany. Except in sprawling India and China, nowhere else has so large a national group ever come under the rule of a single foreign conqueror. Never before has such a small group of men set out to work such fundamental changes in so large a mass of people. The undertaking was gigantic. But the doughty members of the occupation approached their tasks with an enthusiasm and a firmness of purpose that made it seem almost easy.

The tone of the American occupation was set by General MacArthur, who, by his firm domination of his own occupation personnel and the entire Japanese nation as well, gave the whole undertaking a strongly personal flavor. As conscious as the Japanese themselves of the tremendous drama of history, General MacArthur wrote his name on its pages in even larger letters in peace than he did in war. It will stand as one of the great names in Japanese history, surpassed by few in Japan's long annals and unrivaled by any since the stirring days of the Meiji period.

Few men who have found themselves in history's spotlight have better fitted the roles which destiny has given them than General MacArthur in his capacity as American proconsul in Japan and benevolent but absolute master of the fate of eighty million people. He showed all the virtues that the Japanese admire. His strength of will rivaled that of the strongest Japanese hero; his dignity and the firmness of his authority were all that they could hope for in their leaders; his austerity was only matched by his capacity for hard work; his insistence on strict obedience was paralleled by his own careful adherence to the orders that governed his actions in Japan; even his insistence on unwavering personal loyalty on the part of his subordinates and his impatience with any form of criticism were qualities which the Japanese, with their own feeling for personal loyalty, understood and admired.

More important, General MacArthur provided the Japanese with the leadership and also the hope they so desperately needed in their hour of confusion and despair. Just when all hierarchy seemed to be crumbling, all discipline and will power melting away, and the individual Japanese was being cast adrift in the meaningless chaos into which society was disintegrating, there appeared from the least expected quarter a leader who with justness and determination began to create a new and presumably better order and put new purpose into life for the average Japanese. When things seemed blackest, he spoke out in ringing terms, giving a new hope to the Japanese and dignifying their suffering by pointing to the great historical advances to which it might lead. His flair for the dramatic, his thundering phrases, his appreciation of the tremendous historical significance of his own acts, all had a strong emotional appeal for the Japanese. Here was a leader who combined emotional depth with firmness of will.

General MacArthur became to the Japanese the symbol of perfection, the inspired leader, the knight in shining armor, and they repaid him, foreign conqueror though he was, with unlimited respect and often enough with adulation. His quick daily trips by car between his home in the former American Embassy and his headquarters in the Daiichi Building across the moat from the Emperor's burned-out palace in Tokyo drew crowds of admiring Japanese. They showered petitions upon him. While making him the personification of the power of the United States and regarding him as the sole source of all occupation policy, they also looked up to him as the prophet of the future Japan and their own national hero.

General MacArthur's role was not so significant during the latter years of the occupation as at first. As the Japanese, inspired by his strong stand, began to regain their self-confidence and to take hope in the prospect of a democratic Japan, they became less dependent upon him and his resounding phrases. This was demonstrated by the gradual decline of popular interest in him in Japan. In time fewer Japanese than Americans gathered around the entrance of the Daiichi Building to watch him enter or leave. Some of the traits which had made General MacArthur a peerless leader in the first postwar years perhaps became more of a hindrance than aid to the accomplishment of the objectives of the occupation. The development of responsible democratic leadership in Japan may well have been inhibited by his unchallenged authority and prestige, and his very greatness as a leader perhaps helped to perpetuate Japanese habits of blind obedience to authority.

When President Truman suddenly dismissed General MacArthur on April 11, 1951, the Japanese were stunned, but his departure had no effect upon the situation there. The occupation continued as smoothly as before under General Matthew B. Ridgway, the new Supreme Commander for the Allied Powers. In fact, General MacArthur's dramatic disappearance from the scene apparently did far more good than harm in Japan. The summary dismissal of this great military hero and seemingly all-powerful proconsul by a mere civilian politician contrasted sharply with the inability of the prewar Japanese government to control its own generals. The lesson was not lost upon the Japanese, and many of them learned more from this one incident about American concepts of democracy than from the years of American preaching about democracy that had preceded it.

It is still too early to make a final estimate of General MacArthur's unique role in postwar history. As one of America's principal wartime leaders, he has remained a somewhat controversial figure, and wartime attitudes toward him have often influenced personal judgments of his record in Japan. Some of his qualities are less admired by Americans than by Japanese. His insistence on personal loyalty and his intolerance of criticism irritated American and Allied colleagues and subordinates far more than the Japanese. In the broad interpretations of his guiding instructions he undoubtedly made some errors and showed certain blind spots. He has been subjected to severe and sometimes justified attacks from various quarters, though the heavy cross fire from both right and left suggests that he may have remained not too far from the center of the road that he had been instructed to follow.

In any case, there can be no denying that General MacArthur has been one of the great figures of the postwar world and may have accomplished more in Japan than any other man could have. Certainly none of the other leaders of occupation forces elsewhere in the world accomplished proportionately as much, even in their more restricted tasks, and none of the men who were suggested at the end of the war as possible substitutes for General MacArthur had the combination of personal traits which fitted him so well for the post. Thus, as a great military hero in his own land and a still greater peace-time hero in the land he helped to conquer, his place among the great names of history is doubly secure.

General MacArthur was, of course, not the only hero of the occupation. There were literally thousands of others among his headquarters staff, the Military Government teams in the pre-fectures, and even among the tactical troops who first entered Japan. The latter, battle veterans all, won the admiration of the Japanese for their honesty, discipline, and fairness. From the start there was only a negligible number of cases of violence or disorder to be attributed to the conquering army and vir-tually no instances of violence by natives against the American soldiers. The Japanese found moral lessons in the unself-conscious friendliness of the G.I.'s and in their insistence on fair play. When they would indignantly force men to get up on the streetcar and give their seats to baby-burdened mothers, they were as much missionaries of a new ethic as the more self-conscious American reformers in the occupation offices in Tokyo.

Unfortunately, the good work of the first occupation troops was not continued by the teen-age postwar draftees who gradually replaced them. The adolescent antics of some of these soldiers disgusted the Japanese, just at a time when they were becoming more discerning and critical in their estimate of Americans. The Japanese commuting crowds were not edi-fied by the drunken sickness of an unshaven boy or the light-hearted vandalism of his older associates. Every Japanese who had occasion to meet or see Allied soldiers came to have his own petty "atrocity" stories — a harmless old man knocked down by a drunken soldier, a ten-year-old boy robbed of his fishing pole, and occasional incidents of a more serious nature. Naturally, the great majority of Allied troops in Japan remained well behaved, and the Japanese showed great admiration for the polite efficiency and spit-and-polish showmanship of the Military Police, but as a group the troops in Japan during the latter part of the occupation, by serving as a needless irritant to the Japanese public, tended to undermine rather than strengthen the reform program of the United States.

General MacArthur's staff of experts in Tokyo and on the Military Government teams throughout Japan turned in a performance which was uniformly good and sometimes brilliant. Stimulated by the drama of the situation and driven by the desire to do a good job, the great majority of the members of the occupation rose to the occasion, shouldering responsibilities far greater than they had ever known before and trying by sheer effort and enthusiasm to make up for their lack of knowledge and experience. There were among them many who from prewar experience or because of wartime training had some knowledge of Japan and her problems and others who, though uninformed on Japan, were men of the highest caliber and of wide experience in government, business, or the professions in the United States. The occupation forces were also well supplied with Nisei and other American interpreters especially trained during the war for combat and occupation duties. But all in all the story of the occupation was that of the schoolteacher who found himself in charge of the educational system of an entire nation, the bank teller who became the economic czar of a prefecture with several million inhabitants, or the small-town doctor who was suddenly faced with the problem of controlling epidemics and improving health standards in one of the world's largest cities. Normally the entire human resources of a nation must be culled to find leadership capable of handling that nation's problems. That reasonably adequate leadership for a war-torn Japan could be improvised from the limited human resources

available to General MacArthur is a tribute to the versatility
and good judgment of the average American. A group which
for the most part could never hope to achieve positions of
comparable responsibility at home, the occupation authorities
acquitted themselves well in a vastly complicated and difficult
undertaking.

The chief reason for their success was their own attitude.
Most showed sincere enthusiasm for the great experiment
upon which they were embarked. They were as devoted a
band of "revolutionaries" as the world has ever seen, even
though the "revolution" they were leading was for the immediate benefit of another people. Most of them were entirely convinced that the particular reform or reorganization
they themselves were concerned with — industrial deconcentration, land redistribution, local self-government, textbook
revision, or whatever else it may have been — was vital to
the success of the whole experiment. Their enthusiasm and
fundamental optimism carried them over many formidable
obstacles. Their essential good will won the respect and
willing coöperation of their Japanese colleagues, even though
the latter came to feel that the Americans sometimes insisted
on making absurd and costly errors. Their enthusiasm for
their work often grew into a sympathetic interest in the
Japanese and certain aspects of their culture — their drama,
art, or history. It is hard to imagine a conquering army that
could have undertaken the physical and spiritual rehabilitation
of the erstwhile enemy with greater good will and deeper sincerity. The former occupation authorities in Japan deserve
the respect and gratitude both of the Japanese and of their
compatriots for a job well done.

4. THE PROBLEMS OF THE OCCUPATION

A series of problems, however, plagued the occupation and
inevitably impaired its effectiveness. One was the very complexity of the undertaking. The *United States Initial Post-*

Surrender Policy for Japan made it amply clear that General MacArthur was to "exercise his authority through Japanese governmental machinery and agencies" and was not to attempt to set up a military government for the whole of Japan. The policy was "to use the existing form of Government in Japan, not to support it." Although this decision has often been criticized as enabling the old Japanese governing groups to retain enough power to nullify in the long run our reform program, no other decision was possible. Even with the aid of all our allies it would have been quite impossible to bring to Japan enough men with the requisite technical skills and linguistic competence to govern the eighty million people of Japan at both the national and local levels. Any such attempt would have quickly ended in chaos. Our only choice was to utilize the Japanese machinery of government, reserving for ourselves the much more restricted task of policy direction.

But even this was a huge job. General MacArthur's head-quarters staff in Tokyo gradually grew into a tremendous organization. There were the four G's, the General Staff sections, some of which, such as G–2, the intelligence section, were necessarily huge organizations in themselves. Then there were the various technical staff sections, eventually some eighteen in number, some of which, such as the Economic and Scientific Section, the Civil Information and Education Section, the Natural Resources Section, and the Government Section, were during most of the period large and well-staffed groups. Policy decisions emanating from the staff sections were transmitted by way of the Eighth Army, with its headquarters at Yokohama, to the First Corps at Kyoto and the Ninth Corps at Sendai and thence to the Military Government teams, which were the eyes, ears, and also the multifold mouths of the occupation in the forty-six prefectures which constitute postwar Japan.

Liaison with the Japanese authorities grew up at every level, the Emperor occasionally calling on General MacArthur, Cabinet Ministers seeking out Section chiefs, and the rural school principal seeking advice from the lonely education officer on the prefectural Military Government team. There was ample room for confusion when a few thousand men, all comparatively new at their jobs, sought to guide the activities of a bureaucracy more than a hundred times their number and through it a nation of eighty million people, all demoralized by defeat and confused by the rapid changes which were sweeping over them. Our representatives in the prefectures were often embarrassed by local Japanese officials, who had been informed by their colleagues of American policy decisions in Tokyo long before word was transmitted through our circuitous military channels to the interested officers on the Military Government teams. At all levels there was ample reason for feelings of frustration, as the red tape of two parallel bureaucracies became snarled. Frequently, uncoöperative and recalcitrant Japanese officials "dragged their feet," and more frequently the frightened confusion of demoralized Japanese bureaucrats proved even more troublesome than concealed opposition. Dependent on the Japanese for so much of their information and for the final execution of their policies, many American officials felt themselves sinking into a quagmire of Japanese misunderstanding, inefficiency, and even sabotage.

Another major problem was the difficulty of procuring and retaining adequate personnel for all the highly technical and difficult jobs the occupation entailed. The first occupation authorities were the military and naval officers already in General MacArthur's command, but in time, as living conditions in Japan gradually improved and the strictly military phase of the occupation receded into the background, a large proportion of the technical jobs were handed over to civilians. Many of these were the same men, their costumes changed from khaki to mufti, who had held these posts before, but a whole stream of new civilian recruits, both men and women, also started to come from the United States. The occupation began to take on a strongly civilian flavor, with offices filled with girl typists and shirt-sleeved bureaucrats, even though all heads of Military Government teams and most Tokyo Section chiefs remained in uniform. But, whether the staff was primarily military or civilian, General MacArthur had difficulty in retaining the services of many of his best men, with the result that the occupation saw a slow but steady decline in the quality of its personnel.

This situation perhaps was inevitable. The outright civilians and the civilians in uniform tended to grow restive after a year or so and to return to the United States. In fact, the more important the man's normal position was at home or the more ambitious he was to get ahead in his own chosen field, the more likely he was to resign and return to the United States, for, however glorified his post might be in Japan, the occupation was professionally a blind alley, a self-liquidating venture which eventually would leave its members stranded. Moreover, there was the feeling that General MacArthur, with his strong sense of personal loyalty, relied most heavily on his older associates, the so-called "Bataan boys," who included some of the ablest but also some of the most controversial figures in the occupation. Many civilians and nonprofessional officers also became dissatisfied with the military restrictions and discipline of the occupation and preferred to return home to freer though almost invariably less important and less interesting jobs.

Nothing could stop the heavy turnover of occupation personnel or its slow deterioration in quality. As housing became available, the higher civilian officials and all officers and certain noncommissioned officers were allowed to bring their families out to Japan — their "dependents" as the Army calls them. Civil service ratings commonly a full rank above what they could expect to receive in Washington, bolstered for several years by overseas differential pay, gave many of them relatively high incomes, which were further aided by reasonable housing costs, commissary privileges, and extremely cheap domestic service by so-called "indigenous personnel," in other words the Japanese. But still there was a constant drift of

good men away from Japan. Of course, many of the best
of the occupation officials stuck by their fascinating jobs, and
new recruits always brought a fresh outburst of enthusiasm
and often new talents. Special commissions of carefully selected experts were also sent out in large numbers to Japan
and attempted to make up by their virtuosity for the shortness
of their sojourn in the country. But the problem of adequate
personnel remained throughout a growing difficulty for the
occupation.

The most subtle but perhaps the most persistent problem
of the occupation was the inevitably corrupting influence of
any occupation on its members. Living under conditions of
great luxury by postwar Japanese standards, they inescapably
constituted a class set apart — a superior breed of conquerors.
They enjoyed the use of the Japanese telephone network without charge. All the best hotels, the best private homes, the best
trains, the best facilities of every sort were theirs by right of
conquest. Everywhere signs told the Japanese not to do this
"by order of the Allied Army," to keep away from that section of the station platform, to keep off the best cars, not to
ride on the best elevators, even to stay out of certain public
toilets. To parallel his greatly augmented prestige, the average
American in Japan enjoyed vastly more power than he ever
had before and was likely to have again. He was always
right, and the Japanese officials always wrong. He gave orders
to officials whose American counterparts would probably not
have deigned to grant him an interview. The sudden access of
power and prestige was enough to sweep an even moderately
well-balanced man off his feet.

That the corruption of conquest did not eat more deeply
into the occupation forces is a tribute to the balance and honesty of most of its members. Some high-ranking officers were
accused of accepting favors from prominent Japanese which
amounted virtually to bribes. Some Nisei members of the
occupation, whom the Japanese tended to resent more than
their Caucasian compatriots, were accused of taking advan-

tage of their position as interpreters to extort money from the Japanese and to enter the black market. Black market activities for a while after the surrender were common among all ranks of the occupying forces. Many children of American officials and some of the less mentally mature adults developed habits of overbearing arrogance toward the defenseless Japanese. Mild cases of an "infallibility complex" were a common disease in many American offices in Tokyo. But, by and large, the American officials in Japan were saved by their enthusiasm for their work from the most damaging effects of the corrupting influence of power and privilege.

Thus, the occupation had its difficulties but was not submerged by them. One reason for this may be that we Americans seem to have been particularly well adapted to our tasks in Japan. We have the self-confidence such a job demands without being excessively arrogant. We are full of enthusiasm and ready to work hard. While inflexibly set in our own ways, often to the point of provincialism, we tend to be tolerant and friendly toward others. We have a broad humanitarian streak and a sense of fair play. And, perhaps most important, we tend to be genial and generous winners, if not always good losers.

The truly surprising success of the American occupation of Japan might in fact be partially explained in terms of the particular qualifications of the Americans and Japanese for their respective roles. The concept is at best vague and hardly susceptible of proof, but an imaginary substitution of roles will help to indicate its validity. The Japanese, who showed some extraordinary virtues in defeat, demonstrated all too clearly in China and the Philippines how overbearing, unsympathetic, and cruel they would have been in victory. On the other hand, we Americans, who played our part as victors with surprising altruism and good will, would scarcely have made tractable or coöperative losers.

II. Retribution and Reform

1. THE DISMEMBERMENT OF THE EMPIRE

As we have seen, the American program for drawing Japan's fangs and rehabilitating her as a peaceful member of the society of nations fell into three general areas: demilitarization, democratization, and the maintenance of a reasonable degree of economic well-being. The first of these major aims, being largely negative, was the simplest to accomplish. It entailed not only the destruction of the Japanese army and navy and the reduction of Japan's war-making potential by the elimination of all industrial power not considered absolutely essential to the peacetime economy of Japan but also the geographic limitation of Japan to the home islands.

This last objective, which was motivated not only by the wish to reduce Japan's war-making potential but still more by the desire to rectify old wrongs, was actually the first of the Allied aims to be clearly formulated. On December 1, 1943, at the close of the Cairo Conference, the United States, China, and Great Britain issued a statement describing their war aims as being "to restrain and punish the aggression of Japan" and amplifying this purely negative pronouncement by listing the areas which Japan would be forced to disgorge — the Pacific Islands, which she, as one of the Allies, had taken from Germany after the First World War; Korea, which was "in due course" to become "free and independent"; and Manchuria, Formosa, and the near-by Pescadores Islands, which she had taken from China.

The Potsdam Proclamation, which the same three powers issued on July 26, 1945, and which was subsequently adhered to by the Soviet Union, referred to the Cairo statement and specified the limitation of postwar Japan "to the islands of Honshu, Hokkaido, Kyushu, and Shikoku and such minor islands as we determine." Thus, the paring down of the Japanese Empire became one of the conditions enumerated in the Potsdam Proclamation for the "unconditional surrender" of Japan.

It might be said in passing that the doctrine of "unconditional surrender" had been repeatedly enunciated by President Roosevelt and other American leaders, who remembered the unfortunate effects of the belief in Germany after the First World War that Germany had not really been defeated by the Allies. But the phrase "unconditional surrender" unquestionably helped to keep alive the Japanese determination to fight to the bitter end. In the Potsdam Proclamation, without admitting what we were doing, we wisely abandoned this unsound doctrine, allowing it to shrink to the phrase, "the unconditional surrender of all Japanese armed forces," and appealed to Japan to "follow the path of reason." Not only did we enumerate our conditions for surrender, but we also made definite promises — promises that "the Japanese military forces . . . shall be permitted to return to their homes," that "we do not intend that the Japanese shall be enslaved as a race or destroyed as a nation," that "Japan shall be permitted to maintain such industries as will sustain her economy," and that "the occupying forces of the Allies shall be withdrawn from Japan as soon as these objectives have been accomplished and there has been established in accordance with the freely expressed will of the Japanese people a peacefully inclined and responsible government." When the Japanese, addressing us through the Swiss, quibbled on one of the terms, we obligingly clarified its meaning. None of the terms was any more or less than what we considered just and wise, but, by disregarding the unfortunate phrase "unconditional surrender" and by clearly stating our conditions, we helped to ensure the early surrender of Japan, with all that meant in terms of American and Japanese lives saved and the avoidance of further costly destruction.

The *United States Initial Post-Surrender Policy for Japan* did not further elaborate the future geographic limits of Japan, and the Far Eastern Commission was expressly denied the right to discuss territorial adjustments. Thus, the final disposition of the Japanese Empire was left to the 1951 peace conference and even then was defined for the most part only in negative terms. It had proved impossible to agree on which Chinese regime was to be invited to the conference, and India had refused to attend, largely in protest against the absence of the Chinese, while the Soviet Union, though attending the conference, refused to sign the treaty. Under these circumstances, with two of the major recipients of Japanese territory and Japan's three most populous neighbors refusing to take part, all that the treaty could specify for certain former Japanese territories was that Japan herself renounced all claim to them. Nonetheless, the general nature of the postwar territorial settlement has been clear ever since the surrender, and Japan's overseas possessions were for all practical purposes shorn from her already in 1945.

Korea achieved her divided and war-torn independence. China immediately after the surrender proceeded to take over Formosa, the Pescadores Islands, and Manchuria. The Kurile chain and Southern Sakhalin were occupied by the Soviet Union, and the United States took over the Ryukyu and Bonin Islands. Japan's former Mandates in the North Pacific, the Marshalls, Carolines, and Marianas, were also occupied by the United States and in 1947 were formally assigned to us as a trusteeship territory under the United Nations. The remaining small islands around the four main islands of Japan were all left untouched. Despite Korean claims, there could be no doubt that Tsushima, between Kyushu and Korea, had been exclusively Japanese since earliest times. The same was true of the other islands lying off the coast of Honshu and

Kyushu and the Seven Islands of Izu stretching out into the Pacific south of Tokyo Bay. To have taken any of these from Japan could hardly have been justified on moral or practical grounds.

Actually there was no moral or legal justification for the removal from Japan of the Bonin, Ryukyu, and Kurile Islands either, and these the Japanese most certainly have not renounced in their hearts. They promised in the peace treaty to support American proposals for the assignment of the Ryukyu and Bonin Islands to the United States as trusteeship territories, but they still have hopes of getting them back some day. The Bonin Islands, located in the Pacific between Japan and her former Mandates, have been indisputably Japanese since 1875. The Ryukyu Islands are even more thoroughly Japanese. The inhabitants are closely related to the Japanese linguistically and culturally and are in some ways scarcely to be distinguished from the Japanese of the four main islands. Although their kings for centuries paid tribute to China, the Ryukyuans are in no sense Chinese, and they have been politically tied to Japan for a long time. The southern Kyushu fief of Satsuma exercised control over them from the early years of the seventeenth century until they were made an integral part of Japan early in the Meiji period. It is true that the Ryukyuans resented their treatment before the war as second-class citizens of Japan, sometimes exploited at home by Japanese administrators and treated as social and economic inferiors when they migrated to Japan proper. Actually more than 167,000 Ryukyuans residing in Japan proper at the end of the war chose "repatriation" when the opportunity was afforded them by the occupation authorities. Nonetheless, the Ryukyuans unquestionably feel themselves to be Japanese and want to rejoin Japan, if not immediately because of economic reasons, at least some day.

Because of the wishes of the Ryukyuans and the Japanese, the United States did return to Japan at the end of 1953 the Amami group of islands at the northern end of the chain. Dulles, as Secretary of State, also enunciated the concept that

Japan had "residual sovereignty" over the Ryukyu Islands. This was tacit recognition that the whole chain might some day be returned to Japan. President Kennedy in March 1962 made the promise even more specific. However, in the meantime strategic considerations remain paramount. The United States has developed major military establishments on the main island of Okinawa, which are considered essential to the defense of the free world, including Japan. As long as the world situation necessitates such defense establishments, administrative control by the United States over the 900,000 Ryukyuans seems likely to continue.

The Japanese are also not reconciled to the loss of the Kuriles and are still negotiating for the return of the southern islands of the chain, although it seems unlikely that the Russians will relinquish anything but a few small islets close to the coast of Hokkaido, known as the Habomais and Shikotan. In the formal termination of the state of war between the two nations, which finally took place on October 19, 1956, the Russians agreed that Japan had prior claims to these islets, but a full peace treaty could not be concluded at that time just because neither side would retreat on its claims to the Southern Kuriles.

The Soviet Union has strong legal rights to Sakhalin, which the Japanese do not dispute, for Japan took it from the Czars as one of the spoils of war in 1905. On the other hand, the Japanese legal claim to the Kuriles is incontestable. In an amicable agreement in 1875 the Russians relinquished all claims to the Kuriles in return for Japanese relinquishment of her rights to Sakhalin. The present Soviet hold over the islands rests on their strategic location, screening as they do the Siberian coast, and on the simple fact of occupation. Back of the latter lies the Yalta agreement of February 1945. At Yalta, President Roosevelt, in return for a promise on the part of the Russians to enter the war against Japan "two or three months after Germany has surrendered," agreed to give the Soviet Union both Southern Sakhalin and the Kuriles together with the various rights in Manchuria that Japan had won from the

Russians in 1905 and the Russians had previously extorted from the Chinese.

The Yalta agreement has not had many defenders since the end of the war. Even in February of 1945 it was beginning to become clear that Japan could be defeated without Soviet aid, and, as events worked out, the Soviet entrance into the war on August 8, like the dropping of atomic bombs on Hiroshima and Nagasaki on August 6 and August 9, was only a minor incident, perhaps hastening the Japanese surrender by a few days but not determining it. The Japanese leaders in the late spring of 1945 had come to realize that defeat was inevitable and the extermination of a large part of the Japanese people all too probable if the war were continued until American troops had invaded and conquered the home islands of Japan. Japanese soldiers and civilians would soon be reduced to fighting American tanks and planes with antiquated rifles and swords, and famine was sure to kill many more than bullets. After desperate soul-searching and frantic intrigues, the Japanese government naively decided to seek peace through Soviet mediation, but the Russian authorities, backed by the highly advantageous agreement they had signed with the United States and Great Britain at Yalta, were the last people in the world to desire the war to end before they had a chance to enter it. Thus the summer of 1945 witnessed one of the strangest races in history, a race between the Japanese trying to get out of the war and the Russians trying to get in, but, since only the Russians fully realized that a race was on, they of course won.

As it worked out, the Yalta agreement was a bad bargain on our part, but we should not judge President Roosevelt and his advisors too harshly. Certainly there was no assurance in February 1945 that the Japanese would ever surrender, and up to the very end many American leaders retained their doubts as to whether the Japanese forces overseas would respect a surrender made by the Tokyo authorities. While our ultimate victory was already assured, our government made the Yalta agreement with the hope of saving American lives which might otherwise be expended in rooting out bitter-end resistance in Manchuria, Korea, and North China. The bargain proved to be based on inaccurate premises, but these premises seemed reasonable enough when it was made.

In any case, the Yalta agreement, backed by the cold fact of Soviet occupation and *de facto* annexation of Southern Sakhalin and the Kuriles, stands as one of the great blows of the axe which have shorn off Japan's overseas possessions. Once stretching a sixth of the way around the globe from northern Manchuria to the eastern extremities of the Marshalls, the Japanese Empire has been reduced to a thin sliver, scarcely one eighth of its former width and less than half its former length.

Drastic reduction of the geographic spread of Japan was accompanied by the forced return of virtually all Japanese abroad to their homeland. In part this was a humanitarian move, promised in the Potsdam Proclamation, in order to permit Japanese soldiers to return to their families, but an equally important reason was the desire to root out all Japanese influences in neighboring countries, so that Japan could not easily reëstablish political or even economic control over parts of her former empire or lands she had conquered during the war. With great thoroughness and efficiency, the Japanese were rounded up, packed aboard ships, and poured back into Japan in a swelling stream. By the end of 1947, almost six million Japanese had been returned home. Destitute, confused, and usually jobless, they further taxed Japan's collapsing economy and proved to be a disrupting force in Japanese society, but the tremendous transfer of people, probably unmatched in the whole history of maritime transportation, was accomplished with brilliant technical success, and the major aim was achieved. The Far East was for the most part swept bare of all Japanese.

In some respects, however, the program had its flaws. For one thing, the concept of immediate compulsory repatriation was applied somewhat too ruthlessly to all Japanese, regardless of humanitarian considerations and the long-range interests of the countries in which they resided. Civilians and their families who had been legitimate, permanent residents in overseas areas for decades and sometimes for their whole lives were deported on essentially the same terms as soldiers and camp followers. Limited to an inconsequential amount of currency and what personal effects they could themselves carry, they lost virtually all their possessions as well as their means of livelihood and were dumped back into the chaos of postwar Japan to start life entirely anew. Many of these Japanese were technicians essential to the successful operation of industrial plants in Korea, Formosa, Manchuria, and even China proper, and their sudden enforced departure often resulted in the deterioration and sometimes the disintegration of the factories they had served. Only in rare cases did Chinese authorities succeed in persuading the United States to spare certain key Japanese technicians temporarily from the grim efficiency of our repatriation efforts. Although the vast majority of the Japanese unquestionably should have been repatriated and desired repatriation on almost any terms, a less sweeping and more individualized policy for civilian repatriation, while adding greatly to administrative difficulties, would probably have been worth while, not only as a means of strengthening the concept of individual human rights but also because of the crucial aid to the Korean and Chinese economies which some Japanese technicians could have rendered if they had been retained temporarily to work in behalf of the peoples Japan had so long exploited.

Another flaw in the repatriation program was the failure of the Russians to return many of the Japanese they captured. At the end of 1947, it was estimated that some 767,000 Japanese were still to be repatriated, and that more than 99 per cent of these were in Soviet hands. The trifling remainder, most of whom may never be repatriated, consisted primarily of small groups of Japanese soldiers who had been detained by their captors on the continent to fight in the civil wars in China and Indo-China. An intermittent flow of Japanese repatriates from Soviet areas subsequently cut these over-all estimates, but in early 1950 the Japanese claimed that 376,000 men were still to be repatriated, while the Soviet authorities declared that repatriation was ended, and they found only about 1,100 men to be sent back to Japan when finally the state of war between the two countries was officially terminated on October 19, 1956. The discrepancy between the above figures is probably to be attributed largely to a frightful death toll in Soviet prison camps. In any case, the Russians' apparent unwillingness to return some Japanese prisoners and their tardiness in returning others served to create deep resentment on the part of the Japanese against the Russians, which was not lessened by the discovery that those Japanese who were repatriated from the Soviet Union were often selected groups of indoctrinated Communist sympathizers determined to make trouble for both the Japanese and occupation authorities as soon as they had disembarked in Japan.

2. THE DEMILITARIZATION OF THE HOME ISLANDS

The cutting off of Japan's overseas possessions and the repatriation of all Japanese abroad greatly reduced her military potential through a few bold surgical strokes, but the main power of Japanese military expansion has always been generated within the home islands of Japan proper. Reducing this power without killing the patient called for more delicate handling. But one operation was simple enough. This was the destruction of the existing army and navy. Arsenals and factories engaged in producing military weapons were all closed at once by the occupation. Naval bases were destroyed, and Kure near Hiroshima, where the world's two largest battleships were built, was turned into a junk heap of monumental proportions. Over two million officers and men in Japan were demobilized in the opening months of the occupation, after which, in December 1945, the Army and Navy Ministries were transformed into the First and Second Demobilization Ministries. By the following June even these last vestiges of the central organs of the Japanese army and navy were abolished. The repatriation and return to civilian life of more than three million members of the armed services still overseas had, of course, not yet been completed, but this problem was handed over to the civilian authorities. Obviously the attitudes and aspirations of a large proportion of former army and navy officers and many of the enlisted men were not altered by defeat and demobilization. At first there were many rumors of minor military units which in rural areas secretly maintained their entity after demobilization. Formally, however, and to all outward appearances the Japanese army and navy disappeared, leaving no other trace than the fragments of military uniforms which for many years remained an important part of the costumes of many Japanese.

The Potsdam Proclamation did not envisage simply demilitarization of a formal nature but expressly stated, "There must be eliminated for all time the authority and influence of those who have deceived and misled the people of Japan into embarking on world conquest." On the basis of this broader concept a thoroughgoing purge of Japanese leadership was carried out.

The most spectacular phase of this program centered around the war crimes trials and sentences. The trial and punishment of many hundreds of atrocity culprits hardly come under this category, for they were undertaken by the Allied authorities and accepted by the Japanese public as routine criminal procedures, but the trial in Tokyo of a select group of Japanese leaders, headed by Tojo himself, was specifically undertaken to prove that these men were personally responsible for Japan's aggressive wars and subject, therefore, to individual punishments for this crime against humanity. Whether the ponderously slow but impressively staged Tokyo trials established these legal points is a matter for future students of international law to decide. The Japanese public obviously was not convinced. When finally in December 1948 punishment was meted out to the twenty-five defendants, and seven were hanged, and all but two of the others were consigned to life imprisonment, the Japanese were glad that the unhappy matter was finished in time to leave the slate for the new year unsullied, but they seemed to feel only pity for the twenty-five old men and especially for a civilian like former Premier Hirota, who was hanged by the victorious powers as an arch-conspirator but who seemed to many Japanese to have played a compromising role such as many other Japanese bureaucrats might have played in his place. With a realistic appraisal of Japanese politics in the years before the war, the Japanese realized how impossible it was to decide which twenty-five or even which twenty-five hundred men were primarily responsible for the war, and many of them felt that, but for their own obscurity, they might be in Hirota's shoes.

A far more important aspect of the program than the trials was the broad purge directive issued by the occupation authorities in January 1946. Lacking any clear label, such as membership in the Nazi party had been in Germany, to aid in the task of separating the sheep from the goats, the authorities were forced to couch the directive in rather vague but sweeping terms. It called for the dissolution of all organizations which advocated militaristic or imperialistic ideas and the dismissal from public office of any individual "who has shown himself to be an active exponent of militant nationalism and aggression" as well as large groups who were assumed to hold such views because of the positions they had occupied. Such catch-all categories, which accounted for the vast majority of the Japanese purged, included all persons who had ever been commissioned officers in the regular army or navy, all those who had held important posts in the nationalistic political associations founded after the start of the war with China, and all who had held important offices in occupied territories or in development organizations connected with their exploitation. Under these provisions some 1300 organizations were dissolved and almost 200,000 persons barred from public office. A year later the purge was extended down to the local government level and to the influential officers in 246 major Japanese companies, since it was to be assumed that "any persons who have held key positions of high responsibility since 1937 in industry, finance, commerce and agriculture have been active exponents of militant nationalism and aggression." Purged business leaders were of course debarred from private business posts as well as from government office. A purge of teachers in all the schools of Japan was also undertaken, but few were actually dismissed as a result of the screening process, although a large percentage of the Japanese teachers, either frightened by the prospects of the purge or else discouraged by the economic plight of teachers, left the profession before screening procedures were carried out.

Naturally the attempt to eliminate Japan's former militaristic and imperialistic leadership was not entirely successful nor did it avoid serious injustices. Our sweeping purge measures unquestionably caught a large number of the less desirable Japanese leaders, but they as clearly missed a still larger group who, while of like mind with the fallen leaders, stood a rung or two below the purge levels and thus were spared. These men at times secretly sought the advice of the purged political and business leaders, thus permitting the latter to maintain informal but sometimes effective control of the offices or business empires they once directed.

Our purge measures can also be criticized for having caught many who were no more and perhaps no less advocates of militarism and imperialism than practically any other Japanese at the time and a few men who, while occupying posts of prominence because of patriotism or personal ambition, were not in basic sympathy with Japan's aggressive course. Appeal procedures were difficult and were useless for those purged on account of the posts they had held, regardless of what their personal views might have been. We certainly did not strengthen the concept of individual human rights in Japan by sweeping purges by category which paid no attention to individual differences within these groups. We perhaps should have avoided that type of purge or at least instituted adequate appeal mechanisms from the start, so that all those who had been purged could individually seek to clear their names on the basis of their personal acts and statements.

Even during the occupation period the purge was gradually relaxed, and, when the occupation ended, it was dropped completely, whereupon many of the old leaders promptly returned to their old positions of authority. The purge, however, did serve to break at least temporarily the hold of the old leadership and gave a chance for more desirable leaders to emerge. While it was at best only a temporary measure and a most imperfect one at that, it did on the whole serve a very useful purpose in ridding Japan of a large percentage of its least desirable leaders.

Another obvious approach to the broader problem of demilitarization was through the reduction of the economic base for Japanese military power. Of course, the Japanese economy could not be reduced too much without undermining our efforts at democratic reform in Japan. Moreover, Japan's loss of all her overseas possessions had seriously impaired her industrial as well as her strategic position. Our policy-makers, however, felt that the Japanese home islands still had many industrial plants which served to increase Japan's military potential without being absolutely essential to her peacetime economy. An ambitious program of industrial limitation was, therefore, undertaken. We eliminated Japan's whole aircraft industry as well as such industries as synthetic oil and synthetic rubber, which were justified only by wartime conditions. We quite stupidly stopped atomic research and banned certain small industries, such as the production of bearings, which are important for military as well as civilian uses. We went still further by putting drastic limits on major industries, such as steel, chemicals, and machine tools, which, while necessary for a peacetime economy, had in the past been devoted in large part to direct military purposes. In setting levels for

Japanese industry, we rather unreasonably chose as a yard-stick the per capita civilian consumption during the years 1930–1934, when Japanese industry was still suffering from the depression and the great shift to heavy industry had not yet taken place, and we made plans to reduce to these levels all industrial facilities of any great military significance.

This approach to the problem of Japan's future military and economic potential determined the American attitude toward the more controversial problem of reparations, which was closely related to it. It was realized that the tremendous costs of modern war and the desperate economic plight of a bomb-battered and pared-down Japan made it entirely unrealistic to hope for enough reparations from Japan to meet any appreciable portion of Allied war costs or even to compensate for any significant part of the direct war damages suffered by Allied nations. Obviously it was more sensible to let measures designed to prevent a repetion of the war take precedence over entirely useless attempts to make Japan pay for the one just concluded. Thus, reparations proposals were formulated not so much in terms of what the Allied nations might wish to get from Japan as in terms of what should be taken away from Japan as part of the demilitarization program. Specifically, the problem was to determine which industrial plants should be removed and then to decide upon a basis for dividing these between the victor nations.

Few actual transfers of equipment, however, resulted from these proposals. The plants to be removed from Japan were primarily in the field of heavy industry and, therefore, for the most part could be transported from Japan and installed abroad only at prohibitive costs. Furthermore, the countries which were most eager to receive these plants were ill prepared to set them up and operate them successfully, especially under the conditions of economic and political disruption which prevailed in most countries of the Far East at the end of the war. Worst of all, no agreement could be reached among the Allied powers as to a fair division of Japanese reparations payments, the chief bone of contention having been whether the Soviet Union had already taken most of her share when at the end of the war she removed huge quantities of industrial equipment from Manchuria at China's expense under the guise of "war booty." In 1946 the Far Eastern Commission did agree upon an interim removals program, under which some 1100 plants were at one time marked for reparations, and the United States unilaterally authorized the removal of up to 30 per cent of the facilities set aside for this purpose, half to go to China and the remainder to the Philippines and the British and Dutch possessions in the Far East. The United States, however, announced on May 12, 1949, that she would make no further reparations removals of this sort, and consequently this whole aspect of the reparations program came to a virtual end at that time.

The change in the American attitude toward reparations removals of industrial facilities resulted from a reappraisal of the situation. For one thing, the major military powers since the end of the war had been busily producing new weapons which made Japan's wartime armaments seem puny by comparison. It was realized that Japan, unlike Germany, did not have the natural resources to permit her ever again to become an independent military power of major proportions. Experience had also shown that the value of the transfer of old and sometimes obsolescent Japanese industrial facilities to other Far Eastern nations was negligible. Moreover, it had become clear since the end of the war that the problem in Japan was rather whether she could live at all than whether she could wage aggressive war again. Her industrial plant had deteriorated so greatly and her economic plight had become so desperate that few factories, except those devoted specifically to munitions, could be considered to be in excess of her barest needs. Attaining even the production levels of the depression years of 1930–1934 now seemed difficult enough and achieving adequate living standards for Japan's eighty million people well nigh impossible. Naturally there was no thought at that time of permitting Japan to reëstablish strictly military industries, but the emphasis inevitably swung from the elimination of supposedly excess factory power to an attempt to stimulate Japanese industrial production to levels which would afford a minimum subsistence for the Japanese people.

Although thought was given at various times to exacting reparations from current industrial production in Japan, this course was never adopted under the occupation. One reason was the fear that this would recreate Japanese economic hegemony over the rest of the Far East by encouraging Japan's neighbors to depend too much upon her for their manufactured goods. Another reason was the inability of the Japanese economy at that time to pay even for necessary food imports to Japan, much less for a reparations program over and above such import needs. There was no justification for a reparations program from current production so long as the cost eventually would be borne by the American tax payer — and that certainly was the situation in Japan under the occupation. If Japan's neighbors needed the sort of help they could get from Japanese reparations payments from current production, it seemed better to finance such aid directly from the United States rather than indirectly from us through Japanese reparations.

Although reparations payments from Japan herself amounted to little under the occupation, some of the nations she despoiled did receive rich Japanese assets nonetheless. It was agreed, of course, that looted property should be returned to the nation from which it was taken, but, far more important, all Japanese assets located in Allied countries or liberated areas became the property of the country in which they were found. Thus, the Koreans and Chinese received vast capital investments built up over the decades by the Japanese government and private investors in Korea, Formosa, Manchuria, and China proper. The Soviet Union also acquired rich repayment for her brief war effort in the form of Japanese assets in Southern Sakhalin and the Kuriles as well as the industrial "war booty" she removed from Manchuria.

As we have seen, much was done to demilitarize Japan physically, but this, it was feared, might mean little in the long run unless the Japanese abandoned their militaristic penchant of prewar days. The problem was basically one of re-education and was therefore closely associated with our whole long-range reform program. One very specific step, however, was taken which, it was felt, would have considerable bearing on future Japanese attitudes toward war. This was the re-nunciation "forever" of war and "the right of belligerency" and the corollary promise never to maintain "land, sea, and air forces, as well as other war potential," which were made Article Nine of the new Japanese Constitution.

Naturally much skeptical comment has been directed at this portion of the Constitution. At this stage in history, renunciation of war "forever" is clearly nothing more than a pious hope. At the same time, the inclusion of this article in the Constitution struck a responsive note in the hearts of the war-weary Japanese and contributed to the strongly pacifistic sentiments that have swept Japan ever since the war. There was also a certain amount of sheer histrionics in the renunciation of war that caught the Japanese imagination. The loser in war had become the leader in peace. The Japanese, anxious for admiration, had found a new and wholly laudable way of distinguishing themselves. If permanent peace should be achieved, then Japan would be in the forefront of the nations as the first to renounce war unequivocally.

The fact remains, however, that war cannot be exorcised simply by constitutional provisions. Many factors over which the Japanese have little control will unquestionably be far more decisive than this idealistic statement in determining whether or not Japan will ever again resort to war. The ban on armed forces has already been turned by sheer casuistry into an open fraud. The government gets around the Constitution simply by classifying its soldiers, sailors, and airmen as "self-defense forces." There is naturally strong sentiment in Japan for the elimination of the whole of Article Nine in order to bring the Constitution in line with the defense situation in Japan and military realities in the outside world.

The American role in the Japanese renunciation of war has been close to ludicrous. It was one of General MacArthur's most cherished reform measures, but within a few years the United States, faced with a precarious military balance of power in the world, was encouraging the Japanese to rearm in order to relieve the United States of as much of the defense burden in Japan as possible. Many American military men even went further and dreamed of the day when Japan would be our full military partner in holding communism in check in the Far East.

Attitudes toward the problem of Japanese demilitarization have certainly changed greatly in both the United States and Japan since the early postwar years, but Japan still remains a largely defenseless nation. The thoroughness of our disarmament measures at the end of the war meant that rearmament had to start from scratch, while the weakness of the Japanese economy and still more the strong pacifistic sentiments of a large portion of the population have limited rearmament to a snail's pace. The industrial base for rearmament has been largely restored, and the disciplined Japanese people remain a great potential reservoir for first-class fighting men, but the total number of men under arms in Japan today is around 200,000. While the Japanese ground forces have taken over from the United States full responsibility for local ground defense, the Japanese air and naval units remain relatively small, leaving on American shoulders a large part of the responsibility for the defense of Japan from the air and sea. In other words, Japan still lacks adequate military strength for its own defense, much less for exercising military influence abroad.

3. POLITICAL REFORMS

The democratization of Japan was as slow and amorphous a process as demilitarization was rapid and clear-cut. Laws could be changed with ease and political institutions modified, but such acts could not make the Japanese people democratic. They merely set up the rules whereby they could conduct their affairs in a democratic way, if and when they developed democratic attitudes and acquired democratic habits. The latter will require not years but decades. The occupation was a crucial period in which we attempted through careful legal revision, education, and even sweeping social revolution to tip the scales in favor of democracy in Japan. The real test, however, can only come over the decades, when the Japanese see whether or not they can or wish to run their own affairs, in good times and in bad, according to basically democratic procedures.

The first task for the occupation authorities was to revise the formal Japanese political and legal structure, modifying or eliminating every law and institution that stood in the way of democratic development and making new rules which would foster democratic habits. Much of the demilitarization program was also an integral part of the attempt to democratize Japan. When we destroyed the army and navy, we at the same time were eliminating powerful institutions which not only had stood in the way of the development of democratic attitudes but had also played a large role in prewar Japan in undermining parliamentary power and nullifying earlier democratic gains. The purge program was carried out as much to clear the decks for the development of a new democratic leadership as to rid Japan of its old militaristic leaders. In outlawing large numbers of undesirable organizations we sought to cut out one of the most noxious sources of anti-democratic infection in Japanese society — the ultra-nationalistic and so-called "secret" societies, which through mystical dogmas and terroristic tactics had helped to stifle free speech and independent thought in Japan. Somewhat similar acts were dissolution early in the occupation of the "special police," who had been in charge of "thought control," and the abrogation of all laws which limited freedom of thought or expression. These all were primarily negative acts. Our positive efforts to substitute more democratic political institutions for the old, centered around the reform of the Constitution itself.

General MacArthur wisely decided to achieve constitutional reform through the procedures established in the original Meiji Constitution, which required the initiation of amendments by Imperial Ordinance and subsequent Diet approval. With prodding by the occupation authorities, the Japanese government tackled the problem in the autumn of 1945, but its first efforts at revision obviously fell short of what was desired, and direct suggestion if not dictation by the occupation authorities accounted for a large part of the draft Constitution. This was finally announced to the public at the "command" of the Emperor and with the "full approval" of General MacArthur on March 6, 1946, and was adopted with only minor modifications and finally went into effect on May 3, 1947. We may never know exactly which portions of this document originated with the Japanese independently, which were the result of American suggestion or insistence, and which may have been simply drafted by the occupation authorities themselves. To the extent that dictation was involved, the new governmental system cannot be said to have "been established in accordance with the freely expressed will of the Japanese people," as was promised in the Potsdam Proclamation. Significantly enough, the charge of foreign origin has been repeatedly leveled against the Constitution in recent years by those who wished to see it changed.

On the other hand, it is doubtful that the Japanese government early in 1946 was itself representative of the will of the Japanese people. Perhaps in a period of rapidly changing ideas and attitudes, such as the first postwar years inevitably were, no Japanese group could have been sufficiently representative of the popular will, as it was developing, to draw up a Constitution which would fit the Japanese people a few years later, after the effect of our other reforms and our educational program had been felt. In any case, the new Constitution was one of our major reform measures, and it was welcomed and supported by a large proportion of the Japanese, even though, strictly speaking, they had not been entirely free to shape it as they desired. "The freely expressed will of the Japanese people" is still to be seen. The real test of the new Constitution will be its ability over the years to meet the needs of the Japanese people.

The most revolutionary doctrine in the new Constitution is that sovereignty lies with the people and not with the Emperor. In phrases reminiscent of the American Constitution and other famous documents of our own political heritage, it commences with the statement: "We, the Japanese people . . . do proclaim that sovereign power resides with the people. . . . Government is a sacred trust of the people, the authority for which is derived from the people, the powers of which are exercised by the representatives of the people, and the benefits of which are enjoyed by the people. This is a universal principle of mankind."

No less than thirty-one articles, guaranteeing the rights of the people in an expanded and detailed "Bill of Rights," further emphasize the democratic orientation of the new Constitution. There are blanket guarantees, such as, "The people shall not be prevented from enjoying any of the fundamental human rights," and, "Their right to life, liberty, and the pursuit of happiness shall . . . be the supreme consideration in legislation and in other governmental affairs." Many more specific rights are also expressly detailed — equality under the law, which has entailed the scrapping of the whole peerage, the people's "inalienable right to choose their public officials and to dismiss them," "the right to own or to hold property," "freedom of thought and conscience," "freedom of religion," "freedom of assembly," "academic freedom," freedom of the individual "to choose and change his residence and to choose his occupation," and even the equal rights of men and women in marriage, which "shall be based only on the mutual consent of both sexes" and "shall be maintained through mutual cooperation with the equal rights of husband and wife as a basis." There are, of course, all the legal and judicial guarantees we are familiar with in our own country, and in addition there are certain newer rights which our founding fathers did not think of — "the right to maintain the minimum standards of wholesome and cultured living," "the right to receive an equal education," "the right and the obligation to work," and "the right of workers to organize and to bargain and act collectively."

A more important practical innovation in the new Constitution than the changed locus of sovereignty is the clear shift of power from the executive organs, formerly under the Emperor, to the Diet, elected by the people. The new Constitution expressly calls the Diet "the highest organ of state power" and "the sole law-making organ of the State." The Diet consists as before of two houses, but both are now entirely elective and the electorate for both is unlimited by status, income, or sex. The House of Representatives, which is the new name in English for the old Lower House, is elected for a four-year term, and the House of Councillors, which has superseded the old House of Peers, is elected for a six-year term. According to supplementary legislation, the House of Representatives consists of 466 members elected from 117 multiple member electoral districts, and the House of Councillors of 250 members, 100 elected by the nation at large and the remainder from the 46 prefectures into which Japan is divided. The House of Councillors is inferior in legislative powers to the House of Representatives, since bills which it opposes or upon which it fails to act become law when passed a second time by the House of Representatives.

The Premier and his Cabinet, in keeping with British parliamentary usage and Japan's own abortive parliamentary experience three decades ago, are merely the executive organs of the Diet. The Premier is chosen by the Diet from among its own members, and the majority of his Cabinet members must also be from the Diet. As in Great Britain, the Premier and his Cabinet are fully responsible to the Diet, though he can, if he wishes, dissolve the House of Representatives and thus force a new election. Through the Premier and his Cabinet, the vast central bureaucracy is thus subordinated to the Diet, which not only controls its money sources but also the men who are at its head. Naturally Diet inexperience and the old bureaucratic habit of independent leadership and supercilious contempt for the legislative branch of the government has made the actual transfer of leadership from the government bureaus to the Diet halls a more complicated and doubtful procedure than it seems on paper. However, a new civil service code has helped to adapt the bureaucracy to its now subordinate role, and the Constitution has at least established the legal framework for a full parliamentary form of government.

The new Constitution shifts from the British to the American system in setting up the judiciary. While under the old order the executive exercised broad judicial powers and the whole court system was little more than an appendage of the Ministry of Justice, the new Constitution creates an independent judiciary headed by a Supreme Court, which "is vested with the rule-making power" for the whole judicial system and "is the court of last resort with powers to determine the constitutionality of any law, order, regulation or official act." The judges of inferior courts are "appointed by the Cabinet from a list of persons nominated by the Supreme Court." The members of the latter are chosen by the Cabinet, but their appointments "must be reviewed by the people at the first general election of members of the House of Representatives following their appointment" and subsequently at ten-year intervals.

A truly independent judiciary and a strengthened legislature, thus, have deprived the executive of its unchallenged supremacy at the national level, and determined efforts were also made to lessen the actual powers of the central bureaucracy over the people and to strengthen popular support for democracy by increasing local self-government. This was attempted through three principal measures. The first was based on the Constitutional provision that "chief executive officers of all local public entities . . . shall be elected by direct popular vote within their several communities." Prefectural governors thus were made elective officials instead of appointees of the infamous Home Ministry, and the direct control of Tokyo over the local governments was cut at this vital link.

The second measure was to eliminate the compulsory neighborhood associations, which had passed on central government orders directly to the people, and to break up the centrally controlled police force, which had once been the effective tool of the Home Ministry, not only for maintaining public order but often enough for controlling elections and for molding the people to the will of the government. The Home Ministry itself was abolished, and the police force divided between the cities, towns, and villages, except for a residual force of 30,000 men, who were placed under the operational control of the prefectural governors to police sparsely populated rural areas. The atomization of the police force was so complete that police efficiency was drastically reduced and the central government for a while lacked adequate forces to deal with any major domestic emergency. For these reasons, a gradual return to a more integrated police system was inevitable, once the first ardor of the American reformers had cooled.

The third measure was the allocation of far broader legislative powers to the elected assemblies of the prefectural and municipal governments. Before the war such assemblies had only negligible powers, could be dissolved by the higher authorities who were themselves nonelective officials, and could have the laws they passed declared *ultra vires* by these authorities. Despite our efforts, however, local assemblies have not made much use of their new powers since the war. The Japanese, unfamiliar with the concept of broad local self-government, have shown little interest in the increased powers of their local assemblies and have continued to look to Tokyo for leadership even in matters on which local bodies are now empowered to take independent action.

At first, the most controversial aspect of the new Constitution, both in Japan and abroad, was the place it accorded the Emperor. Following the precedent of the document it superseded, the new Constitution devotes its first several articles to the Emperor, but only to strip him of all the vast powers the Meiji Constitution had reserved for him. The latter had described the Emperor as "sacred and inviolable" and "the head of the Empire . . . invested with sovereign power" and had specified among numerous other powers that he "gives sanction to laws," "issues . . . Ordinances," "determines the organization of the different branches of the administration," and "has the supreme command of the Army and Navy." In sharp contrast, the new Constitution in its very first article rules, "The Emperor shall be the symbol of the State and of the unity of the people, deriving his position from the will of the people with whom resides sovereign power." Two further articles make clear that he has no powers whatsoever: "The advice and approval of the Cabinet shall be required for all acts of the Emperor in matters of state," and he "shall not have powers related to government."

Actually these three statements describe with considerable accuracy the Emperor's real position even before the war. For almost a thousand years no Japanese Emperor has actually ruled. Even the Meiji Emperor never exercised the powers assigned him in the Meiji Constitution, and his feeble-minded son, the Taisho Emperor (1912–1926), obviously could take no part in government decisions. The latter's son, the present incumbent, has conducted himself throughout in the spirit of the contemporary British monarchy. A painfully shy and nervous man, he has been far happier in his self-chosen role of naturalist than in his inherited role of Emperor. He never showed any enthusiasm for the extravagant nationalism and chauvinism which characterized the first two decades of his reign, and, except for occasional statements to his leading officials that he preferred peaceful policies to war, his only known effort to influence government decisions was his courageous stand in favor of immediate surrender, which made possible the ending of the war. Thus, the revision of the Emperor's position in the new Constitution, while theoretically drastic, was in fact in general conformity with the present Emperor's own preferences and with accepted Japanese practice over the past several decades.

Many conservative Japanese, however, were more disturbed about this theoretical change than they were about any of the tremendous shifts in actual political power in post-war Japan. In fact, the purely theoretical sovereignty of the Japanese Emperor loomed so large in official Japanese thinking at the end of the war that the Japanese authorities, in first announcing acceptance of the terms of the Potsdam Proclamation on August 10, 1945, singled it out as the one point on which they wished clarification, stating that is was their "understanding that the said declaration does not comprise any demand which prejudices the prerogatives of His Majesty as a Sovereign Ruler." The somewhat equivocal American reply the next day was that "From the moment of surrender the authority of the Emperor and the Japanese Government to rule the state shall be subject to the Supreme Commander of the Allied powers" and that the Emperor would have to ensure the actual surrender of his government and armed forces. The moral of this little side play is that, even when no practical issue was at stake, the Japanese placed tremendous emphasis on the theory of Imperial rule. It indicates, perhaps, the importance to the Japanese of the Emperor as the personification of national unity in an age of division and conflict and also shows how tenaciously they have clung to this one fixed point of unchanging hierarchic order in a time of rapid change.

In the West and particularly in the United States much criticism was directed for a while at the retention of the Emperor in any capacity, and many advocated his trial as a war criminal. In part this attitude was based on a misunderstanding of the Emperor's actual role in prewar Japan. In part it was the result of a justifiable fear that even an Emperor reduced both in theory and in practice to the status of a mere symbol would still provide the Japanese with a rallying point for the type of mystical and jingoistic nationalism which centered around him before the war and that irrational and terroristic acts, such as were committed in his name in the past, could as easily be performed in behalf of an admittedly figurehead Emperor as for one who was a figurehead only in reality. In view of the key role of the Imperial institution in the creation of a militaristic and totalitarian Japan before the war, the innocuous and powerless Emperor conceivably was still a potentially dangerous symbol in postwar Japan.

The chief answer to this argument was that, in the Potsdam Proclamation and our reply on August 11 to the Japanese inquiry regarding the sovereignty of the Emperor, we clearly implied that we would permit the Japanese to continue the Imperial institution in some form, if that was what they wished. The Japanese probably would not have surrendered otherwise, and in a sense we made a clear bargain with them — immediate surrender in return for a promise not to insist that the Japanese throne be abolished entirely, in other words, American lives for an emasculated monarchy.

It can also be argued that, regardless of this bargain, we did well not to insist that the Japanese give up their Emperor. Polls have consistently shown that over 90 per cent of the people have continued to support the Imperial institution ever since the end of the war. With our stated policy "to use the existing form of Government in Japan, not to support it," we left the door open for a republican revolution, but of course nothing of the sort happened. Among the political parties, only the Communists ever espoused abolition of the monarchy, and this stand proved to be so unpopular that even they were forced to abandon it as an immediate issue. Insistence upon abolition of the throne would have won us the determined opposition of the bulk of the Japanese people. We would have been setting our course directly into the teeth of the strong emotional head winds of loyalty to the Emperor. Obviously we were wiser to forge ahead by tacking, aided rather than blown backwards by these winds.

The recent history of Japan also shows that the danger of the Imperial institution does not lie in the acts of the Emperor but in the attitude of his subjects toward him, and this would not have been changed by removing the Emperor and his family by foreign dictate. In fact, the removal of the already remote and mysterious Imperial line to an even more remote exile would have made the institution, in so far as it is an attitude of mind, almost impervious to change. The concept of the "Imperial will," the myth of Imperial sacredness, the burning devotion of the average subject to the Imperial symbol, all could have survived as easily without an actual Emperor on the throne. We had far more chance of reducing these attitudes to safe proportions — of changing mystical devotion to simple affection and respect — with an Emperor on the scene toward whom the Japanese could develop new attitudes. The argument applies as well to the problem of abdication as to complete abolition of the institution. Some Japanese felt that, in accordance with Oriental concepts of personal responsibility, the present Emperor should have abdicated in favor of his son as a measure to strengthen the throne. As long as the heir apparent was a minor, however, abdication would in a sense have put the throne out of public sight and thus helped to preserve it unaltered during the crucial period of rapid change.

Actually much has been accomplished since the war in creating new attitudes toward the throne in Japan. The Emperor's denial of his own "divinity," in an Imperial Rescript on January 1, 1946, created hardly a stir in Japan, because the Japanese, lacking our concept of "divinity," never had believed him to be "divine" as we use the term. His dignified acceptance of the surrender, however, did have a profound influence on his people, as did also his unfeigned friendliness toward the American conquerors, his obvious approval of many of the reforms we undertook, and, most important, his determined though sometimes clumsy efforts at coming down from the mysterious pedestal on which he had been placed and becoming a very human and entirely nonpolitical father of his people. He unquestionably has done much to help cut down the exalted Imperial institution of Japan to the status of a modern constitutional monarchy and in the process has perhaps won more real affection from his people by his embarrassed but well-meant efforts than any Japanese Emperor has ever enjoyed.

4. EDUCATIONAL REFORMS

However spectacular the political changes we instituted in Japan, our whole reform effort was fundamentally a long-range educational program. We had to teach the Japanese people new attitudes as well as new techniques. Democracy depends as much on independence of judgment and a spirit of mature skepticism as on sound electoral procedures and broad Parliamentary experience.

Fortunately for our educational efforts, the Japanese are a literate, newspaper-reading, radio-listening people. There were ample means of bringing new information and new ideas before them. Moreover, at the end of the war they were extremely receptive to new ideas, because the completeness of their defeat had shaken the masses out of their intellectual lethargy and freed them from many of their old concepts. There was a vast intellectual ferment in Japan. Despite the economic chaos of the early postwar years, the Japanese public snatched as hungrily at reading matter as at food. The publishing industry was the one business which prospered, and thousands of intelligent Japanese eagerly presented new ideas to the equally eager millions of the reading public.

Under such circumstances we naturally had considerable initial success in our educational program. Utilizing the great facilities at our disposal for spreading information, we found it a relatively easy task to convince the vast majority of the Japanese that they were grossly misled by their prewar rulers and had been following an unsound and unjustified course in attempting to conquer their neighbors. It was easy to win from most of them lip service and a vague yearning for democracy to replace the old order which had failed so miserably. We greatly influenced their thinking in numberless specific matters and implanted ideas which are having a profound influence in shaping the Japan of the future.

At the same time our greatest single failure in Japan was perhaps our failure to exploit this situation as fully as we could have. We were held back by several factors. One was the essential conflict in motives between our desire to carry through a specific and immediate reform program and our long-term interest in fostering independence of thought on the part of the Japanese public. We inevitably tended more to preach specific concepts than to teach habits of independent thought, substituting often our own dogmas for the authoritarian tradition of prewar Japan. Another problem was that virtually all Americans in Japan, civilians and military alike, came under a strictly military chain of command and, therefore, were themselves not in a position to voice independent judgments and set an example of fearless freedom in speech. Another problem was the inevitable security mindedness of a military organization. Fearful of what an entirely free press might say, our authorities prohibited any criticism of occupation measures or of any of the allied countries, including the Soviet Union. We resorted to a system of post-publication censorship which in practice proved more limiting to free expression of opinion than a frank pre-publication censorship would have been. Determined to exclude dangerous and subversive doctrines and propaganda from Japan, we exercised rigid controls over the importation of printed matter from abroad and the translation of foreign books into Japanese. Communistic propaganda, which presumably was what the authorities wished most to keep out of Japan, poured in clandestinely, but the flow of other materials from abroad, despite an excellent program of American information libraries in major cities, was at times little more than a trickle. Because of economic conditions, until the summer of 1949 almost no Japanese were permitted or were able to go abroad to learn about the rest of the world, and nonofficial visitors to Japan were kept to a minimum. Thus, full freedom of expression was not achieved under the occupation, and Japan for long was kept to a certain extent intellectually isolated from the rest of the world at a time when the Japanese people desperately needed knowledge and ideas from abroad and freedom to develop habits of independent judgment.

One of our major objectives in the educational field was the improvement of methods for spreading knowledge, both in formal education and in other ways, in order that the Japanese people might become better prepared to exercise the independence of judgment on which democracy depends. Quite naturally, we attempted to improve the school system and the school curriculum.

The prewar Japanese educational system, based primarily on the continental European model, was made up of a six-year compulsory and coeducational elementary school, followed for boys by a five-year middle school, a three-year higher school, and a three- or four-year university. Girls usually did not go beyond a girl's higher school, which paralleled the boy's middle school, and at the middle school and higher school levels there were various specialized terminal schools for those who were going no further in their education.

The seventeen- or eighteen-year program leading to graduation from the university produced men who in their technical training were more like American postgraduate students than like our college graduates, but it was estimated at the end of the war that only about 3½ per cent of the students who graduated from the sixth year of the elementary school went beyond the eleventh grade and only half of 1 per cent went on to the university. Thus, merely a select few received a real education, and, as Japanese society was organized before the war, only these few could hope to achieve positions of prestige and importance. The middle schools, which were a necessary step in the education of a would-be university candidate, accommodated only 6 per cent of the elementary school graduates, and less than a tenth of these found their way into the higher schools which prepared students for the university. The vast majority of Japanese children were forced to leave the main educational ladder which led to the all-important university at the end of the sixth grade or else at the end of the eleventh. They could read and write and had some practical training, but they could not become leaders, nor did they usually have enough education to become intelligent citizens.

We attempted to change this situation in several ways. First of all we extended the period of compulsory education to nine years. Since over nine-tenths of Japanese children were already taking some form of schooling beyond the sixth grade and an extension of the period of compulsory education to eight years had already been adopted by the Japanese government, though not enforced because of the war, this part of our program was fully successful.

Another measure was to equalize schools at all levels so that children would not be prevented from going on with their education simply because they had been forced to enter a school which did not qualify its graduates for the next educational level. In the process we scrapped the old school system above the elementary level, creating in its place a three-year compulsory junior high school, a three-year senior high school, and a four-year-college — in other words the American educational system. Japanese educators, however, were for the most part entirely unfamiliar with the American system, and considerable confusion inevitably resulted. The changeover to the new system forced middle schools to add a year to cover the senior high school level and higher schools to add two years to come up to the four-year college level. Lacking adequate facilities, staff, and funds, most schools accomplished this only by lowering standards.

In making schools at each level more uniform, we were forced to broaden their curriculums so that a single type of school could prepare students for the next educational level and at the same time serve as a suitable terminal training for those who went no further. The advantages of such a system for training democratic citizens and ensuring a maximum opportunity for the best potential leadership to rise to the top are offset somewhat in a poor country like Japan by the necessity of supporting a greatly expanded educational program. Before the war education was efficiently but ruthlessly limited to the barest minimum needed to teach the technical skills required by each individual in performing his specific function in society. In the new, more generalized system, more years of schooling are required to teach the specific skills each group needs, because more time is spent in giving all groups a common education. The four-year college naturally has not proved adequate for certain types of professional training, and an extensive system of postgraduate education is gradually developing to meet this need. Whether Japan is rich enough to support this extended system is still to be seen.

One of our biggest educational tasks was to change the teaching methods and materials which had made the Japanese school system such an effective tool for nationalistic propaganda and for inculcating in the people blind obedience to their leaders. We, of course, removed from all schools the small shrines which housed pictures of the Emperor and Empress and stopped enforced visits by school children to Shinto Shrines. We eliminated certain courses, such as the standard courses on "morals" or "ethics," which were in part used for nationalistic indoctrination, substituting social studies in their place. We also had all the textbooks rewritten or at least revised in order to weed out the false propaganda and nationalistic indoctrination which saturated their pages. Writing new textbooks on controversial subjects, however, proved no easy task. Any treatment of history was sure to hurt the national feelings of one Allied people or another, and anything that touched on religion or politics was even more delicate. Thus, in a few instances we failed for some time to produce any textbook at all.

We also introduced new teaching methods in an effort to broaden education beyond the confines of pure memory work and to develop independent inquiry and thought on the part of the student. Even in the elementary grades children were taught to carry out study projects of their own, and the Japanese student for the first time began to ask embarrassing questions of his teachers. Naturally, the children have enjoyed these changes more than their teachers, who, trained in the old system, are baffled and often dismayed by the new approach.

One of the dangers of the old school system was its extreme centralization under the Ministry of Education, which, as we have seen, prescribed for private as well as public schools what courses should be taught in each grade and which textbooks were to be used. We tried to break down this excessive central control by placing a large part of the responsibility for local schools in the hands of municipal school boards, inaugurating the new system with school board elections in the autumn of 1948. Elective school boards, however, were abandoned in 1956 in favor of appointive groups. Moreover, the Japanese educational system has become in some ways more thoroughly dominated by the government today than it was before the war. The many private secondary schools and universities which form an important part of Japan's educational facilities are all in serious economic straits because of the collapse of the moneyed classes which once supported them. In

Article 89 of the new Constitution it is stated that no public funds can be used for any private charitable, educational, or religious institution. This provision was aimed at eliminating state support for the Shinto Shrines, which have been thrown back on whatever popular support they can find. Unfortunately, however, it also prevents the government from giving aid to private educational institutions, and these today are even less able than before the war to offer the healthy competition to government institutions which the Japanese educational system needs.

Because of the unique difficulty of the Japanese writing system, much thought was given by the occupation authorities, and by the Japanese as well, to the problem of writing reform. So much of the Japanese student's time and effort goes into merely learning to read and write that he has less time than his Occidental counterpart for his other studies. Tests also show that many children soon after leaving school lose their ability to read or write except at the most elementary level. There has been much talk of "language reform," but, except for the elimination of certain archaic grammatical forms in newspapers and official documents, there was never any thought of tackling the impossible and pointless task of "reforming" the Japanese language, but only of simplifying the writing system, which is a gigantic task in itself.

The most drastic proposal, which was supported by certain occupation authorities, was to abandon the use of Chinese characters and the native phonetic syllabaries in favor of the use of the Latin alphabet, known in Japan as Romaji or "the Roman letters." This would probably be in the long run the best solution, because spoken Japanese can be written perfectly with only seventeen letters and one or two diacritical marks, and in this form could be mastered by the Japanese child in as many months as it now takes years. There was strong opposition to this proposal, however, because of Japanese aesthetic attachment to the Chinese characters and because it would mean something of a cultural break with the past and would necessitate an extensive modification of the technical vocabulary, which is full of homophones that are indistinguishable in the Latin alphabet. Only half-hearted attempts have been made since the war to utilize Romaji in place of the traditional writing system. Instead, most postwar writing reform has followed earlier precedents in further simplifying the existing system. Spellings in the *kana* syllabaries were made strictly phonetic; variant readings for characters were reduced in number; standard abbreviations were substituted for some of the more complicated characters; and, most important, the number of characters to be used in newspapers and official documents was limited to 1850 and the number to be taught in the nine years of compulsory education to a mere 1300 — a large dose for the child to absorb, but considerably less than previous generations attempted to swallow and digest in the same number of years.

5. SOCIAL REFORMS

Our attempt to democratize Japan did not stop with political and educational measures but also entered the more fundamental and also more controversial field of social reform. We do not usually think of ourselves today as being social revolutionaries, nor does this term figure among the epithets hurled so freely at our heads by our enemies. And yet social revolution formed an integral and essential part of our reform program in Japan. There was none of the violence, the brutal liquidation of individuals, which has accompanied so many social and political revolutions in recent years. But we made fundamental shifts in the economic and political balance of power among the various social groupings in Japan.

It comes as something of a shock to find ourselves in the role of social revolutionaries. We have become so complacently accustomed to our own ideals that they seem anything but revolutionary. We have taken a defensive attitude toward the charge of being nineteenth-century liberals but twentieth-century reactionaries. And yet when one compares the impact of American ideals on Japan with that of Communist ideals on China, there can be no doubt that in an Asian setting ours are the more revolutionary. The Communist concept of a paternalistic dictatorship is nothing new to Asia. The Chinese Communists' attempt to substitute an individual ethic for a family ethic still falls far short of what has already been accomplished in Japan. Their goals of education for the people and industrialization for the nation represent the starting point of our reforms for Japan. Our attitude toward human rights both in individual and collective terms and our righting of the balance of economic and political power in Japan go far beyond anything the Chinese Communists can at present attempt or perhaps even conceive. American democratic concepts as they have continued to grow through the decades represent an ideal to Asia which makes Communist theories seem old-fashioned and unimaginative by comparison.

Our social revolution reached down to the family itself and the relations between the sexes and age groups. Starting with the concept of the individual right to equality, the framers of the Constitution adopted the fundamental equality of men and women as a basic premise. Women were given the franchise and legal equality. Educational opportunities for men and women were equalized. And the women of Japan responded eagerly to their new rights. Broadened economic opportunities in an industrialized society and the urgent wartime demand for women workers in business and industry had given Japanese women some of the economic independence which had helped produce legal equality in the West. Since the war, Japanese women have participated in elections in larger numbers than their menfolk, and they have elected many more of their sex to elective bodies, from municipal school boards to the national Diet, than have ever been elected to comparable bodies in the United States. Many deeply ingrained habits of conduct must be changed before Japanese women achieve full social equality with men, but some of these habits are visibly changing. Women more frequently walk abreast of their husbands, and the latter more frequently carry their share of babies and bundles. There is a long road ahead of them, but the women of Japan, with the laws now giving them an equal chance, seem to be determined to achieve full equality and take their rightful part in society and politics.

Increasing individual independence and responsibility also meant giving greater freedom to the younger age groups and therefore minimizing family controls. The legal power of family heads over adult members of the family was eliminated. The schools now seek to develop greater intellectual independence on the part of the child, so that the young adult can take his place in a democratic society as an independent and responsible individual. It is more a matter of attitudes and habits than of law. How far it has succeeded is a matter of conjecture, but there is behind this attempted reform a long history of incipient revolt by Japanese youth against the tyranny of age and family, and there are signs of fundamental change today. From all parts of the country, both urban and rural, come reports of a rapid shift in the whole concept of marriage from a family-dominated match to a matter of personal choice on the part of the two principals. Japanese society is unquestionably in rapid motion, and the most apparent direction of this motion is toward the freeing of women and young people to become independent individuals, politically and socially the equals of their husbands and fathers.

A more important aspect of our social revolution was the attempt to readjust the balance of power between different economic and social groupings by improving the economic status and stimulating the political development of certain huge underprivileged classes, notably the peasants and urban laborers, and concomitantly reducing the inordinate economic and political power of certain other smaller groups, particularly the great industrialists and the rural landowners. Aiding the underprivileged was, of course, in full accord with our own ideals, but the corollary measure of depriving certain groups of their legally acquired wealth without due compensation did not square with democratic concepts. It did not even square with the new Constitution, but it has been tacitly assumed in Japan that measures adopted at the insistence of the occupation authorities were legalized by the terms of the surrender and therefore did not have to be subjected to the normal test of Constitutionality.

We see in this situation a slight tinge of the dangerous theory that the ends justify the means, which has turned Russian communism into such a travesty of Marxist ideals. On the other hand, there was the valid argument that in Japan the privileged were so rich and powerful and the underprivileged so poor and helpless that more violent measures were called for than we would accept in our own country. There was also the thoroughly justified feeling that after the end of the occupation a swing of the pendulum could be expected, and therefore we should be overly drastic in these reforms while we had the opportunity. These seem to be the reasons why we carried through a program of peaceful social revolution in Japan rather than one simply of evolutionary social reform.

A major problem which the occupation faced was the concentration of a large percentage of Japan's industrial and commercial wealth and power in the hands of a few very rich families and their loyal business executives. It is doubtful that the *zaibatsu* system itself was to be blamed as the chief reason for Japanese imperialism and aggression. This theory was popular in the United States at the end of the war, perhaps on the somewhat Marxian premise that all evil is ultimately traceable to economic villains, but it does not bear close historical scrutiny. But the *zaibatsu* system certainly did not stand in the way of Japanese imperialism, and it unquestionably created an economic and social atmosphere uncongenial to the growth of democracy. Even in the United States undue concentration of economic power in the hands of a few is looked upon as an unhealthy situation, tending to limit the growth of economic and political freedom on the part of the average citizen. In Japan, where the concentration of wealth and power was proportionately much greater and where democracy had far weaker roots, the perpetuation of this situation would have seriously impaired the chances of democracy to survive. It was agreed that the *zaibatsu* families must be reduced in power and their great combines broken up and that, conversely, encouragement should be given to a "wide distribution of income and of the ownership of the means of production and trade."

Restrictions were placed on the financial activities of the *zaibatsu* families, the holding companies, and some 1200 of their subsidiary companies. Subsequently, purge measures forced the members of the *zaibatsu* families and the leading executives of their concerns to sever connections with business enterprises in which they had been active and also barred them from all public posts. The central holding companies were dissolved, and their securities as well as those held directly by the *zaibatsu* families were taken into custody by the government in preparation for their sale to a broader group of "more desirable" owners. The remaining assets of the *zaibatsu* families were frozen, and a heavy capital levy drastically reduced these and all other private concentrations of capital. Starting at 25 per cent for individual holdings over 100,000 yen, it ascended to 90 per cent on holdings in excess of 15,000,000 yen. With the value of the yen dropping rapidly in the early postwar years from around thirty cents to a mere fraction of a cent, this meant the reduction of even modest accumulations of money and the virtual confiscation of all fortunes. Moreover, steeply graduated income taxes and inheritance taxes have been adopted to prevent in the future the accumulation of similar concentrations of wealth. So long as these laws remain in force, it seems improbable that either the *zaibatsu* families or any other individuals or groups can again amass fortunes at all comparable to those of the *zaibatsu* in prewar days.

The dissolution of the holding companies along with the family fortunes behind them brought to an end the great Japanese combines by eliminating their central organs, and laws were passed to prevent their re-creation. Our occupation authorities, however, decided to go beyond this and to break up corporations which could be considered excessive concentrations of economic power and therefore hindrances to the development of a freely competitive economy. In other words, we embarked upon a trust-busting program comparable to but much more thoroughgoing than similar operations in the United States. But after an imposing start, the occupation authorities scaled down the program in the face of the apparent inability of the Japanese economy to recuperate even without further major surgical operations. By the summer of 1949, the list of 325 corporations originally slated for possible dissolution had been reduced to a mere 19.

The so-called *zaibatsu* program, while in general successful, encountered several difficulties. Old loyalties within the former *zaibatsu* combines sometimes continued to hold elements of these combines together in an informal association, and with the end of the occupation a more formal reconstitution of the combines commenced. It seems improbable, however, that they can ever be restored to anything like their old position of complete dominance in the Japanese economy.

Another problem was that the purge of the top business leaders and the dissolution of the combines together with the resultant uncertainty that hung over the whole business world in Japan appreciably reduced the efficiency of Japanese industrial organization. We consequently had to pay a heavy price economically for this particular reform. But this was a passing situation. The industrial deconcentration program had virtually ended by 1949, and a relaxation of purge measures and the emergence of new business leaders combined to produce effective Japanese business leadership again. Throughout 1949 Japanese industrial production mounted steadily, indicating that Japanese business had survived the shock of the reforms and was beginning to regain the vitality lost during the war and early postwar years, and, with the outbreak of the

Korean War the next year, the Japanese economy started to surge forward at an even more rapid rate.

A more touchy problem was the question of the future ownership and control of Japanese big business, because it involved the fundamental question of whether Japan would have a partially socialistic or an entirely competitive economy. For one thing, the resale of former *zaibatsu* assets to new owners did not prove an easy task. Few had capital to invest in this way, and those who did were usually black marketeers who would have made even less desirable owners than the old *zaibatsu* families. The concept that these assets might be disposed of at nominal prices to "desirable" groups was hard to apply because of the difficulty of agreeing on the "desirable" groups to be so benefited. The simplest solution would have been to permit them to remain in the hands of the state, but this, while not repugnant to most Japanese, was a solution that was distasteful to the occupation authorities and raised the specter in some eyes of a rejuvenated statism in Japan. The end result in many cases was that the stocks gravitated into the hands of the banks, which ever since have exercised an inordinate degree of control over Japanese industry.

Another problem was that, right in the midst of our efforts to deconcentrate the control of Japanese industry, we were forced to continue many of the wartime organizations for controlling prices, production, and allocations of scarce materials in the various industries. In fact we often converted these into more official bodies than they had been before. In other words, we in many instances increased rather than decreased government control over certain areas of the Japanese economy and contributed to an even more complete integration of the Japanese economy on an industry-wide basis in place of the old and more haphazard integration through the combines.

The other half of the industrial picture was our attempt to better the economic status of labor and give it a greater stake and voice in politics. This we tried to do through the traditional technique of labor unions. Laws were revised to give the trade union movement much the same legal status it has in the United States, and the Japanese urban workers responded enthusiastically. Unions had been active at two earlier periods in Japanese history — for a short while following the First World War and again after depression conditions had started to spread over Japan in 1927 — but both times workers had for the most part joined the unions only during actual strikes, and the unions, faced with severe police repression and general apathy among the workers, had not become strong, permanent organizations and eventually had withered away completely. Under the occupation, however, they enjoyed not only a mushroom growth but became accepted by labor and management alike as a recognized part of the industrial scene. Starting from almost nothing, the labor unions enrolled more than four and a half million workers in the single year of 1946 alone, and by 1950 their membership was leveling off at about seven millions.

The problems of a rapidly growing labor movement in a politically and economically disrupted Japan were manifold. The rate of growth was too fast for entirely healthy development and surrounding conditions too chaotic to permit Japanese unions to play the same valuable role they have in our more prosperous and politically more stable society. For one thing, the collapsing economy and the virtual bankruptcy of most employers created extremely unfavorable conditions for normal collective bargaining. It was all but useless for workers to attempt to keep up with the inflationary spiral through pressure on individual employers or industries, especially since government wage controls rather than private salary scales were commonly at stake. While labor unions did seek to achieve their political ends through the ballot box, throwing their weight behind Socialist and Communist candidates, this seemed to many Japanese workers a very slow and ineffectual procedure in a time of rapid political change and equally rapid deterioration of the economic situation.

The whole philosophy of trade unionism was not clear to the average union member. Most Japanese workers knew little about labor organization, and the control of many unions passed into the hands of a determined minority of Communist sympathizers, more interested in direct political action than in what we consider traditional trade union activities. Many of the early postwar strikes, some of which were carried out by the peculiarly Japanese technique of taking over a factory and operating it more productively than had the management, were actually attempts to shift policy control of an industry from the owners and managers to the workers themselves. On the national scene, labor unions often showed more interests in attaining their objectives immediately by direct pressure on the government, rather than by slower electoral processes, staging monster demonstrations in an effort to influence government policy or to force the resignation of the cabinet.

The labor movement thus quite naturally created a fundamental conflict of objectives in our own thinking. Strong trade unionism was desired to help redress the old economic and political balance. At the same time, the sometimes violent attempts of many labor unions to exert direct pressure on the government struck at the root of democratic electoral procedures. The occupation authorities, becoming ever more alarmed by Japan's economic plight, were also loath to see labor discord further diminish Japan's industrial output. Moreover, they increasingly displayed the natural distaste of a disciplined military organization for an uninhibited and somewhat obstreperous labor movement. As a result, in occupation thinking a desire to curb the labor movement began to loom larger than our earlier interest in building it up.

We already had discouraged attempts by labor unions to take the policy direction of industries away from their rightful owners. In January 1947 a much more important step was taken when a projected anti-government strike on a nationwide scale was stopped by the occupation. A still more serious situation came to a head in the spring and summer of 1949.

At occupation insistence, government agencies started to dismiss 25 per cent of their employees as an economy measure designed to eliminate unnecessary workers. Since government agencies included, in addition to postal and telegraphic communications, most of the railways and monopolies such as tobacco, huge numbers of workers were involved. The policy also went against the traditional Japanese concept that workers are not dismissed simply because there is no work for them to do. Throughout Japan financially harassed employers had felt obliged to rehire former employees after the war, often employing two or three men to do a job which no longer required the full services of one. Our economy measures, therefore, were not generally popular, and the Communist-dominated unions fought them bitterly. By summer they were resorting to sabotage of the railways, and in July the Director of the Government Railways, who was in charge of the dismissal of some 90,000 workers, was murdered under mysterious circumstances. But the Communists had overplayed their hand. Popular support for them declined, and resistance to the dismissals subsided. The occupation had won a second head-on clash with the labor movement which it had created.

Gradually the labor situation settled down, and since the termination of the occupation the labor unions have achieved a considerable degree of stability, though many of the old problems linger on. Communist domination has declined appreciably, but still remains a serious problem in many unions, particularly in one like the All Japan Teachers Union, which has a very direct influence on education in Japan. Unions are still at a disadvantage in most collective bargaining activities, simply because of the excess supply of Japanese labor. Still worse, the line between justifiable political activities and undemocratic direct action remains a harder one to maintain in Japan than in the United States, because in Japan the government employs more workers and takes a larger part in controlling all wages. Japanese labor unions seem to spend an inordinate amount of time and energy of their members on political demonstrations that have little direct bearing on the unions themselves. At the same time, traditional hostility toward the union movement lingers on in certain sectors of Japanese society. All in all, the unions face many severe tests, and their ultimate role in Japanese society should perhaps still be considered doubtful. On the other hand, the labor movement has shown extraordinary vigor since the war. Its roots, though still shallow, are vastly stronger and more numerous than ever before. It seems improbable that the industrial laboring class can again be politically and economically submerged as it was before the war, unless the whole nation is forced into a totalitarian mold.

The least controversial but from the American point of view the most surprising of our major reforms was our land reform program. Our measures were almost as sweeping as those of the Chinese Communists which originally won them the support of the peasant masses in China, but they were accomplished far more smoothly and without any violence. At the same time our objectives went far beyond those of the Chinese Communists. We were aiming not only at bettering the pitiable economic conditions of the peasant half of Japan's population but also at increasing their interest in and influence over their government. We were trying to give them at least a tiny margin of security which would free them from complete subservience to the landowners and moneylenders and create in them a desire to defend through intelligent participation in democratic procedures the rights they had won.

As we have seen, there were no feudal estates in Japan like those of Eastern Europe and few enough large landholdings, but the land reform program we sponsored encompassed every piece of agricultural property owned by absentee landlords, no matter how small, and in most parts of Japan it affected most other holdings of more than two and a half acres. Absentee landlords were forced to sell all their land to the government and in most parts of Japan all non-cultivating landlords living in the local community had to sell the land they owned above two and a half acres. The lands thus acquired were then resold to the former tenants who had operated them. Cultivating landlords were permitted to keep two and a half acres of tenant-operated land together with the area they and their families cultivated, which was presumed to be no more than about seven and a half acres. Thus, in most of Japan even farmers could not own more than about ten acres of agricultural land and other persons in rural communities no more than two and a half acres. In the less productive northern island of Hokkaido the principle was the same as elsewhere in Japan, but the acreage standards were made four times as large. Since government purchase and resale prices were based primarily on prewar monetary values, without allowances for Japan's runaway inflation, they amounted to virtual confiscation for the former owners, and the tenant farmers had no difficulty in paying for the land outright or meeting the easy credit terms arranged.

The reform was slow in getting under way, but, once started in 1948, efficient local committees elected from among the landlords, owner-cultivators, and tenant farmers rushed it through to virtual completion before the end of the year. Postwar food shortages and inflation had combined to give the rural debtor class temporary surcease from its chronic financial plight, and farm debts had for the most part been liquidated. Now, with the land reform, most tenants easily became peasant owners. The remainder, perhaps a quarter of the number of tenants before the war, had their rents reduced by law to approximately half of what they had been, with rent ceilings established at 25 per cent of the value of the crop on rice paddies and 15 per cent on dry fields. They were also granted the security of written contracts, and credit was made available to them and other peasants on reasonable terms. Thus, the tenancy problem, which was for long one of the most difficult and pressing of the many problems facing Japan, was reduced almost to the vanishing point.

Our land reform was, to say the least, drastic, but it has met only with praise. Actually it was based on plans long advocated by certain Japanese and thus from the start had the understanding and support of most people in Japan. The sincerest compliment it received was the effort on the part of Communist politicians in Japan to give the impression that the Communist party was responsible for it.

At the same time, the land reform created some new problems. The former owners did not receive "just compensation" for their losses, and consequently the reform could not clear the Constitutional hurdle but could only pass through the loophole created by the terms of surrender. The land reform for a while also caused some social dislocation by reducing to the common level a large part of the less impoverished rural families, and it produced certain economic dislocations by breaking up the larger holdings which once served as units for economic coöperation. A further development of rural coöperatives, however, seems already to have compensated for these economic losses.

The land reform was an unquestioned success, and despite many gloomy predictions, there seems little chance of its being undone to any large extent. And yet it did not touch Japan's real agricultural problem. The farms cannot produce enough food to feed the nation; they remain too small to give a decent living even to the owner-farmer; and there are still too many people who lack even such tiny farms. There is also no clear proof that the land reform has developed in the peasant masses the intelligent interest in politics and their own rights on which a healthy democracy depends. Like so many of the basic goals of our reform program, this was a hope, a calculated effort, but not necessarily an accomplished fact. Our reforms, by and large, were daringly conceived and forcefully executed. But Japan's problems remain grave and her future far from certain.

12. The Philosophy of the Occupation

It is far easier to catalogue the successes and failures of the many specific reform measures of the occupation than to estimate the success or failure or our over-all effort to turn Japan into a stable and peaceful democratic nation. Element by element what happened *in* Japan may be fairly clear, but the total picture of what has been happening *to* Japan is by no means so evident. The situation is dynamic. Each factor, influenced by all the other factors and exerting in return an influence on each of them, is constantly changing. It is a pattern of motion in which old and new are still in the process of readjustment to one another. Any interpretation of the picture as a whole depends upon one's philosophy of acculturation or of social change. A philosophy of this sort inevitably underlay all that we attempted to do in our occupation of Japan, but it was never itself discussed or even mentioned. It never reached the surface, though its subsurface configurations could usually be detected in the sharply contrasting conclusions and interpretations which different observers have drawn from the same body of facts concerning Japan.

Perhaps the commonest concept of our undertaking in Japan is the feeling that everything about pre-surrender Japan was bad and that the occupation authorities had the task of wiping the slate clean and constructing a new society virtually from scratch. This attitude has given rise to two very different estimates of the success of the occupation, one strongly pessimistic and the other as strongly optimistic.

The pessimistic interpretation lies behind much of the severest criticism of our occupation efforts, especially criticism by those of leftist sympathies. Any retention of native customs and institutions appeared to these critics to be a highly dangerous compromise with the evil past. The reform of Japan, they felt, must be thoroughgoing — even ruthless, if necessary. The diabolical cunning and unmatched virulence of the evil institutions of prewar Japan made it necessary to achieve virtual perfection in the new system, for anything less than perfection would leave the door open for the return of the old and would thus spell ultimate disaster. It seemed to those who held these opinions that the occupation authorities made fatal blunders time after time, and there was much in the history of postwar Japan which they viewed with the greatest alarm.

Only a slight twist of this same philosophy has produced a completely optimistic view of postwar Japan and its future. Starting with the same assumption that everything in prewar Japan was bad and that the occupation authorities were creating an entirely new Japan, the optimists marveled at the extent of our success in reforming Japan in so short a period. They gave us all the credit for the successful adoption of democratic procedures since the war, forgetting completely the half century of electoral and parliamentary experience the Japanese had had before the war and the influence of a considerable body of strong supporters of democracy within Japan. They assumed that we were entirely responsible for the labor movement in postwar Japan, ignoring the fact that we could have done little without the aid of a corps of experienced and devoted labor leaders who had been active in Japan for several decades. The rapid change in the status of women they attributed solely to American words of wisdom, rather than to the slow improvement of the economic and educational opportunities for women in Japan over the better part of a century. If so much could have been accomplished so quickly, they felt, there was no reason to entertain doubts about the ultimate success of our efforts to democratize Japan. A miracle had been accomplished in changing black into white, and they were willing to accept credit where credit, they felt, was due.

A reaction to this absurdly exaggerated concept of the accomplishments of the occupation slowly grew, especially among the more sophisticated of the observers of postwar Japan. This took the form of a return to the Kipling philosophy of "East is East and West is West." Japan is and always will be essentially Japanese, they held, and reform measures imposed from without are therefore essentially meaningless. The whole occupation effort to reform Japan was sheer folly. No fundamental change was to be expected, nor was it even possible. Americans, they felt, should stop dreaming and return to a common sense acceptance of Japan as she is.

This philosophy breaks down into at least three variants, all united by the central theme that Japan cannot or at least need not be changed. One might be called the anthropological approach in which the terms "good" and "bad" are studiously avoided and hence the concept of "reform" itself is taboo. The second is the military approach in which it is argued that the only thing good or bad about Japan is whether or not she is our friend or enemy and that our major objective should be to get the Japanese back on their feet and effective in the world struggle as our allies. The third and most popular variant is that of many businessmen and old Japan hands. While admitting that some things may have been bad in prewar Japan, they also found much that was good, and, in any case, they felt that not much could be done about it, good or bad. Consequently, they viewed with skepticism all of our reform measures and with unconcealed anxiety and irritation those reforms which they felt were designed to reform things that did not need reforming and therefore created chaos instead.

There is, of course, something to be said for each of these various points of view, and yet the basic concept that everything traditionally Japanese was evil is patently absurd, the idea that we could remake an entirely bad Japan within a few years is ridiculously naive, and the proposition that all societies are immutable entities is historical nonsense. History shows us that societies do change, sometimes radically, and that change can come as a result of external influence as well as from internal evolution. Nowhere is this clearer than in Japan itself during the past century. After we had forced the doors of Japan open in 1854, she could not be the same country that she had been before. Similarly, a thoroughly defeated Japan could not be the same country today as before the war, even if the occupation authorities had not made such a determined effort to effect major changes.

At the same time we should not overestimate the amount of change or the type of change that can be accomplished through external pressure in a few years' time. Any idea that we started from scratch to make an entirely new Japan is obviously absurd. In terms of the total culture, the amount of change was not likely to be great, and specific changes, if they were to last, had to be in general conformity with the over-all pattern of the society as it was slowly evolving. The American occupation obviously could not make of Japan a new nation or a little United States. All we could do was to make some specific readjustments which, while leaving many of the basic elements little changed, would contribute to the creation of some fundamentally new patterns in Japanese society. In other words, we could forcefully tip the scales a bit, hoping that while we were doing so a new balance would be struck which would maintain itself after our hand had been removed. In so far as our efforts were in harmony with natural developments within Japanese society, there was hope that they would succeed. In so far as they had little foundation or support within Japanese society, they would of course fail.

Viewed in this light our efforts in Japan had very limited and also very realistic objectives — to readjust the balance so that in the future the peaceful and democratic forces within Japanese society would gradually win out over the militaristic and authoritarian forces, reversing the history of the 1930's when the balance turned in favor of the latter. The assumption, of course, was that there already were strong peaceful and democratic tendencies in Japan and that a slight readjustment of the rules and a temporary weighting of the scales in their favor would give them a chance to become the dominant tendencies. This was the unstated philosophy which lay behind the *United States Initial Post-Surrender Policy for Japan* and probably accounts for its statesmanlike tone.

With such limited objectives, perfection was, of course, as unnecessary as it was unattainable. All that we had to achieve was a slight preponderance of power for the forces of peace and democracy, with the assumption that, once attained, this preponderance under favorable circumstances would tend to increase decade by decade as it has elsewhere in the democratic part of the world. No one reform and no single aspect of any reform was in itself essential to success. Some obviously were more crucial than others, but all that counted in the long run was the sum total — the preponderance of forces. We had to expect the undoing of a part of all of our reforms and perhaps the complete abandonment of some. To some extend such a process would be a healthy shaking down of the imposed changes to make them fit into the social pattern as a whole.

Looked at from this point of view, the occupation can be judged to have been a decided success. Naturally there were many costly blunders and still more waste motion. We failed to put adequate emphasis at first on economic recovery and were much too slow in correcting this error. An even more serious mistake was our inability to terminate the occupation rapidly enough. MacArthur's original estimate of three years for the occupation was not far from the optimum period for its duration. Instead, it dragged on for almost seven years. Its chief objective was to help the Japanese learn to run their affairs in a basically democratic manner, but there is a limit to the value of dictation and demonstration in teaching a lesson of this sort. The time comes when the pupil must learn for himself, without the heavy guiding hand of the instructor. And foreign conquerors that we were, our presence became a growing irritation to the Japanese. During the latter part of the occupation we not only ran into a period of diminishing returns; our continuing efforts to guide Japan probably did more harm than good.

Part of the blame for this situation lies with ourselves. It is hard for the teacher to realize that he is no longer wanted or needed. An even more important reason lay in the international situation. As early as 1947 the United States proposed the calling of a general conference to discuss a peace treaty that would terminate the occupation but immediately ran into Soviet obstructionist tactics. It soon became apparent that any peace settlement which the United States felt was desirable would meet Russian opposition. We were, therefore, presented with three alternatives, none of which was entirely satisfactory. We could continue the occupation indefinitely; we could give Japan quasi-independence without a peace treaty; or we could conclude a peace treaty without Communist participation. Eventually the last named course was chosen as obviously the least objectionable, and, with the appointment of John Foster Dulles in April 1950 as an advisor to the State Department to arrange for the peace treaty, the stage was set for the formal conclusion of the occupation two years later. In international terms, it was hard enough to end the occupation when we did; in Japanese terms, it lasted about twice as long as it should have.

But despite these major blunders and a host of lesser mistakes, the occupation, by and large, achieved its basic objectives, which were themselves fundamentally sound. It would not have been unreasonable to have predicted that the occupation would end in disaster or at least that the ill will it generated would more than negate its best efforts. An even more probable outcome might have been a confused pattern of grays, in which the remnants of militarism and authoritarianism still outweighed democracy or else social and economic confusion nullified a large part of the reforms attempted. Instead, Japan emerged from the occupation a reasonably well organized democratic nation, strongly inclined to peace and at long last starting to regain its economic legs. The American role of conqueror and reformer in postwar Japan was unique in the history of Japan or any modern nation. It was also a most difficult role, and both we and the Japanese can be profoundly thankful that it was played, on the whole, so well. Allowing for normal human stupidity and ignorance, one can say that the occupation achieved about as much as could reasonably have been hoped for from it.

This is not to say that Japan will undoubtedly remain a peaceful, democratic nation and will become a valuable ally of the democracies in the great world conflict. The occupation authorities for more than six years helped keep the balance of forces weighted in favor of peace and democracy, but the scales will not necessarily continue to tip in this direction now that the foreign hand has been removed. The future of Japan is and always has been essentially in Japanese hands. At most, we Americans could only play a secondary role in giving temporary assistance to the development of Japanese democracy. The eventual success or failure of democracy in Japan depends on the capacities and temper of the postwar Japanese, and only their history, as it slowly unfolds, will give a full answer to this question.

13. Postwar Trends

1. ECONOMIC DEVELOPMENTS

The period since the end of the war has been too short and too confused to offer any definite indication of what will be the eventual fate of Japan and her democratic institutions. Optimists have found much to point to with satisfaction. Pessimists have with equal ease found crucial signs of disaster. Conflicting forces are obviously still at work in Japan today.

One fact, however, does stand out clearly. Japan unquestionably has changed greatly, and the process of change continues apace. The rapidity of motion since the end of the war has been bewildering. The physical and psychological strains of war and defeat caused a confusing pattern of changes of all sorts. So also did the presence of large numbers of foreign troops on Japanese soil, to say nothing of the reforms carried out by the occupation. In fact, there has been so much change in Japan in the last two decades that, when viewed closely year by year, it is hard to see in which direction or directions Japan may actually be moving. Certainly the Japanese themselves, who are in the midst of these changes, are anything but agreed as to what basically is happening to their country.

But if one looks at the whole sweep of the postwar years from the vantage point of Japan's prewar history, a definite direction of general motion does become apparent in the swirling, bubbling waters of postwar Japan. Many of the most spectacular changes are then seen to have been merely momentary eddies of no lasting significance. Other less noticeable currents prove to have persisted throughout the postwar years and in many cases appear to be the continuation of slow drifts that had started decades before. In fact, most of the truly important postwar changes seem to be simply the acceleration of changes that were already taking place in prewar Japan, though less speedily and also less certainly at that time. The war and the occupation between them seem to have swept away certain barriers to the forward motion of these currents. Some that had lain stagnant or even receded during the militaristic reaction of the 1930's are now surging forward again with new force. Herein may lie the true significance of the war and the occupation for Japan. Instead of diverting Japan into a new channel, it cleared the old one of the obstruction of militaristic reaction and changed a slow and meandering flow into a rushing torrent.

Perhaps the most crucial factor in the postwar equation has been the economic situation. A Japan unable to support itself, or a Japan living close to subsistence levels, or again a Japan enjoying rapidly rising living standards presents three very different sets of possibilities. As Chapters 3 and 4 have shown, early postwar estimates of Japan's economic future were indeed black. Even in 1956 I could start this section of the book with the sentence, "Since the war Japan's economy has seemed considerably less firm than her politics and the economic future the darkest spot on the horizon." Today one might better reverse this statement to say that, if Japanese political stability were as assured as its economic success, the future would indeed look rosy.

The economic problems the Japanese faced at the end of the war were almost overwhelming. Their cities were in large part destroyed; industrial production had ground to a virtual halt for lack of raw materials and machinery replacements; even agricultural production, which at best was inadequate for the nation's needs, was declining because of the lack of fertilizers; the merchant marine, which had served as the arteries of Japan's life-giving foreign trade, had disappeared entirely; worst of all, Japan's foreign trade itself was dead, and a hostile world had no desire to see her revive it.

The only thing that saved the Japanese from widespread starvation after the war was large shipments of foodstuffs from the United States. For years after the surrender, Japan lived on an American dole of close to half a billion dollars a year. At first, while wartime attitudes remained strong, this policy of feeding a former enemy people was justified in the United States on the grounds that widespread starvation would cause disease and unrest in Japan, which would in turn endanger the occupation forces. In time, the feeding of the Japanese became accepted as an inescapable concomitant of our efforts to reform and rehabilitate the country.

An American dole was, of course, only a temporary solution to the problem. In the divided world that resulted from Communist intransigence, an economically unhealthy Japan was a serious liability to us rather than an asset. The United States, in view of its world-wide financial commitments, obviously could not permit the indefinite continuance of this drain on its resources. The sum total expended in Japan was not great in terms of the government budget nor even when compared with what we spent on the economic rehabilitation of Europe. We gave the Japanese far less per person than we gave even to such groups as the West Germans or the Italians. But, large or small, the Japanese economic deficit obviously could not be borne permanently by the citizens of the United States. Nor, for that matter, would such a solution of the problem have been any more acceptable to the Japanese than to us. They are not happy receivers of largess.

Ultimately the question was whether Japanese industry could be restored and develop sufficient export markets to pay for necessary imports. In the face of a ruined economy, a hostile world, and the complete disruption of Japan's best prewar markets, this seemed in the early postwar years an almost hopeless task — especially in view of the rapidly increasing population. It is small wonder that the attention of the occupation authorities gradually shifted to economic recovery, sometimes to the neglect of other aspects of occupation policy. While in the first two years after the surrender economic recovery was all but forgotten in our enthusiasm for the demilitarization and democratization of Japan, in time we became more and more alarmed at the continued economic collapse of the country and distressed at the prospect of an indefinite drain on our resources to pay for a bankrupt Japan.

In theory the new emphasis on economic recovery did not require any diminution of our various reform efforts, but in practice reform and recovery met in head-on collision at various points. If Japanese industry was to be restored to levels able to support the nation, a halt had to be called at some place to the dismantling of factories for reparations, the breaking up of going business concerns into smaller and untested units, the purging of experienced business leaders, and many other reforms felt to be desirable for social and political reasons but injurious to the economy as it existed. A serious divergence of opinion immediately developed over the proper balance to be struck between the two highly desirable but inevitably conflicting objectives of reform and recovery. Some felt that we abandoned too much of the original reform program to be sure of success for any part of it. Others felt that we were far too slow in calling a halt to politically unnecessary and economically disastrous reforms. The large amount of criticism from both sides suggests that perhaps the actual balance struck was not an unreasonable one.

One aspect of the new emphasis on recovery was an effort to bring the Japanese budget within bounds by drastically reducing government expenditures. During the course of 1949, under the direction of Joseph Dodge of Detroit, the occupation authorities forced the Japanese government to curtail its activities and to dismiss large numbers of government employees. The budget as a result was balanced, the inflationary spiral was largely checked, and the black market virtually eliminated.

The labor unions, which opposed the dismissals, were soundly defeated, losing some of the prestige and influence we had been at such pains to give them. And the dismissals were in some cases turned into a convenient means of getting rid of employees or teachers who were considered troublesome leftist sympathizers.

The recovery program perhaps laid sound foundations, but no great economic spurt occurred until a turn of the wheel of history abroad suddenly altered Japan's economic position. In June 1950 the Korean War broke out, and immediately the United States began to purchase supplies and services on a very large scale from Japan. The war marked the economic turning point and was the start of a spectacular improvement of economic conditions in Japan, which continued even after the tapering off of the Korean War. Once recovery had reached a certain point, the more that Japan was economically restored, the greater became her recuperative powers. In other words, the more capital investment the Japanese were able to put back into their industry, the greater became the leverage for further capital investment.

Not all of the economic growth was healthy. At first an inordinate amount of the investment went into non-economic amusements from *pachinko* for the millions of pin-ball addicts to swanky night clubs for the *nouveaux riches*. There was also at times a marked tendency for economic recovery to evaporate into inflation.

By the spring of 1955 the Japanese government, worried by the inflationary tendencies, started a second great deflationary effort, and many marginal small businesses were forced into bankruptcy. Just at this point, however, outside influences again provided a powerful economic stimulant. The worldwide boom swept over Japan and, halting the small deflationary recession, turned it into another great economic surge forward. For the first time since the war, there was a definite favorable balance of foreign trade. Moreover, ideal weather conditions in 1955 resulted in the largest rice crop in history, further

improving the economic situation and bringing a decided wave
of prosperity to many farming communities.

At about the same time the Japanese also started to solve
one of their basic economic problems. Trade relations with
Korea and the lands of Southeast Asia had remained stagnant
ever since the war, in part because of the inability of the
Japanese to come to terms on reparation disputes with these
countries. Because of disagreement between the signatory
powers, the 1951 peace treaty had only established the principle that Japan should pay reparations according to her ability
but had not specified amounts. Naturally, the countries expecting such payments demanded far more than the Japanese
felt that they were able to pay. Reparation disputes, thus, became an added barrier to the normalization of trade relations
between Japan and most of her neighbors.

The first major break in this situation was a reparations
agreement signed with Burma in 1954, and it was followed in
the next few years by similar agreements with Thailand, the
Philippines, Indonesia, and South Vietnam. After ten years of
effort a settlement with South Korea was still held up in mid-
1964 by the mutual animosities between the two peoples and
the political instability in Korea. While some trade had grown
up with South Korea during this ten-year period, a larger trade
had also developed between Japan and the Chinese Nationalist
area of Taiwan, which had not demanded reparations. Thus
the artificial barriers to Japan's trade with many of its neighbors gradually fell, and the chief limiting factor became instead
the weak economic position or political instability of some of
these countries.

By the late 1950's the Japanese realized to their surprise that
they were caught up in a lasting economic boom—the biggest
in Japanese history. Living standards had not only reached
prewar levels but were surging far ahead. By the mid-1960's
per capita income, while still far behind that of countries like
England or West Germany, was approximating or passing the
living standards of South Europe. There were occasional slight
recessions. These occurred about every third year when in-

vestments in industry, rising consumer demands, and the import of capital and goods expanded so fast that they caused serious imbalances and forced the government to put a temporary brake on the economy. Despite these setbacks, the gross national product rose at the amazing average of about 10 per cent a year.

In the decade since 1955 the Japanese industrial economy has grown to maturity, becoming able at last to compete in world markets, not just in light industries, but in the heavy industries and in precision machinery. Japan, while remaining a great exporter of traditional light industry goods, such as textiles, has made great strides in other industries. Japan leads the world in shipbuilding, has won third place in steel production, supplies all its own needs for fertilizers from domestic chemical production, with a large surplus for export, and has found strong markets all over the world for its transistor radios and other electronic goods, cameras, binoculars, motorcycles, electric turbines and the like. Where the mark "Made in Japan" had before the war been thought of as the sign of shoddy goods, it has become accepted as a guarantee of high quality in many fields.

The question, of course, is how this industrial "miracle" has been possible. It has certainly confounded all the predictions of earlier years. One thing it clearly shows is that for industrial growth the qualities the Japanese have, that is the capacity for hard work, high levels of education and technical competence, and the ability to maintain political and fiscal stability, are vastly more important than the possession of raw materials. The Japanese, living on their seemingly inadequate physical base, have been able during the past decade to greatly lengthen their lead in industrialization and living standards over the other lands of Asia, which in many cases are far more bountifully blessed by nature.

There have been other factors which help explain Japan's rapid industrial growth. One is the single-minded concentration which the Japanese have devoted to investment in industry. They have allowed investment in the public sector of the

economy — in roads, harbor facilities, schools and social services — to lag behind, while devoting their efforts to building
up industrial capacity. For example the rail network, though
perhaps the finest and most efficiently used in the world, was
allowed to become dangerously overtaxed, and the snarl of
motor traffic on the inadequate road systems of the major
urban centers, especially Tokyo, grew to almost hopeless proportions. The resulting imbalance in the economy will force
the Japanese in the years ahead to put more into the public
sector and therefore probably less into private industry. The
consequence may be some slowing down in the rate of industrial growth.

Another factor in Japan's industrial growth has been a veritable revolution in energy resources. Since the war the Japanese have further expanded hydroelectric power, sometimes
through the construction of large-scale dams. It has also become economically feasible to import large quantities of
superior grades of coal from such distant sources as the United
States and Australia. But cheap petroleum from the Middle
East, transported in huge Japanese tankers and sometimes coming from Japanese-operated oil fields, has made the greatest
difference. The result of all this has been a great expansion in
energy resources available to Japanese industry and a sharp
reduction in dependence on the inadequate domestic coal
supplies.

Still another important factor in Japan's fantastic surge
forward has been its special relationship with the United States.
At a time when most other countries were discriminating
against Japanese goods (many still do), the United States accepted them more freely and became Japan's most important
market. Roughly a quarter of Japanese exports go to the
United States, almost seven times as much as go to any other
country. The flow of goods into Japan, however, has been even
greater. Approximately a third of Japan's imports come from
the United States, making Japan, next to Canada, our second
most important market and our largest cash market for agricultural exports, particularly cotton, soy beans, wheat, and

feed grains. The United States has been of equal importance to the Japanese economy as the supplier of a large part of the capital Japan desperately needed to restore its war-devastated economy and also the provider of technical know-how through hundreds of patent agreements between American and Japanese firms.

The loss of empire also served as a spur to rapid domestic industrial growth, since the cost of defense of overseas areas before the war and the large capital investment Japan made in them more than offset what economic benefits Japan may have derived from its colonial or semi-colonial possessions. Closely allied with this factor has been the light load the Japanese have borne since the war for the defense of their own home islands. The general revulsion against militarism has kept Japanese self-defense efforts to a comparatively low level, made possible by the continuing security arrangements with the United States and the presence of American military power in and around Japan. Whereas the United States in recent years has invested close to 10 per cent of its gross national product in defense efforts and the major Western European countries have averaged around 5 per cent, the Japanese figure has been as low as 1.2 per cent, leaving a much bigger margin for investment in economic growth.

Another factor, which is important but hard to define, is the skillful balance the Japanese have been able to strike between free enterprise and government guidance and control. It is a fact of the greatest significance that the fastest growing economy in Asia — possibly in the whole world — has been an essentially free enterprise system. At the same time, the Japanese have shown remarkable skill at integration within industry and cooperation between industry and government. Government controls over the economy, though considerably liberalized in the past few years, are somewhat greater than we are accustomed to; lingering traces of the *zaibatsu* system and the Japanese tendency toward group leadership and cooperation have given industry greater integration than we would assume normal; and industry has tended to stay close to the counsels of government and to respond voluntarily to suggestions much more than it does in the United States. This has contributed to the ability of the Japanese economy to respond to the needs of each situation, whether it be for deflation, balance of payment adjustments, or slow downs or speed ups in investment, much more rapidly and easily than would be the case in the economies of most of the other industrialized nations.

One could cite other factors, such as the wartime destruction of industrial facilities, which allowed a fresh start in many cases with plants that were more modern than many in the United States. Or again, there is the sociological factor that Japanese women workers throng the factories during the years when they are most nimble of finger and quick of eye. In contrast to the American pattern of women going to work in middle age, after early marriage and the raising of children, Japanese girls tend to work in the five or ten years between graduation from junior high school and marriage. There are thus many reasons for the Japanese industrial miracle, but the most basic remain the high educational and technological levels, the habit of hard work, and political and fiscal stability.

Manufacturing, of course, can never be the whole of a nation's economy. Before the war close to half of the Japanese working force was engaged in agriculture, which though highly productive per square foot was very unproductive per man. In addition, there were millions engaged in traditional industries that were little mechanized or in low-productivity services, such as retailing through myriad tiny shops. While the factory worker greatly increased his productivity through modern machines, these other people increased their productivity very little. The result has been a so-called "dual structure" of the economy.

The surge forward in manufacturing, however, has been so great that it has in a sense carried the less productive forms of economic activity with it. The factory worker has shared in the benefits of his increasing productivity with annual wage increases of around 10 per cent. As a result young people coming on the labor market have flocked to the large new factories, thus drawing population from agriculture and forcing the less productive industries and services to try to match their wages in order to retain an adequate supply of labor. For the first time in history, Japan has been experiencing a labor shortage. Higher wages in the less productive economic fields have had two results. One has been a renewed tendency toward inflation, as workers received higher pay without a commensurate increase in productivity. The other has been a trend toward the rationalizing of these less productive sectors of the economy. For instance, the self-service market is beginning to replace the corner grocery, and service industries are trying to cut down on personnel.

The effect of all this on rural Japan has been perhaps even greater than in the cities. The young people have streamed to city factories, and male members of farm families have often turned into workers who commute to nearby cities or towns. This has meant a drastic reduction in the number of agricultural workers, now well below 30 per cent of the total labor force, and a preponderance of women workers among those who remain. As the agricultural labor force continues to decline, it is reasonable to expect that some marginal lands will go out of cultivation and average farm holdings will begin to increase beyond the present two and a half acres.

The drop in agricultural population has been accompanied not by a decrease in agricultural yields, but by sizable increases. This has been possible because of scientific advances, the greater use of chemical fertilizers, and, most surprising of all, a certain degree of mechanization of farm work. Electricity has long been available to virtually all of rural Japan, making possible the use of small electric threshing machines and the like, as well as domestic appliances, like the washing machine, which reduces the farm wife's work load. While tractors such as we know them are too big for application to Japan's patchwork of tiny fields, a so-called "bean" tractor, hardly larger than a large lawn mower, was developed and met the needs of Japanese agriculture admirably. Even though much of the agricultural expansion of recent years has gone into an increased production of meat, dairy products, and fruit, rice yields, too, have increased and for the first time in many decades are meeting the demands of local consumption, in part because the Japanese are now eating less rice per capita and are enjoying a more varied diet than before the war.

The rapid expansion of Japanese industry and the steady flow of young workers, both boys and girls, from the countryside to the cities has resulted in a fantastic growth of all the urban centers and a heavy concentration in them of young people in their late teens and early twenties. In 1964 the more than 10,000,000 residents of Tokyo made it the largest organized municipality in the world; several million more people in neighboring Yokohama and other cities and in the commuting districts that lie beyond Tokyo's borders made this metropolitan complex probably the largest concentration of people in the world. With the great growth of urban population has gone a tremendous building boom. Hundreds of multistory buildings sprang up like mushrooms in downtown sections of the bigger cities, sprawling new industrial sites were laid out, often on newly .filled-in land along the shores of shallow bays, and the major cities became ringed in the far suburbs with serried rows of four- to six-story concrete apartment houses.

While Japan's economy remains delicately attuned to imports and exports, the economic advance of recent years has produced a veritable consumer's revolution. Housing remains extremely crowded and little if any better than before the war, but the products of Japanese industry are in everyone's hands. The great majority of homes in the city or countryside have television. Japan follows the United States in the percentage of homes with washing machines. The farmer has his motorcycle and the young businessman his family car. Almost everyone seems to own a transistor radio and a camera. The Japanese have become much concerned with the use of leisure time. They crowd movie houses and restaurants, go sightseeing in endless throngs, and in season overrun ski-resorts and beaches.

Not long ago Japan seemed to be engaged in a grim and possibly hopeless race between expanding productive power and a burgeoning population. In the early postwar years millions of Japanese were poured back into Japan from overseas, and there was a frightening jump in births. Since then it has become apparent that the race is going to expanding productive power, as the economy surges ahead and the rate of population increase dwindles. The government, through the dissemination of birth control information and liberal abortion laws, has encouraged the limiting of families, and many big companies have done the same for their workers. More important probably has been the increasing urbanization of the country and other sociological factors which make children more an economic liability than an asset. Even in rural Japan two- or three-children families have become common. As a result, Japan's population, which stood in mid-1964 at 96,600,000, was growing at the rate of less than 1 per cent a year and showed clear signs of leveling off somewhere between 100,000,000 and 110,000,000.

Japan's economic success has been so spectacular in recent years that one runs the danger of painting too rosy a picture. We should not forget that no comparable mass of humanity is balanced on so limited a physical pedestal. Few parts of the world are more subject to the natural disasters of storm and earthquake. Japanese living standards are still far behind those of most of the other advanced industrialized nations. Economic expansion has depended heavily on foreign credit, and Japanese industry, like a sharply tilting bicyclist, has maintained its balance only by the great speed of its forward motion.

Most sobering of all is Japan's greater dependence on foreign raw materials and markets than is the case with the United States and some other countries. While a sharp decline in international trade would seriously threaten our whole economy, for Japan it would be a certain catastrophe. In other words,

Japan remains very much at the mercy of world trade, itself a pawn of international politics. In a far from unitary or peaceful world, this situation remains a constant sword of Damocles in Japanese minds.

2. SOCIAL FERMENT

The shock of war, defeat, and occupation naturally produced great social ferment in Japan, and the decade of rapid economic expansion that followed made the pot continue to boil. The shift from coal to oil as a major source of power blighted the coal producing areas; the swarming of young people to the cities changed the pattern of life both in the cities and in the countryside; and an unaccustomed prosperity brought new opportunities and new problems to millions of Japanese.

Among the great social changes of the postwar years has been the increase in social mobility, that is the chance for people of all classes to rise to positions of responsibility commensurate with their abilities. This change in particular was merely the acceleration of a strong tendency that went back to the very beginning of modern Japan a century ago. Most of the leaders who created Meiji Japan were themselves men of relatively humble origin. The social and educational system they created, while designed to produce an elite of leadership, was so organized that true talent had a chance to rise from most segments of society. The Japanese army itself, as we have seen, was an organization that turned boys from poor and obscure families into national leaders. For several decades before the war there had been a considerable degree of social mobility in Japan, if not as great as in the United States with its strong egalitarian tendencies, certainly as much if not more than in prewar England.

The war and occupation speeded up this process first through social upheavals that tended to mix up the classes and then by more lasting reforms. Much new legislation was designed to help equalize opportunities, and the new educational system in particular, with its extension of the period of compulsory education and its attempt to equalize schools at each level, meant a further chance for social mobility. Actually the Japanese educational system is more democratic in some respects than our own. The high schools and universities that stand at the top in scholarship and prestige are for the most part government institutions which have the lowest tuition fees. In the United States there is a close relationship between wealth and the chance for a superior education, and this is only partially offset by the large amounts of scholarship funds available for students without private means. In Japan the wealthy student obviously has certain advantages, but the great majority of the students in the leading national universities are able scholars from poor homes, while the well-to-do boys who are not of top ability crowd the socially acceptable but scholastically inferior private universities.

Social mobility has been further strengthened since the war by a general leveling of class distinctions that is very different from anything that went on before the war. Most private wealth of any magnitude was wiped out by a combination of three forces — the destruction of war, inflation, and the occupation reforms. The very wealthy were brought down to a position not far above the admittedly poor. At the same time the peerage and most other forms of special privilege were abolished. Former princes became retail merchants, and the wives and daughters of aristocratic households took office jobs to help out the family exchequer. The much larger class of intellectuals and office workers, being city dwellers, were hard hit by wartime destruction and postwar food shortage. For a while, their standard of living was pushed below national averages, until the rush of the economy carried them back to their accustomed position of modest prosperity.

The reverse of the coin has been the rising relative standards of urban workers and farmers. The latter, profiting first from the land reform and extraordinary postwar conditions and subsequently benefiting by their decline in numbers and supplementary factory wages, are far more prosperous than ever before. Urban labor, benefiting as much from Japan's industrial success as from the new labor legislation and its own strong unionization, is in an incomparably stronger position than before the war. Of course, pockets of poverty, even by Japanese standards, continue to exist in marginal agricultural areas, coal mining districts, and the like, and most Japanese farmers and workers would be classified as poor by American standards. At the other end of the scale, the captains of industry, many of them newly risen men, have once again built up considerable fortunes. Still there has been a great economic leveling up and down in Japanese society, producing an overall pattern closer to that of Western Europe than to what existed in Japan before the war.

This great economic change in society would not be so significant if it had not been accompanied by a vast change in attitudes. While the Japanese remain conscious of class distinctions and hierarchy in a way that is quite unknown to Americans, there has been a decided relaxing of the rigidity of these distinctions. Much of the obsequiousness, even the deference, shown before the war by the lower classes to their supposed superiors has disappeared, and the upper classes too have lost a great deal of their unconscious air of superiority. Both attitudes were to a large extent worn down in the grinding confusion of the war and postwar years and have not been easily restored under the postwar reforms. The change is a visible one. It is to be seen in the easier relationships between master and servant and employer and employee. Backed by new legislation and strengthened by changed attitudes, the leveling process in Japanese society shows every promise of continuing, as it has for many decades now in virtually all of the more advanced countries of the world.

Paralleling the breakdown in class distinctions has been a general weakening of all social controls. A great breath of freedom has blown through the tightly knit, cramped society of Japan. Most Japanese, especially younger ones, think and act with a freedom that was not at all common in prewar days. The control of the family over young people has visibly relaxed. Young men and women nowadays are rarely forced into marriages against their will, and often enough they are permitted to select their own mates. Mixed social dancing and a certain amount of dating between young men and women has become common in the cities. Teachers are no longer regarded as awesome oracles by their pupils, and the adult population tends to have scant respect for any of its leaders. Social contacts are less formal and easier than before the war, and there has been a general relaxing of the tensions of all personal relationships.

The changes are most noticeable among two groups, women and young people. The former act with a self-confidence that, if it existed before the war, was carefully concealed. They even walk with a greater freedom than before, in part because of the change from kimonos to Occidental clothing, which they now wear with a style that was entirely lacking in prewar or early postwar days. All in all, the Japanese woman has become much more of an individual, but without losing any of the charm that characterized her before the war.

Young people have changed even more markedly. In fact, one could safely say that in most cases the younger a Japanese is, the more he departs from prewar norms. The old have changed very little, but with each younger age bracket the change becomes more noticeable. Japanese under thirty, whose upbringing and education have been largely postwar, are least like their prewar counterparts. Children are more spontaneous and uninhibited, but these qualities are accompanied by a certain degree of brashness and even rudeness that was virtually unknown before the war.

With the new freedom has gone a great deal of social and emotional confusion. The old iron-bound codes of conduct are now often disregarded, but no new standards have risen to take their place. The postwar Japanese is without doubt more lawless than his police-ridden predecessor. Juvenile delinquency, while in no way as serious as in the United States, has become a real problem for the first time in Japanese history. The Japanese have lost much of their former punctiliousness and with it a certain amount of their politeness. With the relaxing of tensions, there may also have come a certain slackening of will power and even a sloppiness of performance that would not have been tolerated before. In the early postwar years both foreign and Japanese observers were fond of saying that for many people the new freedom simply meant license. This was certainly true, and, while ethical concepts and social customs have tightened up considerably since those days, there is still a great deal of uncertainty as to what standards of ethics and politeness should apply.

The change in the postwar generation of Japan can hardly be overemphasized. For one thing, there has been a vast expansion in education. The extension of compulsory schooling under the occupation from six to nine years has been less of a change than the continuation of more than 60 per cent of the young people on to senior high school, and the great expansion of numbers in junior colleges and four-year colleges. With over 900,000 students at the college level (almost half of them concentrated in Tokyo), Japan ranks only after the United States and Israel in the percentage of its youth that seeks higher education. The postwar generation seems to have changed even physically. Better nutritional standards, perhaps aided by some decline in the habit of sitting on the floor with the feet tucked under the body, has made them visibly taller than their parents. And their carefree, easy, and open manners — their boorishness, their elders might call it — make them seem to resemble their Western contemporaries more than their prewar predecessors.

Thus, the social pot has boiled furiously in postwar Japan, and much has changed in the process. Almost all that has been said in Part Three about the Japanese character requires considerable modification before it can be applied to the postwar

Japanese. For a few, and particularly the old, it is still as valid as before, and for most it is at least partly true today, but the various special traits that distinguished the Japanese personality from what we are accustomed to, have almost all weakened to some degree since the war. Even more significant, the change in each case has brought the Japanese a bit closer to the norms that would apply in the United States and most European countries.

3. INTELLECTUAL TRENDS

The physical changes in Japan wrought by war, defeat, and occupation were no greater than the intellectual changes. The Japanese emerged from these shattering experiences a confused, uncertain, and deeply divided people. And the subsequent economic explosion has in some ways compounded the confusion.

Perhaps the outstanding characteristic of postwar intellectual developments has been their diversity and lack of cohesion. Where the prewar Japanese, subjected to heavy indoctrination, seemed almost parrot-like in their similarity of views, varying groups in postwar Japan appear to be speaking almost in different languages. The differences in thinking between city and rural people and between the various social classes and occupational groups are, of course, pronounced, as they are in any complex society, but the really significant ideological cleavages are those of age. Naturally the different age groups in any modern country show decided differences in their attitudes toward many things, but the contrasts in Japan are far greater than in the United States or most European countries.

Young Japanese and their older compatriots sometimes cannot talk together about certain subjects. The attitude of unconcern or even disrespect of many young Japanese for their Emperor is not only shocking but quite incomprehensible to their elders. A gulf of basic misunderstanding often lies between parents and children or between the university professor and his students. Where a nostalgia for prewar Japan remains strong among the old, it gradually thins out in younger age brackets, until it vanishes entirely in the group now in their twenties. Conversely, a basic satisfaction with the changes resulting from the war and occupation becomes stronger as one goes down the age scale. It is for this reason that it seems improbable that the fundamental changes wrought by the war and occupation will be undone, for the older generation inevitably grows smaller year by year and the new generation larger.

The sharp differences in basic attitudes between the various age groups in Japan are very obvious, and they illustrate another more important point, which itself is not so immediately apparent. Japan today lacks any central core of ethics or any system of guiding ideals. The Japanese religions of Buddhism and Shintoism offer the modern Japanese little solid religious basis for their ethics or ideals; the feudal and Confucian ethics of the past have decayed; and the state-centered system of prewar Japan has been repudiated. Actually what ethics the Japanese have is a composite of old attitudes that have survived piecemeal from the past and elements of the Christian-based ethics of the Occident, with the latter perhaps somewhat in the preponderance, despite the infinitesimal number of professing Christians. The point was strikingly illustrated when the Diet banned organized prostitution — a most surprising step in a country in which the geisha girl and the semi-brothel played very important social and cultural roles up until a few decades ago.

Whatever the origin of modern Japanese ethical concepts, however, there can be no denying that they lack any solid religious basis and vary widely among different social and age groups. And with them goes no generally accepted set of guiding ideals or principles. The Japanese are still self-consciously aware of their national distinctiveness, but the ideal of blind obedience to the state no longer serves as a major unifying principle, and instead they are somewhat apologetic and uncertain in their patriotism. For the most part they are united in their devotion to the concepts of peace and international order, but they are not at all agreed as to how these are to be realized. Most of them approve of democracy, but the principles on which democracy is based do not serve as great unifying beliefs, as they do in such countries as the United States and the United Kingdom. In other words, neither religion, nor ethical principles, nor political and social ideals serve as the great unifying forces they do in many other lands. The keystone appears to be missing in the intellectual or spiritual arch, and this lack in turn gives a certain instability to the whole structure of modern Japan.

The war and early postwar experiences of the Japanese naturally left behind an aura of pessimism and fatalism. Forgetting their former belief in will power, many looked with hopelessness at the grim situation in Japan and the unfriendly world that surrounded it. They became negative rather than positive in their self-consciousness, as sure that anything foreign was superior to anything Japanese as they had been insistent on the opposite before the war. Others bemoaned the supposed loss of Japan's cultural identity. Such attitudes wore off only slowly and still persist in certain circles. It was only after the great economic surge was well advanced that the Japanese seemed to realize what was happening and began to show a normal degree of pride and confidence in their country. Of course, in this as in all other matters, there were sharp differences between age groups. The postwar generation grew up free of the shadow of the past, and their cheerful exuberance now gives the cities at least an optimistic liveliness that is hard to match and contrasts sharply with the early postwar pall of gloom.

Other, more lasting, postwar traits have been internationalism and pacifism. These have been natural reactions to the war and the postwar situation. Few people experienced more fully the horrors of war. None can see more clearly their own complete dependence on the good will and well-being of the rest of the world. They depend on foreign raw materials and markets to live. They have already proved to themselves quite conclusively that they cannot hope to conquer these for themselves. The only alternative is to trade extensively with other nations, and for this peace and international order are necessary. No people could be more devoted to this international ideal than the postwar Japanese, because it is so clearly a matter of life and death to them.

There is, of course, less agreement on how peace is to be maintained. In the early postwar years, Japan's helplessness in a hostile world encouraged the development of pacifism. Faced with overwhelming outside power, the Japanese felt it best to foreswear all armaments and hope that the rest of the world would leave them alone. Pacifism became symbolized by a vigorous "ban the atom and hydrogen bomb" movement, over which the parties of the left have vigorously fought for control in recent years. But as strength surged back into the Japanese economy, many came to realize that Japan itself had a large potential for influencing the world situation and in any case could not simply opt to stand outside all world tensions. The early postwar trust in the efficiency of pure pacifism began to fade. A small military establishment was started in 1950 and in 1954 was named the Self-Defense Force. By the early 1960's it had grown to around 200,000 men. No clear consensus developed, however, as to how Japan could best use its new found economic strength and influence in the cause of world peace. In fact, it is on this point that the Japanese since the war have remained most seriously divided.

Throughout history the Japanese have tended to be a realistic people, less given than many to theoretical conjecture. Even today the bulk of them could be described as pragmatic. For such people, the overwhelming preponderance of American influence in the early postwar years seemed reason enough for Japan to follow in the wake of the American ship of state. Subsequently, the triumph of Japan's free economy, the almost complete alignment of the economy with the United States and the rest of the free world, and the relative success of

Japan's democratic institutions in maintaining an even political keel and in translating the will of the majority into government policy all seemed to justify the continuance of Japan's democratic and free enterprise system and her close defense relationship with the United States. Such pragmatic reasoning was strengthened by a growing ideological devotion to democratic and liberal principles, derived both from postwar roots and from the injection of these ideas into the school system during the occupation.

Against this majority or, as the Japanese would call it, "main stream" point of view, have flowed some strong "anti-main-stream" leftist currents. These elements have sought social revolution and the creation of a socialistic economy at home, and abroad a closer alignment with the Communist world or at least a position of strict neutralism between the Communists and the free world.

In part these leftist points of view derive from the desperateness of early postwar conditions. If Americans during the occupation years felt that the situation was so bad that it called for drastic modifications, it is a small wonder that millions of Japanese longed for some radical cure. The example of the Soviet Union, the great nation that had most recently gone through a major revolutionary change, naturally had a strong appeal, especially when presented with the propagandistic skill of the Communists. Subsequently, the victory of the Chinese Communists had an even greater impact. While the Japanese have had a traditional fear and dislike of the Russians, their attitude toward the Chinese has usually been favorable. Throughout most of their history they have looked to China with respect as the source of much of their higher civilization, and a definite guilt complex over their own imperialistic mistreatment of the Chinese in recent years has contributed to an overly favorable and almost sentimental view of what was happening on the Chinese mainland.

The main source of the leftist trends in postwar Japanese thinking, however, is not to be found in Soviet or Chinese

Communist influence but within Japan itself. As the economy, political system, and society modernized in the decades between 1880 and 1930, thought failed to keep pace. The official dogma became a neo-conservatism, centering around the concept of the state as an extended family responsive to the "will of the Emperor." This proved unsatisfactory to intellectuals, who increasingly showed signs of a passive alienation from society as it was evolving or took refuge in Marxist dogmas. Similarly, enfranchisement of the poor peasants and urban workers after 1925 came too late to give them a sense of meaningful participation in the political process. In so far as they showed political consciousness, they too gravitated toward the revolutionary concepts of Marxism.

Marxist movements remained numerically small before the war, but, while the supporters of liberal democratic belief found themselves ground into ineffectiveness during the 1930's between the intransigence of the then dominant militarists and the dogmatism of the Marxists, the latter established themselves in the public consciousness as the only clear opponents of militarism. Their theories also became all the more attractive by being officially banned. When the war brought the militarists down in ruin and the occupation authorities lifted the lid on all thought and political movements, the bulk of the intellectuals, as well as the newly reorganizing labor unionists, flocked to Marxism as the seemingly obvious alternative to the discredited past.

It has always puzzled Americans that this should have happened at a time when the occupation's reform efforts were helping to remodel Japan along liberal democratic lines. Part of the blame lies in the desperate economic conditions of the early postwar years, which were particularly hard on the city-living intellectuals and workers. The heavy psychological burdens which the Japanese educational system puts on youth might also help explain the radical propensities of students. There is a universal desire for education in Japan and, as a result, tremendous pressure to enter the best schools and universities through the competitive entrance examinations. Consequently, the ambitious young Japanese is exposed to a series of so-called "examination hells," which may well contribute to a jaundiced view of the system into which he is trying to win his way.

Still another reason for the intellectual climate of Japan is the continuing influence of German nineteenth-century philosophy, particularly Hegelianism, which dominated Japanese education before the war. This has helped make the educated Japanese an intellectual artistocrat and pure theoretician rather than a practical leader, standing haughtily and a little tragically aloof from society. The Japanese intellectual thus has tended to be a decided intellectual snob, as proud of his English-derived slang name of *interi* as his American counterpart has been cowed by the term "egghead." Before the war this attitude of aloofness allowed most intellectuals to turn inward and ignore the militaristic trends that few of them could really approve. Since the war, apparently in compensation for their past failures, they have shown strong political consciousness, but their devotion to a highly theoretical approach to Japan's problems has left them with almost as little practical influence as before.

A large part of the blame for the postwar intellectual climate in Japan must also rest with the occupation authorities for not having known how to appeal to Japanese intellectuals. Certainly the occupation, by at first limiting the contacts of the Japanese with the outside world, helped keep the intellectuals divorced from reality. And the latter, accustomed to thinking in theoretical terms, were definitely disappointed at the failure of the American authorities to present a clear and comprehensive philosophy that would explain our actions and clarify our objectives. Japanese intellectuals were disillusioned by the piecemeal explanations offered by individual members of the occupation, who, like most other Americans, took the major tenets of their democratic faith so much for granted that they were unable to formulate them as a coherent philosophy. We left an intellectual vacuum, which the neatly packaged and labeled dialectic materialism of Marxism quickly filled, and many Japanese intellectuals came to accept the mid-nineteenth-century theorizing of Marx as the latest and therefore the most advanced concepts of Western civilization.

Closely allied with postwar leftist trends has been a strong strain of anti-Americanism. This has been inevitable in a country that was first defeated and then occupied for seven years by the United States and still depends very heavily on economic and defense relations with us. It has been all too easy to blame anything that one did not like in postwar Japan on the United States. And the presence of American bases, military planes, and soldiers naturally affords many reasons for specific irritations. Such anti-Americanism takes on added significance when combined with the strong leftist political trend. Communists and many other leftists believe implicitly in the propositions that capitalism inevitably produces imperialism and imperialism war, and therefore the United States, as supposedly the leader of the "capitalist camp," is the chief warmonger in the world, while so-called "socialist" countries, such as the Soviet Union and Communist China, are by nature the forces working for peace.

There are, however, some curious ambivalences in anti-Americanism in Japan. Among conservatives, who are strongest in their support for the close ties maintained with the United States, there is the sharpest criticism of the occupation reforms, which deprived some of these people of the wealth and prerogatives they once enjoyed. On the other hand, leftists, who are loudest in their condemnation of America's supposed baneful influence on Japan and the cause of peace, are strongest in their support of the occupation reforms and the postwar Constitution. The chief focus of debate has been Article 9 of the Constitution, in which the Japanese renounced war and the maintenance of war potential. Many conservatives argue that this and other provisions of the Constitution should be revised because they were imposed by the occupation authorities, while leftists reply that, whatever their source, they are sound provisions which should not be altered.

Another ambivalence in anti-Americanism in Japan is the enthusiasm for most things American that prevails among leftists as well as conservatives. Most Japanese of either political persuasion are personally friendly to Americans if they happen to have any chance for contacts, and probably more feel a greater sense of closeness to the United States than to any other foreign country.

There are, of course, many outward signs of anti-Americanism in Japan. The tone of intellectual magazines and at one time even of the newspapers has tended to be hostile to the United States. There are periodic demonstrations by leftists against American military bases or some aspect of the defense relationship between the two countries. There have also been two major blowups, which seemed at the time to augur ill for Japanese-American relations. The first was the May Day disturbances of 1952, shortly after the restoration of Japanese independence, when American cars and other property were destroyed by rioting leftist demonstrators.

The other crisis in American-Japanese relations was the series of great demonstrations in Tokyo in May and June of 1960. The origin of these was leftist objections to the revision of the security treaty between the United States and Japan. While the new agreement had the benefit for Japan of putting many restrictions on the defense relationship that had not existed in the original 1952 pact and, unlike the latter, was limited to ten years, after which either side could denounce it, the leftists argued that the new agreement was worse than the old because an independent Japan was agreeing to it, whereas the earlier pact had been "forced" on a still occupied nation. The original dispute over the security treaty drew added emotional fuel from certain extraneous happenings, such as the shooting down of an American U-2 reconnaissance plane over the Soviet Union and the subsequent canceling of a planned summit conference in Europe. The tactics of Prime Minister

Kishi in pushing through ratification of the security treaty greatly fanned the excitement, since the leftists regarded his actions as undemocratic and unconstitutional. Finally, the Japanese government arranged to complete ratification of the new treaty on the day on which President Eisenhower was to start a long projected visit to Japan, and this raised in the minds of the Japanese public the issue of "American intervention" in domestic politics.

The demonstrations rose to a frenzy as hundreds of thousands of labor union members, university students organized by the *Zengakuren*, the National Federation of Student Government Associations, and common citizens milled about in frantic protest in the streets of downtown Tokyo. The Japanese government was forced to ask Eisenhower to give up his visit, and shortly after the new treaty went into effect Kishi had to resign as Prime Minister. However the excitement subsided even more quickly than it had risen, leaving behind a calmer atmosphere than had prevailed at any time since the war. There was a general feeling that the demonstrations had been excessive, bringing Japan too close to the brink of political anarchy, and the broadly-based friendship with the United States seemed unimpaired.

Since 1960 attitudes toward the United States have, if anything, improved, and there has been a growing popular acceptance of the concept of close partnership with us. Part of the reason for this has been economic prosperity, which has tended to undercut the dissatisfaction on which leftist theories bred. An increasing awareness of the complexities of the world situation has also contributed, as the Japanese have come back slowly into full contact with the outside world. Most important has been a growing sense of Japan's own strength and ability to influence its fate. But actually the wonder throughout has not been that anti-Americanism existed in Japan but that it has always been so weak in the face of the strong theoretical prejudice against us of the leftists, the irritations engendered by defeat, occupation, enforced reforms, and the continuing presence of American military bases, and the general feeling that the United States exerts economically and in other ways a preponderant influence over Japan.

4. THE POLITICAL SCENE

Postwar Japanese politics have been dominated by the deep cleavage between leftists and conservatives, although the latter have retained the reins of political leadership almost without interruption. A third political group, the Soka Gakkai, which is based on a newly risen Buddhist sect, has recently entered with considerable success into local elections and those for the House of Councillors, and it intends to run candidates in the next general election for the lower house. It is still too early, however, to predict its political future.

The conservatives, as a politically organized group, derive directly from the two major prewar parliamentary parties, which amalgamated as the Liberal Democratic Party in late 1955. They have been traditionally strongest in rural Japan, where many conservative politicians have maintained virtually impregnable constituencies. They have also traditionally been closely allied with the business community, particularly big business. In fact, it is this close association that accounts for some of the skill with which business and government have been able to coordinate national economic policy. There has also been a traditional tie to the bureaucracy, which, while far less powerful than before the war, still exercises much greater influence over government policy than in the United States. Actually many bureaucrats, after reaching retirement age or the top of the ladder as a vice-minister, shift to politics as conservative candidates for the Diet, and a large part of conservative postwar leadership has consisted of such ex-bureaucrats.

The leftists draw their strength primarily from those social groups which even before the war felt themselves alienated from society or left out of leadership, in other words, the city intellectuals and white-collar workers and urban labor, particularly the part that is organized. Even today many of these people feel themselves estranged from the dominant political leadership, which to them seems an alliance between big business and the bureaucracy, backed by uninformed rural voters and dominated by former bureaucrats who were part of the discredited prewar and wartime system.

The postwar leftist parties all derived from relatively small prewar beginnings, but in the two decades since the end of the war there has been a general tendency for the leftist vote to increase and the conservative vote to shrink correspondingly. The rate of shift has on the whole been so steady and apparently so little related to current political issues as to suggest more a sociological than a political change. Apparently, as urban populations grow and rural populations diminish and as the percentage of the working force in union-organized industries increases, the leftist vote expands. In the lower house elections of November 1963 the once overwhelming conservative majority had shrunk to a 60–40 advantage. (Five per cent of the conservative's 60 per cent went to independents.) It should, however, be noted that in local elections the smaller the unit the larger the conservative majority (much of it for independents), showing that at the grass-roots level the Japanese remain decidedly conservative.

Neither the conservatives nor the leftists are closely unified groups, like the Conservatives and Labor Party of the United Kingdom. The Liberal Democratic Party is a looser union, more like the Democratic or Republican Parties of the United States, though the principles of division within the party are quite different. The heart of the party is its Diet membership, which tends to divide vaguely between ex-bureaucrats and men who have risen entirely through the electoral process, and somewhat more sharply between factions consisting of a prominent leader and his followers. In recent years such factions have usually numbered around eight. Sometimes the most hotly contested elections are not those for the lower house of the

Diet, but the elections by the Diet conservatives of the faction leader who, as party president for the next two years, will serve as prime minister.

The divisions among the leftists, while involving some of the same sort of factionalism, are more specifically ideological. Ever since the war, three rather distinct ideological positions have existed among them. On the extreme left have been the Communists, at first under heavy influence from the Soviet Union but in more recent years tending to look toward the Chinese Communists. Next have come those who, while rejecting the Communist label, have tended to support the international position of the Communists against the free world and have stressed the achievement of a socialist economy in Japan through revolutionary change rather than through evolutionary and democratic processes. On the right have been those who have stressed democracy first and foremost and therefore the achievement of a socialist economy only through democratic evolutionary means. In the early postwar years there was considerable flux among leftist parties and splinter groups, but they eventually sorted themselves out in accordance with these three positions into the Communist Party and the Left and Right Socialists. The latter two rejoined late in 1955, but in January 1960 part of the former Right Socialists broke away again to form the Democratic Socialist Party. In the November 1963 elections the Communists won 4 per cent of the popular vote, the Socialists, who ideologically spread all the way from fellow travelers of the Communists to former Right Socialists, won about 29 per cent, and the Democratic Socialists 7 per cent. While the gradual increase of the leftist vote suggests the possibility that it may come to outweigh the conservative vote sometime in the years ahead, the deep ideological cleavages among the leftists make it improbable that any simple majority for them as a whole would result in their immediate take over of political leadership.

Since a large part of the organized strength of the parties of the left rests on organized labor, there has been a vigorous competition among the leftist groups for control of the unions. At one time a large percentage were under the leadership of Communists, and even today many individual unions are dominated or deeply infiltrated by them. The bulk of the labor movement, however, is now affiliated with the Socialists or the Democratic Socialists or stands neutral between these two. The largest organization, Sohyo, which in 1963 embraced 44.8 per cent of the 9,357,179 organized workers, is a staunch supporter of the Socialist Party, while Domei Kaigi (including the older organization known as Zenro), which represents 14.4 per cent of organized labor, supports the Democratic Socialists.

The sharp, sometimes violent, confrontation between the leftist parties and the conservatives ever since the end of the war has often put a brake on the leadership of the latter, despite their usually preponderant numbers in the Diet. By obstructionist tactics in the Diet, not barring even the use of physical force, and by mass demonstrations in the streets, the leftists have repeatedly forced the conservatives to back away from controversial legislation or reach compromises with the opposition. In fact, the Japanese have shown a tendency when possible to avoid decisions by a simple majority vote on highly controversial issues and to seek instead some sort of consensus.

Actually, there is reason to believe that a greater degree of consensus exists in Japanese society as a whole than the stances of the various political parties would indicate. The Liberal Democratic Party, while conservative by Japanese standards, is actually committed to a kind of New Deal and welfare state position that probably is not too far from the viewpoint of many leftist voters. Many of the latter also probably have no real enthusiasm for the stated revolutionary objectives of the parties for which they vote. At the same time, many of the conservative voters no doubt share the pacifistic or neutral yearnings of the left.

Most important in the development of a consensus is the unifying influence of the mass media of communication — the press, television, and radio — which probably are as influential in determining public opinion in Japan as in any country in the world. Television and radio cover the nation with national networks, the largest of which is a semigovernmental agency on the pattern of the British B.B.C. The three largest newspapers, which also blanket the nation, together publish around 10,000,000 copies every morning and only slightly less each evening. All mass media attempt to take an independent stand from the political parties and as a result tend to follow the middle-of-the-road, bringing much of the public there with them.

Certainly the Japanese political situation in recent years seems to have calmed down considerably and the area of agreement between left and right to have increased. Many observers have felt that all except the extreme leftist fringe of the opposition groups have been moving a little toward the center. Perhaps this has been clearest in organized labor, where the emphasis seems to have shifted from political agitation for distant ideological objectives to collective bargaining for immediate economic benefits. The chief reasons for this apparent convergence of left and right has no doubt been economic prosperity, a returning sense of pride and confidence in Japan, and a growing knowledge of the rest of the world, just at a time when the Communist world was being thrown into ideological confusion.

The postwar period can be divided into three main political phases: the occupation, the period between 1952 and 1960 when Japan gradually emerged from under the long shadow of American influence that the occupation had cast, and the period since the great demonstrations of 1960, when the postwar political ferment has begun to subside and Japan has started to resume her natural place as one of the major advanced countries of the world.

The first discernible postwar trend in Japanese politics seemed to be toward the extreme left. This was a natural reaction to defeat and surrender, since the most radical members of Japanese society could most easily prove that they were not contaminated by the past, while conservatives were not sure to what extent their beliefs were discredited by defeat and they themselves would be penalized by the occupation authorities. Communist leaders were hailed as national heroes as they emerged from prison or returned from exile, and Communist publications appeared in large numbers. The Communist bubble, however, was pricked by the first postwar elections on April 10, 1946, in which they won only 3.8 per cent of the vote and five of the 466 seats in the lower house. By that time it had become clear that the Americans, in liberating Communist leaders, were not endorsing Communism and that it was by no means necessarily the wave of the future.

The two major conservative parties, the Liberals and Progressives (or Democrats), who were the successors respectively of the prewar Seiyukai and Minseito, together with a host of minor conservative parties and independents, won three-quarters of the vote. Although much of the conservative leadership had been lost through the purge, the grass-roots organization of the conservative parties obviously remained intact. And to replace the lost leaders, new men emerged who for the most part had been the "liberals" of the 1920's and 1930's. Significantly, those at the top were often former diplomats, because the chief function of the Japanese government at that time was to deal diplomatically with the occupation authorities. Shidehara of the Progressive Party, who was Prime Minister from October 1945 until the next spring, had been a famous "liberal" Foreign Minister in the 1920's, and he was succeeded in May 1946 by Yoshida of the Liberal Party, who was another former diplomat.

The Socialist Party proved itself far stronger than the Communists in the 1946 election, winning 17.8 per cent of the vote and virtually tying with the Progressives for second place in the lower house. Because of Japan's long tradition of government participation in business, socialist ideas were congenial to many Japanese and seemed to fit postwar conditions, since economic collapse had necessitated the continuation of strict government controls over the economy. Moreover, some of the socialist leaders, such as Katayama, were Protestant Christians, whose influence seemed enhanced by their close association with the United States. In the election of April 25, 1947, the Socialists did still better, winning 25.8 per cent of the vote and emerging ahead of the Liberals and Democrats as the plurality party in the lower house with 143 seats. Katayama became the new Prime Minister in a coalition cabinet with the Democrats and the small People's Cooperative Party.

This centrist coalition, however, did badly, being internally divided by ideological differences and unable in any case to put through its own program, because ultimate leadership remained in the hands of the occupation authorities. In February 1947 Katayama yielded the post of Prime Minister to Ashida, another former diplomat and the leader of the Democratic Party. Ashida organized a new Democratic-Socialist coalition cabinet, but it too foundered the next October. The centrist groups had become thoroughly discredited by their year and a half of ineffective leadership, and a pronounced trend toward the two political extremes set in.

Yoshida returned as Prime Minister and led his party, renamed the Democratic Liberals after being joined by defectors from the Democrats, to a smashing victory in the elections of January 23, 1949, winning an absolute majority of 264 seats in the lower house. At the other end of the political spectrum the Communists reached their postwar high-water mark with 9.6 per cent of the votes and 34 seats.

Perhaps this trend away from the center and toward the political extremes was inevitable as long as the economy stagnated and the government remained under the strict control of the occupation authorities. But by 1950 the economy had begun to surge forward and occupation controls were being rapidly relaxed. Communist excesses in acts of sabotage and Moscow insistence on a more militant stand also undercut the Communist Party. In the next general election of October 1, 1952, which followed the restoration of independence to Japan, the Communist vote dropped to 2.6 per cent, and both the Progressives (the former Democrats) and the Socialists, even though the latter had split the previous October into left and right parties, gained seats. The Liberals, however, managed to maintain their absolute majority in the lower house, and Yoshida continued as Prime Minister. In the next general election of April 19, 1953, there were no great changes in the balance of power.

The lifting of the purge bars, for the most part in 1951, had returned many prewar leaders to the political scene. Among them was Hatoyama, who, except for his sudden debarment by purge in 1946, would at that time have become Prime Minister in place of Yoshida. In an effort to regain control, Hatoyama had formed a splinter Liberal Party in March 1953, and in November 1954 he took leadership of a reorganized Democratic Party. These maneuverings led Yoshida at last to resign in December, after a total of seven years as Prime Minister, and Hatoyama took his place, leading the Democrats to victory as the plurality party in the election of February 27, 1955. The Left Socialists also registered strong gains, while the Communists slipped still further to 2 per cent of the vote.

The Japanese electoral system has from the start usually been based on electoral districts in which each voter has a single vote but three to five candidates are elected to the lower house. (In 1964 it was decided to increase the membership from 467 to 486 elected from 123 districts.) Such a system results in a form of proportional representation, favoring minority parties and facing large parties with the difficult task of splitting their votes evenly between several candidates. Despite this situation, however, there has been a steady tendency, both before and after the war, toward the development of a two-party system. The two Socialist parties knew that, until they rejoined forces, they had no chance of winning a majority in the lower house, and the two conservative parties realized that united they could better beat off the steady encroachment of the left. In October 1955, the Socialists reunited, and a month later the two conservative parties joined as the Liberal Democratic Party. The latter has remained effectively united ever since, and when the Socialists split again in January 1960, it was only part of the former Right Socialists which seceded as the Democratic Socialist Party.

Hatoyama, who had become the head of the Liberal Democratic Party, was forced by ill health to resign as Prime Minister in December 1956. He was succeeded by Ishibashi, but the latter also soon fell ill and was replaced by Kishi in February 1957. In the general election of May 22, 1958, the Liberal Democrats retained a solid majority in the lower house, but the struggle in the Diet over the renewal of the security treaty with the United States in the first half of 1960 and the violent demonstrations that swept Tokyo that May and June discredited Kishi in the eyes of the public, and he was forced to pass on the Prime Ministership to Ikeda in July.

Ikeda helped quiet the political excitement by adopting what he called a "low posture" toward both the public and the opposition. In other words, he sought to develop a consensus on controversial issues rather than utilize his Diet majority to push through legislation. Aided by the rapid expansion of the economy, he also diverted public attention from political controversy to his plan to double incomes within a decade. Under Ikeda the Liberal Democrats maintained their strong Diet majority in the general elections of November 20, 1961, and November 21, 1963. In July 1964 Ikeda was re-elected Party President for a third term by a slim majority but was forced by ill health to resign in November and was succeeded by Eisaku Sato.

14. Japan and America: The Future

The most critical days of Japanese-American relations probably lie in the past. It seems unlikely that the two countries will ever again be pitted against each other in mortal combat, as in the Second World War, or that one will have such complete control over the other, as we had over Japan during the occupation period. The influence of those fateful years will long be felt. They have set the general course of Japanese-American relations for the foreseeable future — and a much more promising course it is than might have been expected to emerge from a bitterly fought war and an occupation by a conquering army.

There have been three phases in postwar American attitudes toward Japan. As we have seen, in the early years of the occupation we felt that we were rehabilitating a miscreant Japan for possible membership in a united family of nations. In the latter years of the occupation, and during the remainder of the 1950's, we felt that we were helping Japan develop into a healthy member of the free world and sponsoring her return to full membership in international society. Since 1960 it has become progressively clear that Japan has regained its full independence and is winning back, not just full membership, but a place of leadership among the nations of the world. Our relations with Japan have become that between equals. Fortunately, as equals we have found that we share enough common interests and ideals to be essentially partners rather than rivals.

The chief reason for Japan's recent emergence as a potential world leader has been its spectacular economic success, buttressed by a relatively high degree of efficiency in meeting the political and social problems of an advanced society. With this has gone a restoration of Japanese self-confidence and a significant increase in respect for Japan on the part of other nations, particularly its neighbors. Important early steps in Japan's return to an international position commensurate with its potentialities were, first, the peace treaty of 1952, then the reparations agreements with its neighbors from 1954 on, and then Japan's admission to the GATT (General Agreement on Tariffs and Trade) in 1955 and to the United Nations in 1956. It was only after 1961, however, that Japan won recognition as a major supplier of technological knowledge and aid to the less developed countries, set up cabinet-level committees for consultation, first with the United States, and then with other leading Western powers, and began to exchange visits of foreign ministers regularly with the leading Western nations. In April 1964, Japan also became a full-fledged member of the OECD (Organization for Economic Cooperation and Development). Significantly, Japan is the only member of this group — often called the club of the advanced nations — not in the Atlantic Community.

And yet the American public, to say nothing of the people of Europe and most other parts of the world, seems to have remained unaware of the full importance of Japan for the future of the Far East and perhaps the whole of Asia. Attention has continued to be riveted on the twin problems of the hostility toward us of the Communist Chinese colossus and the instability and continuing crises of some of the relatively weak and undeveloped lands of Southeast Asia. Many people failed to see that, while these two areas stagnated or crept slowly ahead economically, Japan was rapidly building up an economic potential that might well prove more decisive for the future of that part of the world than anything happening in Communist China or Southeast Asia. The long-run significance of the political and social patterns being established in Asia's one major advanced nation was all but ignored, while attention continued to be directed to the far less successful political and social experiments in the less developed areas.

If Japan's growing economic potential and the example of her political and social institutions may some day prove decisive factors in the Far East, it becomes a matter of greatest concern to all the peoples of the world how Japan uses this economic potential and the direction in which its political and social institutions develop. It could be convincingly argued that Chinese Communist hostility and Southeast Asian crises are matters of less serious consequence to the United States and the rest of the world than Japan's friendship or hostility.

There is no room for easy complacence about Japan's future. The question of whether Japan should align itself with the United States and the free world, or with the Communists, or should maintain strict neutralism between the two, has been the most divisive issue in Japanese politics ever since the end of the war. Anti-Americanism has been a steady feature of the postwar scene. The vote of the parties of the left has been increasing. Japan's authoritarian and totalitarian tendencies of the past, as well as the totalitarian leanings of the extreme left today, all indicate that democratic and liberal institutions may not be securely established. And Japan's complete dependence on the maintenance of a high level of international trade, itself dependent on international order, adds a note of continuing uncertainty.

Even given these reasons for concern, however, Japan remains one of the corners of the world where optimism seems best justified. As we have seen, there is reason to discount to some extent the anti-Americanism and apparent sharp cleavage on foreign policy in Japanese society. Japan has shown itself to be politically and socially a more united and stable country than a superficial reading of the political situation would indicate. Japan's defense relationship with the United States has given it security over the past two decades and, before the Japanese could safely abandon it, they would probably have to make a defense effort of a magnitude that they have so far shown little desire to undertake. More important, Japan's economy and financial structure are overwhelmingly aligned with that of the free world and, by the very nature of things, are likely to continue to be so oriented. The trade on which Japan depends has been, and is likely to continue to be, more than nine-tenths with the non-Communist parts of the world and most heavily of all with the United States.

This may sound like a rash statement in view of the periodic efforts of many Japanese to expand trade with both Communist China and the Soviet Union and the desire of a large part of the public for the complete normalization of relations with both countries. Of course, Japan already has virtually full relations with the Soviet Union, although a peace treaty concluding the Second World War has not as yet been signed because of the Soviet's refusal to countenance Japan's demands for the return of the two large southern islands in the Kurile chain. In the case of Communist China, there are trade and cultural contacts but no diplomatic relations. The chief inhibiting factor has been Japan's full recognition of the Nationalist Chinese government on Taiwan. One reason Japan is not inclined to withdraw recognition from Nationalist China is the fact that trade with Taiwan has tended to be larger than with the mainland. The Japanese also have a sentimental attachment for Taiwan because of the large investment they made in the development of the island when it was a part of their empire, and the high esteem for Japan of the native Taiwanese, which is a flattering departure from the usual attitude of once colonial peoples toward their former rulers.

There is no reason, however, why the incompleteness of political relations with the Soviet Union and Communist China should limit economic relations if both sides desire it, as they say they do. The vast natural resources of Siberia and the huge expanse and population of China, both next door to Japan, would seem to hold out promise of almost unlimited trade. But the economic realities are far different. The chief inhibitor of trade is the nature of Communism itself. The Communist countries strive for self-sufficiency within their respective borders and therefore limit foreign trade to the minimum, while most free world countries attempt to maximize trade as the way to achieve mutual prosperity. Moreover, both Siberia and continental China would require heavy Japanese investment to become major trading partners, and this neither the Soviet Union nor Communist China is likely to permit on terms acceptable to Japan. And the propensity of Communist countries to turn trade off or on in order to achieve political objectives has served as a warning against dependence on them for raw materials.

As a result, Japan's trade with both the Soviet Union and Communist China has grown only slowly. Lumber, oil, and other raw materials have flowed from the Soviet Union to Japan but in no great quantity. There is little limit to what the Chinese Communists might wish to acquire from Japan, especially since their economic contacts with the Soviet Union have dwindled, but there are strict limits to what they can sell to Japan to pay for imports. They are capable of providing Japan with such raw materials as coal, iron ore, soy beans, and salt, but these products so far have competed poorly both in quality and price in the Japanese market. In 1963 only $320 million of Japan's trade was with the Soviet Union, which was 2.6 per cent of Japan's total trade. Already by 1956 trade with the China mainland had risen to the level of $157 million per year, but the Chinese Communists saw fit to cut it off in May 1958 in an unsuccessful effort to exert political pressure on Japan. By 1963 the figure had crept back only to $137 million, which was only 1.1 per cent of Japan's rapidly expanding world trade.

Another important reason why Japan is likely to remain aligned with us and the free world is that the bulk of the Japanese have come to share with us our basic ideals of a free, democratic society and a peaceful world order made up of truly independent nations, settling their problems, without recourse to force, through international institutions such as the United Nations. Despite the sharp confrontation between the various political parties of Japan, the great bulk of the people unquestionably believe in both ideals. Since the devotion to domestic and international democracy is even stronger among the young than among the old, it is hard to think that Japan will abandon either — at least under existing world conditions.

This is perhaps the most significant fact about Japan today. In a world in which some countries have not abandoned the use of military power in one form or another to subvert or subject other nations and in which the newly rising countries are for the most part finding the achievement of prosperity and democracy a hard and dubious road, it is indeed encouraging that Asia's one major modernized nation, after some decades of conflict between the forces of totalitarianism and democracy, seems to have firmly chosen the latter and to have ranged itself uncompromisingly on the side of peace through international law and order. As Japan's lead lengthens over the other nations of Asia, the influence of its ideas and institutions, as well as of its economy, will undoubtedly grow. The experience as well as the influence of Japan are reasons to hope that the other nations of Asia will in time win their way through their present difficulties to the same general position.

One other hope that Japan gives Asia is in the field of culture. In the early days of Japan's Westernization, the native culture seemed at times in danger of being swamped by foreign imports, and many Japanese have ever since feared that Japan will lose its cultural identity. Today, however, with the supposed process of Westernization far more advanced, Japan shows its cultural identity as clearly as ever, and much of Japan's traditional culture, such as music, dance, drama, literature, and the fine arts, has regained its old vigor. In fact, the cultural flow is now decidedly in two directions. There is a world-wide interest in Japanese art, literature, and drama, and Japanese canons of design, interior decoration, and landscape gardening have become as influential as any in the world. Thus, Japan has shown its ability to add much of Western culture, such as Western music, without losing its own.

The experience of modern Japan suggests that the common concept that the whole world is becoming Westernized is not correct. In the early phases of Western influence, this may seem to be the case, but now we can see that a very large percentage of the changes that have swept Japan during the past century are better described as modernization than as Westernization. Industrialization has developed in the West too only during the past two centuries. Transistor radios or air travel are as natural a part of contemporary Japanese society as of our own. So also are such strictly modern institutions as universal education, universal suffrage, or labor unions. A highly modernized Japan remains distinctively Japanese, and the West today seems as ready to make cultural borrowings from Japan as Japan from the West. All this gives hope to other less modernized non-Western countries that they too can modernize without losing their cultural distinctiveness.

In making this generally optimistic estimate of where Japan stands today and what its influence is likely to be, I would not wish to imply that there are not serious problems. In addition to those already mentioned, there is the continuing animosity of many people for the Japanese, which still limits their potential influence. There is also their difficulty of communication with the outside world. Few other people know the Japanese language, while the Japanese themselves, for a variety of reasons, have difficulty in mastering English, the *lingua franca* of Asia, or the other major international languages. No people stands behind a more serious language barrier, which they must overcome both for the sake of the trade that is so important to them and in order to assume the role they might play in the future of Asia.

There are also a series of problems existing specifically between the United States and Japan. The latter's defense still depends in large part on us, and the resultant American bases in Japan, with their inevitable possibilities for political friction, call for the continuance of tact and tolerance on both sides. Natural American desires to see the Japanese assume their full defense load, or even participate in the broader defense of the free world, must be tempered by an understanding of psychological and political conditions in Japan.

In the military field there is also the particularly difficult problem of the Ryukyu Islands, or Okinawa, as the Japanese call them collectively after the name of the principal island. The United States and Japan are cooperating effectively over the economic development of the islands, and we have promised continuing efforts to expand the area of local autonomy and ultimately to return the islands to Japan. But the time when the relaxation of world tensions or other factors so changes military necessities as to permit the return of the islands to Japan still seems over the horizon. In the meantime, the continued administrative control by the United States over 900,000 people who regard themselves as Japanese and are accepted as such by the Japanese presents the two countries with the need for the greatest degree of tact, forbearance, and wisdom.

In the economic field, which underlies all other possibilities in Japan, direct trade with the United States and the influence of our economy on the economic health of the world are almost decisive factors. The shadow of American economic influence still lies long in Japan. And the imbalance of trade in our favor, even if more than made up in balance of payments by American military expenditures and investment in Japan, creates many economic irritations for the Japanese. A large part of our exports to Japan, such as grains, soy beans, cotton, coal, scrap iron, and certain types of machinery, could not be supplied, at least in sufficient quantity, by Japan itself; yet almost everything Japan can export in quantity to us is something we ourselves produce. As a consequence, Japanese exports to us are more likely than are our exports to her to run into barriers of one sort or another or at least demands for such barriers.

Actually, the great two-way flow of trade between Japan and the United States, now worth well over 3 billion dollars a year, is the great success story of international commerce — the largest transoceanic trade the world has ever seen. But just because it is so great there is a correspondingly wide fringe of problems which serve as irritants on both sides. Both we and the Japanese must constantly strive to keep these problem areas to the minimum, and we, in particular, who are less dependent on this flow of trade, must always bear in mind that it is not only mutually beneficial, but is one of the chief factors that makes Japan the healthy country it is, capable of playing a significant role in the achievement of world peace and prosperity.

Perhaps the most difficult area in the relations between the United States and Japan is the psychological one. We are a much bigger country than Japan, with twice the population and about ten times the productive capacity. This imbalance in size, when underlain by a recent past in which we controlled Japan, makes the Japanese sensitive to our possible domination of them, and Americans sometimes seem unconsciously dominating in their attitudes. We must never forget that Japan is now not simply an international equal, but one of our five or six most important partners in facing the problems of the world. While once we controlled Japan and later sought to lead her, today we must expect her to make her decisions strictly in her own interests and as these are seen by Japanese themselves. If we can remember to conduct ourselves in accordance with this situation and if we can avoid the other pitfalls in our relations with Japan, we shall probably find that the interests and ideals we now share with the Japanese will make them staunch partners of ours in the quest for world peace and prosperity.

APPENDIXES

Appendix I. The Potsdam Proclamation

July 26, 1945

(1) WE–THE PRESIDENT of the United States, the President of the National Government of the Republic of China, and the Prime Minister of Great Britain, representing the hundreds of millions of our countrymen, have conferred and agree that Japan shall be given an opportunity to end this war.

(2) The prodigious land, sea and air forces of the United States, the British Empire and of China, many times reinforced by their armies and air fleets from the west, are poised to strike the final blows upon Japan. This military power is sustained and inspired by the determination of all the Allied Nations to prosecute the war against Japan until she ceases to resist.

(3) The result of the futile and senseless German resistance to the might of the aroused free peoples of the world stands forth in awful clarity as an example to the people of Japan. The might that now converges on Japan is immeasurably greater than that which, when applied to the resisting Nazis,.necessarily laid waste to the lands, the industry and the method of life of the whole German people. The full application of our military power, backed by our resolve, *will* mean the inevitable and complete destruction of the Japanese armed forces and just as inevitably the utter devastation of the Japanese homeland.

(4) The time has come for Japan to decide whether she will continue to be controlled by those self-willed militaristic advisers whose unintelligent calculations have brought the Empire of Japan to the threshold of annihilation, or whether she will follow the path of reason.

(5) Following are our terms. We will not deviate from them. There are no alternatives. We shall brook no delay.

(6) There must be eliminated for all time the authority and in-

fluence of those who have deceived and misled the people of Japan into embarking on world conquest, for we insist that a new order of peace, security and justice will be impossible until irresponsible militarism is driven from the world.

(7) Until such a new order is established *and* until there is convincing proof that Japan's war-making power is destroyed, points in Japanese territory to be designated by the Allies shall be occupied to secure the achievement of the basic objectives we are here setting forth.

(8) The terms of the Cairo Declaration shall be carried out and Japanese sovereignty shall be limited to the islands of Honshu, Hokkaido, Kyushu, Shikoku and such minor islands as we determine.

(9) The Japanese military forces, after being completely disarmed, shall be permitted to return to their homes with the opportunity to lead peaceful and productive lives.

(10) We do not intend that the Japanese shall be enslaved as a race or destroyed as a nation, but stern justice shall be meted out to all war criminals, including those who have visited cruelties upon our prisoners. The Japanese Government shall remove all obstacles to the revival and strengthening of democratic tendencies among the Japanese people. Freedom of speech, of religion, and of thought, as well as respect for the fundamental human rights shall be established.

(11) Japan shall be permitted to maintain such industries as will sustain her economy and permit the exaction of just reparations in kind, but not those which would enable her to re-arm for war. To this end, access to, as distinguished from control of, raw materials shall be permitted. Eventual Japanese participation in world trade relations shall be permitted.

(12) The occupying forces of the Allies shall be withdrawn from Japan as soon as these objectives have been accomplished and there has been established in accordance with the freely expressed will of the Japanese people a peacefully inclined and responsible government.

(13) We call upon the government of Japan to proclaim now the unconditional surrender of all Japanese armed forces, and to provide proper and adequate assurances of their good faith in such action. The alternative for Japan is prompt and utter destruction.

Appendix II.   United States Initial Post-Surrender Policy for Japan*

PURPOSE OF THIS DOCUMENT

This document is a statement of general initial policy relating to Japan after surrender. It has been approved by the President and distributed to the Supreme Commander for the Allied Powers and to appropriate U. S. departments and agencies for their guidance. It does not deal with all matters relating to the occupation of Japan requiring policy determinations. Such matters as are not included or are not fully covered herein have been or will be dealt with separately.

Part I—Ultimate Objectives

The ultimate objectives of the United States in regard to Japan, to which policies in the initial period must conform, are:

(*a*) To insure that Japan will not again become a menace to the United States or to the peace and security of the world.

(*b*) To bring about the eventual establishment of a peaceful and responsible government which will respect the rights of other states and will support the objectives of the United States as reflected in the ideals and principles of the Charter of the United Nations. The United States desires that this government should conform as closely as may be to principles of democratic self-government but

---

* Prepared jointly by the Department of State, the War Department, and the Navy Department and approved by the President on September 6, 1945. The document in substance was sent to General MacArthur by radio on August 29 and, after approval by the President, by messenger on September 6.

it is not the responsibility of the Allied Powers to impose upon Japan any form of government not supported by the freely expressed will of the people.

These objectives will be achieved by the following principal means:

(*a*) Japan's sovereignty will be limited to the islands of Honshu, Hokkaido, Kyushu, Shikoku and such minor outlying islands as may be determined, in accordance with the Cairo Declaration and other agreements to which the United States is or may be a party.

(*b*) Japan will be completely disarmed and demilitarized. The authority of the militarists and the influence of militarism will be totally eliminated from her political, economic, and social life. Institutions expressive of the spirit of militarism and aggression will be vigorously suppressed.

(*c*) The Japanese people shall be encouraged to develop a desire for individual liberties and respect for fundamental human rights, particularly the freedoms of religion, assembly, speech, and the press. They shall also be encouraged to form democratic and representative organizations.

(*d*) The Japanese people shall be afforded opportunity to develop for themselves an economy which will permit the peacetime requirements of the population to be met.

Part II—Allied Authority

1. *Military Occupation*

There will be a military occupation of the Japanese home islands to carry into effect the surrender terms and further the achievement of the ultimate objectives stated above. The occupation shall have the character of an operation in behalf of the principal allied powers acting in the interests of the United Nations at war with Japan. For that reason, participation of the forces of other nations that have taken a leading part in the war against Japan will be welcomed and expected. The occupation forces will be under the command of a Supreme Commander designated by the United States.

Although every effort will be made, by consultation and by constitution of appropriate advisory bodies, to establish policies for the conduct of the occupation and the control of Japan which will satisfy the principal Allied powers, in the event of any differences of opinion among them, the policies of the United States will govern.

2. *Relationship to Japanese Government*

The authority of the Emperor and the Japanese Government will be subject to the Supreme Commander, who will possess all powers necessary to effectuate the surrender terms and to carry out the policies established for the conduct of the occupation and the control of Japan.

In view of the present character of Japanese society and the desire of the United States to attain its objectives with a minimum commitment of its forces and resources, the Supreme Commander will exercise his authority through Japanese governmental machinery and agencies, including the Emperor, to the extent that this satisfactorily furthers United States objectives. The Japanese Government will be permitted, under his instructions, to exercise the normal powers of government in matters of domestic administration. This policy, however, will be subject to the right and duty of the Supreme Commander to require changes in governmental machinery or personnel or to act directly if the Emperor or other Japanese authority does not satisfactorily meet the requirements of the Supreme Commander in effectuating the surrender terms. This policy, moreover, does not commit the Supreme Commander to support the Emperor or any other Japanese governmental authority in opposition to evolutionary changes looking toward the attainment of United States objectives. The policy is to use the existing form of Government in Japan, not to support it. Changes in the form of Government initiated by the Japanese people or government in the direction of modifying its feudal and authoritarian tendencies are to be permitted and favored. In the event that the effectuation of such changes involves the use of force by the Japanese people or government against persons opposed thereto, the Supreme Commander should intervene only where necessary to ensure the security of his forces and the attainment of all other objectives of the occupation.

3. *Publicity as to Policies*

The Japanese people, and the world at large, shall be kept fully informed of the objectives and policies of the occupation, and of progress made in their fulfilment.

Part III—Political

1. *Disarmament and Demilitarization*

Disarmament and demilitarization are the primary tasks of the military occupation and shall be carried out promptly and with determination. Every effort shall be made to bring home to the Japanese people the part played by the military and naval leaders, and those who collaborated with them, in bringing about the existing and future distress of the people.

Japan is not to have an army, navy, air force, secret police organization, or any civil aviation. Japan's ground, air and naval forces shall be disarmed and disbanded and the Japanese Imperial General Headquarters, the General Staff and all secret police organizations shall be dissolved. Military and naval matériel, military and naval vessels and military and naval installations, and military, naval and civilian aircraft shall be surrendered and shall be disposed of as required by the Supreme Commander.

High officials of the Japanese Imperial General Headquarters, and General Staff, other high military and naval officials of the Japanese Government, leaders of ultra-nationalist and militarist organizations and other important exponents of militarism and aggression will be taken into custody and held for future disposition. Persons who have been active exponents of militarism and militant nationalism will be removed and excluded from public office and from any other position of public or substantial private responsibility. Ultranationalistic or militaristic social, political, professional and commercial societies and institutions will be dissolved and prohibited.

Militarism and ultra-nationalism, in doctrine and practice, including para-military training, shall be eliminated from the educational system. Former career military and naval officers, both commissioned and non-commissioned, and all other exponents of militarism and ultra-nationalism shall be excluded from supervisory and teaching positions.

2. *War Criminals*

Persons charged by the Supreme Commander or appropriate United Nations agencies with being war criminals, including those charged with having visited cruelties upon United Nations prisoners or other nationals, shall be arrested, tried and, if convicted, punished. Those wanted by another of the United Nations for offenses against its nationals, shall, if not wanted for trial or as witnesses or otherwise by the Supreme Commander, be turned over to the custody of such other nation.

3. *Encouragement of Desire for Individual Liberties and Democratic Processes*

Freedom of religious worship shall be proclaimed promptly on occupation. At the same time it should be made plain to the Japanese that ultra-nationalistic and militaristic organizations and movements will not be permitted to hide behind the cloak of religion.

The Japanese people shall be afforded opportunity and encouraged to become familiar with the history, institutions, culture, and the accomplishments of the United States and the other democracies. Association of personnel of the occupation forces with the Japanese population should be controlled, only to the extent necessary, to further the policies and objectives of the occupation.

Democratic political parties, with rights of assembly and public discussion, shall be encouraged, subject to the necessity for maintaining the security of the occupying forces.

Laws, decrees and regulations which establish discriminations on ground of race, nationality, creed or political opinion shall be abrogated; those which conflict with the objectives and policies outlined in this document shall be repealed, suspended or amended as required; and agencies charged specifically with their enforcement shall be abolished or appropriately modified. Persons unjustly confined by Japanese authority on political grounds shall be released. The judicial, legal and police systems shall be reformed as soon as practicable to conform to the policies set forth in Articles 1 and 3 of this Part III and thereafter shall be progressively influenced, to protect individual liberties and civil rights.

PART IV—ECONOMIC

1. *Economic Demilitarization*

The existing economic basis of Japanese military strength must be destroyed and not be permitted to revive.

Therefore, a program will be enforced containing the following elements, among others; the immediate cessation and future prohibition of production of all goods designed for the equipment, maintenance, or use of any military force or establishment; the imposition of a ban upon any specialized facilities for the production or repair of implements of war, including naval vessels and all forms of aircraft; the institution of a system of inspection and control over selected elements in Japanese economic activity to prevent concealed or disguised military preparation; the elimination in Japan of those selected industries or branches of production whose chief value to Japan is in preparing for war; the prohibition of specialized research and instruction directed to the development of war-making power; and the limitation of the size and character of Japan's heavy industries to its future peaceful requirements, and restriction of Japanese merchant shipping to the extent required to accomplish the objectives of demilitarization.

The eventual disposition of those existing production facilities within Japan which are to be eliminated in accord with this program, as between conversion to other uses, transfer abroad, and scrapping will be determined after inventory. Pending decision, facilities readily convertible for civilian production should not be destroyed, except in emergency situations.

2. *Promotion of Democratic Forces*

Encouragement shall be given and favor shown to the development of organizations in labor, industry, and agriculture, organized on a democratic basis. Policies shall be favored which permit a wide distribution of income and of the ownership of the means of production and trade.

Those forms of economic activity, organization and leadership shall be favored that are deemed likely to strengthen the peaceful disposition of the Japanese people, and to make it difficult to command or direct economic activity in support of military ends.

To this end it shall be the policy of the Supreme Commander:

(*a*) To prohibit the retention in or selection for places of importance in the economic field of individuals who do not direct future Japanese economic effort solely towards peaceful ends; and

(*b*) To favor a program for the dissolution of the large industrial and banking combinations which have exercised control of a great part of Japan's trade and industry.

3. *Resumption of Peaceful Economic Activity*

The policies of Japan have brought down upon the people great economic destruction and confronted them with the prospect of economic difficulty and suffering. The plight of Japan is the direct outcome of its own behavior, and the Allies will not undertake the burden of repairing the damage. It can be repaired only if the Japanese people renounce all military aims and apply themselves diligently and with single purpose to the ways of peaceful living. It will be necessary for them to undertake physical reconstruction, deeply to reform the nature and direction of their economic activities and institutions, and to find useful employment for their people along lines adapted to and devoted to peace. The Allies have no intention of imposing conditions which would prevent the accomplishment of these tasks in due time.

Japan will be expected to provide goods and services to meet the needs of the occupying forces to the extent that this can be effected without causing starvation, widespread disease and acute physical distress.

The Japanese authorities will be expected, and if necessary directed, to maintain, develop and enforce programs that serve the following purposes:

(a) To avoid acute economic distress.

(b) To assure just and impartial distribution of available supplies.

(c) To meet the requirements for reparations deliveries agreed upon by the Allied Governments.

(d) To facilitate the restoration of Japanese economy so that the reasonable peaceful requirements of the population can be satisfied.

In this connection, the Japanese authorities on their own responsibility shall be permitted to establish and administer controls over economic activities, including essential national public services, finance, banking, and production and distribution of essential commodities, subject to the approval and review of the Supreme Commander in order to assure their conformity with the objectives of the occupation.

4. Reparations and Restitution

Reparations

Reparations for Japanese aggression shall be made:

(a) Through the transfer—as may be determined by the appropriate Allied authorities—of Japanese property located outside of the territories to be retained by Japan.

(b) Through the transfer of such goods or existing capital equipment and facilities as are not necessary for a peaceful Japanese economy or the supplying of the occupying forces. Exports other than those directed to be shipped on reparation account or as restitution may be made only to those recipients who agree to provide necessary imports in exchange or agree to pay for such exports in foreign exchange. No form of reparation shall be exacted which will interfere with or prejudice the program for Japan's demilitarization.

Restitution

Full and prompt restitution will be required of all identifiable looted property.

5. Fiscal, Monetary, and Banking Policies

The Japanese authorities will remain responsible for the management and direction of the domestic fiscal, monetary, and credit policies subject to the approval and review of the Supreme Commander.

6. *International Trade and Financial Relations*

Japan shall be permitted eventually to resume normal trade relations with the rest of the world. During occupation and under suitable controls, Japan will be permitted to purchase from foreign countries raw materials and other goods that it may need for peaceful purposes, and to export goods to pay for approved imports.

Control is to be maintained over all imports and exports of goods, and foreign exchange and financial transactions. Both the policies followed in the exercise of these controls and their actual administration shall be subject to the approval and supervision of the Supreme Commander in order to make sure that they are not contrary to the policies of the occupying authorities, and in particular that all foreign purchasing power that Japan may acquire is utilized only for essential needs.

7. *Japanese Property Located Abroad*

Existing Japanese external assets and existing Japanese assets located in territories detached from Japan under the terms of surrender, including assets owned in whole or part by the Imperial Household and Government, shall be revealed to the occupying authorities and held for disposition according to the decision of the Allied authorities.

8. *Equality of Opportunity for Foreign Enterprise within Japan*

The Japanese authorities shall not give, or permit any Japanese business organization to give, exclusive or preferential opportunity or terms to the enterprise of any foreign country, or cede to such enterprise control of any important branch of economic activity.

9. *Imperial Household Property*

Imperial Household property shall not be exempted from any action necessary to carry out the objectives of the occupation.

Appendix III.　The Constitution of Japan

We, the Japanese people, acting through our duly elected representatives in the National Diet, determined that we shall secure for ourselves and our posterity the fruits of peaceful cooperation with all nations and the blessings of liberty throughout this land, and resolved that never again shall we be visited with the horrors of war through the action of government, do proclaim that sovereign power resides with the people and do firmly establish this Constitution. Government is a sacred trust of the people, the authority for which is derived from the people, the powers of which are exercised by the representatives of the people, and the benefits of which are enjoyed by the people. This is a universal principle of mankind upon which this Constitution is founded. We reject and revoke all constitutions, laws, ordinances, and rescripts in conflict herewith.

We, the Japanese people, desire peace for all time and are deeply conscious of the high ideals controlling human relationship, and we have determined to preserve our security and existence, trusting in the justice and faith of the peace-loving peoples of the world. We desire to occupy an honored place in an international society striving for the preservation of peace, and the banishment of tyranny and slavery, oppression and intolerance for all time from the earth. We recognize that all peoples of the world have the right to live in peace, free from fear and want.

We believe that no nation is responsible to itself alone, but that laws of political morality are universal; and that obedience to such laws is incumbent upon all nations who would sustain their own sovereignty and justify their sovereign relationship with other nations.

We, the Japanese people, pledge our national honor to accomplish these high ideals and purposes with all our resources.

CHAPTER I. THE EMPEROR

Article 1. The Emperor shall be the symbol of the State and of the unity of the people, deriving his position from the will of the people with whom resides sovereign power.

Article 2. The Imperial Throne shall be dynastic and succeeded to in accordance with the Imperial House Law passed by the Diet.

Article 3. The advice and approval of the Cabinet shall be required for all acts of the Emperor in matters of state, and the Cabinet shall be responsible therefor.

Article 4. The Emperor shall perform only such acts in matters of state as are provided for in this Constitution and he shall not have powers related to government.

The Emperor may delegate the performance of his acts in matters of state as may be provided by law.

Article 5. When, in accordance with the Imperial House Law, a Regency is established, the Regent shall perform his acts in matters of state in the Emperor's name. In this case, paragraph one of the preceding article will be applicable.

Article 6. The Emperor shall appoint the Prime Minister as designated by the Diet.

The Emperor shall appoint the Chief Judge of the Supreme Court as designated by the Cabinet.

Article 7. The Emperor, with the advice and approval of the Cabinet, shall perform the following acts in matters of state on behalf of the people:

> Promulgation of amendments of the constitution, laws, cabinet orders and treaties.
>
> Convocation of the Diet.
>
> Dissolution of the House of Representatives.
>
> Proclamation of general election of members of the Diet.
>
> Attestation of the appointment and dismissal of Ministers of State and other officials as provided for by law, and of full powers and credentials of Ambassadors and Ministers.
>
> Attestation of general and special amnesty, commutation of punishment, reprieve, and restoration of rights.
>
> Awarding of honors.
>
> Attestation of instruments of ratification and other diplomatic documents as provided for by law.
>
> Receiving foreign ambassadors and ministers.
>
> Performance of ceremonial functions.

Article 8. No property can be given to, or received by, the Imperial House, nor can any gifts be made therefrom, without the authorization of the Diet.

Chapter II. Renunciation of War

Article 9. Aspiring sincerely to an international peace based on justice and order, the Japanese people forever renounce war as a sovereign right of the nation and the threat or use of force as means of settling international disputes.

In order to accomplish the aim of the preceding paragraph, land, sea, and air forces, as well as other war potential, will never be maintained. The right of belligerency of the state will not be recognized.

Chapter III. Rights and Duties of the People

Article 10. The conditions necessary for being a Japanese national shall be determined by law.

Article 11. The people shall not be prevented from enjoying any of the fundamental human rights. These fundamental human rights guaranteed to the people by this Constitution shall be conferred upon the people of this and future generations as eternal and inviolate rights.

Article 12. The freedoms and rights guaranteed to the people by this Constitution shall be maintained by the constant endeavor of the people, who shall refrain from any abuse of these freedoms and rights and shall always be responsible for utilizing them for the public welfare.

Article 13. All of the people shall be respected as individuals. Their right to life, liberty, and the pursuit of happiness shall, to the extent that it does not interfere with the public welfare, be the supreme consideration in legislation and in other governmental affairs.

Article 14. All of the people are equal under the law and there shall be no discrimination in political, economic or social relations, because of race, creed, sex, social status or family origin.

Peers and peerage shall not be recognized.

No privilege shall accompany any award of honor, decoration or any distinction, nor shall any such award be valid beyond the lifetime of the individual who now holds or hereafter may receive it.

Article 15. The people have the inalienable right to choose their public officials and to dismiss them.

All public officials are servants of the whole community and not of any group thereof.

Universal adult suffrage is guaranteed with regard to the election of public officials.

In all elections, secrecy of the ballot shall not be violated. A voter shall not be answerable, publicly or privately, for the choice he has made.

Article 16. Every person shall have the right of peaceful petition for the redress of damage, for the removal of public officials, for the enactment, repeal or amendment of laws, ordinances or regulations and for other matters; nor shall any person be in any way discriminated against for sponsoring such a petition.

Article 17. Every person may sue for redress as provided by law from the State or a public entity, in case he has suffered damage through illegal act of any public official.

Article 18. No person shall be held in bondage of any kind. Involuntary servitude, except as punishment for crime, is prohibited.

Article 19. Freedom of thought and conscience shall not be violated.

Article 20. Freedom of religion is guaranteed to all. No religious organization shall receive any privileges from the State, nor exercise any political authority.

No person shall be compelled to take part in any religious act, celebration, rite or practice.

The State and its organs shall refrain from religious education or any other religious activity.

Article 21. Freedom of assembly and association as well as speech, press and all other forms of expression are guaranteed.

No censorship shall be maintained, nor shall the secrecy of any means of communication be violated.

Article 22. Every person shall have freedom to choose and change his residence and to choose his occupation to the extent that it does not interfere with the public welfare.

Freedom of all persons to move to a foreign country and to divest themselves of their nationality shall be inviolate.

Article 23. Academic freedom is guaranteed.

Article 24. Marriage shall be based only on the mutual consent of both sexes and it shall be maintained through mutual cooperation with the equal rights of husband and wife as a basis.

With regard to choice of spouse, property rights, inheritance, choice of domicile, divorce and other matters pertaining to marriage and the family, laws shall be enacted from the standpoint of individual dignity and the essential equality of the sexes.

Article 25. All people shall have the right to maintain the minimum standards of wholesome and cultured living.

In all spheres of life, the State shall use its endeavors for the promotion and extension of social welfare and security, and of public health.

Article 26. All people shall have the right to receive an equal education correspondent to their ability, as provided by law.

All people shall be obligated to have all boys and girls under their protection receive ordinary education as provided for by law. Such compulsory education shall be free.

Article 27. All people shall have the right and the obligation to work.

Standards for wages, hours, rest and other working conditions shall be fixed by law.

Children shall not be exploited.

Article 28. The right of workers to organize and to bargain and act collectively is guaranteed.

Article 29. The right to own or to hold property is inviolable.

Property rights shall be defined by law, in conformity with the public welfare.

Private property may be taken for public use upon just compensation therefor.

Article 30. The people shall be liable to taxation as provided by law.

Article 31. No person shall be deprived of life or liberty, nor shall any other criminal penalty be imposed, except according to procedure established by law.

Article 32. No person shall be denied the right of access to the courts.

Article 33. No person shall be apprehended except upon warrant issued by a competent judicial officer which specifies the offense with which the person is charged, unless he is apprehended, the offense being committed.

Article 34. No person shall be arrested or detained without being at once informed of the charges against him or without the immediate privilege of counsel; nor shall he be detained without adequate cause; and upon demand of any person such cause must be immediately shown in open court in his presence and the presence of his counsel.

Article 35. The right of all persons to be secure in their homes, papers and effects against entries, searches and seizures shall not be impaired except upon warrant issued for adequate cause and particularly describing the place to be searched and things to be seized, or except as provided by Article 33.

Each search or seizure shall be made upon separate warrant issued by a competent judicial officer.

Article 36. The infliction of torture by any public officer and cruel punishments are absolutely forbidden.

Article 37. In all criminal cases the accused shall enjoy the right to a speedy and public trial by an impartial tribunal.

He shall be permitted full opportunity to examine all witnesses, and he shall have the right of compulsory process for obtaining witnesses on his behalf at public expense.

At all times the accused shall have the assistance of competent counsel who shall, if the accused is unable to secure the same by his own efforts, be assigned to his use by the State.

Article 38. No person shall be compelled to testify against himself.

Confession made under compulsion, torture or threat, or after prolonged arrest or detention shall not be admitted in evidence.

No person shall be convicted or punished in cases where the only proof against him is his own confession.

Article 39. No person shall be held criminally liable for an act which was lawful at the time it was committed, or of which he has been acquitted, nor shall he be placed in double jeopardy.

Article 40. Any person, in case he is acquitted after he has been arrested or detained, may sue the State for redress as provided by law.

CHAPTER IV. THE DIET

Article 41. The Diet shall be the highest organ of state power, and shall be the sole law-making organ of the State.

Article 42. The Diet shall consist of two Houses, namely the House of Representatives and the House of Councillors.

Article 43. Both Houses shall consist of elected members, representative of all the people.

The number of the members of each House shall be fixed by law.

Article 44. The qualifications of members of both Houses and their electors shall be fixed by law. However, there shall be no discrimination because of race, creed, sex, social status, family origin, education, property or income.

Article 45. The term of office of members of the House of Representatives shall be four years. However, the term shall be terminated before the full term is up in case the House of Representatives is dissolved.

Article 46. The term of office of members of the House of Councillors shall be six years, and election for half the members shall take place every three years.

Article 47. Electoral districts, method of voting and other matters pertaining to the method of election of members of both Houses shall be fixed by law.

Article 48. No person shall be permitted to be a member of both Houses simultaneously.

Article 49. Members of both Houses shall receive appropriate annual payment from the national treasury in accordance with law.

Article 50. Except in cases provided by law, members of both Houses shall be exempt from apprehension while the Diet is in session, and any members apprehended before the opening of the session shall be freed during the term of the session upon demand of the House.

Article 51. Members of both Houses shall not be held liable outside the House for speeches, debates or votes cast inside the House.

Article 52. An ordinary session of the Diet shall be convoked once per year.

Article 53. The Cabinet may determine to convoke extraordinary sessions of the Diet. When a quarter or more of the total members of either House makes the demand, the Cabinet must determine on such convocation.

Article 54. When the House of Representatives is dissolved, there must be a general election of members of the House of Representatives within forty (40) days from the date of dissolution, and the Diet must be convoked within thirty (30) days from the date of the election.

When the House of Representatives is dissolved, the House of Councillors is closed at the same time. However, the Cabinet may in time of national emergency convoke the House of Councillors in emergency session.

Measures taken at such session as mentioned in the proviso of the preceding paragraph shall be provisional and shall become null and void unless agreed to by the House of Representatives within a period of ten (10) days after the opening of the next session of the Diet.

Article 55. Each House shall judge disputes related to qualifications of its members. However, in order to deny a seat to any member, it is necessary to pass a resolution by a majority of two-thirds or more of the members present.

Article 56. Business cannot be transacted in either House unless one-third or more of total membership is present.

All matters shall be decided, in each House, by a majority of those present, except as elsewhere provided in the Constitution, and in case of a tie, the presiding officer shall decide the issue.

Article 57. Deliberation in each House shall be public. However, a secret meeting may be held where a majority of two-thirds or more of those members present passes a resolution therefor.

Each House shall keep a record of proceedings. This record shall be published and given general circulation, excepting such parts of proceedings of secret session as may be deemed to require secrecy.

Upon demand of one-fifth or more of the members present, votes of the members on any matter shall be recorded in the minutes.

Article 58. Each House shall select its own president and other officials.

Each House shall establish its rules pertaining to meetings, proceedings and internal discipline, and may punish members for disorderly conduct. However, in order to expel a member, a majority of two-thirds or more of those members present must pass a resolution thereon.

Article 59. A bill becomes a law on passage by both Houses, except as otherwise provided by the Constitution.

A bill which is passed by the House of Representatives, and upon which the House of Councillors makes a decision different from that of the House of Representatives, becomes a law when passed a second time by the House of Representatives by a majority of two-thirds or more of the members present.

The provision of the preceding paragraph does not preclude the House of Representatives from calling for the meeting of a joint committee of both Houses, provided for by law.

Failure by the House of Councillors to take final action within sixty (60) days after receipt of a bill passed by the House of Representatives, time in recess excepted, may be determined by the House of Representatives to constitute a rejection of the said bill by the House of Councillors.

Article 60. The budget must first be submitted to the House of Representatives.

Upon consideration of the budget, when the House of Councillors makes a decision different from that of the House of Representatives, and when no agreement can be reached even through a joint committee of both Houses, provided for by law, or in the case of failure by the House of Councillors to take final action within thirty (30) days, the period of recess excluded, after the receipt of the budget passed by the House of Representatives, the decision of the House of Representatives shall be the decision of the Diet.

Article 61. The second paragraph of the preceding article applies also to the Diet approval required for the conclusion of treaties.

Article 62. Each House may conduct investigations in relation to government, and may demand the presence and testimony of witnesses, and the production of records.

Article 63. The Prime Minister and other Ministers of State may, at any time, appear in either House for the purpose of speaking on bills, regardless of whether they are members of the House or not. They must appear when their presence is required in order to give answers or explanations.

Article 64. The Diet shall set up an impeachment court from among the members of both Houses for the purpose of trying those judges against whom removal proceedings have been instituted.

Matters relating to impeachment shall be provided by law.

CHAPTER V. THE CABINET

Article 65. Executive power shall be vested in the Cabinet.

Article 66. The Cabinet shall consist of the Prime Minister, who shall be its head, and other Ministers of State, as provided for by law.

The Prime Minister and other Ministers of State must be civilians.

The Cabinet, in the exercise of executive power, shall be collectively responsible to the Diet.

Article 67. The Prime Minister shall be designated from among the members of the Diet by a resolution of the Diet. This designation shall precede all other business.

If the House of Representatives and the House of Councillors disagree and if no agreement can be reached even through a joint committee of both Houses, provided for by law, or the House of Councillors fails to make designation within ten (10) days, exclusive of the period of recess, after the House of Representatives has made designation, the decision of the House of Representatives shall be the decision of the Diet.

Article 68. The Prime Minister shall appoint the Ministers of State. However a majority of their number must be chosen from among the members of the Diet.

The Prime Minister may remove the Ministers of State as he chooses.

Article 69. If the House of Representatives passes a non-confidence resolution, or rejects a confidence resolution, the Cabinet shall resign en masse, unless the House of Representatives is dissolved within ten (10) days.

Article 70. When there is a vacancy in the post of Prime Minister, or upon the first convocation of the Diet after a general election of members of the House of Representatives, the Cabinet shall resign en masse.

Article 71. In the cases mentioned in the two preceding articles, the Cabinet shall continue its functions until the time when a new Prime Minister is appointed.

Article 72. The Prime Minister, representing the Cabinet, submits bills, reports on general national affairs and foreign relations to the Diet and exercises control and supervision over various administrative branches.

Article 73. The Cabinet, in addition to other general administrative functions, shall perform the following functions:

> Administer the law faithfully; conduct affairs of state.
>
> Manage foreign affairs.
>
> Conclude treaties. However, it shall obtain prior or, depending on circumstances, subsequent approval of the Diet.
>
> Administer the civil service, in accordance with standards established by law.
>
> Prepare the budget, and present it to the Diet.
>
> Enact cabinet orders in order to execute the provisions of this Constitution and of the law. However, it cannot include penal provisions in such cabinet orders unless authorized by such law.
>
> Decide on general amnesty, special amnesty, commutation of punishment, reprieve, and restoration of rights.

Article 74. All laws and cabinet orders shall be signed by the competent Minister of State and countersigned by the Prime Minister.

Article 75. The Ministers of State, during their tenure of office, shall not be subject to legal action without the consent of the Prime Minister. However, the right to take that action is not impaired hereby.

CHAPTER VI. JUDICIARY

Article 76. The whole judicial power is vested in a Supreme Court and in such inferior courts as are established by law.

No extraordinary tribunal shall be established, nor shall any organ or agency of the Executive be given final judicial power.

All judges shall be independent in the exercise of their conscience and shall be bound only by this Constitution and the laws.

Article 77. The Supreme Court is vested with the rule-making power under which it determines the rules of procedure and of practice, and of matters relating to attorneys, the internal discipline of the courts and the administration of judicial affairs.

Public procurators shall be subject to the rule-making power of the Supreme Court.

The Supreme Court may delegate the power to make rules for inferior courts to such courts.

Article 78. Judges shall not be removed except by public impeachment unless judicially declared mentally or physically incompetent to perform official duties. No disciplinary action against judges shall be administered by any executive organ or agency.

Article 79. The Supreme Court shall consist of a Chief Judge and such number of judges as may be determined by law; all such judges excepting the Chief Judge shall be appointed by the Cabinet.

The appointment of the judges of the Supreme Court shall be reviewed by the people at the first general election of members of the House of Representatives following their appointment, and shall be reviewed again at the first general election of members of the House of Representatives after a lapse of ten (10) years, and in the same manner thereafter.

In cases mentioned in the foregoing paragraph, when the majority of the voters favors the dismissal of a judge, he shall be dismissed.

Matters pertaining to review shall be prescribed by law.

The judges of the Supreme Court shall be retired upon the attainment of the age as fixed by law.

All such judges shall receive, at regular stated intervals, adequate compensation which shall not be decreased during their terms of office.

Article 80. The judges of the inferior courts shall be appointed by the Cabinet from a list of persons nominated by the Supreme Court. All such judges shall hold office for a term of ten (10) years with privilege of reappointment, provided that they shall be retired upon the attainment of the age as fixed by law.

The judges of the inferior courts shall receive, at regular stated intervals, adequate compensation which shall not be decreased during their terms of office.

Article 81. The Supreme Court is the court of last resort with power to determine the constitutionality of any law, order, regulation or official act.

Article 82. Trials shall be conducted and judgment declared publicly.

Where a court unanimously determines publicity to be dangerous to public order or morals, a trial may be conducted privately, but trials of political offenses, offenses involving the press or cases wherein the rights of people as guaranteed in Chapter III of this Constitution are in question shall always be conducted publicly.

CHAPTER VII. FINANCE

Article 83. The power to administer national finances shall be exercised as the Diet shall determine.

Article 84. No new taxes shall be imposed or existing ones modified except by law or under such conditions as law may prescribe.

Article 85. No money shall be expended, nor shall the State obligate itself, except as authorized by the Diet.

Article 86. The Cabinet shall prepare and submit to the Diet for its consideration and decision a budget for each fiscal year.

Article 87. In order to provide for unforeseen deficiencies in the budget, a reserve fund may be authorized by the Diet to be expended upon the responsibility of the Cabinet.

The Cabinet must get subsequent approval of the Diet for all payments from the reserve fund.

Article 88. All property of the Imperial Household shall belong to the State. All expenses of the Imperial Household shall be appropriated by the Diet in the budget.

Article 89. No public money or other property shall be expended or appropriated for the use, benefit or maintenance of any religious institution or association, or for any charitable, educational or benevolent enterprises not under the control of public authority.

Article 90. Final accounts of the expenditures and revenues of the State shall be audited annually by a Board of Audit and submitted by the Cabinet to the Diet, together with the statement of audit, during the fiscal year immediately following the period covered.

The organization and competency of the Board of Audit shall be determined by law.

Article 91. At regular intervals and at least annually the Cabinet shall report to the Diet and the people on the state of national finances.

CHAPTER VIII. LOCAL SELF-GOVERNMENT

Article 92. Regulations concerning organization and operations of local public entities shall be fixed by law in accordance with the principle of local autonomy.

Article 93. The local public entities shall establish assemblies as their deliberative organs, in accordance with law.

The chief executive officers of all local public entities, the members of their assemblies, and such other local officials as may be determined by law shall be elected by direct popular vote within their several communities.

Article 94. Local public entities shall have the right to manage their property, affairs and administration and to enact their own regulations within law.

Article 95. A special law, applicable only to one local public entity, cannot be enacted by the Diet without the consent of the majority of the voters of the local public entity concerned, obtained in accordance with law.

CHAPTER IX. AMENDMENTS

Article 96. Amendments to this Constitution shall be initiated by the Diet, through a concurring vote of two-thirds or more of all the members of each House and shall thereupon be submitted to the people for ratification, which shall require the affirmative vote of a majority of all votes cast thereon, at a special referendum or at such election as the Diet shall specify.

Amendments when so ratified shall immediately be promulgated by the Emperor in the name of the people, as an integral part of this Constitution.

CHAPTER X. SUPREME LAW

Article 97. The fundamental human rights by this Constitution guaranteed to the people of Japan are fruits of the age-old struggle of man to be free; they have survived the many exacting tests for durability and are conferred upon this and future generations in trust, to be held for all time inviolate.

Article 98. This Constitution shall be the supreme law of the nation and no law, ordinance, imperial rescript or other act of government, or part thereof, contrary to the provisions hereof, shall have legal force or validity.

The treaties concluded by Japan and established laws of nations shall be faithfully observed.

Article 99. The Emperor or the Regent as well as Ministers of State, members of the Diet, judges, and all other public officials have the obligation to respect and uphold this Constitution.

CHAPTER XI. SUPPLEMENTARY PROVISIONS

Article 100. This Constitution shall be enforced as from the day when the period of six months will have elapsed counting from the day of its promulgation.

The enactment of laws necessary for the enforcement of this Constitution, the election of members of the House of Councillors and the procedure for the convocation of the Diet and other preparatory procedures necessary for the enforcement of this Constitution may be executed before the day prescribed in the preceding paragraph.

Article 101. If the House of Councillors is not constituted before the effective date of this Constitution, the House of Representatives shall function as the Diet until such time as the House of Councillors shall be constituted.

Article 102. The term of office for half the members of the House of Councillors serving in the first term under this Constitution shall be three years. Members falling under this category shall be determined in accordance with law.

Article 103. The Ministers of State, members of the House of Representatives and judges in office on the effective date of this Constitution, and all other public officials who occupy positions corresponding to such positions as are recognized by this Constitution shall not forfeit their positions automatically on account of the enforcement of this Constitution unless otherwise specified by law. When, however, successors are elected or appointed under the provisions of this Constitution, they shall forfeit their positions as a matter of course.

Appendix IV. Treaty of Peace with Japan

Whereas the Allied Powers and Japan are resolved that henceforth their relations shall be those of nations which, as sovereign equals, coöperate in friendly association to promote their common welfare and to maintain international peace and security, and are therefore desirous of concluding a Treaty of Peace which will settle questions still outstanding as a result of the existence of a state of war between them;

Whereas Japan for its part declares its intention to apply for membership in the United Nations and in all circumstances to conform to the principles of the Charter of the United Nations; to strive to realize the objectives of the Universal Declaration of Human Rights; to seek to create within Japan conditions of stability and well-being as defined in Articles 55 and 56 of the Charter of the United Nations and already initiated by post-surrender Japanese legislation; and in public and private trade and commerce to conform to internationally accepted fair practices;

Whereas the Allied Powers welcome the intentions of Japan set out in the foregoing paragraph;

The Allied Powers and Japan have therefore determined to conclude the present Treaty of Peace, and have accordingly appointed the undersigned Plenipotentiaries, who, after presentation of their full powers, found in good and due form, have agreed on the following provisions:

CHAPTER I

PEACE

Article 1

(a) The state of war between Japan and each of the Allied Powers is terminated as from the date on which the present Treaty comes into force between Japan and the Allied Power concerned as provided for in Article 23.

(b) The Allied Powers recognize the full sovereignty of the Japanese people over Japan and its territorial waters.

CHAPTER II

TERRITORY

Article 2

(a) Japan, recognizing the independence of Korea, renounces all right, title and claim to Korea, including the islands of Quelpart, Port Hamilton and Dagelet.

(b) Japan renounces all right, title and claim to Formosa and the Pescadores.

(c) Japan renounces all right, title and claim to the Kurile Islands, and to that portion of Sakhalin and the islands adjacent to it over which Japan acquired sovereignty as a consequence of the Treaty of Portsmouth of September 5, 1905.

(d) Japan renounces all right, title and claim in connection with the League of Nations Mandate System, and accepts the action of the United Nations Security Council of April 2, 1947, extending the trusteeship system to the Pacific Islands formerly under mandate to Japan.

(e) Japan renounces all claim to any right or title to or interest in connection with any part of the Antarctic area, whether deriving from the activities of Japanese nationals or otherwise.

(f) Japan renounces all right, title and claim to the Spratly Islands and to the Paracel Islands.

Article 3

Japan will concur in any proposal of the United States to the United Nations to place under its trusteeship system, with the United States as the sole administering authority, Nansei Shoto south of 29° north latitude (including the Ryukyu Islands and the Daito Islands), Nanpo Shoto south of Sofu Gan (including the Bonin Islands, Rosario Island and the Volcano Islands) and Parece Vela and Marcus Island. Pending the making of such a proposal and affirmative action thereon, the United States will have the right to exercise all and any powers of administration, legislation and jurisdiction over the territory and inhabitants of these islands, including their territorial waters.

Article 4

(a) Subject to the provisions of paragraph (b) of this Article, the disposition of property of Japan and of its nationals in the areas referred to in Article 2, and their claims, including debts, against the authorities presently administering such areas and the residents (including juridical persons) thereof, and the disposition in Japan of property of such authorities and residents, and of claims, including debts, of such authorities and residents against Japan and its nationals, shall be the subject of special arrangements between Japan and such authorities. The property of any of the Allied Powers or its nationals in the areas referred to in Article 2 shall, insofar as this has not already been done, be returned by the administering authority in the condition in which it now exists. (The term nationals whenever used in the present Treaty includes juridical persons.)

(b) Japan recognizes the validity of dispositions of property of Japan and Japanese nationals made by or pursuant to directives of the United States Military Government in any of the areas referred to in Articles 2 and 3.

(c) Japanese owned submarine cables connecting Japan with territory removed from Japanese control pursuant to the present Treaty shall be equally divided, Japan retaining the Japanese terminal and adjoining half of the cable, and the detached territory the remainder of the cable and connecting terminal facilities.

CHAPTER III

SECURITY

Article 5

(a) Japan accepts the obligations set forth in Article 2 of the Charter of the United Nations, and in particular the obligations

(i) to settle its international disputes by peaceful means in such a manner that international peace and security, and justice, are not endangered;

(ii) to refrain in its international relations from the threat or use of force against the territorial integrity or political independence of any State or in any other manner inconsistent with the Purposes of the United Nations;

(iii) to give the United Nations every assistance in any action it takes in accordance with the Charter and to refrain from giving assistance to any State against which the United Nations may take preventive or enforcement action.

(b) The Allied Powers confirm that they will be guided by the principles of Article 2 of the Charter of the United Nations in their relations with Japan.

(c) The Allied Powers for their part recognize that Japan as a sovereign nation possesses the inherent right of individual or collective self-defense referred to in Article 51 of the Charter of the United Nations and that Japan may voluntarily enter into collective security arrangements.

Article 6

(a) All occupation forces of the Allied Powers shall be withdrawn from Japan as soon as possible after the coming into force of the present Treaty, and in any case not later than 90 days thereafter. Nothing in this provision shall, however, prevent the stationing or retention of foreign armed forces in Japanese territory under or in consequence of any bilateral or multilateral agreements which have been or may be made between one or more of the Allied Powers, on the one hand, and Japan on the other.

(b) The provisions of Article 9 of the Potsdam Proclamation of July 26, 1945, dealing with the return of Japanese military forces to their homes, to the extent not already completed, will be carried out.

(c) All Japanese property for which compensation has not already been paid, which was supplied for the use of the occupation forces and which remains in the possession of those forces at the time of the coming into force of the present Treaty, shall be returned to the Japanese Government within the same 90 days unless other arrangements are made by mutual agreement.

CHAPTER IV

POLITICAL AND ECONOMIC CLAUSES

Article 7

(a) Each of the Allied Powers, within one year after the present Treaty has come into force between it and Japan, will notify Japan which of its prewar bilateral treaties or conventions with Japan it wishes to continue in force or revive, and any treaties or conventions so notified shall continue in force or be revived subject to such amendments as may be necessary to ensure conformity with the present Treaty. The treaties and conventions so notified shall be considered as having been continued in force or revived three months after the date of notification and shall be registered with the Secretariat of the United Nations. All such treaties and conventions as to which Japan is not so notified shall be regarded as abrogated.

(b) Any notification made under paragraph (a) of this Article may except from the operation or revival of a treaty or convention any territory for the international relations of which the notifying Power is responsible, until three months after the date on which notice is given to Japan that such exception shall cease to apply.

Article 8

(a) Japan will recognize the full force of all treaties now or hereafter concluded by the Allied Powers for terminating the state of war initiated on September 1, 1939, as well as any other arrangements by the Allied Powers for or in connection with the restoration of peace. Japan also accepts the arrangements made for terminating the former League of Nations and Permanent Court of International Justice.

(b) Japan renounces all such rights and interests as it may derive from being a signatory power of the Conventions of St. Germain-en-Laye of September 10, 1919, and the Straits Agreement of Montreux of July 20, 1936, and from Article 16 of the Treaty of Peace with Turkey signed at Lausanne on July 24, 1923.

(c) Japan renounces all rights, title and interests acquired under, and is discharged from all obligations resulting from, the Agreement between Germany and the Creditor Powers of January 20, 1930, and its Annexes, including the Trust Agreement, dated May 17, 1930; the Convention of January 20, 1930, respecting the Bank for International Settlements; and the Statutes of the Bank for International Settlements. Japan will notify to the Ministry of Foreign Affairs in Paris within six months of the first coming into force of the present Treaty its renunciation of the rights, title and interests referred to in this paragraph.

Article 9

Japan will enter promptly into negotiations with the Allied Powers so desiring for the conclusion of bilateral and multilateral agreements providing for the regulation or limitation of fishing and the conservation and development of fisheries on the high seas.

Article 10

Japan renounces all special rights and interests in China, including all benefits and privileges resulting from the provisions of the final Protocol signed at Peking on September 7, 1901, and all annexes, notes and documents supplementary thereto, and agrees to the abrogation in respect to Japan of the said protocol, annexes, notes and documents.

Article 11

Japan accepts the judgments of the International Military Tribunal for the Far East and of other Allied War Crimes Courts both within and outside Japan, and will carry out the sentences imposed thereby upon Japanese nationals imprisoned in Japan. The power to grant clemency, to reduce sentences and to parole with respect to such prisoners may not be exercised except on the decision of the Government or Governments which imposed the sentence in each instance, and on the recommendation of Japan. In the case of persons sentenced by the International Military Tribunal for the Far East, such power may not be exercised except on the decision of a majority of the Governments represented on the Tribunal, and on the recommendation of Japan.

Article 12

(a) Japan declares its readiness promptly to enter into negotiations for the conclusion with each of the Allied Powers of treaties or agreements to place their trading, maritime and other commercial relations on a stable and friendly basis.

(b) Pending the conclusion of the relevant treaty or agreement, Japan will, during a period of four years from the first coming into force of the present Treaty

(1) accord to each of the Allied Powers, its nationals, products and vessels

(i) most-favored-nation treatment with respect to customs duties, charges, restrictions and other regulations on or in connection with the importation and exportation of goods;

(ii) national treatment with respect to shipping, navigation and imported goods, and with respect to natural and juridical persons and their interests — such treatment to include all matters pertaining to the levying and collection of taxes, access to the courts, the making and performance of contracts, rights to property (tangible and intangible), participation in juridical entities constituted under Japanese law, and generally the conduct of all kinds of business and professional activities;

(2) ensure that external purchases and sales of Japanese state trading enterprises shall be based solely on commercial considerations.

(c) In respect to any matter, however, Japan shall be obliged to accord to an Allied Power national treatment, or most-favored-nation treatment, only to the extent that the Allied Power concerned accords Japan national treatment or most-favored-nation treatment, as the case may be, in respect of the same matter. The reciprocity envisaged in the foregoing sentence shall be determined, in the case of products, vessels and juridical entities of, and persons domiciled in, any non-metropolitan territory of an Allied Power, and in the case of juridical entities of, and persons domiciled in, any state or province of an Allied Power having a federal government, by reference to the treatment accorded to Japan in such territory, state or province.

(d) In the application of this Article, a discriminatory measure shall not be considered to derogate from the grant of national or most-favored-nation treatment, as the case may be, if such measure is based on an exception customarily provided for in the commercial treaties of the party applying it, or on the need to safeguard that party's external financial position or balance of payments (except in respect to shipping and navigation), or on the need to maintain its essential security interests, and provided such measure is proportionate to the circumstances and not applied in an arbitrary or unreasonable manner.

(e) Japan's obligations under this Article shall not be affected by the exercise of any Allied rights under Article 14 of the present

Treaty; nor shall the provisions of this Article be understood as limiting the undertakings assumed by Japan by virtue of Article 15 of the Treaty.

Article 13

(a) Japan will enter into negotiations with any of the Allied Powers, promptly upon the request of such Power or Powers, for the conclusion of bilateral or multilateral agreements relating to international civil air transport.

(b) Pending the conclusion of such agreement or agreements, Japan will, during a period of four years from the first coming into force of the present Treaty, extend to such Power treatment not less favorable with respect to air-traffic rights and privileges than those exercised by any such Powers at the date of such coming into force, and will accord complete equality of opportunity in respect to the operation and development of air services.

(c) Pending its becoming a party to the Convention on International Civil Aviation in accordance with Article 93 thereof, Japan will give effect to the provisions of that Convention applicable to the international navigation of aircraft, and will give effect to the standards, practices and procedures adopted as annexes to the Convention in accordance with the terms of the Convention.

CHAPTER V

CLAIMS AND PROPERTY

Article 14

(a) It is recognized that Japan should pay reparations to the Allied Powers for the damage and suffering caused by it during the war. Nevertheless it is also recognized that the resources of Japan are not presently sufficient, if it is to maintain a viable economy, to make complete reparation for all such damage and suffering and at the same time meet its other obligations.

Therefore,

1. Japan will promptly enter into negotiations with Allied Powers so desiring, whose present territories were occupied by Japanese forces and damaged by Japan, with a view to assisting to compensate those countries for the cost of repairing the damage done, by making available the services of the Japanese people in production, salvaging and other work for the Allied Powers in question. Such arrangements shall avoid the imposition of addi-

tional liabilities on other Allied Powers, and, where the manufacturing of raw materials is called for, they shall be supplied by the Allied Powers in question, so as not to throw any foreign exchange burden upon Japan.

2. (I) Subject to the provisions of sub-paragraph (II) below, each of the Allied Powers shall have the right to seize, retain, liquidate or otherwise dispose of all property, rights and interests of

(a) Japan and Japanese nationals,

(b) persons acting for or on behalf of Japan or Japanese nationals, and

(c) entities owned or controlled by Japan or Japanese nationals,

which on the first coming into force of the present Treaty were subject to its jurisdiction. The property, rights and interests specified in this sub-paragraph shall include those now blocked, vested or in the possession or under the control of enemy property authorities of Allied Powers, which belonged to, or were held or managed on behalf of, any of the persons or entities mentioned in (a), (b) or (c) above at the time such assets came under the controls of such authorities.

(II) The following shall be excepted from the right specified in sub-paragraph (I) above:

(i) property of Japanese natural persons who during the war resided with the permission of the Government concerned in the territory of one of the Allied Powers, other than territory occupied by Japan, except property subjected to restrictions during the war and not released from such restrictions as of the date of the first coming into force of the present Treaty;

(ii) all real property, furniture and fixtures owned by the Government of Japan and used for diplomatic or consular purposes, and all personal furniture and furnishings and other private property not of an investment nature which was normally necessary for the carrying out of diplomatic and consular functions, owned by Japanese diplomatic and consular personnel;

(iii) property belonging to religious bodies or private charitable institutions and used exclusively for religious or charitable purposes;

(iv) property, rights and interests which have come within its jurisdiction in consequence of the resumption of trade and financial relations subsequent to September 2, 1945,

between the country concerned and Japan, except such
as have resulted from transactions contrary to the laws
of the Allied Power concerned;

(v) obligations of Japan or Japanese nationals, any right,
title or interest in tangible property located in Japan, interests in enterprises organized under the laws of Japan,
or any paper evidence thereof; provided that this exception shall only apply to obligations of Japan and its
nationals expressed in Japanese currency.

(III) Property referred to in exceptions (i) through (v) above
shall be returned subject to reasonable expenses for its preservation
and administration. If any such property has been liquidated the
proceeds shall be returned instead.

(IV) The right to seize, retain, liquidate or otherwise dispose
of property as provided in sub-paragraph (I) above shall be exercised in accordance with the laws of the Allied Power concerned, and the owner shall have only such rights as may be given
him by those laws.

(V) The Allied Powers agree to deal with Japanese trademarks
and literary and artistic property rights on a basis as favorable to
Japan as circumstances ruling in each country will permit.

(b) Except as otherwise provided in the present Treaty, the
Allied Powers waive all reparations claims of the Allied Powers,
other claims of the Allied Powers and their nationals arising out of
any actions taken by Japan and its nationals in the course of the
prosecution of the war, and claims of the Allied Powers for direct
military costs of occupation.

Article 15

(a) Upon application made within nine months of the coming
into force of the present Treaty between Japan and the Allied
Power concerned, Japan will, within six months of the date of
such application, return the property, tangible and intangible, and
all rights or interests of any kind in Japan of each Allied Power
and its nationals which was within Japan at any time between December 7, 1941, and September 2, 1945, unless the owner has
freely disposed thereof without duress or fraud. Such property
shall be returned free of all encumbrances and charges to which
it may have become subject because of the war, and without any
charges for its return. Property whose return is not applied for by
or on behalf of the owner or by his Government within the pre-

scribed period may be disposed of by the Japanese Government as it may determine. In cases where such property was within Japan on December 7, 1941, and cannot be returned or has suffered injury or damage as a result of the war, compensation will be made on terms not less favorable than the terms provided in the draft Allied Powers Property Compensation Law approved by the Japanese Cabinet on July 13, 1951.

(b) With respect to industrial property rights impaired during the war, Japan will continue to accord to the Allied Powers and their nationals benefits no less than those heretofore accorded by Cabinet Orders No. 309 effective September 1, 1949, No. 12 effective January 28, 1950, and No. 9 effective February 1, 1950, all as now amended, provided such nationals have applied for such benefits within the time limits prescribed therein.

(c) (i) Japan acknowledges that the literary and artistic property rights which existed in Japan on December 6, 1941, in respect to the published and unpublished works of the Allied Powers and their nationals have continued in force since that date, and recognizes those rights which have arisen, or but for the war would have arisen, in Japan since that date, by the operation of any conventions and agreements to which Japan was a party on that date, irrespective of whether or not such conventions or agreements were abrogated or suspended upon or since the outbreak of war by the domestic law of Japan or of the Allied Power concerned.

(ii) Without the need for application by the proprietor of the right and without the payment of any fee or compliance with any other formality, the period from December 7, 1941, until the coming into force of the present Treaty between Japan and the Allied Power concerned shall be excluded from the running of the normal term of such rights; and such period, with an additional period of six months, shall be excluded from the time within which a literary work must be translated into Japanese in order to obtain translating rights in Japan.

Article 16

As an expression of its desire to indemnify those members of the armed forces of the Allied Powers who suffered undue hardships while prisoners of war of Japan, Japan will transfer its assets and those of its nationals in countries which were neutral during the war, or which were at war with any of the Allied Powers, or, at its option, the equivalent of such assets to the International

Committee of the Red Cross which shall liquidate such assets and distribute the resultant fund to appropriate national agencies, for the benefit of former prisoners of war and their families on such basis as it may determine to be equitable. The categories of assets described in Article 14 (a) 2(II) (ii) through (v) of the present Treaty shall be excepted from transfer, as well as assets of Japanese natural persons not residents of Japan on the first coming into force of the Treaty. It is equally understood that the transfer provision of this Article has no application to the 19,770 shares in the Bank for International Settlements presently owned by Japanese financial institutions.

Article 17

(a) Upon the request of any of the Allied Powers, the Japanese Government shall review and revise in conformity with international law any decision or order of the Japanese Prize Courts in cases involving ownership rights of nationals of that Allied Power and shall supply copies of all documents comprising the records of these cases, including the decisions taken and orders issued. In any case in which such review or revision shows that restoration is due, the provisions of Article 15 shall apply to the property concerned.

(b) The Japanese Government shall take the necessary measures to enable nationals of any of the Allied Powers at any time within one year from the coming into force of the present Treaty between Japan and the Allied Power concerned to submit to the appropriate Japanese authorities for review any judgment given by a Japanese court between December 7, 1941, and such coming into force, in any proceedings in which any such national was unable to make adequate presentation of his case either as plaintiff or defendant. The Japanese Government shall provide that, where the national has suffered injury by reason of any such judgment, he shall be restored in the position in which he was before the judgment was given or shall be afforded such relief as may be just and equitable in the circumstances.

Article 18

(a) It is recognized that the intervention of the state of war has not affected the obligation to pay pecuniary debts arising out of obligations and contracts (including those in respect of bonds) which existed and rights which were acquired before the existence of a state of war, and which are due by the Government or nationals of Japan to the Government or nationals of one of the Allied Powers, or are due by the Government or nationals of one of the Allied Powers to the Government or nationals of Japan. The intervention of a state of war shall equally not be regarded as affecting the obligation to consider on their merits claims for loss or damage to property or for personal injury or death which arose before the existence of a state of war, and which may be presented or re-presented by the Government of one of the Allied Powers to the Government of Japan, or by the Government of Japan to any of the Governments of the Allied Powers. The provisions of this paragraph are without prejudice to the rights conferred by Article 14.

(b) Japan affirms its liability for the prewar external debt of the Japanese State and for debts of corporate bodies subsequently declared to be liabilities of the Japanese State, and expresses its intention to enter into negotiations at an early date with its creditors with respect to the resumption of payments on those debts; to encourage negotiations in respect to other prewar claims and obligations; and to facilitate the transfer of sums accordingly.

Article 19

(a) Japan waives all claims of Japan and its nationals against the Allied Powers and their nationals arising out of the war or out of actions taken because of the existence of a state of war, and waives all claims arising from the presence, operations or actions of forces or authorities of any of the Allied Powers in Japanese territory prior to the coming into force of the present Treaty.

(b) The foregoing waiver includes any claims arising out of actions taken by any of the Allied Powers with respect to Japanese ships between September 1, 1939, and the coming into force of the present Treaty, as well as any claims and debts arising in respect to Japanese prisoners of war and civilian internees in the hands of the Allied Powers, but does not include Japanese claims specifically recognized in the laws of any Allied Power enacted since September 2, 1945.

(c) Subject to reciprocal renunciation, the Japanese Government also renounces all claims (including debts) against Germany and German nationals on behalf of the Japanese Government and Japanese nationals, including inter-governmental claims and claims for loss or damage sustained during the war, but excepting (a) claims in respect of contracts entered into and rights acquired before September 1, 1939, and (b) claims arising out of trade and financial relations between Japan and Germany after September 2, 1945. Such renunciation shall not prejudice actions taken in accordance with Articles 16 and 20 of the present Treaty.

(d) Japan recognizes the validity of all acts and omissions done during the period of occupation under or in consequence of directives of the occupation authorities or authorized by Japanese law at that time, and will take no action subjecting Allied nationals to civil or criminal liability arising out of such acts or omissions.

Article 20

Japan will take all necessary measures to ensure such disposition of German assets in Japan as has been or may be determined by those powers entitled under the Protocol of the proceedings of the Berlin Conference of 1945 to dispose of those assets, and pending the final disposition of such assets will be responsible for the conservation and administration thereof.

Article 21

Notwithstanding the provisions of Article 25 of the present Treaty, China shall be entitled to the benefits of Articles 10 and 14(a)2; and Korea to the benefits of Articles 2, 4, 9 and 12 of the present Treaty.

CHAPTER VI

SETTLEMENT OF DISPUTES

Article 22

If in the opinion of any Party to the present Treaty there has arisen a dispute concerning the interpretation or execution of the Treaty, which is not settled by reference to a special claims tribunal or by other agreed means, the dispute shall, at the request of any party thereto, be referred for decision to the International Court of Justice. Japan and those Allied Powers which are not already parties to the Statute of the International Court of Justice will deposit with the Registrar of the Court, at the time of their respective ratifications of the present Treaty, and in conformity with the resolution of the United Nations Security Council, dated October 15, 1946, a general declaration accepting the jurisdiction, without special agreement, of the Court generally in respect to all disputes of the character referred to in this Article.

CHAPTER VII

FINAL CLAUSES

Article 23

(a) The present Treaty shall be ratified by the States which sign it, including Japan, and will come into force for all the States which have then ratified it, when instruments of ratification have been deposited by Japan and by a majority, including the United States of America as the principal occupying Power, of the following States, namely Australia, Canada, Ceylon, France, Indonesia, the Kingdom of the Netherlands, New Zealand, Pakistan, the Republic of the Philippines, the United Kingdom of Great Britain and Northern Ireland, and the United States of America. The present Treaty shall come into force for each State which subsequently ratifies it, on the date of the deposit of its instrument of ratification.

(b) If the Treaty has not come into force within nine months after the date of the deposit of Japan's ratification, any State which has ratified it may bring the Treaty into force between itself and Japan by a notification to that effect given to the Governments of Japan and the United States of America not later than three years after the date of deposit of Japan's ratification.

Article 24

All instruments of ratification shall be deposited with the Government of the United States of America which will notify all the signatory States of each such deposit, of the date of the coming into force of the Treaty under paragraph (a) of Article 23, and of any notifications made under paragraph (b) of Article 23.

Article 25

For the purposes of the present Treaty the Allied Powers shall be the States at war with Japan, or any State which previously formed a part of the territory of a State named in Article 23, provided that in each case the State concerned has signed and ratified the Treaty. Subject to the provisions of Article 21, the present Treaty shall not confer any rights, titles or benefits on any State which is not an Allied Power as herein defined; nor shall any right, title or interest of Japan be deemed to be diminished or prejudiced by any provision of the Treaty in favor of a State which is not an Allied Power as so defined.

Article 26

Japan will be prepared to conclude with any State which signed or adhered to the United Nations Declaration of January 1, 1942, and which is at war with Japan, or with any State which previously formed a part of the territory of a State named in Article 23, which is not a signatory of the present Treaty, a bilateral Treaty of Peace on the same or substantially the same terms as are provided for in the present Treaty, but this obligation on the part of Japan will expire three years after the first coming into force of the present Treaty. Should Japan make a peace settlement or war claims settlement with any State granting that State greater advantages than those provided by the present Treaty, those same advantages shall be extended to the parties to the present Treaty.

Article 27

The present Treaty shall be deposited in the archives of the Government of the United States of America which shall furnish each signatory State with a certified copy thereof.

Appendix V.   Treaty of Mutual Cooperation and Security Between the United States of America and Japan (1960)

The United States of America and Japan,

Desiring to strengthen the bonds of peace and friendship traditionally existing between them, and to uphold the principles of democracy, individual liberty, and the rule of law,

Desiring further to encourage closer economic cooperation between them and to promote conditions of economic stability and well-being in their countries,

Reaffirming their faith in the purposes and principles of the Charter of the United Nations, and their desire to live in peace with all peoples and all governments,

Recognizing that they have the inherent right of individual or collective self-defense as affirmed in the Charter of the United Nations,

Considering that they have a common concern in the maintenance of international peace and security in the Far East,

Having resolved to conclude a treaty of mutual cooperation and security,

Therefore agree as follows:

ARTICLE I

The Parties undertake, as set forth in the Charter of the United Nations, to settle any international disputes in which they may be involved by peaceful means in such a manner that international peace and security and justice are not endangered and to refrain in their international relations from the threat or use of force against the territorial integrity or political independence of any state, or in any other manner inconsistent with the purposes of the United Nations.

The Parties will endeavor in concert with other peace-loving countries to strengthen the United Nations so that its mission of maintaining international peace and security may be discharged more effectively.

ARTICLE II

The Parties will contribute toward the further development of peaceful and friendly international relations by strengthening their free institutions, by bringing about a better understanding of the principles upon which these institutions are founded, and by promoting conditions of stability and well being. They will seek to eliminate conflict in their international economic policies and will encourage economic collaboration between them.

ARTICLE III

The Parties, individually and in cooperation with each other, by means of continuous and effective self-help and mutual aid will maintain and develop, subject to their constitutional provisions, their capacities to resist armed attack.

ARTICLE IV

The Parties will consult together from time to time regarding the implementation of this Treaty, and, at the request of either Party, whenever the security of Japan or international peace and security in the Far East is threatened.

ARTICLE V

Each Party recognizes that an armed attack against either Party in the territories under the administration of Japan would be dangerous to its own peace and safety and declares that it would act to meet the common danger in accordance with its constitutional provisions and processes.

Any such armed attack and all measures taken as a result thereof shall be immediately reported to the Security Council of the United Nations in accordance with the provisions of Article 51 of the Charter. Such measures shall be terminated when the Security Council has taken the measures necessary to restore and maintain international peace and security.

ARTICLE VI

For the purpose of contributing to the security of Japan and the maintenance of international peace and security in the Far East, the United States of America is granted the use by its land, air and naval forces of facilities and areas in Japan.

The use of these facilities and areas as well as the status of United States armed forces in Japan shall be governed by a separate agreement, replacing the Administrative Agreement under Article III of the Security Treaty between the United States of America and Japan, signed at Tokyo on February 28, 1952, as amended, and by such other arrangements as may be agreed upon.

ARTICLE VII

This Treaty does not affect and shall not be interpreted as affecting in any way the rights and obligations of the Parties under the Charter of the United Nations or the responsibility of the United Nations for the maintenance of international peace and security.

ARTICLE VIII

This Treaty shall be ratified by the United States of America and Japan in accordance with their respective constitutional processes and will enter into force on the date on which the instruments of ratification thereof have been exchanged by them in Tokyo.

ARTICLE IX

The Security Treaty between the United States of America and Japan signed at the city of San Francisco on September 8, 1951 shall expire upon the entering into force of this Treaty.

ARTICLE X

This Treaty shall remain in force until in the opinion of the Governments of the United States of America and Japan there shall have come into force such United Nations arrangements as will satisfactorily provide for the maintenance of international peace and security in the Japan area.

However, after the Treaty has been in force for ten years, either Party may give notice to the other Party of its intention to terminate the Treaty, in which case the Treaty shall terminate one year after such notice has been given.

Appendix VI. Suggested Reading

Books on Japan in the English language are still somewhat spotty in coverage and quite uneven in quality. The situation, however, is much better than it was a decade or two ago, and reasonably adequate materials in English can be found on most aspects of Japanese culture.

A good starting point for those who wish to do some further reading would be Herschel Webb's *An Introduction to Japan* (Columbia University Press, New York, 1955), which contains brief essays and short bibliographies on various aspects of Japanese life. Donald Keen's *Living Japan* (Doubleday, Garden City, 1959), is also good as a general introduction to the various facets of modern Japanese life.

The geographical substructure of Japanese civilization is presented comprehensively and authoritatively in Glenn Thomas Trewartha's *Japan, a Physical, Cultural and Regional Geography* (University of Wisconsin Press, Madison, 1945), and I gratefully acknowledge my debt to this work for many of the factual statements made in Chapters 4 and 5.

In the field of history one might start with my own brief *Japan Past and Present* (Knopf, New York, third revised edition 1964). For more detailed accounts of premodern history there are the chapters on Japan in *East Asia: The Great Tradition* by John K. Fairbank and myself (Houghton Mifflin, Boston, 1960); and Sir George Sansom's classic work, *Japan, A Short Cultural History* (Appleton-Century, New York, revised edition 1943). For a detailed account of modern history there are the chapters on Japan in "East Asia: The Modern Transformation" (to be published shortly by Houghton Mifflin, Boston) by John K. Fairbank, Albert Craig, and myself, *Japan's Modern Century* (Ronald Press, New York, 1955) by Hugh Borton, and *A History of Modern Japan* (Penguin Books, Baltimore, 1960) by Richard Storry. Among the more specialized works on modern Japan are William

W. Lockwood's *The Economic Development of Japan: Growth and Structural Change 1868–1938* (Princeton University Press, Princeton, 1954), *Democracy and the Party Movement in Prewar Japan* (University of California Press, Berkeley, 1955) by Robert Scalapino, and *The Beginnings of Political Democracy in Japan* (Johns Hopkins Press, Baltimore, 1950) by Nobutaka Ike. *Sources of the Japanese Tradition* by Tsunoda Ryusaku, edited by William Theodore De Bary, and Donald Keene (Columbia University Press, New York, 1958) is a valuable series of translated readings from early and modern Japanese history.

Sir George Sansom's *The Western World and Japan* (Knopf, New York, 1950) gives an account of early Western influence on Japan, and Payson Jackson Treat's writings, *Japan and the United States 1853–1921, Revised and Continued to 1928* (Stanford University Press, Stanford, 1928), and his three volume work *Diplomatic Relations Between the United States and Japan* (Stanford University Press, Stanford, 1932, and 1938), cover in detail the earlier phases of Japanese-American relations. A more recent brief survey of the relationship is to be found in *America Encounters Japan, From Perry to MacArthur* (Johns Hopkins Press, Baltimore, 1963) by William L. Neumann.

Among the books on the Second World War and its background are Richard Storry's *The Double Patriots* (Chatto and Windus, London, 1957), *Japan's New Order in East Asia: Its Rise and Fall, 1937–1945* (Oxford University Press, London, 1954) by F. C. Jones, *The Road to Pearl Harbor* (Princeton University Press, Princeton, 1950) by Herbert Feis, *Tojo and the Coming of the War* (Princeton University Press, Princeton, 1961) and *Japan's Decision to Surrender* (Stanford University Press, Stanford, 1954), both by Robert J. C. Butow, and *Japan Subdued: The Atomic Bomb and the End of the War in the Pacific* (Princeton University Press, Princeton, 1961) by Herbert Feis.

Among the spate of books on the occupation period, perhaps the best balanced comprehensive account is *Japan's American Interlude* (Chicago University Press, Chicago, 1960) by Kazuo Kawai. Other more specialized works on postwar Japan are: *Japan's Economic Recovery* (Oxford University Press, London, 1958) by G. C. Allen; *Japan's Economy in War and Reconstruction* (University of Minnesota Press, Minneapolis, 1949) and *Japan's Postwar Economy* (Indiana University Press, Bloomington, 1958) both by Jerome B. Cohen; *Japanese People and Politics* (Wiley, New York, 1956) by Chitoshi Yanaga, *Japanese Politics: An Introductory Survey* (Knopf, New York, 1957) by Nobutaka

Ike, *The Government of Japan* (Crowell, New York, 1961) by Ardath W. Burks, *Parties and Politics in Contemporary Japan* (University of California Press, Berkeley, 1962) by Robert A. Scalapino, and Junnosuke Masumi, and *Land Reform in Japan* (Oxford University Press, London, 1959) by Ronald P. Dore.

In the field of sociology Ruth Benedict's effort in *The Chrysanthemum and the Sword* (Houghton Mifflin, Boston, 1946) to analyze the prewar Japanese personality proved a considerable stimulus to me in writing Chapters 7 and 8 of this book. On the postwar scene there are *Village Japan* (Chicago University Press, Chicago, 1959) by R. K. Beardsley, J. W. Hall, and R. E. Ward, *City Life in Japan* (University of California Press, Berkeley, 1958) by Ronald P. Dore, and *The Population of Japan* (Princeton University Press, Princeton, 1958) by Irene B. Taeuber.

In the field of religion, Masaharu Anesaki's *History of Japanese Religion* (Kegan Paul, London, 1930) is still a useful survey. In the field of literature, a most useful brief survey is provided in Donald Keene's *Japanese Literature* (Grove Press, New York, 1955), and this work is backed up by two excellent anthologies in translation by the same author, *Anthology of Japanese Literature from the Earliest Era to the Mid-Nineteenth Century* (Grove Press, New York, 1955) and *Modern Japanese Literature; an Anthology* (Grove Press, New York, 1956).

Index

INDEX

Date Due

Date Due